THE PRIVATE LIVES OF
ALBERT EINSTEIN

The Private Lives of

ALBERT EINSTEIN

ROGER HIGHFIELD
PAUL CARTER

St. Martin's Press
New York

To
JULIA, DORIS AND RON
and
DR GORDON RUSTIN
and his team at Charing Cross Hospital, London

ISBN 0-312-11047-2

First published in Great Britain by Faber and Faber Limited.

First U.S. Edition: May 1994
10 9 8 7 6 5 4 3 2 1

Contents

List of Illustrations

Acknowledgements

THERE have been hundreds of books that popularize the theory of relativity and many biographies that have dealt with the life of Albert Einstein. With only one or two exceptions, all portray him as he would have wanted – as an individual who turned his back on personal matters to seek scientific enlightenment.

Our interest in Einstein was stimulated in the late 1980s during research for a previous book, The Arrow of Time. We were fortunate to draw on the love-letters between Einstein and the woman who would become his first wife, Mileva Marić. Published in 1987 in Volume 1 of the Collected Papers of Albert Einstein (Princeton University Press), the letters dented the prevalent image of Einstein as a man so dedicated to science that he had no time for other passions.

The correspondence gives a vivid picture of his affair with Mileva Marić, one that led to an illegitimate child, then to a marriage which finally ended in divorce. We had planned to write a biography of Mileva, but, as more papers have been published and new material has been uncovered, our project has evolved to focus more on Einstein, illuminating his personal story by dealing with those who were closest to him: his family, wives and children. To underline why this is a somewhat mysterious side of Einstein, we also deal with the censorship that protected his name until recently.

We have drawn on interviews with those who knew Mileva Marić and Albert Einstein, conversations with historians and archivists, and translations of original material from individuals and archives in Boston, Zurich, Oxford, Edinburgh and Berlin. Other key sources were the volumes of collected papers produced by the Einstein papers project (notably Volumes 1 and 5) and a manuscript containing excerpts of letters written by Einstein after the year of his separation from Mileva.

We are indebted to a number of people listed below, but would like to stress that any errors in this book must be our own and that the views we express are not necessarily held by those who have assisted us.

Robert Schulmann, one of the heads of the Einstein papers project at Boston University, and his colleagues Jürgen Renn and John Stachel, have provided a great deal of generous guidance, information and advice during interviews conducted in Boston, London and Berlin and over the telephone. They also read and commented on the draft manuscript, providing priceless feedback and criticisms.

The contribution of Einstein's granddaughter, Evelyn, whom we visited in Zurich and California, also stands out. Evelyn gave us access to new material, provided many important insights, and made available a range of photographs, some of which have not been published before.

Doris Highfield provided invaluable support through her tireless efforts to conduct German-language interviews and to translate documents and letters, many of which were handwritten and very difficult to decipher — for instance, Einstein's correspondence with his colleague Heinrich Zangger.

Ze'ev Rosenkranz, curator of the Albert Einstein Archives in the Hebrew University, Jerusalem, has also been of great help in advising us.

Through faxes, letters, face-to-face interviews and telephone calls we have drawn on the help, either direct or indirect, of a large number of people for our research.

In the United States, Robert Schulmann's colleagues at the Einstein papers project in Boston University gave us particular help during three visits. We are indebted to Rita Lübke, Annette Pringle and Adam Bryant for their assistance with inquiries.

We also benefited from the advice of Gerald Holton, whom we met at Harvard University, and from interviewing Don Howard of the University of Kentucky, who provided invaluable notes on work he had done while he was with the Einstein papers project in Boston.

At the Institute for Advanced Study, Princeton, a visit organized by Rachel Gray at the invitation of Phillip Griffiths and Peter Kann ensured that we could benefit from the views of physicists such as Frank Wilczek. The Institute's archivist, Mark Darby, also provided invaluable background material and helped track down information.

In Princeton, Louise Sayen was also helpful in putting us in touch with her son Jamie, biographer of Einstein's life in America.

During a visit to Berlin, we interviewed various members of the Max Planck Institut für Bildungsforschung Arbeitsstelle Albert Einstein, including Peter Damerow, Tilman Sauer and Werner Heinrich. In particular, we are indebted to Giuseppe Castagnetti, who provided background on Einstein's Berlin days and some important leads to other archive information.

Also in Berlin, we tracked down Einstein's former maid, Herta Waldow. During telephone interviews (conducted by Doris Highfield), she provided invaluable background information to her published account of life with Einstein. We also met Angela and Karlheinz Steinmüller, who were working on a biography of Einstein, and visited Einstein's summer house in Caputh. The latter visit was possible only with the kind help of Gary Smith of the Einstein Forum, Erika Britzke and Robert Schulmann.

During two visits to Switzerland we interviewed a range of people who knew Mileva and her son Eduard Einstein. We would like to offer our thanks to Hilde Jost, Waltrud Kappeler, Maja Schucan, Maria Grendelmeier, Hans Freimüller, and Nora Herzog. In addition, we received great help from Beat Glaus at the ETH Bibliothek, Zurich, which contains the papers of Carl Seelig, notably his correspondence and research on Einstein.

Others who offered us assistance in Switzerland were Hans Koch of the ETH Bibliotek Mediothek, Sibylle Franks and Morten Guddal of the ETH Bibliothek, Vladimir Prelog of the ETH, Pierre Speziali and Charles Enz of the University of Geneva, Werner Zimmermann, Meret Tavernaro-Zürcher, Eduard Rübel, and Rolf Mösli and Victoria Owen of the Burghölzli. We would also like to thank Helmut Ograjenschek of *Blick* for publishing an appeal in his paper for information on Mileva Marić.

In Vienna, Wolfgang Mader Thaner of the Verein für die Geschichte der Arbeiterbewegung and Rudolf Ardelt of the Institut für Neuere Geschichte und Zeitgeschichte, Linz University, provided assistance with our efforts to hunt down some Friedrich Adler correspondence.

We had hoped to pursue research in the former Yugoslavia but were prevented from doing so by the recent ethnic unrest. Dord Krstić and Milan Popović offered help and assistance, as did Milisav Stanković of the Embassy of the Federal Republic of Yugoslavia, London.

We paid several visits to the National Library of Scotland in Edinburgh to examine the papers, photocopies and interviews used by Ronald Clark for his biography of Einstein. Sheila Mackenzie provided invaluable assistance, and we are also grateful to Ronald Clark's widow, Elizabeth Clark, for her help and permission to draw on his papers.

At Nuffield College, Oxford, we examined the correspondence of Elnstein with Professor Frederick Lindemann (Lord Cherwell). We received assistance from Eleanor Vallis and Richard Temple.

Thanks are also due to the following: James Albisetti of the University of Kansas; Dorothea Barfknecht of the Staatsbibliothek zu Berlin; Micha Battsek; Peter Bergmann, Professor Emeritus and research professor at Syracuse University; Adrian Berry; Anne Blumberg; Marianne Borsutzky of the Archiv zur Geschichte der Max-Planck Gesellschaft, Berlin; Charles Boyd of New Jersey's University of the Health Sciences; Gulshan Chunara for her unstinting secretarial help; Mary Creese of the University of Kansas; Marian Diamond of the University of California, Berkeley; Douglas Egan of the Emilio Segrè Visual Archives; Einstein's great-grandson, Paul Einstein; his granddaughter-in-law Aude Einstein; Hazel Gaskin and Richard Williams of Sandy Lane; Sam Guntley; Lutz Haber; Evan Harris Walker of the Walker Cancer Research Institute; Enda Jackson; Laurie Kaufman of the American Arbitration Association; Walter Lippincott, Alice Calaprice and Florence Slade of Princeton University Press; Sue Mallia; Susanne McDadd and Julian Loose of Faber; James Lyle; Terry Manners; Jagdish Mehra; Claudia Meier of the Bauer au Lac; Vivian Nutton of Wellcome; Dorinda Outram of University College, Cork; David Perry; Mike Shaw of Curtis Brown & John Farquharson and James Woodhouse.

Several people read the draft manuscripts to provide feedback and advice, to whom we are grateful: Peter Coveney, Bob Davenport, Evelyn Einstein, Doris Highfield, David Johnson, Eamonn Matthews, Susanne McDadd, and Gerald Whitrow. Michael Wright provided especial support in this area, and during many hours of discussion gave sensitive and penetrating criticism.

We would also like to thank our editors, Max Hastings of the *Daily Telegraph* and Sir Nicholas Lloyd of the *Daily Express*, for allowing us to pursue this project.

Julia Brookes gave invaluable assistance in the proof-reading, and in helping to arrange travel to Switzerland and California. She also gave crucial support in the final marathon edit. Most important of all, she provided her husband (RH) with love and encouragement during another drawn-out and exhausting project.

We also owe an outstanding debt to Yasmine Khan (PC's wife) who was closely involved in the project from its beginning. Without her constant stream of insights, her talent for analysis, and her unstinting support, this book would be immeasurably poorer. Only she and her husband can realize how much she had to put up with, and how many invaluable ideas she contributed.

The following have granted permission to quote various sources: The Albert Einstein Archives, The Hebrew University of Jerusalem, Israel; Buchverlag Der Morgen (Friedrich Herneck, *Einstein privat, Herta Waldow errinert sich an die Jahre 1927 bis 1933*); Butterworth Heinemann (Anton Reiser, *Albert Einstein: a Biographical Portrait*); The Cabinet Office and English-Speaking Union (Cherwell correspondence, Crown Copyright. Published with the permission of the controller of HMSO); Carol Publishing Group (Albert Einstein, *The World as I See It*); A. P. French (*Einstein: a Centenary Volume*, Heinemann); Handschriftenabteilung, Staatsbibliothek zu Berlin (Nachlaß 165, Maja Winteler); Carl Hanser Verlag (M. Grüning, *Ein Haus für Albert Einstein*); Elsevier Science Publishers (Martin Klein, *Paul Ehrenfest, Volume 1, The Making of a Theoretical Physicist*); HarperCollins Publishers (Paul Schilpp, *Albert Einstein, Philosopher-Scientist, Volume 1*); Paul Haupt Publishers (Desanka Trbuhovic-Gjuric, *Im Schatten Albert Einsteins: das tragische Leben der Mileva Einstein-Marić*, and Eduard Rübel, *Eduard Einstein*) Princeton University Press (*The Collected Papers of Albert Einstein, Volumes 1, 2 and 5*; the English translations of Volumes 1 and 2; *Albert Einstein/ Mileva Marić, the Love Letters*; and *Albert Einstein, the Human*

Side); The University of Iowa and Dord Krstić (Elizabeth Roboz Einstein, *Hans Albert Einstein: Reminiscences of his Life and our Life Together*); University of Oklahoma Press (Morris Goran, *The Story of Fritz Haber*, © 1967); Oxford University Press (Abraham Pais, *Subtle is the Lord . . . the Science and Life of Albert Einstein*); Peters Fraser and Dunlop (Ronald Clark, *Einstein: the Life and Times*); Peter Plesch (Janos Plesch, unpublished memo on Einstein, and his autobiography *Janos: the Story of a Doctor*); Lewis Pyenson, IOP Publishing and Adam Hilger (Lewis Pyenson, *The Young Einstein*); Russell & Volkening Inc. (Leopold Infeld, *Albert Einstein: his Work and its Influence on our World*); Rutgers University Press (Pnina Abir-Am and Dorinda Outram, *Uneasy Careers and Intimate Lives*, © 1987 by Rutgers, The State University); Jamie Sayen and The Crown Publishing Group (Jamie Sayen, *Einstein in America*, © Crown Publishers); Harry Woolf (Harry Woolf, *Some Strangeness in the Proportion*, © Addison-Wesley, 1980).

THE PRIVATE LIVES OF
ALBERT EINSTEIN

The Inheritance

HANS Albert Einstein lay in a coma for four weeks after the heart attack that struck him in the summer of 1973. The only surviving son of the century's greatest scientist was sixty-nine, and had been warned by doctors that his heart was weak. He had ignored them, and told his children that the indignity of being kept alive artificially was 'his greatest fear'. Eighteen years earlier, his dying father had refused emergency surgery, saying that it was tasteless to prolong life beyond its natural term. In this, as in so much else, Hans Albert bore the emotional legacy of a man whom by turns he had worshipped and despised. To cling to life smacked of sentimentality, and Hans Albert had been taught by his father to show a stoical resistance towards sentiment. Nothing would have dismayed him more than to think of his second wife, Elizabeth, sitting day and night at his hospital bedside, waiting for a recovery that would never come.

He had collapsed in a canteen queue after delivering a lecture on a visit to the Woods Hole Oceanographic Institution, Massachusetts. Like his father, who even on his deathbed called for writing material, intent on working to the last, Hans Albert had taken refuge from the world by devoting himself to academic study. He was an hydraulic engineer who had become an international authority on sediments and flood control. An assistant recalled that he never spoke of his famous father, his family or his private life. Only if the topic was music would he allow himself to stray beyond professional matters. Music and sailing were his twin recreations – just as they had been those of his father, whom he so strongly resembled, stocky and muscular, at the helm of his wooden sloop on San Francisco Bay. A less experienced sailing companion wrote that the rule with Hans Albert was simple: one was allowed to make the same mistake twice, but on the third occasion one had to bow before a storm of temper. At the piano he kept strictly to the classics, shying away from anything he thought too modern or mawkish.

Hans Albert was respected by his colleagues and friends as a man of exceptional gifts, and was loved and admired in his own right. Yet on everything he did there was the stamp of his father, and he was never able to shake off the weight of his great name. He once admitted that the constantly repeated question 'Are you related to Albert Einstein?' had become like the drip-drip of a Chinese water torture. He hid his feelings behind a permanent slight smile, but his daughter, Evelyn, sensed a suppressed resentment that fed on the many family secrets that his father had left behind.

Albert Einstein has become so much of a modern icon that it is hard to see him afresh. He was only twenty-six when he published the special theory of relativity in 1905, but the most famous images of him date from his last years, half a century later. Einstein's face in old age has been described so often that the phrases seem to arrive prefabricated: the tangles of white hair are almost invariably described as 'a mane' or 'a halo', the eyes below that famously wrinkled forehead have so often been called 'mild' and 'gentle' that we easily miss a glint of something altogether harsher and more sardonic. We tend to carry with us a slightly blurred picture, something between Lewis Carroll's amiably absurd White Knight and Aslan, the lion-Christ of C. S. Lewis's Narnia. The writer C. P. Snow called it 'at first glance the face of an inspired and saintly golliwog'.

This was a nice summary point. Einstein has become a popular epitome of the eccentric genius, poking his tongue out for the cameras and wandering around in shoes without socks. He often joked that he had also turned into a Jewish saint. It was not only that his discoveries transformed our view of space and time, rebuilding the foundations of twentieth-century scientific thought: his readiness to describe his work in religious terms, despite his own decidedly unorthodox views on religion, was accompanied by an enthusiasm for pronouncing on politics and morals. Einstein's reputation rests on not only his scientific triumphs but also his record as a campaigner for pacifism and human rights. He gave the appearance of great humility and gentleness, of being entirely at ease with himself. In a secular age, he took on the aura of a holy man.

This was not the father that Hans Albert knew. He had lived with the private Einstein – a man whose public words and private deeds were often at odds, and whose outward serenity concealed inner confusion. He was a man whose combination of intellectual vision and emotional myopia left behind him a series of damaged lives.

Saints tread a lonely road, and the idea of personal relationships playing an important part in Einstein's life is alien to the conventional picture of him. He cast himself as a naturally solitary man, describing himself in German as an *Einspanner*, a one-horse cab. In a much-quoted passage, he contrasted his crusading interest in social justice with his lack of desire for direct human contact:

> I have never belonged wholeheartedly to any country or state, to my circle of friends, or even to my own family. These ties have always been accompanied by a vague aloofness, and the wish to withdraw into myself increases with the years. Such isolation is sometimes bitter, but I do not regret being cut off from the understanding and sympathy of other men. I lose something by it, to be sure, but I am compensated for it in being rendered independent of the customs, opinions, and prejudices of others, and am not tempted to rest my peace of mind upon such shifting foundations.

Bertrand Russell, like many others who knew him, took Einstein at his word, proclaiming, 'Personal matters never occupied more than odd nooks and crannies in his thoughts.' A more clear-eyed analysis was provided by C. P. Snow, who wrote, 'No one has stripped away the claims of self more ruthlessly . . . But it is wrong to romanticize anyone, even Einstein. It seems to me that a man has to possess a pretty hefty ego to need to subdue it so totally.' He must have power-ful emotions, too, if the wish to suppress them is as strong as Ein-stein's self-description suggested. Avowals of self-sufficiency and emotional detachment pepper his writings, but their very frequency should call their conviction into doubt. The private Einstein was a man of fierce passions, whose efforts to deny them never succeeded.

Einstein described his dedication to science as an attempt to escape what he called 'the merely personal' by fixing his gaze on the objective universe. The desire to locate a reality free of human uncertainties was fundamental to his most important work. His two theories of relativity attempt to provide a consistent description of the universe that is independent of human observers, and unaffected by changing frames of reference. Equally, his stubborn opposition to quantum mechanics grew from a refusal to accept that uncertainty was intrinsic to sub-atomic physics, and that some aspects of quantum reality could be determined only by observation. Today it is clear that these features are indeed intrinsic to the quantum world – a world that Einstein helped to discover. In science, much as in life, even he was unable to eliminate the human element.

The desire for impersonal detachment and the desire for intimacy were secretly at war within Einstein – just as his idealism was at war with a bleak cynicism, and his modesty was at war with arrogance. Few understood these contradictions better than Hans Albert's mother – Mileva Marić – who met Einstein while both were physics students in Switzerland. Their marriage, from 1903 to 1919, spanned the most important years of Einstein's life, covering the majority of his creative activity. Yet Mileva has always remained a shadowy figure in Einstein biographies, and it is only in the last few years that the full story of their relationship has begun to emerge. In the early stages, it is the story of an amorous young man rebelling against his background to pursue a woman of exceptional drive and intelligence. This includes Einstein's attempt to use Mileva as a means to break free from his mother, whose emotional grip was exceptionally strong and marked him throughout his life. It includes the birth of an illegitimate daughter whom he gave away and whose existence remained secret until 1987 – but who possibly could still be alive today. Most controversially, recent scholarship has suggested how heavily Einstein leaned on Mileva as he began to develop the first outlines of relativity. He referred to his early studies as 'our work', casting her as his co-conspirator in what became a scientific revolution. Einstein hailed Mileva as his 'right hand', his equal, one who was as strong and as independent as himself, without whom he was unable to function.

Mileva emerged from this relationship with her spirit crushed and her own academic dreams abandoned. She was divorced from

Einstein in the year that he gained his fame, and had no share in it. Newly released documents make it possible to chart the decline of the marriage, and to show how Einstein deceived Mileva in a secret liaison with the cousin who later became his second wife. His behaviour during the separation, when Mileva suffered a mental and physical breakdown from which she never fully recovered, dismayed his closest friends. Yet it was to her that Einstein then gave the money from his Nobel prize for physics – the greatest honour that the scientific world can bestow. In this way, he hoped to secure the future of their two sons, who formed a link between the couple for the rest of their lives.

Hans Albert was the elder of the boys, and was fifteen at the time of the divorce. He developed a bitterness towards his father that he never mastered, and which hurt Einstein badly. The arguments between them helped to open a split between Hans Albert and his father's followers that still rankles among his descendants today. But the unluckiest member of the family was Einstein's younger son, Eduard, whose emotional turmoil in the years after the divorce eventually developed into mental illness. He seemed to friends and teachers to have inherited the spark of his father's genius, directed away from science towards literature and the arts. But Einstein was never at ease with Eduard's great gifts, and possessed a horror of illness and modern medicine that led him to turn his back on his son. Eduard spent many years detained in a Swiss psychiatric clinic, unvisited by his father, and died in miserable circumstances.

Other relationships show further unexpected sides of Einstein's character. It is now possible to describe his first unhappy romantic attachment, before he met Mileva, which established many of the emotional themes that were to run through his later life. A large amount of new material has also emerged in recent years regarding his second marriage. His cousin Elsa became more of a mother than a wife, organizing his daily life and shielding him from the relentlessly inquisitive public. In return, he came to show a casual disregard for her feelings. His philandering became part of his family's private folklore, with his granddaughter Evelyn speaking of him as 'quite the ladies' man . . . a rake'. Yet his love for women's company often seemed combined with a scorn for their intellect and character that bordered on misogyny.

Einstein touched on these questions a month before his death in 1955, in a letter of condolence that he sent to the grieving son and sister of his dearest friend, Michele Besso, who had just died. The seventy-six-year-old's words were heavy with a sense of his own mortality. He was extremely frail and had known for several years that there was a blister-like growth on his main artery which one day would burst and kill him. Besso, he wrote, had merely 'preceded me briefly in bidding farewell to this strange world'. He offered by way of comfort his conviction as a physicist that 'the distinction between past, present and future is only an illusion, however persistent' – that death had no greater reality than the life it seemed to end. But his most revealing words were those that he chose as a personal epitaph for his friend. 'What I most admire about him as a human being', said Einstein, 'is that he managed to live for many years not only in peace but in harmony with a woman – an undertaking in which I twice failed rather disgracefully.'

When Hans Albert finally died, on 26 July 1973, the key to this 'disgrace' and many more of his father's secrets sat in a shoebox in a kitchen drawer at his home in Berkeley, California. The box contained family correspondence dating back to the end of the last century – including Einstein's love-letters to Mileva, and many other letters that he sent to her and his sons after their separation. The collection was so sensitive that the executors of Einstein's estate, who had legal control of the publication of his words, had gone to court to stop Hans Albert and his first wife from publishing selected details. Not even Einstein's son could be allowed to reveal such intimate material.

This was only one example of a sustained campaign by the guardians of Einstein's reputation – 'the Einstein priests' as one researcher has called them – to suppress information that revealed his personal flaws. Only recently, and after much detective work by a team of scholars, have the letters begun to be published as part of Einstein's *Collected Papers*. The massive Einstein papers project at Boston University, under the leadership of Professors Martin Klein, A. J. Kox and Robert Schulmann, has provided the first compelling arguments for a fundamental reappraisal of Einstein's character. In the light of their pioneering efforts, many clues left by his early biographers now take on a new significance. By re-examining their work and drawing on a wide range of archival material, together with interviews with family members, scholars and those who knew Einstein, it is now possible to move closer to understanding the private man – the Einstein that Hans Albert knew, and who left him such a mixed inheritance.

2

First Love

ASKED once why her household ran so smoothly, Einstein's mother smilingly replied, 'It is discipline.' Pauline Einstein was an ample and commanding figure, and it is from her that young Albert seems to have inherited his distinctively fleshy nose, as well as that unruly bundle of hair. Her grey eyes stared out at the world with a mocking glint, and she presided over family affairs with caustic wit. Einstein's letters give several hints of her fondness for teasing him, and her spirit was reflected in his own propensity to sarcasm. One friend described the penetrating ridicule that Einstein often deployed in otherwise amiable conversations, leaving people unsure whether to smile or to take offence. His laughter was infectious, but sometimes had an unpleasantly critical edge. In this, and in other ways, Einstein was very much his mother's son.

When Einstein was born, in the southern German city of Ulm, at 11.30 a.m. on 14 March 1879, Pauline regarded her baby with alarm. His head was so big and so angular that she thought he was deformed. Later the slowness with which this quiet, fat child learned to speak made her fear he was mentally retarded. As he grew, so did Pauline's pride in him and her ambition for his future. But she was never an indulgent parent, and it was her domineering personality that defined much of the atmosphere of Einstein's childhood. This period of his life has been described before, but many new details are now available. Moreover, it is only with the release of his private correspondence that Einstein's attachment to his parents has come into full focus. Despite his protests to the contrary, it is now possible to see that family bonds – as a source of both tension and security – were of immense importance to him. Many of those who knew Einstein said that he retained a childlike quality all his life. Intellectually, it showed in his penetrating directness and his readiness to question what others took for granted. Emotionally, its effects were not always so benign.

Einstein was once invited to say whether Pauline or his father, Hermann, was head of the family. 'Cannot be answered,' came the reply. He was equally brusque when asked on another occasion to which parent he owed his great gifts. His only gift was extreme inquisitiveness, he said, so the question did not arise. Einstein was noticeably less defensive when questioned solely about his father. Asked to outline Hermann's qualities, he listed 'good humour, patience, goodness, charm'. When the same questioner returned to the point, suggesting his father might have been severe, Einstein was insistent: 'Exceedingly friendly, mild and wise.' He said that Hermann had a moral influence on him, although not an intellectual one.

It is hard to find any public testimonials by Einstein to his mother's merits. One can understand why his friend Janos Plesch wrote that it was to Hermann that he was more strongly attached. The biography of Einstein by his stepson-in-law, Rudolf Kayser, which seems to have given the approved account of his childhood, agrees that he 'sought his bearings from his father', but we should read this in the light of Hermann's own habitual style of navigation. He would choose the route for the family's Sunday excursions, but the final destination was always where Pauline wanted to go.

Kayser wrote that Pauline did not always see the world through Hermann's 'optimistic eyes'. For this she had good reason, since her husband's life was dogged by failure. Behind his pince-nez and formidable moustache, Hermann was placid and passive. He was well liked by those who knew him ('particularly by women', says Kayser) but careless about life's practicalities. He was thirty-one at the time of his son's birth and had drifted into business as a partner in a cousin's feather-bed firm. This might seem a fitting job for a man of such soft and accommodating character, but no one as docile as Hermann could be a successful entrepreneur. He is said to have shown an early aptitude for mathematics, but was prevented from pursuing his studies by the financial limitations that a large family imposed on his father. His daughter Maja, Einstein's younger sister, considered him too dreamy to take decisions and too kind-hearted to resist stronger wills. His younger brother Jakob possessed such a will, and in 1880 he persuaded Hermann to join his plumbing and electrical business in Munich. The family moved when Einstein was just a year old, and initially the new firm enjoyed some success. In 1888 it supplied the electrical system to give power and light for the entire town of Schwabing, with ten thousand inhabitants. Most of Einstein's early years were spent in considerable material comfort at the family villa, a lavish two-storey building complete with roof-top sun terrace and surrounded by landscaped gardens.

Though Jakob had technical flair, his ambition overreached itself. A larger plant was set up to construct a dynamo that he had designed, but rivals with greater financial muscle squeezed the Einstein brothers out of the capital-intensive market. Their estate was sold and their Munich factory liquidated in 1894, but once again Hermann was swept along by his more dynamic sibling. Jakob persuaded him to shift their activities to northern Italy, where they had already enjoyed some success, conjuring up dreams of installing and running a hydro-electric power station in Pavia. Two years later, after the massive family upheaval entailed by moving across the Alps, this new venture also failed. For all the wisdom later praised by his son, Hermann Einstein was to be troubled by financial problems for the rest of his life.

Jakob accepted defeat and took a job as an engineer with another company, but Hermann ploughed on alone and set up yet another electrical factory, this time in Milan. It brought with it new debts and new worries – but again a stronger personality was driving him on. Hermann feared that Pauline could not tolerate the lower social status if he lost professional independence. His wife was a woman accustomed to wealth and success, and she found it hard to accept the reduced circumstances that his failures slowly produced. She had brought considerable financial means to the marriage, and large sums invested by her relatives were lost in her husband's ventures.

Pauline's family history gives many clues to her character. Her father, Julius Koch, had risen from being a baker to make a sizeable fortune as a grain-trader with his brother. According to Maja Einstein's account, he was forceful and shrewd but not at all given to theorizing. He enjoyed his wealth and even dabbled as a patron of the arts, but this was in such conflict with his instinct for a bargain that he ended up buying copies rather than original paintings. Koch headed an extraordinarily close family: he and his brother and their wives and children shared a single household under one roof, with each wife cooking in alternate weeks. Maja wrote that the arrangement lasted for decades without friction, for which she gave the credit to Einstein's maternal grandmother, Jette. A quiet, clear-headed and methodical woman, she was in Maja's words 'the soul of that odd household'. The families of Hermann and Jakob also shared one house when they moved to Munich, and they were joined there by Julius Koch after Jette died in 1886. Close families, with powerful women at their centre, were a tradition with which Einstein grew up.

Like her mother, Pauline was the soul of her household. With significant qualification, Maja wrote that she 'basically' had a warm and caring nature. But the picture she paints is of someone hardened by experience (Pauline 'learned early about the realities of life') and who possessed a sceptical outlook. According to her daughter, Pauline's inner feelings were seldom given free expression, and it is clear that she was less interested in showering her son with love than in making sure he developed more backbone than his father. Maja recalled the rigour with which Einstein was trained to be self-reliant, and remarked what a contrast this made to the 'over-anxious tutelage' of most European parents. At three or four, her brother was sent off alone to navigate Munich's busiest streets. Having been shown the route once, he was left to find his own way over the road-junctions, all the time being secretly observed to check his performance. When he was five, his parents hired a woman teacher to instruct him at home, apparently determined that he should jump straight into the second grade when he entered primary school a year later. Maja remembered the absolute strictness with which he was made to finish his homework before turning to play. No excuses were tolerated. Hermann and Pauline were trying to create a child at once independent and dependently obedient. It was bound to be a combustible mixture.

By his own description, Einstein was a lonely and dreamy child who did not easily find companions. He would avoid the rough-and-tumble games when the children of relatives came to play in the

Einsteins' garden, unless it was to act as arbiter in disputes. Maja compared his mother's taste for complicated needlework with his own devotion to solitary and taxing pastimes. Besides assembling complicated constructions with his building blocks, he made houses of cards up to fourteen stories high. His sister believed that this lone persistence was reflected in the tenacity with which Einstein later approached his scientific problems.

Little Albert's reaction on first meeting Maja after her birth in November 1881 was unenthusiastic. He had been told he would now have a sister to play with, and had imagined she was some kind of toy. 'Yes, but where are its wheels?' he asked bemusedly. In many ways, he appears to have been something of a trial to his sister. Like his grandfather, Julius Koch, he was prone to tantrums – colourful ones, in which his face went completely yellow and the tip of his nose turned white. Maja found herself at the receiving end of violent attacks: once having a large bowling-ball thrown at her, another time being thumped about the head with what she described as a child's hoe. 'Nothing more is needed to show that a sound skull is needed to be the sister of a thinker,' she wrote. If it was any comfort, she was not the sole target of her brother's eruptions. He also hit his private teacher with a stool – frightening her so much that she ran away and was never seen again, according to Maja.

When gripped by these rages, which subsided during his early years at school, the young Einstein seemed unable to control himself. At other times he showed an almost unnatural calm. His nurse had nicknamed her seemingly placid charge 'Pater Langweil' – Father Bore. It was this apparent inertia that fuelled concern about his mental development. After starting to talk comparatively late, he would softly repeat every sentence he uttered – a habit that continued until he was seven. Even when he was nine he lacked fluency of speech. The problem seems to have been as much a reluctance to communicate as any inability to do so.

Except in his sudden explosions of rage, the young Einstein kept his feelings under an even tighter rein than his mother did hers. One of the few means of expression they found was music – an activity that carried his mother's strong approval. Music meant little to his father, but Pauline had talent and liked to perform piano duets with engineers from her husband's factory. Her son showed an early aptitude, starting to learn the violin at the age of five. By his own account his progress was only workmanlike until about thirteen, but he persisted, with his mother acting as eager accompanist at the keyboard. Music became for him an 'inner necessity', and the violin a constant companion. As a young man he would refer to his violin as his child, joking once that when he left it unplayed on holiday 'it probably thinks it has got a stepfather'. He called the instrument 'my old friend, through whom I say and I sing to myself all that which I often do not admit to myself at all, but which at best makes me laugh when I see it in others.' Many years later, Hans Albert would recall, 'He often told me that one of the most important things in his life was music. Whenever he felt that he had come to the end of the road or faced a difficult challenge in his work, he would take refuge in music and that would resolve all his difficulties.' Mozart, Bach and Schubert were among his favourite composers, with Einstein praising the last of these for his 'superlative ability to express emotion'. But he always wanted emotion to be tempered by a sound musical structure, and he was reluctant to discuss what moved him in a composer's work. His motto was simple: 'Listen, play, love, revere – and keep your mouth shut.'

At the age of seven Einstein was sent to a public primary school, a Catholic institution where he was the only Jewish boy in his class. Jews were a well-established community in the region of his birth, but made up only about 2 per cent of Munich's population. Although his parents were far from devout, and never discussed religion, this served only to isolate them further. There is a famous story, which Einstein approved as true, that one of his teachers once produced a large nail, with the assurance that this was the type used to pin Christ to the Cross. However, it seems that the teacher did not, as was sometimes done, blame the Crucifixion on the Jews. In a draft letter written in 1920, Einstein recalled that the school was liberal and showed no discrimination. It was his classmates, not the teachers, who were anti-Semitic. Violent attacks and abuse were frequent on his way to lessons. Even though most were 'not too malicious', he wrote that they intensified his feeling of being an outsider. He later suggested that he was made fully conscious of his Jewishness only after the First World War, when he was recruited to the cause of Zionism. But his Zionist convictions did not spring from thin air, and Einstein grew up well aware of his heritage. As a young man searching for an academic job in 1901, he wrote that one of the main obstacles was the anti-Semitism he felt sure he would encounter in German-speaking countries.

It was compulsory for primary-school pupils in Bavaria to undergo instruction in the Catholic faith, and Einstein was given lessons on the Jewish religion at home by a relative. These lessons seem to have tapped passions that he had previously kept hidden. The boy is said to have been irritated by his father's own indifference towards religion, and was now fired with enthusiasm. Alone in his family he refused to eat pork, and at around the age of eleven he was so filled with faith that he composed songs of praise to God and sang them in the street. He identified God with nature, leading Maja to write that his instruction had unleashed fervent feelings without them being integrated into orthodox dogma. Einstein later described this phase as one of 'deep religiosity', hinting that there was an element of childish posturing. The ardour was genuine, but its means of expression were not fully worked out.

Einstein would always be a great self-dramatist, but this early choice of role is one of his most interesting. In his own scanty biographical notes, he said, 'It is quite clear to me that the religious paradise of youth . . . was a first effort to free myself from the chains of the "merely personal", from an existence which is dominated by wishes, hopes and primitive feelings.' This was Einstein writing at the age of sixty-seven and with the implicit conviction that he had indeed shaken off these 'chains'. He did not question whether this was an achievable goal: there was no apparent doubt in his words that a man really could live free of emotions and desires. Nor did he choose to dwell on why this objective should appeal to a child so young. It seems that Einstein was a boy whose upbringing left him unable to understand or easily express emotions, except in music. Their sublimation in religious zeal was a tremendous release – although surely not, as he later thought, a form of escape. The joy that his 'religiosity' brought him came not from discarding his primitive feelings but from giving them voice. Nor was it an escape from the personal. By embracing religion so ardently in a family of non-believers, he was making an emphatic statement of individuality. This was no retreat into the impersonal – it was the carving of a personal niche.

Einstein's purported dimness as a schoolboy is one of the most seductive parts of his legend: it gives hope to the rest of us. Classmates at primary school taunted him with the nickname 'Biedermeier', which roughly translates as 'Honest John', because of his blunt and unsophisticated manner. His sister remarked that he was considered only moderately talented because he took so long to mull things over. She wrote, 'Nothing of his special aptitude for mathematics was noticeable at the time; he wasn't even good at arithmetic in the sense of being quick and accurate, though he was reliable and persevering.' Stories of this early backwardness are easily overplayed, however, and at as early as seven he had started to show real promise. Pauline wrote to her own mother in August 1886 that he had been placed top of the class 'once again' and had received a 'splendid' school report. It became part of family folklore that she had declared that her little Albert would become a great professor one day.

Einstein spoke bitterly about his formal schooling at the Luitpold Gymnasium, which he entered at the age of nine and a half. He was one of 1,330 pupils in a regime he later presented as authoritarian and devoted to dully mechanical teaching methods. 'I preferred to endure all sorts of punishments rather than to learn gabble by rote,' he said. In his autobiographical notes, Einstein admitted that 'every reminiscence is coloured by today's being what it is, and therefore by a deceptive point of view.' The Luitpold Gymnasium was in fact progressive for its time, and Einstein proved a successful pupil with good grades. He was consistently excellent at mathematics, scored top marks in Latin, and came close to doing so in Greek. Indeed, his only weak spot was sports, which made him feel tired and dizzy. It remains true that he did not entirely fit in, and found Pauline's maternal discipline more tolerable than that of his schoolmasters. His Greek professor earned immortality by saying that nothing would ever become of him. 'And in fact,' his sister Maja observed, 'Albert Einstein never did attain a professorship of Greek grammar.'

In addition to the influence of his masters, notably his mathematics teacher, Josef Zametzer, a key part of Einstein's education took place outside the classroom. Although Einstein would later deny that anyone in his family had real scientific knowledge, he was surrounded by adults involved in telecommunications and electrotechnology. These fields were then at the forefront of contemporary technology, as computers and lasers are today. His father's partner, Uncle Jakob, had received a higher education, being a graduate of the Stuttgart Polytechnic Engineering School. It was Jakob who introduced Einstein to geometry and algebra, portraying the latter as a jolly game, hunting for the animal 'x' whose name we do not know.

The scholars of the Einstein papers project are also placing renewed emphasis on the young boy's reading of popular science books, some of which were given him by Max Talmey, a poor Jewish medical student whom his parents took under their wing. From the time Albert was ten until he turned fifteen, Talmey would engage him in intellectual debate during weekly visits to have dinner with the family. Maja recalled her brother working through a series of simple guides to science by Aaron Bernstein that had been recommended by Talmey. Einstein himself said that he read them 'with breathless attention'. As Kayser remarked, 'They were a gay-coloured, beautiful atlas of nature within the limits of a child's comprehension. To Albert, these books were veritable revelations. He consumed them with the same passion with which other boys devour Indian stories.' For today's Einstein scholars, study of Bernstein's books has revealed striking parallels to some of Einstein's most important ideas. As Jürgen Renn and Robert Schulmann have commented, 'Bernstein discusses the corpuscular theory of light that Einstein would revive . . . and he even mentions the possibility of light deflection by a gravitational field, which eventually became one of the key proofs of the general theory of relativity.' Einstein never cared for painting in the details of science for their own sake: he worked on a big canvas. Bernstein's books allowed him to grasp the pressing issues of current research without becoming overwhelmed by minutiae. One of their themes dear to his heart was their emphasis on the way that unseen forces gave unity to the universe. Renn has pointed out another – the idea that the world can be described in terms of atomic behaviour, a theme that underpinned Einstein's revolutionary papers in 1905.

Einstein said that it was his reading of popular science which ended his 'religiosity' abruptly at the age of twelve. He decided that the stories of the Bible could not be true, and swung to the opposite extreme of fervent doubt. The young boy went through a fit of fanatical freethinking, convinced that he had been fed lies. He later suggested that this bred a suspicion of authority and a scepticism towards the established social order that never left him. At the same time, his feelings of reverence focused more strongly on the inanimate world. Here is how he described it in his autobiographical notes, immediately after the passage on his religious phase:

> Out yonder there was this huge world, which exists independently of us human beings and which stands before us like a great, eternal riddle, at least partly accessible to our inspection and thinking. The contemplation of this world beckoned like a liberation, and I soon noticed that many a man whom I had learned to esteem and to admire had found inner freedom and security in devoted occupation with it.

Here, according to Einstein, was the means of escape into the 'extrapersonal world' that would sustain him for the rest of his life. The boy who had found neither security nor freedom in human relationships, and whose attempt to find them in religion had failed, would seek them now in science. Yet one is struck by Einstein's emphasis on the sympathy he felt with those he thought like-minded. 'Similarly motivated men of the present and past', he went on, were 'the friends which could not be lost.'

Einstein would frequently return to the language of religion to describe his feelings of awe towards the physical world. His saintly image is due in part to the way that he lent his scientific efforts the appearance of a holy mission. He famously explained his scepticism about quantum mechanics with the remark that 'God does not play dice with the world.' Almost as celebrated is his statement of faith that no secrets of physics are ultimately inaccessible: 'The Lord God is subtle, but not malicious.' His declared aim was 'to know how God created the world', and he once wrote that scientists of his kind were 'the only deeply religious people' of the age. What Einstein called his 'cosmic religious experience', a worship of the beauties of physics, has become the common faith of a generation of physicists. The British cosmologist Stephen Hawking, for example, has spoken in strikingly similar terms of his own desire to penetrate 'the mind of God'. But there was something slippery about Einstein's vocabulary. One biographer has written that his use of the word 'God' recalled the attitude to words of Lewis Carroll's Red Queen. In fact it was Humpty Dumpty who told Alice that words meant what he wanted them to mean, but the point is otherwise well made. Einstein's views were atheistic in almost every important respect. He found it impossible to conceive of a personal deity, had no belief in an afterlife, and considered morality an entirely man-made affair. His worship of cosmic harmony was genuine; his claims that this was the face of God were at best a benign affectation. Einstein gave a strong hint of this when he was asked how he would have reacted if his theory of relativity had not been backed by experiment: he said he would have felt 'sorry for the dear Lord'. It was as if he felt that only religious language would prevent his surrender to the mundane, the unspiritual, the crassly earthbound. The truth was that he had never quite put behind him the 'religiosity' of youth.

One of the most celebrated anecdotes about Einstein suggests that his reverence for nature's secret powers was aroused when he was as young as four or five. It was then, while ill in bed, that he was presented by his father with a compass, and was filled with wonder at the way in which its needle was compelled by an invisible force to point northwards. It has often been remarked that Einstein, when recounting this incident, expressed a lingering worry that 'the deep and abiding impression' he thought it made might be an embellishment of memory, tacked on in the retelling. But a similar impact appears to have been made on Einstein at the age of twelve by what he called – with another flash of religiosity – the 'holy geometry book.' This standard mathematics text, of the kind from which countless schoolchildren have shrunk away in horror, dazzled him with its display of the power of pure thought. He wrote of the indelible memory left by the 'lucidity and certainty' with which seemingly groundless assertions could be proved. Over the next four years he familiarized himself with the other elements of mathematics, including calculus.

When his family set off on the ill-fated move to Italy in 1894, the fifteen-year-old Einstein was left behind in Munich in lodgings, to avoid interrupting his education. It was a harsh decision, suggesting how Pauline and Hermann's ambition for Einstein outweighed their need to be close to him, and it provoked one of the great emotional crises of his life. In the spring of the following year, without having consulted his parents, Einstein suddenly abandoned school a year and a half before his final examination and crossed the Alps to rejoin them. He effected his escape by presenting his teachers with a medical certificate stating he was suffering from nervous disorders. According to the authorized version of his life, as recorded by Kayser, this was a 'necessary lie' – a wily trick carried out with the help of a sympathetic doctor. Einstein, so we are told, simply wanted an excuse to enjoy the charms of Italy, which younger cousins from Genoa had depicted as an earthly paradise. However, it is just as likely that his mental anguish was genuine. His sister made no hint of trickery in her own description of the episode, stating that Einstein was depressed and nervous, and suggesting that his laconic letters to his parents should have warned them of his unhappiness. Reasons for this included his dissatisfaction with school and the approaching threat of military service. It also appears that his Greek master had told him that his disrespectful attitude was disruptive, and that he would do well to leave. But the point that most accounts overlook is perhaps the most obvious: Einstein missed his parents.

It is clear that Einstein remembered chafing against his family's intellectual limitations, and a constant theme of his letters to Mileva is how narrow-minded and stultifying he found life at home. This is reflected in Kayser's biography, with its description of the 'well-to-do philistine atmosphere' in which Einstein was raised. The word 'philistine' became Einstein's shorthand for everything he detested about his family, and Kayser writes of the boy living in a foreign world, surrounded by conversation unrelated to his dreams and wishes. Nevertheless, this home was enormously important to him: he had no real life outside it, and could remember having only one friend at school. For all its faults, his home provided him with the material comforts and cosiness – the *Gemütlichkeit* – that was such a great South German tradition.

Maja leaves us in no doubt how painful his family's move to Italy must have been. The attractive villa where her brother had 'spent a happy childhood' was sold to a building contractor 'who immediately turned the handsome grounds into a construction site, cutting down the magnificent old trees and erecting an entire row of ugly apartment houses. Until the time of their move the children had to watch from the house as these witnesses to their most cherished memories were destroyed.' Little wonder that Einstein had no desire to stay behind in Munich.

Hermann and Pauline were alarmed by their son's abrupt trans-formation into a school drop-out, and also by his declaration that he would now give up German citizenship. This liberated him from the military obligations that would have become unavoidable after his seventeenth birthday. His lifelong anti-militarism seems to have had its roots in early childhood, not in any horror of violence, but in revulsion from the regimentation that allowed soldiers no will of their own. Young Albert, so the story goes, was filled with fear and hatred by the sight of troops parading in the street. Yet whether this entirely explains his renunciation of German citizenship is doubtful. In 1901, he would present himself meekly enough for military service in Swit-zerland, only to be declared unfit due to varicose veins and flat, sweaty feet. His repudiation of the country of his birth involved something more than reluctance to be a soldier: it seems to have been a rejection of all the 'philistine' formality with which Germany was associated in his mind. Perhaps it should also be seen as an attempt to kick against his family, in whom he saw the same faults, and to reassert his independence after following them to Italy. There remained in his character much more of the German stereotype than he cared to admit – especially his iron self-discipline and his impatience with those whom he considered more feeble than himself.

Einstein sought to reassure his parents by promising to apply for a place at the Swiss Federal Polytechnical School at Zurich, one of the best centres for technical education in Europe (now called the Eidgenössische Technische Hochschule or ETH). Bowing to their wishes, the target he set himself was to become an electrical engineer or technician. Einstein already wanted to pursue a more theoretical path, but was told by his father to forget such 'philosophical non-sense' and apply for a sensible trade. He gave in only reluctantly, and retained unhappy memories of the disagreement. Ironically, many years later, he acted out a mirror image of the same confrontation with Hans Albert.

Pauline Einstein set about pulling what strings she could to advance her son's progress, and asked a family friend, Gustav Maier, to use his influence in Zurich. Maier persuaded the Polytechnic's director, Albin Herzog, to let Einstein take the entrance examination despite being two years under the normal age of eighteen and lacking a secondary-school leaving certificate (matura). The claims he made for the boy can be sensed from Herzog's doubtful reply, with its withering reference to this 'so-called child prodigy'. Passing the entrance examination would have put Einstein's life back on course. Instead, he failed. If we are to believe his own recollections, he was so unenthusiastic at the career his parents had chosen for him that he did little to prepare himself outside his fields of interest. His performance seems to have been worst on general-knowledge questions, but he shone in mathematics and science. The Polytechnic's physics professor, Heinrich Weber, was impressed enough to invite Einstein to attend his lectures as a visitor. However, Director Herzog advised him to go back to secondary school, pass the matura, then enter the following year.

On 26 October 1895 Einstein enrolled as a third-year pupil in the technical division of the cantonal school in Aarau, twenty miles to the west of Zurich. Once again he was separated from his parents, but this time he found two surrogates who would change his life. Professor Jost Winteler taught Greek and history in a different division of the Aarau school. He and his wife, Pauline, were accustomed to taking pupils as boarders, and it was agreed that young Albert would lodge at their home, Rossligut, opposite the school building. Einstein remained with the Wintelers throughout his three semesters in Aarau, and they became a second family to him. His sister Maja eventually married the couple's son Paul, and his best friend Michele Besso married their daughter Anna. Most significantly of all, their daughter Marie was Einstein's first sweetheart.

It was one of the happiest periods of his life, and he described the town as 'an unforgettable oasis in that European oasis, Switzerland'. Professor Winteler shared with Einstein's father an easy-going manner and was unusually kind. It was typical that neither man felt inclined to discuss Albert's boarding costs until the boy was already well settled. Intellectually, however, the difference was marked. While Hermann Einstein's education had been limited to technical school, Winteler was the son of a teacher and had received a rigorous academic training at the universities of Zurich and Jena. Although his areas of expertise lay far from science (he had studied history, German and philology), he could provide the young Albert with a new level of mental stimulation. Under his leadership, the entire family would regularly gather round the table to debate topics of the day. Hermann Einstein was clearly in awe of the 'Esteemed Herr Professor', and hoped that these 'stimulating discussions' would be of special benefit in broadening his son's knowledge. Hermann was unconcerned about politics, but Professor Winteler had a strong liberal outlook which chimed with Einstein's own developing views. In particular, he shared the teenager's suspicions of Germany and its militarism. He had a spiky integrity which inspired Einstein's respect, and had resigned as director of one school after conflict with its hard-line Catholic governors. It may be that he affected a greater freedom of thought than he possessed: Einstein would later grumble to Mileva that Winteler remained 'an old village schoolmaster, whatever he says'. Indeed, Einstein let it be known that he found the professor rather self-willed and complacent, but these were faults that he complained of in almost everyone at one time or another. His underlying respect for the intelligence and decency of the man he called 'Papa' Winteler never wavered.

The professor's wife had a much warmer personality than Einstein's mother. Where Pauline Einstein was sceptical and reserved, Pauline Winteler was indulgent and open-hearted. Already mother to seven children of her own, she accepted Albert as one more addition to her brood. He in turn came to call her 'Mamerl', or Mummy, and would have painfully happy memories of the times they sat sharing confidences in Rossligut's sunny peace and calm. After his departure he sent her letters overflowing with affection, typically ending with 'A thousand greetings and kisses'. It is unlikely that Einstein would have written to his natural mother that a play made him cry like a child, 'half in bliss, half in pain'. He did so to Pauline Winteler. It is unlikely that he would have written to his mother that his life seemed 'so philistine that people could use it for setting their watches – except that their watches would be somewhat late in the morning'. Pauline Winteler could share the joke, and understand what he meant by 'philistine' without being offended. She in turn sent him letters full of love, together with presents, poems and lilies of the valley.

Soon after his son's arrival at Rossligut, Hermann Einstein told Jost Winteler of his deep gratitude for the hospitality Albert was receiving. Hermann could see that Albert already felt as comfortable in Aarau as he did at home. The point was made when his son decided to stay there for the Christmas holidays of 1895.

It seems that the Wintelers brought out in Einstein an emotional side that was not always obvious to his classmates, who still regarded him as a loner. One friend, Hans Byland, left behind a rather intimidating picture of this 'unregenerate mocker', a cocksure youth with thick black hair, who strode about in the 'rapid, I might almost say crazy, tempo of a restless spirit which carries the whole world in itself'. Here was a confident clear-thinker who voiced his opinions 'whether they offended or not', and whose witty ridicule 'lashed any conceit or pose'. The sarcastic curl to his lip 'did not encourage philistines to fraternize with him', and he loathed any display of sentimentality. Yet one day Byland had a glimpse of something very different, when Einstein played Mozart sonatas on his violin in the school refectory. The grace and conviction of the performance seemed impossible to reconcile with the intellectual bruiser of the classroom. Byland's conclusion was shrewd. 'He was one of those split personalities who know how to protect, with a prickly exterior, the delicate realm of their intense emotional life.'

Byland remarked upon the happy way in which fate had pitched a boy of this kind with such a 'romantically inclined' family. The Wintelers had a warmth and openness of heart that marked them out from their cool Swiss neighbours. At best this showed itself in a beguiling eccentricity – Jost Winteler, a keen ornithologist, is said to have enjoyed holding conversations with birds. At worst there were hints of mental instability, which emerged with terrifying consequences a decade after Einstein's stay. In November 1906 Pauline was shot dead by her son Julius, a ship's cook, who had become deranged and ran amok after returning from America. He then killed his sister

Rosa's husband, Ernst Bandi, before committing suicide. The incident left deep scars on the survivors, and Einstein's sweetheart Marie was to spend the final years of her life under psychiatric care. According to one account, Professor Winteler claimed that mental illness had been brought into the family by his wife, much as Einstein would later blame Mileva for their son Eduard's mental illness. In his letter of condolence after the shooting, Einstein placed the blame more tactfully on 'blind fate'.

Marie was the prettiest of the three Winteler daughters, and two years older than Einstein. Their names are linked in a letter to the family from his mother, little more than two months after his arrival in Aarau. Following a new-year greeting to the family at large, and an expression of relief that Albert was under 'such exquisite care', Pauline turned to address 'dear Miss Marie'. She acknowledged a 'little letter' the two had jointly sent her, saying that it had brought her 'immense joy', and promised to reply to Marie soon. Four months later, back in Italy for the school holidays, Einstein wrote to Marie with all the yearning one would expect of a lovelorn seventeen-year-old.

> Many, many thanks for your charming little letter, which made me endlessly happy. It is so wonderful to be able to press to one's heart such a bit of paper which two so dear little eyes have lovingly beheld and on which the dainty little hands have charmingly glided back and forth. I was now made to realize to the fullest extent, my little angel, the meaning of homesickness and pining. But love brings much happiness – much more so than pining brings pain. Only now do I realize how indispensible my dear little sunshine has become to my happiness . . . You mean more to my soul than the whole world did before.

Einstein's excursions into the language of love always tended towards the treacly, and this letter – the only one to Marie that survives – sets a tone that is echoed in his later correspondence with Mileva. Einstein tended to be most affectionate when the objects of his love were at a safe distance, as if he could then make of them what he wanted.

Pining for Marie and 'homesickness' for Aarau went hand in hand. The town was a splendid stage for an adolescent romance. Set at the end of the magnificent Jura mountains, its old centre with its maze of narrow streets rises in terraces from the river Aare. It is known as 'the town of the beautiful gables', and its fine buildings are embellished with oriel windows, wrought-iron emblems, frescos and decorated eaves. Open countryside is all around, and Einstein enjoyed long Sunday walks with Jost, Marie and the rest of the family. Rudolf Kayser would later write that Einstein was 'fascinated' by Marie, whose light-hearted nature provided an alluring distraction from his studies. Her elder sister Anna recalled that their 'agreeable house-guest' spent much of his time hard at work, and seldom went out. For all that, he was never dull and enjoyed an excuse for a laugh. Einstein welcomed Marie's efforts to prise him away as he sat tired and pensive over his books. One thing that drew them together was a mutual love of music. An examiner remarked around this time upon the sparkling quality of Einstein's violin playing, praising the 'deep understanding' he showed for a Beethoven sonata. Marie was a pianist, like his mother, and they would often play duets.

In comparison, his family's new home of Pavia was dull indeed. Einstein's April letter took a cantankerous swipe at the city, in which he wondered how its essence could be given mathematical expression. He suggested that the formula would involve the sum of the ramrods its unbending inhabitants appeared to have swallowed, plus the downward pressure exerted on the spirit by its grimy walls and streets. Einstein was grumbling about exactly the kind of stuffiness that he appears to have hated so much in Germany. How different it was to play music with Marie in Aarau than to perform for 'decked-up Pavia ladies' who expected both perfection and breakneck speed!

Looming behind the scenes was the figure of Einstein's mother. He told Marie that Pauline had taken her to heart, even though they had not met. He even admitted giving his mother two of Marie's letters to read. She had laughed at him, and teased her son for the way he had grown out of previous lesser infatuations. But a personal seal of approval came in the conspiratorial tone of a maternal postscript: 'Without having read this letter, I send you cordial greetings!'

Marie later wrote of her relationship with Einstein, 'We loved each other fervently, but it was a completely ideal love.' The tone of their surviving letters is ardent but restrained. Just as Einstein spoke of pressing Marie's letters to his heart, so she wrote of longing to stroke his tired brow. In Marie's memory he was 'as pretty as a picture', but she clearly felt overwhelmed by the burgeoning intellect of her 'clever darling curlyhead', the 'great dear philosopher'. Einstein was moved to remonstrate after she described herself to him as an 'insignificant silly little sweetheart that knows nothing and understands nothing'. The kiss he proposed as punishment seems a rather complacent response, but he was not interested in intellectual partnership with Marie. Instead, he was happy to bask in her affection and feed off her high spirits. 'And as to whether I will be patient? What other choice do I have with my beloved, naughty little angel? The more so since the little angels are always weak ... and you are, after all, and should be, my little angel.' Einstein treated Marie as if she was several years his junior, rather than his senior. He called her 'my beloved child'.

The growth of Einstein's intellectual self-confidence around this time reflects in part the excellence of the Aarau school. By the middle of the nineteenth century, the canton of Aargau had become known as 'the culture state' of Switzerland, and its education system was celebrated for its progressive methods. When Einstein arrived in October 1895, the cantonal school consisted of two parts: a gymnasium, or classical school, with fifty-six pupils learning mandatory Latin, alongside a technical/commercial school with another ninety pupils. Einstein joined the latter, and found no trace of the authoritarianism that had offended him in Munich. Pupils were treated as individuals and were encouraged to think for themselves. During his year there, a new building was opened with a physics laboratory boasting equipment that a small university might envy. Einstein had written his first scientific essay the previous summer (proudly sending it off to one of his uncles), and he now began to read up on theoretical physics. He recalled that it was as a sixteen-year-old that he wondered what it would be like to chase a light ray through the sky. This was a crucial stimulus: the first childish 'thought experiment' that touched on the mysteries of relativity.

In the summer of 1896, Einstein joined a school field-trip to the mountains in north-eastern Switzerland. He sent Marie a letter from the Toggenburg valley, telling her that he wanted the relationship to continue, even though their paths were now beginning to diverge. At the end of September, he sat and passed his final examination, entitling him to move on to higher education. A glimpse of his ambitions was given in his French test, whose title was 'My Future Plans'. Einstein wrote that he hoped to become a teacher in mathematics and physics, leaning towards the 'theoretical part of these sciences'. He left Aarau in October to enrol at the Polytechnic in Zurich. The following month, Marie took up a short-term post as a teacher in Olsberg, a village in the north-west of Aargau. She remained thoroughly smitten and fancied that one of her first-grade pupils, whom she described as a bunch of blockheads, resembled her beloved Einstein. Every glimpse of the child, who shared the name Albert, would conjure up his image. Needless to add, the boy received particular help from his teacher.

Marie's two letters to Einstein from Olsberg were sad little affairs. The first began with her looking forward breathlessly to a projected reunion. 'I really thank you, Albert, for wanting to come to Aarau, and I don't have to tell you that I will almost be counting the minutes until that time. Tomorrow is Thursday and after that is Friday and then finally finally Saturday and then you will come with your fiddle, your dear child, and your other child (also dear?) will come from the other side.' A few lines later, reality suddenly intruded. 'My love, I do not quite understand a passage in your letter. You write that you do not want to correspond with me any more, but why not sweetheart? You said already in your Toggenburg letter that we would want to write to each other again when I'll be in Olsberg ... You scold me rudely that I don't want to write to you how and why I've come here. But you dear wicked one, don't you know that there exist a lot more beautiful and more clever things one can chatter and talk about than something so stupid ...'

Marie's letter suggests that Einstein had accused her of trying to end their romance by moving away. This was a piece of fine hypocrisy, given his own move to Zurich, but, as she went on to point out, even her clever darling curlyhead was not always logical. At this point Einstein was still sending Marie his dirty laundry so she could wash it and mail it back to him. She was determined to win back his heart with the sheer extravagance of her affection. 'I could never describe, because there are no words for it, how blissful I feel ever since the dear soul of yours has come to live and weave in my soul,' she told him. 'All I can say is that I love you for all eternity, sweetheart, and may God preserve and protect you.'

A reply from Einstein, now lost, threw Marie into an ecstasy of repetition. 'My dear, dear sweetheart,' she began. 'Finally, finally I felt happy happy, something only your dear, dear letters can bring about.' Nevertheless, she knew that something was amiss. She had been forced to wait 'terribly long' for a message, and had even asked her mother to see if Einstein was ill. Her sense of intellectual inferiority was more painful than ever. She did not give a thought to her own happiness, 'but the only reason for this is that I don't think at all, except when it comes to some tremendously stupid calculation that requires, for a change, that I know more than my pupils.' Marie had sent Einstein a teapot as a present, only to receive a peevishly ungrateful response. She now felt that she could see Einstein's angry face looking at her from all sides of the writing-paper. How much angrier that face must have become when he read of her plans to visit him in Zurich. 'Then I will arrange everything the way I like it, and you will enjoy your little study room twice as much,' promised Marie. In fact Einstein always detested the idea of a woman organizing his working conditions.

Quite when this romance expired is unclear, since its terminal phase was drawn-out. A couple of weeks after Marie's second letter, Einstein's mother wrote to her in a tone of woman-to-woman exasperation. Life as a student had changed her son, she said. 'The rascal has become frightfully lazy, one can notice the absence of loving admonition, for the regularity of his letters leaves much to be desired.' She promised to give him a good talking-to, adding without much conviction, 'Will it help?' Pauline had strongly approved of the match and seems to have done her best to help it continue. She wrote again to Marie three months later, in March 1897, reporting that Einstein was back at home for the holidays and in fine fettle. He had developed a vast appetite, and was so full of boisterous energy that 'maternal authority' was being totally subverted. The cheery tone of this note must have made bitter reading for its recipient.

The first clear indication of an ending came in May, when Einstein wrote to Pauline Winteler to 'cut short an inner struggle'. He had been invited to visit Aarau at Whitsun, but had decided not to go. It would, he told Pauline, 'be more than unworthy of me to buy a few days of bliss at the cost of new pain, of which I have already caused much too much to the dear little child.' His words implied that the pain would be Marie's alone, and that for him the joyful prospect of visiting Aarau and his 'Mummy Number Two' remained untarnished. Only because this visit was now impossible was he sharing Marie's distress.

Perhaps. The ardour of Einstein's letters to Pauline Winteler suggests that his feelings for her were almost as strong in their own right as those he had for her daughter. His pleasure in Marie's affection and admiration had collided with his growing awareness of how dependent on him she had become. No such problem existed with her mother. Nevertheless, Einstein's note to Pauline leaves little doubt that his romance with Marie had shaken him more than his opening remarks admitted. The central passage is one of the most intriguing he ever wrote:

> It fills me with a peculiar kind of satisfaction that now I myself have to taste some of the pain that I brought upon the dear girl through my thoughtlessness and ignorance of her delicate nature. Strenuous intellectual work and looking at God's nature are the reconciling, fortifying, yet relentlessly strict angels that shall lead me through all of life's troubles. If only I were able to give some of this to the good child. And yet, what a peculiar way this is to weather the storms of life – in many a lucid moment I appear to myself as an ostrich who buries his head in the desert sand so as not to perceive the danger. One creates a small little world for oneself, and as lamentably insignificant as it may be in comparison with the ever-changing greatness of real existence, one feels miraculously large and important, just like a mole in his self-dug hole. – But why denigrate oneself, others take care of that when necessary. Therefore let's stop.

Einstein's talk of devoting himself to the 'strict angels' of science (instead of his 'naughty little angel' Marie) is familiar. This is ostensibly the same retreat into the impersonal that he later wrote of having attempted as a child. However, it is clear that he had not yet

29

succeeded in it, otherwise this piece of rededication would have been unnecessary.

The Einstein scholar Robert Schulmann is in no doubt that this was a sincere declaration of intent. 'I take him at his word when he says to Marie's mother that he will find his destiny in the stars,' he says. 'Of course it is arch and theatrical, but I think that is him.' Yet this is to ignore the second part of the passage, dwelling on the absurdity of behaving like an ostrich, which quite undercuts the first part and seems far more perceptive, witty and convincing. The first three sentences are grandiose, complacent and patronizing towards Marie. They suggest nothing more than an adolescent throwing himself into a pose, and it is strange that they should set the tone for much of Einstein's life. In his autobiographical notes – despite their hints of inconsistency – he showed no doubt that it was both desirable and possible to escape the 'merely personal'. Here, as a much younger man, he wrote of the lucid moments in which he could see the folly of what he was proposing. Einstein did not write of submerging himself in science, or of dedicating himself to a greater cause that would consume him. He wrote of becoming a mole in a self-dug hole. If he could define the limits of his world, he would always be the most important person in it, untroubled by the demands of others. Like his religious phase as a child, this would be an escape not into the impersonal but into the personal.

Einstein's next letter to Pauline Winteler, written over Whitsun when he had hoped to stay with her, was almost as remarkable as the last, but less for its clear exposition of ideas than for its nervous and overwrought tone. His 'strict angels' were unable to contain a flood of nostalgia for Aarau so powerful that it poured out in an incoherent torrent. He wrote of his head ringing 'in a delightfully mad way', of feeling 'so silly', and of 'curiously vacillating between laughter and tears'. In rococo images that quite defy translation, he pictured 'a thousand memories' of the old days dancing before his eyes. These, he said, could still grab him by the nose as he sat in his room pursuing 'golden scholarship', just as Marie herself had once distracted him. He even seemed to hear the sound of her at the piano, the notes ringing out 'calmly or madly' with his own changing mood. Here again we find talk of angels. God, he wrote, had directed him to 'one of those angels who do not menace sensitive souls with the dangerous two-edged sword'. This was another safely mature woman, 'already a grandmother' and 'marvellously grand and yet truly feminine in her attitudes', with whom he seems to have been performing at musical evenings in Zurich. In such company, he did not have time 'to torment myself with sweet thoughts on how would it be now if . . . and if not . . . etc.'

According to Marie, Einstein would once happily have married her. All that prevented it, she said, was her own obstinacy and reluctance to follow 'the path of duty'. She made this claim many years after the event, when she was no longer an entirely reliable source. Nevertheless it seems that both sets of parents would have been very happy if a marriage had resulted, and the eventual betrothal of Maja Einstein to Marie's brother Paul can only have sharpened their regrets. Long after the romance ended, Einstein admitted to Mileva that Marie still preyed on his mind. The confession came in September 1899, when Maja was following in his footsteps as an Aarau pupil. Einstein was still in close contact with the family, but promised Mileva that he would not be returning so often 'now that the critical daughter with whom I was so madly in love four years ago is coming back home'. In words that might have been calculated to send a shiver down Mileva's spine, he added, 'For the most part, I feel quite secure in my high fortress of calm. But I know that if I saw her a few more times, I would certainly go mad. Of that I am certain, and I fear it like fire.'

It may be that Marie was referring to Mileva when she later wrote that the romance had been broken by another woman. When Marie was writing her letters from Olsberg, Einstein and Mileva had already met. Although their friendship was yet to grow close, news of his new liaison placed great strain on his relationship with the Winteler family. Two years later, he still found himself apologizing to Pauline Winteler for the distress he had caused. A point was reached where a mutual friend thought it better not to mention him in the Wintelers' presence, and Einstein complained that they seemed to think he was living a life of debauchery. He even alluded to the matter in his letter to Professor Winteler after the shooting of 1906.

Marie never did find lasting love. She continued teaching, working at a primary school in Murgenthal, Aargau, from 1902 to 1905, and later giving organ and piano lessons. When Professor Robert Schulmann studied her employment records, he found that she was often off sick – perhaps with one of those mysterious 'nervous illnesses' that were prevalent at the time. One present member of the Einstein family is convinced that Marie's unhappy affair with Einstein 'confused' her, and the tragedy of 1906 brought new despair. In 1911 Marie married another Albert – Albert Müller, a watch-factory manager in Buren, in the canton of Berne. The couple had two boys (one of whom bore a passing resemblance to Einstein) but were divorced in 1927. When Marie was living in Zurich in the 1940s, she approached Einstein for help to emigrate to the United States. But she remained in Switzerland, and lived out her final years of mental illness in the tourist centre of Meiringen. It was there that she died in an asylum on 24 September 1957.

No doubt Marie would have been struck by the advice that Einstein gave to another young woman with whom he played music while staying with the Wintelers. His friendship with Julia Niggli, the daughter of a town clerk and music historian, became intimate enough for her to seek his counsel about an affair with an older man. She was upset because her lover did not intend to marry her. Einstein's response was sharp:

> What a strange thing must be a girl's soul! Do you really believe that you could find permanent happiness through others, even if this be the one and only beloved man? I know this sort of animal personally, from my own experience as I am one of them myself. Not too much should be expected from them, this I know quite exactly. Today we are sullen, tomorrow high-spirited, after tomorrow cold, then again irritated and half-sick of life – but I have almost forgotten the unfaithfulness and ingratitude and selfishness, things in which almost all of us do significantly better than the good girls . . .

By the time he wrote those words, in August 1899, the twenty-year-old Einstein had already embarked on his romance with Mileva.

3

Johnnie and Dollie

LARGE, dark and deep set, the eyes of the young Mileva Marić glowed with quiet intensity. Their intelligence and determination shine out from a photograph taken in her first year as a student. She is smartly dressed, with a bright, quietly pretty face perched warily above a great bow at her collar. Her features are pleasantly rounded, even soft, but finish in an emphatically firm chin. The mouth is broad and sensual but unsmiling. Her dark, shining hair is swept back from the slightly frowning brow, under which those powerful eyes stare out. Whereas Einstein often seems to be looking through the observer, far away into space, Mileva's eyes are alert and watchful. They are the eyes of a formidable young woman.

Mileva was a Serb from the province of Vojvodina, in the north of the former Yugoslavia. This is a region of endless corn and sunflower fields, sweeping north of Belgrade across the Pannonian Plain, a vast lowland formed from the floor of a prehistoric sea. For years it stood on the fault line where the great Habsburg and Ottoman empires collided, and at the time of Mileva's birth, on 19 December 1875, it was part of southern Hungary. Settlers had long been encouraged on these drained marshlands in order to form a human bulwark against the Turks. So many came as colonists or refugees that the area has been said to resemble a microcosm of central Europe. Its twenty or so minorities include Croats, Slovaks, Romanians, Ruthenians, Albanians, Gypsies and Greeks. Many of the first colonists came from Einstein's Swabian homeland in Germany, and their descendants made up a large part of the population of Novi Sad, the local capital.

It was near here that Mileva's father, Miloš, was born in 1846. He was descended from one of the forty thousand Serbian families who fled north from Turkish rule in what became known as the Great

Migration of 1690. The refugees – a mixture of prosperous traders, craftsmen and farmers – followed in the wake of Habsburg troops who were forced to retreat after a deep incursion into enemy territory. Led by their Orthodox Christian patriarch, they crossed the Danube and began to exploit the natural fertility of the local soil. They and their descendants were so successful that, until the recent troubles that have torn apart Yugoslavia, this was known as the country's granary.

Mileva joked to Einstein that she came from a 'little land of outlaws'. The rebel hajduks who had terrorized the Turks were part of Serbian folklore, and there was a touch of the Wild West about the whole region. The stretch of the Danube where she was born was famous for the Serbian sailors armed with rifles and bayonets who once patrolled it in gunboats. Vojvodina – or 'The Dukedom' – was part of Hungary's so-called Military Frontier, with settlers receiving a plot of land in return for service in the imperial army. Frontier life encouraged a tough-minded pragmatism among Mileva's forefathers that still endures. 'You don't ask a Vojvodina man what ideals he has,' one twentieth-century traveller was told, 'you ask him what he earns.'

The early settlers knew that they were regarded with suspicion within their adopted country. In order to discourage subversive gatherings in doorways, the Habsburgs insisted that houses should not open on to the street, save for a single 'gossiping window'. The decree helped to give the region's villages a private atmosphere, but the Serbs were more interested in exploiting the empire than in plotting against it. Society was more open than under the Turks, and military service brought with it opportunities for education and advancement. A Serb intelligentsia began to develop, and Vojvodina emerged as the centre of a national renaissance. Novi Sad even became known as the 'Serbian Athens'. It was this cultural revival – together with Vojvodina money and ammunition – that fuelled the Ottoman Serbs when they rose up across the border in 1804. They eventually achieved independence there three years after Mileva was born.

Her father was a tall, thin, imposing man with a high forehead, a jutting chin and a confident stare. The martial heritage of Vojvodina ran through his soul. His birthplace, the small town of Kać, was approached by roads which twisted and turned to impede attackers, and the broken paving-stones of its church testified to its use as a stable by Hungarian cavalry. It was almost inevitable that at the age of sixteen Milos would enter military school at Novi Sad. His army career occupied him for the next thirteen years and brought him to Titel, a town on the Tisa river. There he met Marija Ruzic, one of three daughters of a prosperous local family, of whom little is known. He married her in October 1867.

There was nothing in this background to provide the young Mileva with a scientific stimulus, in the way that Einstein benefited from his family's interests in technology. However, Miloš appears to have been a keen reader and something of an autodidact, and he was ambitious enough to see the army as a stepping-stone rather than a job for life. He went on to accumulate considerable wealth and prestige as an official in the Hungarian civil service. Hans Albert Einstein wrote, 'I remember my grandfather as a kind but rather serious man whom one could both trust and fear . . . My grandmother was quiet, kind, and always busy.' A Novi Sad contemporary maintained that Miloš was 'very affable, cheerful and fond of jokes', but also confirmed the picture of a proud and perhaps arrogant man. Even in maturity he bore himself like a soldier, and he wore the short top hat that was a mark of social distinction. As an official at the city's Serbian reading-room, he was happy to hold court to the younger generation about his army days. One listener recalled that his manner was slightly condescending, full of patriarchal self-assurance.

Mileva was the couple's first child. The priest who christened her was the one who had christened her mother and officiated at her parents' wedding. A sister, Zorka, arrived in 1883, and a brother, Miloš Junior, in 1885. But she always remained her father's favourite child, whom he called by the pet name 'Mitza', which one day Einstein too would use.

Miloš was discharged from the forces one month after Mileva's birth. He became an official at the district courts in Ruma, an agricultural town between Novi Sad and Belgrade, and here his elder daughter began four years of elementary school in 1882. Mileva was a small and shy girl, already conscious of the limp on her left side that she would carry all her life. She had been born with a dislocated hip joint, but the disability seems not to have been noticed until she began to walk. Local doctors were unable to correct it, and the same problem afflicted her younger sister. It is likely that her shyness, and the impediment that her limp must have posed to active games, encouraged Mileva to retreat into her own world. We are told by one Serbian biographer that her intelligence and thirst for knowledge were already evident at this early age. An elderly teacher is said to have told Miloš, 'Watch out for this child. She is a rare phenomenon!' – a heartwarming testimonial if true, but one that could be matched by the proud teachers and parents of countless children destined for mediocrity. From the same source, though, it appears that Miloš tried hard to encourage Mileva's education. Military service had enabled him to master German, and it was spoken at home. The young Mileva is said to have read German-language editions of the Grimms' fairy tales and the works of Hans Christian Andersen. Her father recited Serbian folk poetry for her to learn by heart, and from the age of eight she was given piano lessons.

Mileva's school record now began to resemble a Cook's tour of the region, suggesting the way that Miloš pushed her on in search of excellence. In 1886 she moved into the first form of the Serbian girls' high school in Novi Sad. One classmate, Jelisaveta Barako, remembered her as the outstanding pupil, whose high marks and studious attitude won her the nickname 'the woman saint'. The following year she switched to the second class of another school in Sremska Mitrovica, where she stayed until 1890, when her father sent her across the border into Serbia. Miloš wanted his daughter educated at a gymnasium, but those in Austria-Hungary were for boys only. The same barriers no longer existed in Serbia, and Mileva entered the fifth form of the gymnasium at Sabac.

Mathematics and physics were the subjects in which she excelled, but her interests ranged widely. After initially choosing to study German, in March 1891 she won permission to take up the new challenge of French. She also showed great talents at drawing. Among her schoolmates was another ambitious and gifted young woman, named Ružica Dražić. A few years later they would share the same lodgings as students in Zurich, but for now their friendship was brief, as Miloš was appointed to a new job at the high court of justice in Zagreb in December 1891. He sought special permission for his daughter to enrol as a private pupil at the city's all-male Royal Classical High School. It was a remarkable step, which made her one of the first young women in the Austro-Hungarian Empire to sit alongside boys in a high-school classroom.

Mileva passed the entrance exam and entered the school's tenth grade during the academic year of 1892. The first hurdle to overcome was her ignorance of Greek. A request from Miloš that she be excused the subject was turned down, but she swiftly mastered it. Her next success was to win permission to attend physics lectures with her male peers. This too needed special permission, which was granted in February 1894 on the recommendation of her class master and the mathematics and physics teacher. The Einstein scholar Gerald Holton speaks from his own more recent experience as a schoolboy in Vienna in the 1930s to underline the move's significance. 'I studied at a gymnasium – a boy's gymnasium, of course – and the idea of a girl sitting in on a class is so, oh, bizarre,' he says. 'If this had happened, the poor girl would have been the subject of attacks in the early years and seduction in the later years. In either case, it would have been a struggle to learn any physics.' Despite such distractions, Mileva emerged triumphant in her final examination at the start of September 1894. Her marks in mathematics and physics were the highest awarded.

Around this time – exactly when is unclear – Mileva fell seriously ill. All that seems to be known is that she suffered a heavy cold that was followed by a severe inflammation of the lungs. This was one reason, according to her Serbian biographers, why she now decided to leave her family behind and move to Switzerland. The curative effect of the clean Alpine air was an article of faith among doctors, particularly for the treatment of tuberculosis. It is possible, although by no means certain, that this was Mileva's illness. There are many suggestions by Einstein that she had a history of the disease, which he held responsible for a motley collection of troubles. He told his biographer Carl Seelig that her 'depressive' nature was partly due to a 'a certain physical disability, that was evidently traced back to childhood tuberculosis'. However, since this seems to be a reference to Mileva's limp, which all other accounts state was congenital, there are good grounds to be sceptical. Tuberculosis is mentioned only once in the fullest account of Mileva's childhood, and then the sufferer is her schoolfriend at Sabac, Ružica Dražić.

The strongest reason for Mileva's move to Switzerland was her driving ambition for further academic success. Swiss schools had a reputation for excellence that extended across Europe, and higher education was free of many of the obstacles to women still in place elsewhere. Miss Mileva Marić from Agram (the name then given to Zagreb) was provisionally admitted to the girls' high school in Zurich on 14 November 1894, a little short of her nineteenth birthday. Besides mathematics and physics, her lessons included Latin, singing, natural history, Swiss history and shorthand. She was excused from gymnastics and some other subjects, but her admission form recorded that she was also to undergo private instruction in French, history, geography, zoology and botany.

In the spring of 1896 Mileva passed her matura exam, which qualified her to enter higher education. In the light of subsequent claims made for her ability in physics, it is significant that she did not immediately throw herself into further study of the subject. Instead, she started out as a medical student at Zurich University, which nineteen years earlier had become among the first in Europe to admit women. Mileva would never show the same almost fanatical fascination with physics as Einstein, and this is the first hint that, despite her cleverness, her true vocation lay elsewhere. Medicine was a subject that attracted her brother Miloš and later her younger son. Her letters to Einstein would show an abiding interest in psychology, and it may be that this was where her deeper interests lay. However, the course offered at the University seems to have disagreed with her, for she studied it for only that one summer term. In October she switched to Section VIA of the Swiss Federal Polytechnical School, reading for a diploma that would qualify her to teach mathematics and physics at secondary schools. This was the same diploma for which Einstein was studying, and was less an end in itself than a ticket to higher academic posts.

Mileva, now almost twenty-one, was the only woman to join Section VIA that year and only the fifth to do so since a pioneering Norwegian five years before. She had already travelled a long way from her relatively humble origins, defying the prevailing sexual prejudices of her era to enter one of central Europe's élite technical schools. It was a journey that had required all the strength and steel hinted at in her photograph, but Mileva rarely put these qualities on public display. Her Zurich contemporaries described her as 'a dear, sympathetic, shy girl' and 'a modest, unassuming creature'. Her fellow Serb, Milana Bota, wrote home that Mileva was 'a very good girl but too serious and quiet. One would hardly suppose that she had such a clever head.' Bota soon discovered that there was a far warmer and more irreverent face to her new friend. She told her parents how they had sat together imitating 'an odd Bulgarian', who lived in Bota's lodging-house, and 'laughed a lot about it'. But there was something elusive and self-effacing about Mileva, who was not thought by her friends to be very physically attractive. In another letter, Bota described her as small, delicate and plain. She also noted Mileva's limp and her strong Novi Sad accent, although she graciously conceded that Mileva had a 'very nice manner'.

Einstein, by contrast, was now a handsome teenager exuding casual charisma. Far from the shaggy-haired figure of later years, whom one writer has likened to a superannuated sheepdog, he possessed what a friend of his second wife would describe as 'masculine good looks of the type that played havoc at the turn of the century'. He was five feet six inches tall, with regular features, warm brown eyes, a mass of jet-black hair and a slightly raffish moustache. Despite his indifference to most forms of exercise, his physique was impressive – and would remain so well into his maturity. 'He looks fleshy,' wrote his Berlin friend Janos Plesch, 'but in fact his build is muscular and quite powerful.' C. P. Snow, whom Einstein met in 1937 wearing only a pair of shorts, noticed with surprise that his host had 'a massive body, very heavily muscled . . . he was still an unusually strong man.'

The student Einstein had learned how to be charming with women, and to engage them with his provocative sense of humour. Margarete von Uexküll, a biology student who became a friend of Einstein and Mileva, left a vivid picture of her first meeting with him. She had spent the whole of a warm June afternoon wrestling with an experiment in the Polytechnic's laboratories. Frustration overwhelming her, she was drawn into an argument with a small, fat physics professor, who refused to let her seal a test-tube with a cork for fear it would break. Suddenly she noticed 'a pair of the most extraordinarily large shining eyes that were clearly warning me'. These belonged to Einstein, who quietly assured her that the professor was mad and had recently fainted during an angry fit in front of his class. He suggested that she give him her laboratory notes so he could cook up some better results. At the next review, the professor exclaimed, 'There, you see. With a little goodwill, and despite my impossible methods, you can apparently work out something useful.'

It has to be said that von Uexküll may have varnished this anecdote, since she claimed that when Einstein borrowed her notebook he already had eight others awaiting similar doctoring. He certainly seems to have been on his best behaviour in her presence. She thought him shy, modest and (despite casting aspersions on the professor's sanity) 'mild in his judgement, even of our teachers'. This is far from how he appears in his letters to Mileva, but von Uexküll remains an intriguing witness, since she and Mileva shared the same lodgings at the house of Johanna Bächtold. She remembered watching in the living-room as Mileva would sew or play the piano, with Einstein sitting attentively next to her. He already had the ability to explain difficult problems with clarity, she recalled, and would pour out his ideas as they walked home from the laboratories. 'I believe', said von Uexküll, 'that Mileva was the first person who believed in his theories. When I once remarked that I found Einstein's theories quite fantastic, she answered confidently: "But he can prove his theory." Quietly I thought to myself, she must really be in love!"

It is unclear when this love took root. Mileva and Einstein met during that first winter term at the Polytechnic. Over the next year they followed the same compulsory courses side by side – differential and integral calculus, analytical geometry, descriptive geometry, projective geometry and mechanics. But, instead of returning to the Polytechnic at the start of her second year, Mileva formally withdrew on 5 October 1897. She travelled to Germany and spent the winter term at the country's oldest and most famous university, Heidelberg. One suggestion is that she did so because her relationship with Einstein was already threatening to overwhelm her: that she wanted time to reconsider her feelings, safely outside the field of his magnetism. This is a little patronizing, and it is more likely that the attractions of Heidelberg were purely academic. It is premature to suggest that Mileva had been swept away by Einstein's charms. Her first surviving letter to him, some time after her move, suggests a definite romantic interest but nothing like the passion seen later.

Mileva was replying to a four-page letter, now lost, that Einstein had sent after a hike with her during the summer. Her words show coquettish self-confidence rather than love-struck confusion. Einstein had told her not to write until she began to feel bored, and Mileva said, 'I waited and waited for boredom to set in, but until today my waiting has been in vain, and I'm not sure what to do about it.' Her tone was teasing. Gossiping about a colleague who had withdrawn from their course, apparently in the grip of unrequited love, she observed that it served him right, since what was the point of falling in love nowadays? However, she had already given full details about Einstein to the other man in her life – her father. 'Papa gave me some tobacco that I'm to give to you personally,' she wrote. 'He's eager to whet your appetite for our little land of outlaws. I told him all about you – you absolutely must come back with me someday – the two of you would have a lot to talk about! But I'll have to play the role of interpreter.'

Women were barred from matriculating at Heidelberg but since 1891 they had been allowed to sit in on courses as auditors. Among the lecturers was the future Nobel prizewinner Philipp Lenard, still only in his mid-thirties but already assistant professor of experimental physics. Lenard was to be one of Einstein's most venomous opponents after the First World War, lending his scientific authority to the Jew-baiters who tried to discredit relativity. An early and enthusiastic supporter of the Nazis, he would dismiss Einstein's 'botched-up theories' as perversions 'estranged from nature'. Yet it was Lenard who paved the way for Einstein's own Nobel prize, by discovering that light beamed at certain metals kicked electrons out of the surface. Einstein's explanation of this 'photoelectric effect' was one of the first great successes of quantum theory. Mileva saw Lenard in his prime, and her letter to Einstein contained an enthusiastic report on one of his lectures.

The professor had been describing the kinetic theory of gases, which explains their properties by the behaviour of their constituent molecules. This was just the kind of problem that would be central to much of Einstein's work in 1905, but Mileva's account suggests a certain scientific naïvity. She wrote, 'It really was too enjoyable in Professor Lenard's lecture yesterday . . . It seems that oxygen molecules travel at a speed of over 400 metres per second, and after calculating and calculating, the good professor set up equations, differentiated, integrated, substituted and finally showed that the molecules in question actually do move at such a velocity, but that they only travel the distance of 1/100 of a hair's breadth.' This irreverent tone is appealing, but it seems that Mileva had missed the key points of what Lenard was saying. The mathematics that apparently dazzled her would not have been directed at determining the velocity of the molecules – since this can be obtained quite simply – and the tiny distance they travelled between collisions should hardly have come as a surprise to her. It depends on how many collisions each molecule experiences with others within a given time interval. Although this was only a light-hearted anecdote, it suggests that Mileva lacked Einstein's intuitive grasp of physics.

However, this first letter does show Mileva at her most attractive. In the words of the Einstein scholars Robert Schulmann and Jürgen Renn, she had 'a high degree of self-consciousness and independence, discipline in her studies, and a healthy measure of impudence'. To this list one might add a quirky, romantic turn of mind. As she wrote, thick fog shrouded Heidelberg's picturesque setting on the wooded Neckar valley. The grey desolation sent Mileva into a reverie on the mysteries of infinite space. She wrote:

> I don't think the structure of the human skull is to be blamed for man's inability to understand the concept of infinity. He would certainly be able to understand it if, when young, and while developing his sense of perception, he were allowed to venture out into the universe, rather than being cooped up on earth or, worse yet, confined within four walls in a provincial backwater. If someone can conceive of infinite happiness, he should be able to comprehend the infinity of space – I should think it much easier.

There is a genuinely visionary quality to these lines – and a faith in the power of the human intellect – that must have attracted Einstein. No one wished more than he did 'to venture out into the universe' instead of being confined to the mundane. Nevertheless, the impression the passage leaves is of an imaginative sensibility rather than a strictly scientific one. Mileva's words are saved from seeming precious by their straightforward simplicity and optimism. Her tone became more fatalistic as her relationship with Einstein evolved.

After the winter semester, Mileva returned from Heidelberg and rejoined classes at the Polytechnic in April 1898. However much she wanted to see Einstein again, she appears to have been in some doubt about resuming her studies in Zurich. He wrote in February welcoming her decision, and reassuring her that it was the right one. His own advice – which he admitted might not be 'entirely unselfish' – was to return without delay. He offered a summary of the lectures she had missed, but insisted she could catch up easily by reading the information 'tightly packed in our notebooks'. His use of the plural is significant. As much as his own notes, Einstein relied on those of his classmate Marcel Grossmann, who would later provide crucial mathematical help on the general theory of relativity. While Grossmann conscientiously attended lectures and recorded their contents, Einstein tended to play truant and read what interested him instead. He later wrote that in the few months before his examinations he was able to brush up the basics by borrowing Grossmann's books. This was only the first instance of Einstein's lifelong habit of leaning heavily on close colleagues, who found themselves carrying out the more menial work while he concentrated on bigger questions.

Mileva's need to make up lost time, and Einstein's obvious affection for his 'little runaway', led them to work increasingly closely. Mileva borrowed his notes and he borrowed her textbooks, passing on pungent criticism. The young Einstein was no respecter of reputations. He told Mileva that the work of Paul Drude, one of the leading theorists of the day, was 'stimulating and informative' but lacked clarity and precision in the detail. Albin Herzog, the Polytechnic director who handled his first application, taught clearly but too superficially. Wilhelm Fiedler, an expert in projective geometry, was brilliant and profound but an impenetrable pedant. Einstein wanted freshness and the ruthless application of basic principles to fundamental problems. His heroes included Hermann von Helmholtz, famous for his contributions to establishing the law of conservation of energy. This was a man with the originality and independence to which Einstein aspired. He began exploring Helmholtz's work while on holiday in the summer of 1899, but assured Mileva 'out of my fear of you (as well as for my own pleasure)' that they would reread it together. Joint study had become a habit. He told her, 'When I read Helmholtz for the first time I could not – and still cannot – believe that I was doing so without you sitting next to me. I enjoy working together very much, as well as finding it soothing and less boring.'

Einstein's letters to Mileva would increasingly present her as his intellectual comrade, matching him stride for stride on his journey through science. At this point he was clearly ahead of her, though ready to cover old ground again as she caught up. The surviving correspondence between them does not suggest that Mileva was bringing new ideas and insights to his work, but she made it much more congenial. Here at last – after his philistine parents and the unassuming Marie Winteler – was someone with the intelligence and interest to share the ideas that excited him.

In the two years after Mileva's return from Heidelberg the relationship began to move from friendship to romance. At first things were a little prim. Notes from Einstein were addressed to '*Liebes Fräulein*' or '*LFM*' (*Liebes Fräulein Marić*). Both used 'Sie' – the German formal term for 'you' – until as late as 1900, when there is the first letter from Mileva with the familiar 'du'. Some months before this, Einstein began to call Mileva by a pet name, 'Doxerl', which can best be translated as 'Little Doll' or 'Dollie'. With gathering momentum he moved on from '*LD*' (*Liebes Doxerl*, or Dear Dollie) in August 1899 to '*LSD*' (*Liebes Süßes Doxerl*, or Dear Sweet Dolly) that October. The following August, she became his 'sweet little one' and his 'dearest little sweetheart'. This was far from the limit of his invention: at one time or another, Einstein called Mileva his little witch, his little frog, his dear kitten, his little street urchin, his dear little angel, his little right hand, his dearest little child, his little black girl and numerous variations on these themes. She appears to have been more consistent, usually calling him 'Johonesl', or Johnnie. This first appeared in her 1900 letter addressing him as 'du', which was one of the shortest and sweetest that she wrote:

My dear Johnnie,

Because I like you so much, and because you're so far away that I can't give you a little kiss, I'm writing this letter to ask if you like me as much as I do you? Answer me immediately.

A thousand kisses from your Dollie

The answer, if one was given, does not survive.

Both Einstein and Mileva often used their pet names to write of themselves in the third person – so that he would refer to 'that Johnnie boy' almost as if this was someone else. Johnnie and Dollie seemed to take on a life of their own, expressing feelings in which Einstein and Mileva did not normally deal. The two creations seemed to represent only the best qualities of their alter egos, and allowed their faults to be overlooked.

Einstein's attraction to this small, silent, limping girl must have taken many of his contemporaries by surprise: a young man of his good looks and wit would have found it easy to make other, more conventionally attractive, conquests. Referring one day to Mileva's limp, a colleague is reported to have said, 'I should never have the courage to marry a woman unless she was absolutely sound.' Einstein replied calmly, 'But she has such a lovely voice.'

Mileva's fine singing and their shared love of music were indeed a powerful bond between them. Just as in his childhood, and his relationship with Marie Winteler, it was through music that Einstein found his own emotional voice most easily. But this exchange also suggests how he had created an idea of Mileva in his mind and was ready to block out anything that disagreed with it. The Harvard scholar Gerald Holton feels that Einstein's pleasure at finding a potential soulmate made him ready to overlook Mileva's possible shortcomings. 'She limped, she was moody, and she was very dark-complexioned, which at the time was not very fashionable,' he com-

45

ments. 'But to him this did not count, because she had a mind.' The danger here is of suggesting a purely intellectual bond, but Einstein was not drawn to Mileva's mind alone – a letter from him in March 1899 ended roguishly, 'Best wishes etc., especially the latter.' Although in later life he was brutally insulting towards Mileva's looks, he found no fault with them in youth. He told Mileva that he liked her to be 'plump as a dumpling' and wanted to shower her with the 'biggest kisses'.

The pair shared an innocent delight in life's simpler sensual pleasures – both liked comforting food and drink. There are several references in their letters to the inspiring qualities of freshly ground coffee, with Einstein describing himself to Mileva as 'your good colleague and fellow coffee-guzzler'. He told her, 'We understand each other's dark souls so well, and also drinking coffee and eating sausages etc. . . .' Einstein's stomach was always a sure way to his heart, and it does not seem coincidental that this was one of the main ways his mother showed her affection for him. Pauline often sent food parcels to her student son, packed with cakes and pastries, and Mileva noted 'what a magnificent effect' their arrival had on him – he would walk proudly through the streets, with eyes only on the package cradled in his hands. Otherwise, Einstein subsisted on an allowance of 100 Swiss francs each month, sent to the 'little professor' by his aunt Julie in Genoa. He enjoyed tobacco – a few years later his smoking habits were described as repulsive – but did not drink alcohol and usually dined in temperance restaurants. Often he was reduced to snatching a slice of tart from a bakery and bolting it in his room. His uneven diet has been blamed for the stomach problems that dogged him throughout his life – what Mileva would call his 'famous ailment'. Shared indigestion at a dinner party led him to tell her 'how closely knit our psychic and physiological lives are'.

Einstein was already very absent-minded – forever forgetting his keys or umbrella, or leaving behind his nightshirt and wash things when he went home in the holidays. Mileva, three and a half years older, was well suited to offer him a guiding hand. Her domestic skills seem to have been honed at an early age by helping to care for her siblings (her sister was more than seven years younger), and as a student she was an accomplished cook who made her own clothes to save money. One of the smaller injustices done to Mileva is the suggestion that she was guilty of what Einstein's biographer Ronald Clark called 'the unpardonable Slav tendency of letting things slip'. Clark based his judgement on another writer's report that Mileva was 'hardly the typical Swiss-German house-sprite, the height of whose ambition is a constant war against dust, moths and dirt'. In reality her motherly competence was one of her charms for Einstein, whose letters are full of tributes to Mileva's housewifely industry, her 'skilled hands', and the 'hen-like enthusiasm' with which she looked after him. Once he even sent her a sketch of his foot so that she could knit him some socks. 'Since you have such a great imagination and are accustomed to astronomical distances,' he observed, 'I think this work of art will suffice.'

An authentic flavour of the way in which Mileva mothered him may have been captured in one of the few Einstein biographies to pay her more than passing attention. Einstein: Profile of the Man, published in 1962, was written in a highly popular style and was dismissed by Einstein's secretary Helen Dukas as complete nonsense. Yet the author, Peter Michelmore, based his account on private conversations with Hans Albert, who later said that he knew of no errors in it. At the very least, it suggests how Mileva saw things and what she told her children. The student Einstein is described as 'hopelessly impractical' and never able to make up his mind on everyday matters – strikingly similar to Maja Einstein's description of their father. Mileva's character, on the other hand, sounds rather like that of Pauline Einstein – 'decisive about everything'.

> She judged people more quickly and was firm in her likes and dislikes. She had a definite viewpoint in any argument. She planned her studies and her routine well ahead. She tried to bring a sense of order into Albert's life, too ... She made him eat regularly and told him how to budget his allowance properly. Frequently, she was infuriated with his absent-mindedness. He would look at this angry little girl stamping her foot and a glint of devilment would come into his eyes. He would make a joke or pull a face and slowly charm her out of her mood.

Although a third-hand account, this sounds very much like the subverting of 'maternal authority' that Pauline Einstein mentioned in her letter to Marie Winteler. In many ways her son was allowing Mileva to take Pauline's place.

Einstein's first surviving letter to Mileva began with him cringing before her 'critical eye' for not having written sooner. The second – just two sentences long – begged 'don't be angry' after he had borrowed a textbook without permission. 'Please don't be angry with me,' echoed his third letter, only a few days later, when illness confined him to his room. He was forever expecting Mileva's disapproval: 'bitter resentment' about not keeping in touch, or scowling anger at his failure to lend her some notes. 'Don't pout about it, you little witch,' he would tell her. 'Don't fret and frown about it . . . don't make angry faces.' He was joking, of course, but only up to a point. For all her sweetness his girlfriend had a fierce temper, and one that Einstein found strangely nostalgic. 'You came vividly to my mind during a harsh scolding I just received,' he wrote while staying with his mother in March 1899, before going on to picture Mileva's 'tight-lipped smile' if a promised present had not arrived. Something in Einstein liked her to boss him about, while at the same time he was poking his tongue out. 'I'm beginning to feel the absence of your beneficent thumb under which I'm always kept in line,' he wrote to her from Milan. In Zurich, he said, she was 'the mistress of our house'.

Einstein and Mileva did not live together as students, but he was soon writing of 'our household' just as if they did. He had warned Mileva before she returned from Heidelberg that her old room at the Bächtold lodging-house had been taken by someone else ('a Zurich philistine'). She registered there initially but soon moved to the Pension Engelbrecht on Plattenstrasse, which was already the home of Ružica Dražić, her schoolmate from Sabac, and the Serbian psychology student Milana Bota. Bota recorded that she was introduced to Mileva's 'good friend' Einstein in May 1898, after which he became a constant visitor. The following year he considered moving into the same street ('but not into your house – we don't want to start any rumours') before eventually making do with a room on nearby Unionstrasse. Einstein took to calling Mileva's lodgings 'our place', and during the summer holidays of 1899 both found it agreeable to write of this as their true home. Einstein, staying with his family in Italy, said that 'our place' was 'the nicest and cosiest place I can think of'. Mileva, with her parents in Vojvodina, told him his letters gave her 'warm memories of home'. Einstein seemed particularly pleased when his mother recognized the new focus of his loyalties by promising to redirect her food parcels: henceforth, he reported, she would post 'something for the household' direct to Plattenstrasse rather than his own address.

The summer of 1899 was a time of immense stress for Mileva. Like all diploma students, she faced two academic hurdles during her Polytechnic course: the intermediate examination and finals. The former was a series of oral tests that Einstein had sat at the start of his third year, in October 1898, as was normal. He had come top of his group, with an average mark of 5.7 out of 6, but Mileva had not taken part. The interruption of her second year of studies by her stay at Heidelberg forced her to wait until October 1899, sitting the exam with the next set of entrants. She spent the preceding summer revising at home in Kać, on the farm to which her father had retired. At the start of August she told Einstein that the hard work was agreeing with her, but this early bravado did not last and her next letter was mournful. The weather was oppressively hot and she dared not go into town because the area was gripped by scarlet fever and diphtheria. Her work was progressing only slowly, with Fiedler's geometry – which Einstein punningly dubbed 'fiddling' – causing her the most frustration. She was desperate for advice on what questions to expect, and anxious to borrow Einstein's notes. Her apprehension was unmistakable as she wrote of returning to Zurich with 'mixed feelings' and plaintively asked, 'Don't you feel sorry for me?'

Einstein sent her a series of messages full of sympathy and support. She was a poor girl having to 'stuff her head with grey theory' and 'swallow a lot of book dust', but soon it would be over and she would have 'yet another success'. The other students were harmless competition, after all, and his Dollie was a girl who 'knows what she wants and has demonstrated this frequently.' He agreed that Mileva 'had it a lot harder' in sitting the exam after her classmates. He remembered how he and Marcel Grossmann had kept each other's spirits up the previous year by exchanging wisecracks – even though they were 'laughing on the outside while crying on the inside'. Yet it seems that Einstein was rather unnerved by the intensity of Mileva's gloom, preferring the perky resilience seen in her letter from Heidelberg. He joked rather hopefully that his determined Dollie was bound to scoff at his needless words of reassurance, but he constantly praised her toughness – her 'divine composure', her 'hard little head', her 'robustness' – as if she needed reminding that she possessed it. It is clear that Mileva found her exams far more of a trial than had her boyfriend. She earned a pass but came only fifth out of the six candidates, with a personal average of 5.05. She was most impressive in physics, where she scored 5.5 – the same as Einstein. He had not fallen below that level in any subject, and in two of them (analytical geometry and mechanics) had gained a straight 6. Mileva's other marks were straight 5s and a 4.75 in the dreaded 'fiddling'.

Einstein's mind was already alive with aspects of physics far beyond the confines of the Polytechnic curriculum, which he found frustratingly narrow. While Mileva was revising, he had written to her that he was more and more convinced that current thinking did not 'correspond to reality' in a key area: electrodynamics. This is the branch of physics dealing with the way that the motions of charged bodies such as electrons are influenced by electric and magnetic fields. Einstein's doubts about it would lie at the heart of his 1905 paper explaining special relativity, which carried the title 'On the Electrodynamics of Moving Bodies'. He would deal in this paper with an anomaly that meant that the fields and forces at work in a motor, which converts electricity into motion, were explained differently from those in a dynamo, which converts motion into electricity. This was puzzling, given that the two devices are physically essentially the same, both depending on the relative motion of an electrical conductor and a magnet. By unifying the description of the phenomena underlying both devices, Einstein was to demolish the 300-year-old foundations of Newtonian physics.

In the summer of 1899 this was still far in front of him, but Einstein was already sharing with Mileva the beginnings of his ideas. He told her that he was sure that the subject could be dealt with 'in a simpler way'. One focus of his attention was the ether: the material that scientists of the day believed carried light and other electromagnetic waves through space, in much the same way that water carries ripples on its surface. This ghostly medium was believed to fill not only the air but also vacua and solid material such as glass through which light could shine. In 1905 Einstein would dismiss its existence in a single sentence, with a casualness that shocked science, but his doubts were already there in 1899. He told Mileva, 'The introduction of the term "ether" into theories of electricity led to the notion of a medium of whose motion one can speak without being able, I believe, to associate a physical meaning with this statement.' He sketched out his ideas to her, with the help of a formula, and in other letters spoke of experiments that he had devised to test them.

This is the first evidence of Einstein making a sustained attempt to wrestle with the questions that would one day be answered by his theory of relativity. Mileva was the first person to share his ideas – a dramatic confirmation of the extent to which she had become his intellectual confidante. Einstein's pleasure in being able to spill his thoughts into a sympathetic ear was almost palpable. Mileva, however, had her sights set on her impending examinations and was in no position to engage in a dialogue with him about such advanced problems. He seemed aware of this, and content merely to unburden himself without reply. 'But enough of that!' he told Mileva after one outburst. 'Your poor little head is already crammed full of other peoples' hobby-horses that you've had to ride. I won't bother you with mine as well.'

The limits to their relationship were visible elsewhere. Rather than be with her, he spent much of the summer holidays of 1899 with his 'mother hen and sister' at the Hotel Paradise in Mettmenstetten, a small resort to Zurich's south-west. It would not be the last stressful period for Mileva when he preferred to spend time with his family, in spite of his ambivalent feelings towards them. The reports he sent to Mileva were scathing about the 'mindless prattle' surrounding him and the unpleasantness of his mother's friends and relatives. Worst of these was the same Aunt Julie who kindly paid his allowance. She was 'a veritable monster of arrogance and insensitive formalism' according to her grateful nephew. However, Einstein's disenchantment was all-encompassing. He told Mileva:

My mother and sister seem somewhat petty and philistine to me, despite the sympathy I feel for them. It is interesting how gradually our life changes us in the very subtleties of our soul, so that even the closest of family ties dwindle into habitual friendship. Deep inside we no longer understand one another, and are incapable of actively empathizing with the other, or knowing what emotions move the other.

The flattering implication was that Einstein felt real empathy only with Mileva, and that together they stood apart from the stuffy banalities of his family circle. But Einstein hardly felt as oppressed as this would suggest, and admitted to Mileva that he was enjoying 'each and every day of my vacation'. It is striking that his sympathy for her in the approach to her examinations found no practical expression. He made a brief foray into Zurich at the start of September, before she returned from Kać, but claimed he was too busy to leave behind the notebook she had asked for. 'I would so much like to be in Zurich to make your exam period more pleasant,' he assured her, 'but that would understandably cause my parents a great deal of pain.' Instead, he returned to Italy until the start of term. For all his talk of 'our place' and 'our household', he could not shake off the grip of his family home.

There were also other calls on his affection. Einstein was a flirt, and one of the attractions he found in Mettmenstetten was the company of a girl three years his junior. Anna Schmid was the sister-in-law of the Hotel Paradise's owner, Robert Markstaller, with whom Einstein became sufficiently friendly for the two men to go hiking together through the mountains. It appears that he became even friendlier with the seventeen-year-old Anna. On his departure he left some verses in her personal album, which read:

> Little girl, small and fine,
> What should I inscribe for you here?
> I could think of many things
> Including a kiss
> On your tiny little mouth
>
> If you're angry about it

Do not start to cry.
The best punishment is
To give me one too

This little greeting
Is in remembrance of your rascally little friend.

This shows an unexpected intimacy from a man who at much the
same time was sending Mileva 'my thousand warmest wishes'.

Julia Niggli, the friend from Aarau whom he had advised on the
unreliability of the male heart, was another target of his charm. To
her astonishment, Einstein invited her to join him at the Mettmenstetten hotel. 'How could a young man even think of inviting me to go
with him into Paradise?' she recalled. He laughed away her embarrassment, promising that everything was above board since his
mother and sister would be in attendance. She finally gave in and
agreed to visit – but only because she knew that her strict mother
would never allow her to keep her promise. In Zurich, too, Einstein
was keen to seek out female company. He enjoyed playing music with
Susanne Markwalder, the daughter of one of his landladies, and gave
her copies of some Mozart piano sonatas with the dedication 'in
friendship and admiration'. He also took her for sailing trips on Lake
Zurich – showing the lifelong devotion to boats that he later recalled
had begun at around the age of twelve, when he sailed toy vessels on a
tin tub one metre wide. He often joined Mileva for tea with her
girlfriends whom he would then gallantly walk home, particularly
one called Marie Rohrer, whose books he insisted on carrying back
from the library.

Mileva remained by far his closest companion, however – to the
extent that his constant presence became an irritant to her girlfriends,
Milana Bota and Ružica Dražić. They had formed a close-knit three-
some: gossiping together over coffee, helping each other with their
sewing, and travelling home by train together during the vacation.
Later they posed for a photograph to commemorate their 'common
life' at the Pension Engelbrecht. Bota's first impressions of Einstein
were favourable: she told her parents that he 'plays beautiful violin,
one can say that he is an artist, and so I will be able to play music with

someone again.' But Mileva had no intention of seeing her position as Einstein's accompanist usurped. Bickering ensued, and, although she was soon able to write that Mileva was once more 'very amiable with me', Bota's own feelings towards Einstein were poisoned. In the summer of 1900 she told her mother, 'I see little of Mitza because of the German, whom I hate.' It was then that she and Dražić announced that they intended to move out. Mileva noted, 'The girls seem somewhat cross with me . . . though I have not the slightest idea why; maybe I must atone for other people's sins.' Einstein, she added, had written a satirical poem about the pair – 'very good but very wicked' – which he intended to give them.

Einstein's mother had at first seemed to smile on her son's relationship. He had showed her Mileva's photograph in March 1899 and reported that it had 'quite an effect', adding that he pressed home the advantage by declaring with great conviction, 'Yes, yes, she is certainly a clever one.' At the end of his letter he added with quiet triumph, 'My old lady sends her best.' Similar postscripts appeared twice that summer, in addition to a terse 'Best wishes to your family' from 'P. Einstein', written on one of the envelopes. This did not disguise an underlying tension. The first possible hint of friction came in August, with Einstein reassuring Mileva in an oblique remark that he probably 'only imagined the story about you and Mama'. Evidently wary, Mileva insisted that he should not let anyone else read her letters. Perhaps he had admitted showing his mother those from Marie Winteler. Mileva was firm: 'You said once you don't like disrespect, and if I feel this is being disrespectful, you can do it for me!' He told her that his parents teased him for writing so much to her without reply.

Pauline's outright hostility emerged when it became clear that this relationship was more substantial than his previous flirtations. She did not seem to care that Mileva was not Jewish – neither was Marie Winteler – but she seems to have held the common German prejudice against Serbs. The belief that Slavs were inferior was deep-rooted long before the rise of Hitler. Pauline also distrusted Mileva as an older woman, tainted by physical handicap, who was leading her son astray. Despite having agreed to send parcels to Mileva's address, her decency was outraged by the implication that they were already sharing rooms. News of her hardening attitude was relayed to Mileva not by Einstein but through a mutual friend, Helene Kaufler. Kaufler, a history student at Zurich University, had met the couple after coming to live at the Pension Engelbrecht. She visited the Einstein home in Milan while on holiday at Lake Garda, and found that Pauline's antagonism towards Mileva had emerged in characteristic expression in ridicule. Mileva was thrown into despair by Kaufler's account of her stay and wrote:

Do you think that she does not like me at all? Did she make fun of me really badly? You know, I seemed to myself so wretched just now, so thoroughly wretched, but then I comforted myself all the same, because after all the most important person is of a different opinion, and when he paints beautiful pictures of the future, then I forget all my wretchedness.

These lines were written at some point in June or July 1900. Only one brief note between the couple survives from early October 1899 until at least a week after this period. Such a gap makes it impossible to follow the development of their relationship with any accuracy over these crucial months. Mileva's words suggest that, with the end of their student days in sight, Einstein was now talking of marriage. His loyalty to his parents remained ominously strong, however. It appears from the rest of Mileva's letter that Kaufler had found them very amiable hosts, and even admitted being drawn into the mockery of her friend. Mileva, who showed no resentment, noted that Einstein was 'extraordinarily pleased' that Kaufler had liked his 'old lady' so much.

A crisis was inevitable, and arrived without delay. The summer of 1900 saw Einstein and Mileva sit their final examination – a daunting mixture of more oral tests and a written thesis. They worked closely as they prepared for this ordeal, on which both their futures depended, and wrote their theses on the same subject of heat conduction. But when the results were announced at the end of July, they fared very differently. The marks are not strictly comparable across the five candidates (the other three were majoring in mathematics rather than physics), but they show that Mileva had lost her academic momentum. In theoretical physics, she was second only to Einstein. In astronomy, however, she was joint last with Grossmann. She and Einstein gained similar marks for the thesis: 18 for him and 16 for her, out of a possible 24. But these were the worst thesis grades of the group, with the rest scoring in the 20s. It was mathematics that proved her downfall: in the theory of functions she scored fewer than half the marks of the other four candidates. Mileva's final average grade was 4.00 compared with Einstein's 4.91. Even his performance was undistinguished, given that the others' ranged from 5.14 to 5.45. But the examiners, who are thought to have set a pass mark of around 5, duly granted diplomas to the four male candidates, including Einstein. Only Mileva was failed.

Perhaps the oral presentations before the all-male examiners had prejudiced her chances. She was always at a disadvantage within the male-dominated Polytechnic, with most of the professors having little expectation that women would succeed. Even the brightest female student was unlikely to be encouraged and brought on in the same way as a male contemporary. It may be, though, that Mileva had simply not mastered her subject. Unlike her colleagues, she sat her finals at the end of the same academic year as her intermediate exams, galloping from one fence straight on to the other. Her self-confessed difficulty with Professor Fiedler's geometry suggests how hard she found some of the work, although it was Einstein himself who branded Fiedler 'impenetrable' and a 'terrible pedant'. He would tell his biographer Carl Seelig that Mileva lacked 'ease of understanding', despite being intelligent and thirsty for knowledge. Elsewhere Einstein confessed to having precisely the same flaw as a student, but Mileva evidently lacked his flair. His eagerness to read around the subject may have encouraged her to skimp on duller coursework, without having his ability to skim off the essentials at the last moment.

Mileva returned home to Vojvodina, tired and depressed. But her spirit was not yet extinguished, and she was determined to retake the examination the following year. Einstein set off to join his mother and sister on holiday at the Swiss resort of Melchtal, accompanied by his despised Aunt Julie. He was covered in kisses when he arrived at the railway station in nearby Sarnen, but the friendly mood was deceptive. As a horse-drawn carriage took the party to their hotel, Maja

Einstein alighted with her brother and issued an urgent warning while they walked along alone. So tense was the atmosphere that she had been too scared to mention the 'Dollie affair' in their mother's presence. She begged him to keep his mouth shut and to spare Pauline's feelings. All in vain. Einstein was looking for a fight, and was carrying with him a piece of news that he knew would provoke one. We owe our knowledge of what happened next to the description he scribbled down for Mileva with immense relish as he sat later in bed. He faced his mother in her hotel room and the conversation began, not unexpectedly, with a discussion of the Polytechnic exams. Despite his success, Einstein had no job and an uncertain future ahead of him. 'So, what will become of your Dollie now?' his mother asked him innocently. 'My wife,' responded Einstein.

It was a challenge thrown with some deliberation in his mother's face, and one that she had just as deliberately invited. Einstein, who wrote that he had assumed an innocence matching her own, was steeled for the inevitable storm. He was not disappointed:

> Mama threw herself on the bed, buried her head in the pillow and wept like a child. After regaining her composure she immediately shifted to a desperate attack: 'You are ruining your future and destroying your opportunities.' 'No decent family will have her.' 'If she gets pregnant you'll really be in a mess.' With this last outburst, which was preceded by many others, I finally lost my patience. I vehemently denied that we had been living in sin and scolded her roundly ...

One doubts that Einstein was quite as composed as his account suggested, or that his mother would allow herself to be scolded in the magisterial manner he implied. However, other details have the ring of truth. He reported that he was ready to march out of the room, but was denied his grand gesture by the arrival at the door of one of his mother's friends. In the presence of Mrs Bär, a small and lively woman whom he evidently liked, there was a comical transformation in the manner of mother and son. All at once, with the greatest eagerness, they set to making polite conversation about the weather, their fellow guests, even the bad behaviour of certain children. The philistine chattering that Einstein so despised sprang easily to his lips, and his great confrontation with his mother dissolved into absurdity. Soon it was time to eat, and then the illusion of cordial relations was maintained as the guests gathered to play music. Only later, when he and his mother came to say goodnight, did the exchanges resume 'più piano'. Pauline Einstein's greatest fear was that the couple had 'already been intimate'; if not, some hope remained that disaster could be averted. Her son's denials gave her limited reassurance, but she continued to heap invective on Mileva's head. 'Like you she is a book – but you ought to have a wife,' she told him, adding for good measure, 'By the time you're thirty she'll be an old witch.'

Einstein scoffed at the crudeness of his mother's assaults, which he told Mileva had succeeded only in enraging him. Picking an argument like this, however, had hardly been likely to help his own avowed cause. His tactics suggest that he wanted to provoke a crisis so dramatic that it would finally break his mother's hold on him. Recounting it in such detail was calculated to upset Mileva rather than reassure her, but his main concern was to show his fiancée, and himself, how bravely he had defied his mother. Put to the test, he found it impossible to carry his strategy through.

4

The Delicate Subject

No sooner had these initial hostilities died down than Einstein began to pander to his mother's every whim. He became the epitome of a dutiful son, playing music for their fellow hotel guests and smothering everyone around him with flattery. The popularity he won himself seemed to restore Pauline's good humour: it was 'balm on her wounded mother-in-law's heart', he told Mileva. Within a few days he felt that they had 'more or less' made up again, and soon he reported that the atmosphere was downright cosy. He chose not to think too hard about why this was: he confidently told Mileva that his mother was gradually becoming resigned to the inevitable. The 'delicate subject' of the engagement was no longer mentioned, and his time was divided between walks with his sister, over mountainsides scattered with edelweiss, and contented study when the frequent rain kept him indoors. Soon Pauline was acting as if nothing had happened, politely handing Einstein letters from Mileva and affecting not to notice when he sat down to reply.

Slowly it dawned on him that this was only a tactical retreat. His mother had given up open warfare but was preparing to fire 'the big philistine guns' when reinforced by her husband. Einstein had written to his father, telling him of the proposed marriage, but had airily assured Mileva that Hermann's certain opposition was of no importance. Hermann responded with an indignant letter, dismissed by his son as a sermon, and the promise of a longer homily when Einstein returned to Italy with his mother at the end of August. Einstein complained to Mileva that his parents regarded wives as a luxury, in which men should indulge only after they had made a comfortable living. This left a wife and a whore on much the same level, he said, save that the wife had a contract for life. Einstein was starting to regret his rash announcement of the engagement, and he urged Mileva not to break the news to her own parents, though he conceded that the judgement was best left to her. There were signs in his letters of a reluctant recognition that she had already shown more wisdom and maturity on the subject than he had. 'I would have been smarter to have kept my mouth shut,' he admitted.

Conflicting emotions were tearing at his conscience. He told Mileva that he wanted to spare his parents – but without giving up anything he considered to be good: 'and that means you'. The pressure intensified when, after a few days back in Zurich, he made his way to Milan. One of the objects of his trip was to be instructed in the running of his father's business. He mocked this as an unwelcome ritual – 'partaking of the holy sacraments' – which he was undertaking only in case Hermann fell ill and needed someone to take his place. Nevertheless, it suggests how near he came to being lost to science and sucked into the family firm.

Two days after his arrival in Italy, Einstein had convinced himself that the so-called Dollie affair had blown over. He had still not received the 'treatment' from his parents and declared, 'As far as I can tell, they have nothing against our relationship any more.' He told Mileva that he had dropped her name into the conversation now and again, without response, and boasted that his parents must at last have realized he would not be influenced by them. A fond illusion. A few days later his confusion was complete as he told his 'dear kitten':

> My parents are very worried by my love for you. Mama often cries bitterly and I don't have a single moment of peace here. My parents weep for me almost as if I had died. Again and again they complain that I have brought misfortune upon myself by my devotion to you, they think you are not healthy . . . Oh Dollie, it's enough to drive one mad! You wouldn't believe how I suffer when I see how much they both love me . . .

These were the big guns that Einstein had feared, and the barrage quickly breached his flimsy defences. Before this, he had bragged that Hermann and Pauline had less obstinacy in their entire bodies than he had in his little finger. 'I understand my parents quite well,' he had announced complacently. Now the force of their conviction dazed him. It was as if he could not believe that this was the same couple of whose commonplace spirits he was accustomed to be so patronizing and dismissive. He told Mileva that they were behaving as though bewitched – just as they thought him to be bewitched by her. He felt like a criminal, he said, rather than a man who had done 'what my heart and conscience irresistibly prompted me to do'. Plans had previously been made for him to join his father on a tour of the family's power plants. Deflated and depressed, and perhaps seeking a way to strike back, he spoke of refusing to go. But this upset his parents so much that he became 'quite frightened' and fell back into line.

The irony was that this conflict with his family intensified Einstein's passion for Mileva and the fear that he could lose her. The lack of letters in the first half of 1900 makes direct comparisons impossible, but a sense of heightened emotion and intimacy is clear immediately after his first clash with his mother. In an echo of his April 1896 letter to Marie Winteler, he told Mileva that 'only now' could he see how madly he loved her. There was an ardent sexuality in his words as he yearned to hug and squeeze her, mischievously remarking how he pitied the chaste Catholic nuns he had seen near his holiday hotel in Melchtal. His letters always ended now with kisses – 'colossal kisses', 'heartfelt kisses', 'tender kisses'. His insistent theme was that without Mileva he felt directionless, incomplete. From the hotel he wrote, 'When I'm not with you, I feel as if I'm not whole. When I sit, I want to walk; when I walk, I'm looking forward to going home; when I'm amusing myself, I want to study; when I study, I can't sit still and concentrate; and when I go to sleep, I'm not satisfied with how I spent the day.'

The message was the same during his brief return to their common territory of Zurich. There he was free to go where he wanted – 'but I belong nowhere, and I miss your two little arms and that glowing mouth full of tenderness and kisses.' He complained of wasting away his days by staying in bed, loitering listlessly waiting for meals and thinking half-heartedly about physics. Studying now seemed unappetizing without Mileva to encourage him. Without her, he said, 'I lack self-confidence, pleasure in work, pleasure in living – in short, without you my life is no life.'

Einstein's abuse towards his relatives and their 'hangers-on' also gained a new intensity. His tone was so strident that it sometimes resembles that of a hard-line ideologist railing against the decadent bourgeoisie. These were 'people gone soft', turned 'mouldy', whose lives were idle and whose minds had atrophied. It was the women most of all whom he attacked: lazy, dressed-up and always complaining about something. Not that Einstein was one to complain, of course – it was just that his companions were stupid, cold and 'hopelessly dull', their daily round centred on enormous meals that each lasted an hour or more. The problem, he wrote in one of his more generous moods, was that the feelings of his parents and most other people were dominated by the primitive senses. He implied that they were a lower form of social evolution. The more refined minority could do little more than remind themselves how much they depended on these lesser beings for their own material comfort.

Underlying Einstein's comments was his growing vision of himself as something very similar to Nietzsche's Superman – a lonely intellectual, alienated from the common herd of humanity, who must live in the 'ice and high mountains' of spiritual solitude. His most direct inspiration in this direction was Schopenhauer, the great predecessor of Nietzsche, to whom his letters in this period contain a number of warmly approving references. There is much in Schopenhauer's aphorisms and essays that can also be found in Einstein – from an indifference to book-learning and an emphatic belief in 'thinking for yourself', to an enthusiasm for the idea of polygamy and a disdain for bourgeois attitudes to marriage. But the most suggestive link is the emphasis on the solitary destiny of the genius, surrounded by uncomprehending lesser beings. It is clear that the young Einstein liked to think of himself in these terms, making a stark contrast to the image he projected in maturity, full of amiable self-deprecation. As Schopenhauer wrote, 'If your abilities are only mediocre, modesty is mere honesty; but if you possess great talents, it is hypocrisy.'

Einstein's disdain for his female relatives recalls Schopenhauer's notorious misogyny – stimulated by the philosopher's own difficulties with his mother. In later years, Einstein would often seem to echo Schopenhauer's view that women 'taken as a whole, are and remain thorough and incurable philistines'. But at this stage he was anxious to stress that Mileva belonged with him in the elite. He assured her that there was no one 'as talented and industrious' as her 'in this entire ant hill' of the Melchtal hotel. However strongly solitude attracted him, it was not so strongly that he wished to forgo Mileva's love and support. His one comfort as he looked at his fellow hotel guests was to think, 'Johnnie, your Dollie is a different kind of girl.'

The danger for Einstein was that he would create an image of Mileva that she could not sustain when their long separation ended. His letters showed flashes of recognition of the strain under which events had placed her. Her health was poor and her confidence was badly bruised. Einstein urged her to rest, and expressed repeated pleasure that Mileva's mother was 'fattening her up' with home cooking. It was as if he drew vicarious strength from this maternal nurture, now that supplies closer to home were in doubt. Mileva's mother and father were proof, he said, that not everyone's parents had to turn out like his own. He told her not to study too much – there would be plenty of time to do that with him later on. Their present difficulties, he wrote, would only make it all the more agreeable when they were together in Zurich, working away over mugs of fragrant coffee. 'I can hardly wait to be able to hug you and squeeze you and live with you again,' he wrote. 'We'll happily get down to work right away, and money will be as plentiful as manure.' He assured Mileva that when he thought of her now he was determined never again to tease or provoke her. 'What a nice illusion!' he added.

Throughout this period, Einstein swung between feverish optimism and despair. He was at his most cheerful on 20 August 1900, just after his return to Milan. His cheery certainty that he had defeated the opposition of his parents poured out in the form of a dialect poem:

> O my! That Johnnie boy!
> So crazy with desire,
> While thinking of his Dollie,
> His pillow catches fire.
>
> When my sweetie mopes around the house
> I shrivel up so small,

But she only shrugs her shoulders
And doesn't care at all.

To my folks all this
Seems a stupid thing,
But they never say a single word
For fear of Albert's sting!

My little Dollie's little beak,
It sings so sweet and fine;
And afterwards I cheerfully
Close its song with mine.

This is an engaging piece of silliness, and oddly revealing. Even as he boasted of not being cowed by his parents at home, Einstein was basking in memories of being cowed by Mileva in his other 'household'. The thought of her sulky strength seemed to thrill him just as much as his more sentimental picture of her as a sweet little bird. A poem such as this hardly bears detailed textual analysis, but its very soppiness is itself suggestive. The babyish tone (even more pronounced in the German original) contrasts oddly with Einstein's portrayal of their relationship as a high-minded alliance against the philistines.

This was the posture to which he returned only a few days later, after the counter-attack by his parents. He told Mileva that science was his only distraction and she was his only hope. Without the thought of her, he wrote, he would not want to live any longer 'among this sorry herd of humans'. Then again, a few days after that, we find more childishness – and an entertaining insight into the roles each of them adopted when together. Einstein wrote, 'Do you know I've been shaving myself for quite some time now, and with great success? You'll see, Dollie! I can always do it while you're making coffee for lunch so that I don't pound the books as usual while poor Dollie has to cook, and while lazy Johnnie lolls about after hastily obeying the rapidly uttered command: "Grind this." '

Quite apart from his troubled romance, Einstein faced the small matter of arranging his future career. After passing his examinations he pinned his hopes on obtaining an assistantship at the Polytechnic, the most junior of all academic posts. In September, after hearing that a potential rival had found work elsewhere, he wrote to press his services on Professor Adolf Hurwitz, the head of his old section. Hurwitz told him that he had a chance – despite having skipped some obligatory seminars – but it turned out not to be a winning one. The professor announced that there were no entirely suitable candidates and recommended that the post be split between two of them. Neither of them was Einstein. He became the only one of the four 1900 graduates from Section VIA not to secure a position. He had fallen at the first fence of the course.

At the start of October, one week before Hurwitz announced his choice, Einstein insisted to Mileva that he had 'hardly any doubts' of success. This was bravado: he knew that his cocky manner and irregular attendance at classes had not endeared him to the Polytechnic staff. Professor Heinrich Weber, his physics lecturer, had told him that his cleverness was marred by one great fault: 'You'll never let yourself be told anything.' Einstein retaliated by addressing him as 'Herr Weber', instead of 'Herr Professor', rather as he had once irritated his childhood music teacher by calling him 'You, Herr Schmied' using the familiar German 'du' . His protestations of confidence to Mileva were mingled with assurances that failure hardly mattered so long as they were together, free to study, answering to no one. It was with the same insouciant air that he now returned to Zurich on 7 October. He supported himself by giving private lessons in mathematics, about eight a week, and began studying thermoelectricity (the study of the electricity produced by temperature differences) for a doctorate. This involved trying hard to be charming towards Professor Weber, whose laboratory had the best facilities.

Mileva was now steeled to retake her final examinations. She joined Einstein three days after his arrival, accompanied by her younger sister, Zorka. Despite Einstein's announcement that he had bought two new coffee-spoons especially to impress her, Zorka made her visit only after a certain amount of nagging. 'There's nothing like a female,' Einstein told Mileva – hastily adding that 'as a dear little scientist' she was naturally exempted from such stereotypes. Before their reunion he had been filled with dreams of domesticity, with the two of them saving up to buy some bicycles for country outings. The reality was rather different. He was forced to admit that private tuition was an unreliable source of income, and that their 'gypsy's life' was hardly satisfactory.

The only comfort as the year moved to a close was the progress he had made in science. His attention had focused on capillarity, the phenomenon that accounts for the way that the surface of a liquid is raised or depressed when it touches something solid like the sides of a pipe. His ideas were based on a theory of molecular forces of his own devising. Given that the very idea of molecules was still controversial, these notions seemed to him entirely new. They formed the contents of his first scientific paper, which in early December he sent to *Annalen der Physik*, the premier journal of German physics. 'You can imagine how proud I am of my darling,' Mileva told her newly married friend Helene Savić (formerly Kaufler), declaring that this was 'not just an everyday paper but a very important one'.

In the words of Professor John Stachel, who has made a close study of Mileva's scientific relationship with Einstein, her praise was excessive by the standards of physics, if not by those of love. Einstein himself would later dismiss this as one of his two worthless beginner papers. His later colleague and biographer Abraham Pais has described it as 'justly forgotten', and significant only for the interest it showed in a possible connection between molecular forces and gravitation. This was evidence of his desire to find universal principles, a feature of the extraordinary work that would follow.

Despite its limitations, the paper's publication was the first feather in Einstein's scholarly cap, and there are some grounds for believing that Mileva helped him with it. In October he had promised that they would work together on the topic in Zurich, collecting 'empirical material', and added, 'If a law of nature emerges from this, we will send it to [the] Annalen.' In subsequent letters, Einstein would write of 'our paper' and 'our theory of molecular forces'. He showed particular interest in whether 'our view' would hold good for gases as well as liquids. Mileva told Helene Savić that 'we' had sent a copy of the paper to the great Austrian physicist Ludwig Boltzmann, hoping that he would give 'us' his comments. Of course, the use of the collective pronoun is hardly proof of an intellectual partnership. When Einstein was addressing other audiences, such as his friend

Marcel Grossmann, he wrote of 'my theory' as entirely personal property. Nor did Mileva's expression of her pride in him suggest any attempt to claim co-authorship: she was happy to hand him full credit ('Albert has written a paper,' she told Savić). Any direct contribution she made to the paper probably lay in helping to obtain experimental evidence for conclusions that he had already drawn. What these hints do suggest, though, is the emotional commitment she was investing in his work, and the comfort he gained by drawing her into his private world. 'Even my work seems pointless and unnecessary if not for the thought that you are happy with what I am and what I do,' he had told her in September. One must always be sceptical of Einstein's hyperbole, which was often a better guide to the depth of his youthful confusion than to the strength of his convictions, but Mileva's faith and support were like a rock beneath him, at a time when he had little else to be sure of.

The trouble with being as dependable as a rock is that you get stood upon. However much weight Einstein placed on Mileva, he was unable to offer her anything like the same unconditional support in return. Since her examination failure, and the emergence of the hostility of Einstein's parents, Mileva's self-belief seems steadily to have eroded. Failing to obtain her diploma had been the first serious setback in her otherwise very successful academic career. She now knew that, even if she were to pass at the second attempt, she was no longer regarded as a high-flier. Moreover, the difficulties she openly admitted with much of the course material were a warning that further academic progress would be a deepening struggle. Her comments on Einstein's capillarity paper suggest that her own ambitions were now being subsumed in his. Instead of being the self-possessed partner on whom he could depend for mothering and support, without having to do much more in return than be boyishly charming, Mileva had come to depend on him just as strongly. Yet his ability to provide the support she needed was clearly compromised – partly by his failure to secure work, partly by his failure to reconcile his parents to her, and partly by the limitations of his character.

With the prospect of a job as far off as ever, Einstein decided to return to his parents in Milan. He seems to have persuaded Mileva that from there he would be better able to hunt for a position, making use of his family's contacts. She told Helene Savić that he would be 'taking half of my life with him', but added, 'It is better so for his career and I can't stand in its way. I love him too much for that, but only I know how much I suffer because of it. Both of us have had much to endure lately, but the forthcoming separation is almost killing me.'

Mileva longed to 'acknowledge our love before the whole world' and envied Helene's marriage that November. Helene's husband, an engineer called Milivoj Savić, had been a persistent suitor but was despised by Einstein, who predicted that she would 'suffocate in his fat'. To Mileva all that mattered was that Helene's letters shone with happiness, of a kind that she hardly believed she would live to see herself. Her spirits rose only slightly when Einstein announced that he would stay in Zurich until he finished his doctoral thesis in the new year. Even then he chose to return home for Christmas, which he had previously promised to spend with her. Mileva knew Einstein's vacillating nature and was frightened that his parents would turn him against her. She was also embittered by the 'slanders and intrigues' she believed were denying him the academic post he deserved. His own mood was altogether more buoyant, as was shown in another of his impromptu verses:

> The lass cried
> because the lad must split
> but we thought
> we won't grumble about it.

After Christmas, which appears to have passed without undue incident, the couple shared a few happy days hurtling down a hillside above Zurich on a sled. Einstein in particular took a childlike delight in speeding along 'like the devil'. He gained Swiss citizenship the following February. He had been stateless for almost four years when he first applied, a move prompted in part by his admiration for the Swiss political system and partly by more pragmatic reasons, not least that it would make positions in the civil service available, notably teaching. However, his prospects were uncertain. 'We haven't yet the slightest idea what fate has in store for us,' Mileva told Helene Savić.

Einstein returned to Milan in March 1901 and spent the ensuing weeks applying unsuccessfully for an assistantship with physicists across Europe. His known targets ranged as widely as Vienna, Leipzig, Göttingen, Stuttgart, Bologna and Pisa. 'Soon I will have honoured all physicists from the North Sea to the southern tip of Italy with my offer,' he said. Mileva helped by posting off reprints of his first paper, but the couple both suspected that his former physics lecturer Professor Weber was thwarting his chances by spreading bad opinions of him. At Mileva's prompting, Einstein wrote to Weber emphasizing how much he depended on the professor's references. No good came of it, and he grumbled that he would have found a job long ago 'had it not been for Weber's underhandedness'.

Life at home only added to the pressure upon him, since he could see the financial position of his parents deteriorating. They were being harried over Hermann's business debts by his chief creditor, the uncle that Einstein called 'Rudolf the Rich'. Einstein's growing desperation fed theirs, and his father secretly wrote to Professor Wilhelm Ostwald, one of two academics at Leipzig from whom Einstein had sought a job. Hermann Einstein pleaded in vain with Ostwald to give his twenty-two-year-old son a few words of encouragement, since he was 'profoundly unhappy' and felt that his career had been derailed. In addition, his father said, 'he is oppressed by the thought that he is a burden on us, people of modest means.'

Einstein's sympathy for his parents' plight was clear in the first letter he sent back to Mileva. It dwelt on the fact that, despite their own constant worries, 'the poor souls' were doing their best to calm his nerves. In this time of common stress there was a great temptation to retreat into his family in search of old certainties. As if in answer to Mileva's fears, however, he was soon insisting that he felt 'quite a stranger' at home, and could now see 'quite clearly what a little sweetheart's love is compared with parental love. This is as different as day and night. I kiss you therefore with all my heart and you should know that your devotion makes me so happy that without it my life would be unspeakably bleak.'

Mileva remained concerned that he was no longer sharing his feelings with her. She believed that his optimism had faded, leaving the way open for his parents to drive between them a wedge of doubt.

The brave face he put on in reply to her probings was not entirely convincing. He assured her that he was 'not discouraged in the least' by the rejections he had encountered, and had 'already set aside my anger, which was rooted in injured pride for the most part'. If he had been upset, he promised, 'I would have certainly poured out my heart to you, as I've so long been accustomed to doing, my dear, good soul.' Those words were written on 10 April 1901. Only five days later Einstein was apologizing to Mileva for failing to keep an assignation at the Swiss holiday town of Lugano, close to the Italian border. He said that he had been too depressed at the failure of several more applications.

As Einstein struggled to get an assistantship, the lowest rung on the academic ladder, Mileva worked towards resitting her final examinations, and hoped to build the work of her diploma thesis into a doctorate. Writing to her about physics was far more agreeable to Einstein than writing about his feelings, and his letters during this period teemed with science, despite his personal troubles and his complaint that home life made sustained study difficult. A great spate of ideas continued to flow out of him in her absence. There was a flash of insight about heat and energy that struck him during the train journey to Italy; fundamental doubts about radiation that arose as he read an article by Max Planck; a 'wonderful idea' he had arrived at for applying 'our theory of molecular forces' to gases. His mind was in flux as he announced a series of revisions and extensions to his previous views. This creative flow hardly suggested that Mileva's presence was necessary to his inspiration, but his desire to share his thoughts with her was as strong as ever. He asked her to look up data in the library and to send him a key textbook. He wrote of the investigations they could carry out together to develop his new insights. Above all there is one sentence that leaps from the page of a letter written in 1901, and that has been seized on as proof that he and Mileva were already collaborating closely on the theory that would make his name. 'I'll be so happy and proud', he wrote, 'when we are together and can bring our work on relative motion to a successful conclusion!'

It is important to step back and look at this remark in context. It was almost two years since Einstein had written to Mileva as she revised for her intermediate examination, voicing some of the thoughts that would lead to his revolutionary paper in 1905. Since then the theme of the electrodynamics of moving bodies had largely disappeared from his letters, but not from his mind. He discussed it not only with Mileva but also with Marcel Grossmann, with whom he had studied mathematics, and with his friend Michele Besso. When his great work was finally published, Besso was the only one of these three whose help he formally acknowledged. He is a major figure in Einstein's story.

They had met in 1896 at a musical evening in Zurich, where Besso studied engineering at the Polytechnic before starting work at an electrical-machinery factory in Winterthur. He was a short man, with a full beard and thick, dark, curly hair. His background was cosmopolitan – a Jewish family with origins in seventeenth-century Spain, now living in Italy, but with Swiss citizenship. Besso himself was born in Riesbach, near Zurich, and had shown an outstanding ability in mathematics early in his childhood. Although Einstein constantly complained about his friend's lack of ambition and drive – 'Michele is an awful schlemiel', he remarked – he had enormous respect for his intelligence and wide scientific knowledge. Besso was also a poetic, sensitive and emotional man. Einstein called him 'almost unbalanced', but liked him all the more for it, in the manner in which he was so often drawn to people whose passions flowed freer than his own. It was through an introduction by Einstein that Besso married Anna Winteler in 1898. At the start of 1901 he was working in Milan as a consulting engineer for the Society for the Development of Electrical Enterprises.

Einstein had written to Mileva of 'our work on relative motion' on 27 March of that year. A few days later, on 4 April, he told her that he had discussed 'our research' with Besso. The two men had sat for four hours debating the ether, the definition of absolute rest, molecular forces and other issues. Einstein did not disguise the 'great enjoyment' the encounter had given him, but surrounded his remarks with barbs about Besso being 'a terrible weakling' with no common sense and a mind that was 'disorderly' in its workings, although 'extraordinarily keen'. By way of example, Einstein told a story of how Besso had been sent out by his manager to inspect a power station. He set off in the evening, 'to save valuable time', but missed his train. The next day he forgot about his assignment and again arrived too late at the station. On the third day he arrived in good time for departure, but realized with horror that he could not remember what he was supposed to do when he arrived, and had to send a note to his office asking for fresh instructions. 'I don't think this fellow is normal,' said Einstein, apparently forgetting his own similar absent-minded lapses.

It was an anecdote that gently undermined his friend's credibility as a scientific partner. 'He's interested in our research, though he often misses the big picture by worrying about petty things,' Einstein told Mileva. 'This pettiness is a natural part of his character, and constantly torments him with all sorts of nervous ideas.' Implicit in this was the reassurance that Mileva was free of such blinkers – a fellow visionary. Einstein seemed anxious to ensure that she was not made jealous by his confiding in someone else. Why this was so important becomes clearer if we return to his previous letter about 'our work', and set out the quotation in full. Einstein had again been writing about Besso, whose help he had sought while job-hunting at Italian universities. He went on:

> You don't have to worry about me saying anything to him or anyone else about you. You are and will remain a shrine for me to which no one has access: I know that of all people, you love me the most, and understand me the best. I assure you that no one here would dare, or even want, to say anything bad about you. *I'll be so happy and proud when we are together and can bring our work on relative motion to a successful conclusion!* When I see other people I can really appreciate how special you are!

By italicizing the key sentence, one shows how it sat marooned, not in one of Einstein's many passages of close scientific argument, but amid an outpouring of reassurance that his love for Mileva remained absolute despite their separation. Besso was hardly the most obvious threat to his lasting loyalty, so long as Einstein stayed living with his parents, but he was included here in the list of suspects. The two men's scientific friendship already posed a threat to the idea that Mileva and Einstein were facing the rest of the world alone.

Einstein's reference to 'our work' may best be seen as an attempt to reassert this exclusive bond between them: to prove to Mileva that no one else had intruded into the shrine. In his own analysis of this passage, pointing out its wider context, Professor John Stachel has suggested that Einstein was 'a young man, deeply in love, who has relaxed his own ego boundaries to include Marić within them . . . although he maintains a wary and perhaps even hostile sense of separation between the two of them and the outside world.' Stachel believes that it was natural for Einstein to overvalue the accomplishments of the woman he loved and to identify his own achievements as those of them both. Yet, for all its insight, this explanation overlooks the defensive, protesting tone of Einstein's words. They suggest a young man repeating an article of faith precisely because that faith was being sorely tested. Once again, in the last line, there was the implication that he fully appreciated Mileva only when he saw the true awfulness of other people. Was this really, as Stachel suggests, a man 'deeply in love'? Or was this a twenty-two-year-old deeply loved by Mileva, and nervously clinging to that love, but far less sure than he pretended of his own feelings towards her? Reading Einstein's love-letters to Mileva, one often begins to wonder whether they should be described as 'love-letters' at all. He showed every sign of wanting to be in love, but of finding it very hard work.

Einstein's career worries were eventually eased in April 1901 by Marcel Grossmann, whose father was an old colleague of Friedrich Haller, the director of the Swiss Patent Office in Berne. Grossmann Senior recommended Einstein to Haller as a possible employee, and the message came back that a post could probably be found for him before too long. During the previous summer Einstein had turned down the offer of a vacation job in an insurance office, saying that the drudgery of an eight-hour day was too stultifying to endure. The Patent Office offered a similar grinding routine and only marginally more intellectual stimulation, but academic disappointment had made him less fastidious. In the present circumstances this seemed 'a wonderful job', and he told Marcel that he was 'deeply moved' by the loyalty 'which did not let you forget your old luckless friend'. All at once — again thanks to a recommendation by friends from the Polytechnic — he was also offered a two-month teaching position at a secondary school in Winterthur, about ten miles north-east of Zurich, while one of the staff was away on military service. The prospect of thirty hours in the classroom each week – and having to teach descriptive geometry, Mileva's pet hate – was not especially appealing, but Einstein needed money. 'The valiant Swabian is not afraid', he proclaimed, and accepted the post. The good news swung his mood back to loving ebullience, and he summoned Mileva to a celebratory reunion at Lake Como, near the Italian border. She was given orders to bring a blue nightshirt that he had left behind in Zurich, so that together they could wrap themselves up in it. 'You'll see for yourself how bright and cheerful I've become and how all my frowning has been forgotten,' he told her. 'And I love you so much again! It was only out of nervousness that I was so mean to you. You'll hardly recognize me now that I've become so bright and cheerful and am longing so much to see you again, dearest Dollie.'

Mileva was making inquiries about her own future. She had been considering a return home to teach at a secondary school in Zagreb – assuming, that is, that she passed the exam for her teacher's certificate. Einstein's sudden elation made this ambition seem absurd in his eyes: what need did she have of an independent career, when he could appoint her 'my dear little scientist' in Berne? 'You are a thousand times more important to me than you could ever be to all the people of Zagreb!' he said. Not only was his confidence restored, it soared to new heights. His every word breathed his conviction that Mileva was gloriously lucky to be part of his life. 'If you knew what you mean to me, you wouldn't envy any of your girlfriends at all,' he told her, 'because with all modesty I believe you have more than all of them combined.'

The sheer gusto of his self-satisfaction overwhelmed Mileva's initial resistance. Before being subjected to its full intensity she had written of having lost 'all desire, not only for having a good time but for life itself', and told him to make the Como trip by himself. 'I'm going to lock myself up and work hard, because it seems I can have nothing without being punished,' Mileva wrote. 'Farewell, be cheerful, and if you find any pretty flowers, bring me a few.'

This bout of gloom had its immediate cause in a letter Mileva had received from home, which does not survive. But this had only added to a deeper hopelessness which had been growing in her as she studied alone in Zurich. Her tone was self-pitying, even petulant, and a pointed reminder to Einstein that his own happiness did not necessarily ensure her own. However, the mood soon passed. 'I became a little more cheerful, since I see how you love me, and I think that we'll take that little trip after all,' she wrote the day after refusing him.

Now Mileva was desperate that he should not oversleep and delay the moment of their meeting. 'You have so much love for your Dollie, and you long for her so!' she told Einstein. 'She's always so happy with your little letters full of passionate love, showing her that you are once again her dear sweetheart, and my God! what sweet little kisses she's saved for you! . . . Awaiting you with a thousand pleasures, your tormented Dollie.'

Their reunion was one of the most passionate and intensely physical moments of their relationship, and Mileva recounted it in breathless detail to Helene Savić. Einstein had met her 'with open arms and a pounding heart'. They stayed half the day in the town of Como, relaxing among the cafés and hotels that look out over the water and its mountain setting. Then they took a boat towards Colico, near the north-eastern end of the lake, stopping on the western shore to visit the famous Villa Carlotta. Together they admired the villa's collection of marble statues by Canova, including a group showing Cupid and Psyche, before strolling amid the lush vegetation of its terraced gardens. Mileva had told Einstein how much she looked forward to 'practising our botany' along the lake's shores, and she was not disappointed. The gardens – renowned for their azaleas, camelias and rhododendrons – were ablaze in the brilliant spring sunshine. 'I have no words to describe the splendour we found there,' she recalled, and joked, 'We were not allowed to swipe even one single flower.'

The next day they set out north to cross the Splügen pass over the Alps. It was a spectacular journey as the road wound steeply through a series of hairpin bends, past a romantic landscape of ravines and waterfalls. The mild weather was soon left behind them, the pass being more than two thousand metres above sea level and covered in snow up to six metres deep. Mileva described how they hired a sleigh with 'just enough room for two people in love'. They rode on through the snow flurries with the coachman standing behind them on a little plank, chatting away charmingly and calling her 'signora' as if Einstein and she were already man and wife. Snow was falling all around them, she recalled. 'We were driving now through long galleries, now on the open road, where there was nothing but snow and more snow as far as the eye could see, so that this cold, white infinity gave me the shivers and I held my sweetheart firmly in my arms under the coats and shawls with which we were covered.'

They travelled for a few hours to the pass and then continued on foot. It was hard marching through the snow, and the weather grew increasingly gloomy, but they found too much pleasure in each other's company to care. Together they triggered snow slides to terrify the hapless occupants of the Rhine valley below. 'How happy I was again to have my darling for myself a little, especially because I saw that he was equally happy!' wrote Mileva.

After returning to collect his belongings in Zurich – where one hotel refused to admit him after inspecting his shabby appearance – Einstein set off to take up his temporary teaching job at Winterthur. He found clean and roomy lodgings with the landlady of an old friend, Hans Wohlwend, who was a frequent companion during his stay. Each morning he would give classes at the technical school, leaving him fresh enough to continue his own studies in the library or at home. Sundays were usually reserved for seeing Mileva, who was working on a new diploma thesis under Professor Weber's supervision. By submitting a dissertation, Mileva could obtain a doctorate from the University of Zurich, provided she graduated.

Einstein soon became frustrated by the limited scientific knowledge of his fellow teachers, and continued to tell Mileva that only she gave his life any meaning. Their loving intimacy on the trip from Como had left him eager for more. 'How beautiful it was the last time you let me press your dear little person against me in that most natural way,' he wrote. 'Let me kiss you passionately for it, my dear sweet spirit!' Mileva was equally impatient for his next visit. 'I'll work very hard so that I'm free to enjoy our time together – my God, how beautiful the world will look when I'm your little wife, you'll see. There will be no happier woman in the whole world – in which case the man must also be happy.'

Then Mileva discovered she was pregnant. To a young woman who increasingly saw herself as a victim, accustomed to reverses whenever she dared to start feeling optimistic, the news was dismaying. She was alone and far from her family, only two months away from retaking the exams that were so important to her self-esteem and her hopes for an independent career. Her lover was an impecunious dreamer to whom marriage remained only a dim prospect, whose parents detested her, and who had yet to be confirmed in a permanent job. Although Mileva had a powerful maternal instinct, which was later to find full expression in the care of her sons, and although she was proud to be carrying the child of a man she adored, the happy future that she had been dreaming of had suddenly been thrown into even greater uncertainty than before.

Mileva probably broke the news to Einstein during one of his weekend visits to Zurich, and his first surviving reference to it was in a letter that has been dated to 28 May 1901. He began with an exclamation of touching and unfeigned pleasure – but not about his impending fatherhood. Instead, Einstein wrote of the latest physics article to have inspired him, and only then turned to Mileva's predicament.

> My dear kitten,
> I have just read a wonderful paper by Lenard on the generation of cathode rays by ultraviolet light. Under the influence of this beautiful piece I am filled with such happiness and joy that I absolutely must share it with you. Be happy and don't fret, darling. I won't leave you and will bring everything to a happy conclusion. You just have to be patient! You'll see that my arms aren't so bad to rest in, even if things are beginning a little awkwardly. How are you, darling? How's the boy? Can you imagine how pleasant it will be when we're able to work again, completely undisturbed, and with no one around to tell us what to do! You will be well compensated for your present worries with much joy, and the days will pass peacefully.

There was no sign that Einstein realized how thoroughly parenthood threatened to transform his life, and how unlikely it was that the arrival of a child would allow him and Mileva 'to work again, completely undisturbed'. Moreover, his assumption that she would be in the mood to share his excitement over Lenard's paper could hardly have been more misjudged. The facetious and indirect manner in which he referred to the baby – hiding behind the conceit that it was bound to be a boy – reflected a determination to treat the situation as lightly as possible. A little later in the same letter, he asked, 'How is our little son? And your dissertation?'

Mileva's pregnancy held Einstein's attention only fleetingly over the following weeks. His main concern was his first direct challenge to the scientific establishment through an attack on Paul Drude, editor of *Annulen dor Physik.* In a long letter, he sent Drude a series of objections to his electron theory of metals (in which thermal and electrical properties are explained in terms of an electron gas). Einstein proudly told Mileva that his points were too straightforward to be refuted. He had come up with a similar theory to Drude's himself, so he felt it quite proper to approach him as an equal and 'point out his mistakes'. Once again, these scientific matters took precedence over the personal. 'Do you still remember how awkward I was the last time?' he asked Mileva. 'But you can bet I didn't write Drude anything about that. How are your studies going, and the child, and your mood? I hope that all three are as well as is to be expected. I'm sending you kisses especially, so you'll never be lacking in good cheer. What the present leaves to be desired will be compensated for in the future – and how.'

Einstein hoped that the brilliance of his letter to Drude might earn him the offer of a job: he made clear in it that he needed one. Instead, Drude's reply dismissed Einstein's objections out of hand. It was no more than a stand-in schoolmaster could expect after taking on one of the scientific giants of his day, but it came as a stinging rebuff to Einstein's pride. Three months earlier he had told Mileva that Drude was without doubt 'a brilliant man'; now he saw him as a 'sad specimen' whose response proved his wretchedness. More than ever he was convinced that the dunces of the world were in confederacy against him. 'It is no wonder that little by little one becomes a misanthrope,' he told Mileva. To Jost Winteler he wrote that he would 'make it hot' for Drude by publishing his criticisms in a skilfully humiliating article. 'Unthinking respect for authority is the greatest enemy of truth,' he declared.

Einstein's threats ultimately turned out to be empty: he never would publish an attack or cause Drude the least bit of discomfort. In his most revolutionary paper of 1905, on light quanta, Einstein would cite Drude's work in the very first reference without taking a single swipe at his methods. His threats were similar to the theatrical behaviour that Mileva had witnessed before, when he described his confrontations with his mother. However, there was one important consequence of Drude's snub: it threw Einstein into defiance, and he now vowed to marry his pregnant girlfriend at any cost. He told Mileva that he had made an 'irrevocable decision' to accept any job, however modest, and however much at odds with his 'personal vanity' and scientific goals. As soon as he found work, they would marry and set up home together secretly, presenting a fait accompli to their families. 'Then no one can cast a stone upon your dear head,' he told her, 'and woe unto him who dares to set himself against you.' Einstein would later claim that he had married Mileva only out of a sense of duty – but these comments suggest a more passionate commitment than he was ready to admit in old age. After suffering a humiliating reverse, he wanted Mileva at his side in his battle against the philistines.

Mileva's pleasure in reading his promises was tempered by scepticism. She was too sensible to endorse his histrionics wholeheartedly, and she cautioned him not to set his sights too low: to take 'a really bad position' would be foolish and, 'would make me feel terrible . . . I couldn't live with it.' He seriously considered joining an insurance company, enlisting the help of Michele Besso's father, who was the director of a large firm in Trieste. At the prompting of Jost Winteler, he applied for a vacancy at a technical school in Burgdorf, near Berne, but was rejected. He was beaten to another job at a secondary school in Frauenfeld by none other than Marcel Grossmann. Hopes of work at the Swiss Patent Office were still unfulfilled, and he was turned down flat when he put himself forward for an administrative post there. All he could find was more temporary work, teaching at a private boarding-school in Schaffhausen. For the most part it meant coaching a nineteen-year-old English boy, Louis Cahen, to prepare him for the high-school examinations.

Mileva sat her finals again at the end of July 1901. In the circumstances, perhaps disaster was inevitable. Pregnancy had placed her under great stress, and a letter she wrote to Einstein, in the thick of her revision, suggests that yearning for his company was a major distraction. She told him of her hard work, and how she must study Weber, only to add that she spent 'every moment' looking forward to his next visit, 'when I can see you and kiss you again in the flesh, not only in my thoughts, and almost as it pours out of my heart, and everywhere, everywhere.' Rather than being at her side to bring comfort, Einstein was once again holidaying with his mother and sister at the Hotel Paradise in Mettmenstetten. A letter that he sent to wish Mileva luck also carried news of his rejection by the Patent Office and a dark hint that his mother remained suspicious of their relationship. Neither item can have made encouraging reading. Mileva also admitted having 'a few spats' with Professor Weber in the period before the examinations. It is possible that their academic relationship was soured by her resentment over Weber's treatment of Einstein. Mileva's own chances, already damaged by her weakness in mathematics, may have been harmed further by her readiness to see her lover's battles as her own.

Whatever the reasons, Mileva failed her exams a second time. Her average mark was 4.0, exactly the same as the year before. Once again she was the only candidate to be refused her teaching certificate, with the others in her group of six all scoring averages of 5 or more. Mileva abandoned her doctoral dissertation and vowed never again to work with Weber. She returned to Vojvodina in low spirits but ready to tell her parents all her 'unpleasant news' – both academic and personal. It was agreed that Einstein should send ahead a letter to her father, outlining their plans to marry. Mileva asked to check what he had written before she left, and told him to keep the message short – past evidence of his diplomatic skills made such precautions wise. There had been further clashes with his mother during his holiday, although Mileva refused to believe that Pauline would never give up her hostility. 'She would have to be motivated by ambition and self-love alone, not by love, and such mothers don't exist,' Mileva wrote.

With studied optimism, the twenty-five-year-old insisted that she could win over Einstein's parents and dispel the false impression they had gained of her, however long this took. Mileva hinted that she had devised a number of cunning strategies to this end, but her only example was the rather lame idea of ingratiating herself with someone the Einsteins admired, as if their own approval would magically follow. It was little more than a comforting daydream. Mileva had real faith in no one other than Einstein himself, who had told her that even their friend Besso was likely to have misgivings about her pregnancy. Her response was to rank Michele with the rest of their philistine opponents, so bogged down in humdrum existence that they had 'left the plane of pure human feelings behind'.

Her reunion with her mother and father was no doubt painful, and Einstein later made a cheeky reference to the thrashing that Marija Marić had promised to bestow on him. It seems, though, that Mileva's family was ready to accept her situation with resigned understanding. What threw them into fury was a letter sent to them that autumn by Pauline Einstein, bitterly attacking their daughter's character. It reviled Mileva with a vehemence the victim found hard to believe: no longer could she pretend to trust in Pauline's essential goodness. Vainly attempting to restrain her anger with irony, she told her friend Helene Savić that 'the charming behaviour of my dear mother-in-law' had filled her with misery. 'That lady seems to have made it her life's goal to embitter as much as possible not only my life but also that of her son. Oh, Helene, I wouldn't have thought it possible that there could exist such heartless and outright wicked people!'

Those words were written from Novi Sad some weeks after the crisis broke, and Mileva explained that she had torn up other attempts to set down her feelings, fearing they were too bleak to send. Her first response had been to travel back to Switzerland to be at Einstein's side. Since the start of September he had been teaching in Schaffhausen, twenty miles north of Zurich. In early November, Mileva set off to join him. She checked into the Hotel Steinerhof at Stein am Rhein, a few miles away from Schaffhausen, anxious to avoid detection by Einstein's parents. As ever, she lived in fear of his indiscreet tongue, and she issued strict instructions that he should give his family no clues to her presence. Even confiding in his sister was too dangerous, so anxious was Mileva to prevent another onslaught by his mother. 'No more fights; I dread the mere thought of it,' she wrote. 'The peace right now is pleasant and soothing . . . Tell them I am in Germany!'

Her stay lasted only a few weeks. Einstein was strangely reluctant to see her, despite her obvious distress, and two letters survive in which her indignation was clear. He claimed that he was too short of money to visit her, but Mileva was unimpressed, reminding him that he earned 150 francs a month with room and board provided. She offered to send him money herself, and warned that she would leave if he continued to stay away. 'If you only knew how much I want to see you again,' she wrote. 'I think about you all day long, and even more at night . . .'

Mileva gave him flowers and he gave her books, on which her comments were revealing. A volume on thermodynamics by the German physicist Max Planck inspired from her the insipid remark, 'It seems to be interesting.' In contrast her imagination was fired by a study of hypnotism by August Forel, the director of the Burghölzli psychiatric clinic in Zurich. During her Polytechnic days Mileva had attended a course on psychology, in which hypnosis had been dismissed as immoral by the lecturer. She now felt the 'same feeling of disgust' towards Forel's ideas, which seemed to her 'a violation of human consciousness'. There was more conviction in her discussion of the subject than can be found in any of her surviving comments on physics. Here she almost matched Einstein in her magisterial dismissal of authority, denouncing Forel as a quack who fooled the 'stupid herd' but did not fool her. Many of Einstein's letters to Mileva include promises to explain his ideas to her at some later date, in the manner of a teacher to his favourite pupil. With the same poise, she promised to explain to him later why Forel's experiments were dishonest.

Mileva returned home towards the end of November, seven months pregnant. Her limited contact with Einstein had been enough to raise her spirits slightly, but she still saw little hope of his obtaining secure employment. His handicaps were all too clear – he had 'a very wicked tongue' and faced prejudice as a Jew. They were still 'a sorry little couple', she told Helene, even though she could not help loving him 'quite frightfully much'.

After the breakdown of his relations with Professor Weber, Einstein had resumed work under the supervision of Alfred Kleiner, a physicist at Zurich University who was interested in his theoretical work. Mileva's faith in Einstein's ability was undimmed, and she was full of praise for the 'magnificent' study of molecular forces in gases that he submitted as his doctoral dissertation (only to withdraw it later). Mileva read the work with 'great joy and admiration for my little sweetheart who has such a good head on his shoulders'. Her opinion of it was surpassed only by Einstein's own, but the long wait for Kleiner's verdict jangled his nerves. 'I'm sure he won't dare reject my dissertation, otherwise the short-sighted man is of little use to me,' he wrote at the end of November. Three weeks later he was even more exasperated, complaining, 'It's really terrible, all the things these old philistines put in the path of people who aren't of their ilk.' The thesis probably contained his earlier criticism of Drude, and Einstein was determined not to accept another rebuff. 'I'll publish his rejection along with my paper and make a fool of him,' he threatened. 'But if he accepts it, then we'll see what good old Herr Drude has to say.' Einstein had developed a cold contempt for the scientific establishment, convinced that men such as Kleiner considered every intelligent youth as a threat to their dignity. He took a solemn oath that in future he would give help to any 'gifted young men' who found themselves in a similar plight.

Einstein's reluctance to visit Mileva at Stein am Rhein was in marked contrast to the eagerness with which he pursued her by post in the following weeks. He claimed to live in almost total isolation at Schaffhausen, speaking to no one save his student, Cahen. This was a characteristic exaggeration, and he spent particularly happy hours at local concerts and music evenings, both as listener and performer. Nevertheless, Mileva's letters were his most substantial human contact – in his words, 'the only human pleasures here to warm my soul' – and each one was greedily devoured. A three-day lapse in the correspondence was enough for him to joke that the postmen must be using them for kindling, or some other more unspeakable purpose. He asked Mileva to write in detail about her daily life so that he could fantasize about her, and he acknowledged that her letters provided an agreeable substitute for reality. 'They must take the place of wife, parents, friends, and companions,' he told her, 'and they do a good job of it.' This was followed by the immediate qualification that it would 'of course' be nicer to have Mileva there in the flesh. In another letter, he admitted finding his best company when alone, only to add 'except when I'm with you'. There seems no reason to doubt that Einstein had decided, as he put it in the same passage, that 'every regular fellow should have a girl'; but it is also clear that he found the theory much easier than the practice.

Einstein sometimes took a positive pleasure in engineering his isolation, as if to prove to himself his inner independence. At Schaffhausen he picked a fight with the director of his boarding-school, Jakob Nüesch, that recalled his first great clash with his mother. Einstein took his evening meal with Dr Nüesch, his wife and their four children, but it was not an arrangement he enjoyed. He asked instead to be paid enough to buy his meals out, thinking that he could save some money in the process. Dr Nüesch responded with an angry and rude refusal, but backed down after Einstein vowed to take his services elsewhere. It was an entirely empty threat, given the trouble he had found in getting any job at all, but this only made the young man prouder of himself. 'Long live impudence!' he told Mileva. 'It's my guardian angel in this world.'

His description of the episode had the same theatrical flair as his account of his battle with his mother, with Dr Nüesch 'flushed with anger' but immediately crumbling in the face of Einstein's masterly counter-attack. The Nüesches were left 'in a vicious rage' against him, but it was agreed that Einstein would take his meals at a nearby inn. Here he continued true to form. His first visit was a great success, and he made friends with two pharmacists among the other diners. Days later, however, every fellow customer seemed stupid and commonplace. Einstein described toying with his cutlery between courses while looking out the window. 'These people must think I've never laughed in my life,' he told Mileva, 'but then they've never seen me with my Dollie.'

His last meal at the home of Dr Nüesch, one Wednesday evening early in December, offered the first glint of hope for his future. Propped against his soup dish was a letter from Marcel Grossmann, announcing that the long-awaited vacancy at the Patent Office was about to be advertised. Most importantly, Grossmann was certain that Einstein would be chosen to fill it. Einstein pronounced himself 'dizzy with joy', and was thrown into even greater ecstasies a week later when his prospective boss, Haller, wrote personally asking him to apply. The position of engineer, second class, was advertised in Switzerland's federal gazette on 11 December. Einstein applied a week later but had to wait until June before being elected. He was subsequently told that Haller had tailored the requirements especially to fit his rather limited qualifications. The salary would be from 3,500 to 4,500 Swiss francs a year. Einstein's friend Jakob Ehrat warned that this was too little to support a wife in an expensive city such as Berne, but Einstein was in no mood to heed such advice. He told Mileva that Ehrat (who would not himself marry until 1914) spoke of wedlock 'as if it were a bitter medicine that has to be taken dutifully'. How funny, he added, that they could see something so differently.

As so often in the past, Einstein's feelings towards those around him were given new warmth by his sudden burst of optimism. That summer he had grumbled that friends tended to desert you when times were hard. Now his gratitude to Grossmann – 'who never stopped thinking of me' – knew no bounds. Professor Kleiner no longer appeared a philistine establishment figure, bent on frustrating his progress. Though he still had not read Einstein's dissertation, he was now an enlightened mentor full of encouragement for the younger man's ideas on relative motion. 'He is not quite as stupid as I'd thought, and, moreover, he's a good fellow,' Einstein said. Most noticeable of all was the characteristic upsurge in his love for Mileva. 'Now our troubles are over,' he declared. 'Only now that this terrible weight is off my shoulders do I realize how much I love you.' What did it matter that he had 'once again' forgotten her birthday? Soon he would take his faithful Dollie in his arms 'and call her my own in front of the whole world'. A golden future seemed assured – although his vision of it was little more than a return to the past. His first reaction to Grossmann's tip-off had been to tell Mileva that now they could be 'students . . . as long as we live' and ignore the rest of the world. After Haller's letter he promised, 'Soon you'll be my "student" again, like in Zurich. Looking forward to it?'

The looming reality of Mileva's baby was largely ignored. Einstein's favourite joke was to call the unborn child 'Hanserl', or little Hans, in his playful insistence that it was bound to be a boy. Mileva referred to it as 'Lieserl', a diminutive of Elisabeth, in equally firm insistence that it would be a girl. Einstein asked Mileva to draw him a picture of the 'funny figure' which she told him she was developing. Only once in the surviving letters did he strike a more serious note, but this was ominous. In the midst of his celebrations over Grossmann's letter, Einstein wrote, 'The only problem that still needs to be resolved is how to keep our Lieserl with us; I wouldn't want to have to give her up. Ask your Papa; he's an experienced man, and knows the world better than your overworked, impractical Johnnie.' These lines were followed by a jocular warning that the baby 'shouldn't be stuffed with cow's milk, because it might make her stupid.'

The sting was hardly removed from what he had already written. It is impossible to know whether the couple had already broached the subject of giving their baby away. The option may have been touched on in an earlier letter from Mileva, which spoke of the need to keep on good terms with Helene Savić 'because she can help us with something important'. However, this phrase is so vague that it is impossible to place much weight on it. Einstein's words were specific, and have a slightly disingenuous air that hints that this was a choice for which he wished to win support. Mileva was now close to giving birth, but there was still no suggestion of an imminent marriage. Nor was there even a chance of their imminent reunion. Einstein had made up his mind to follow Kleiner's advice and publish his ideas for experiments to investigate the ether before the post at the Patent Office became free. That meant staying at Schaffhausen over the winter holiday, apart from a short Christmas break with his sister at the Hotel Paradise in Mettmenstetten. 'If only you could be there too,' he told Mileva. 'But our own paradise will follow soon enough.'

Einstein later made clear that his stay at the hotel was not a success. Mileva had sent him a parcel packed with Christmas treats of tobacco and food, which he guzzled almost immediately. In his thank-you

note, he set down a marker for their own future as he complained
how dull he had found his sister's company:

> When you're my dear little wife we'll diligently work on science
> together so we don't become old philistines, right? My sister
> seemed so crass to me. You'd better not get that way – it would
> be terrible. You must always be my witch and street urchin . . .
> Everyone but you seems foreign to me, as if they were separated
> from me by an invisible wall.

5

My Only Companion

MILEVA gave birth to a daughter some time around the end of January 1902. It was a difficult labour, which left her too ill and exhausted to write to Einstein. There are no records of the birth, but it is thought it took place far from Switzerland, probably at the home of Mileva's parents. Her father broke the news in a letter to Einstein, who admitted to being 'frightened out of my wits'. He had suspected all was not well, and evidently feared the worst when he saw Miloš Marić's handwriting on the envelope.

In a reply that made every show of sympathy for his 'poor, dear sweetheart', Einstein deplored the miserable way in which 'our dear Lieserl' had entered the world. 'All other fates are nothing compared with this,' he declared, throwing out a series of questions befitting a concerned father. Was the baby healthy? Was she hungry? Which of them did she most resemble? Who was feeding her milk? Even without seeing his daughter, Einstein pronounced himself completely in love with her. He asked Mileva to send him a photograph of the child, or draw a picture of her, as soon as she had recovered her own health. It amused him to treat the birth as a scientific phenomenon, announcing, 'I'd like to make a Lieserl myself sometime – it must be fascinating!' He urged Mileva to 'make observations' on the baby's development, and added, 'She's certainly able to cry already, but won't know how to laugh until much later. Therein lies a profound truth.'

There is no evidence that Einstein and his daughter ever set eyes on one another. For all his apparent enthusiasm after the birth, it seems that his main concern was to free himself of this burden at the earliest opportunity. Lieserl's existence was kept hidden even from his closest friends, and within months she had disappeared from his life without trace. Einstein was never to talk of her publicly, and Lieserl might have been erased from history had it not been for the discovery of his letters to Mileva by the Einstein papers project. No other references to her have been found in all the vast bulk of Einstein's papers. Nor has any official record of her birth yet been located, despite the determined efforts of Robert Schulmann from the Einstein project and Professor Milan Popović of Belgrade University, the grandson of Mileva's friend Helene Savić. In the summer of 1986 Schulmann travelled to Yugoslavia to search through local civic archives. No trace of Lieserl existed in either Novi Sad, where the Marić family lived in winter, or in Kać, their home in summer. Since then, Schulmann's hunt has extended to the Hungarian capital of Budapest, still without success. The turmoil in what was Yugoslavia has made it impractical to continue his inquiries, although he hopes to resume them.

Mileva did not join Einstein in Switzerland until several months after the birth. When she did so, Lieserl was not with her. We do not know who cared for the child in her mother's absence (although Mileva's relatives are the most obvious candidates) because there is complete silence about her during the first year and a half of her life. She is not mentioned in her parents' surviving letters until September 1903, and to make any judgement on her fate one must briefly leap forward to this point. Mileva had returned to her family home, apparently discovering there that the child had contracted scarlet fever. Word was passed to Einstein, who replied as follows: 'I'm very sorry about what has befallen Lieserl. It's so easy to have lasting effects from scarlet fever. If only this will pass. As what is the child registered? We must take precautions that problems don't arise for her later.'

This is the most substantial clue to the mystery, but is frustratingly inexplicit. One explanation of Lieserl's disappearance would be that her illness proved fatal, which was a real danger in the days before antibiotic drugs. However, Einstein's emphasis on longer-term dangers suggests that her life was not thought to be at risk. The dangers that seemed to preoccupy him were unconnected to the child's illness: his question about registration strongly suggests that she was being surrendered for adoption, and that Einstein was eager to cover his tracks. The lack of any official record of the birth would appear to be a tribute to the thoroughness of the precautions that he referred to.

Lieserl's birth posed a threat to Einstein's new start as a patent examiner in Berne. He had gained Swiss citizenship only a year earlier, and the stigma of an illegitimate child would have harmed his prospects both in the country's civil service and in the socially conservative environment of its capital. Illegitimate births were not uncommon in Switzerland, making up 11.8 per cent of all live births in Zurich in 1901, the year of Lieserl's conception. Only around half these children were born to Swiss mothers, however, with the rest belonging to foreigners like Mileva. They remained an affront to polite society, and Einstein had been forced along a path requiring compromise with convention. 'Illegitimacy was acceptable in certain populations, and it was very widespread,' says Robert Schulmann. 'But if you were to be a civil servant in Berne it was not a good idea.' The couple's meagre income may have provided another motive for giving the child away, although this did not prevent them establishing a family after their subsequent marriage. Perhaps Einstein's attitude would have been different if Lieserl had been a Hanserl, as he had hoped. Perhaps she was handicapped by her illness. However, all this lies even further within the realm of speculation.

What cannot be doubted is that the birth had transformed Einstein's relationship with Mileva. Her claim on him was now stronger than ever before – Lieserl's arrival threw on him a heavy responsibility for two other lives. At the same time, Lieserl threatened to compromise his own exclusive enjoyment of Mileva's maternal care. In addition, there was unstinting parental pressure on Einstein to distance himself from Mileva and thus her child. It is unclear whether Pauline even knew of Lieserl's birth, but a few weeks after it she wrote, 'This Miss Marić is causing me the bitterest hours of my life. If it were in my power, I would make every possible effort to banish her from our horizon, I really dislike her.' The issue was now dividing the entire family. Einstein's sister, Maja, had provoked a violent argument by speaking up in Mileva's defence, and had parted from her mother on the frostiest of terms. 'She knows that we strongly oppose the liaison of Albert and Miss Marić, that we don't want ever to have anything to do with her, and that there is constant friction with Albert because of it,' Pauline Einstein wrote. Significantly, these words come from a letter to Pauline Winteler – her son's 'Mummy Number Two'. Einstein's mother could not bear the thought of Maja mentioning his engagement in Aarau, where memories of his jilting Marie Winteler were still vivid. Her greatest misery was that she had 'lost any influence' over her son, but in that she was probably mistaken. While he refused to part from Mileva, his decision to dispense with Lieserl may in part have reflected a desire to contain his mother's wrath. Echoing in his mind must have been Pauline's warning, 'If she gets pregnant, you'll really be in a mess.'

Professor Schulmann suspects that Mileva's friend Helene Savić assisted in the adoption, but this again is largely guesswork, based almost entirely on Mileva's reference in November 1901 to her friend's possible help 'with something important'. Einstein and Mileva may or may not have been checking on Lieserl when they visited Savić in Belgrade in the late summer of 1905. However, the letters that survive do not neatly fit this theory, as Professor John Stachel points out. Mileva wrote to Savić shortly after her marriage to Einstein in January 1903, saying how well things were going and making no mention of her daughter. If Savić knew about the child, says Stachel, 'it would have been a strange thing to write.' On the other hand, it is also known that some letters from Mileva were destroyed by Savić's daughter, perhaps to wipe out any reference to Lieserl and her fate.

Einstein did receive a letter in 1909 offering 'compliments to your lady wife and your daughter'. This was written by a Japanese student called Ayao Kuwaki, but, like so much else in the story, is a false lead. It seems to reflect an innocent mix-up about the couple's son Hans Albert, born in 1904, whom contemporary photographs show dressed in a unisex smock. So girlish was his appearance that Hans Albert's own daughter, Evelyn Einstein, thought for some time that these pictures showed Lieserl rather than her father. The remarkable possibility remains that Einstein's secret daughter may be living today, in her nineties, under another identity. Gerald Holton jokes, 'Some day she might walk in and say "My name is Anastasia, I want my parents' letters." '

There is strong circumstantial evidence that Einstein himself believed this could happen. Once again we must move briefly forward in time, to the years of his second marriage. It was then that a woman came forward claiming to be his long-lost daughter and bearing a son alleged to be his grandchild. In 1935 she approached contacts of Einstein in England, including his distinguished scientific admirer Frederick Lindemann, later Viscount Cherwell. The woman claimed that she was unable to approach Einstein directly due to the hostile presence of her 'stepmother', Elsa. Lindemann was suspicious but found the woman sufficiently plausible to send a warning telegram to Princeton, where Einstein was living after his departure from Berlin three years earlier

Among the others she approached was Janos Plesch, a close friend of Einstein in his Berlin years, who had moved to England to escape Nazi persecution in the summer of 1933. He too found her surprisingly persuasive:

> I even began to see family resemblances between Einstein and the child, an intelligent wide-awake and attractive little lad. Well, she convinced me, so with the assistance of friends, who were also convinced, we set to work to help her, found her a position and sent the boy to school. Then I wrote a tactful letter to Einstein explaining the situation and giving him news of his daughter and grandchild. To my great mystification Einstein showed no proper interest, and so in order to move his paternal and grandfatherly heart I sent him one or two really clever and delightful little coloured sketches the boy had made and a photo. There! I thought, the features of the boy will move him. I then received a letter telling me that the whole thing was a swindle. It amused Einstein greatly and made me blush for months.

Plesch told this story ostensibly as a joke against himself and 'to show what famous men have to put up with'. Einstein's friend Max von Laue, who was also drawn in, felt anger that Lindemann had been fooled and bemoaned the gullibility of the English. He too passed off the episode as 'extraordinarily comic', but there is rather more to it than that. For all his own outward show, Einstein took the allegations seriously enough to call in a private investigator.

The events have been pieced together from documentary records by

Professor Don Howard of the University of Kentucky. Lindemann did
not send his telegram directly to Einstein but to his close colleague
Hermann Weyl, who was asked to question the professor personally
and to cable an immediate reply. It appears that Einstein disavowed
all knowledge of the woman, named in Lindemann's message as 'Mrs
Herrschdoerffer'. Soon afterwards, however, she was identified as
Grete Markstein, a Berlin actress. Einstein's secretary, Helen Dukas,
engaged an acquaintance to act as 'Jewish detective' and locate Markstein's true family. It took between eight and nine months before the
work was complete. The investigator's report, on two poorly typed
pages, revealed that Markstein was too old to be Lieserl. She had been
born in Vienna in August 1894. Her father, Samuel, was a Hungarian
bank worker who had died at the end of the First World War, followed in 1925 by her mother. Markstein's reputation was 'somewhat
lacking', remarked the detective, who concluded 'this is the right
person.'

So Markstein was a fraud. Indeed, it appears that she had feared
exposure as soon as Lindemann sent his telegram, telephoning him to
plead for greater discretion. Nevertheless, questions remain. Professor
Howard believes that Einstein's behaviour suggests that he thought
Lieserl was alive – backing the adoption hypothesis – and was uncertain about her fate. 'The other thing that is puzzling me', he says, 'is
what could Markstein have known that would have enabled her to be
so persuasive?' There is documentary evidence that Einstein had made
contact with Markstein while both were still in Berlin, well before the
approaches to his friends. A letter he wrote to a city trade association
on 29 September 1932 shows that he made a payment to her of eighty
Reichmarks. The context of his words suggests that this was in some
semi-official capacity (Markstein was described as a 'female lecturing
artist'), but their full significance is unclear.

Also intriguing is a snatch of doggerel that Einstein sent to Plesch
after the hoax was exposed. It is in slightly slewed German, but this is
a fair translation,

> All my friends are hoaxing me
> – Help me stop the family!
> Reality's enough for me,

> I've borne it long and faithfully.
> And yet it would be nice to find
> That I'd possessed the strength of mind
> To lay eggs on the side – so long
> As others didn't take it wrong.

This was signed 'A. Einstein, Stepfather'.

Whatever shadow the Lieserl affair cast over Einstein's life, there seems little doubt that Mileva fell under a darker one. Their son Hans Albert left behind heavy hints of this, years before the existence of his secret sister was revealed. Drawing on conversations with him in 1962, the Einstein biographer Peter Michelmore wrote of a 'mysterious pre-marital incident' that opened a rift between Albert and Mileva. Only now does its meaning seem plain:

> Friends had noticed a change in Mileva's attitude and thought that the romance might be doomed. Something had happened between the two, but Mileva would only say that it was 'intensely personal'. Whatever it was, she brooded about it and Albert seemed to be in some way responsible. Friends encouraged Mileva to talk about her problem and to get it out in the open. She insisted that it was too personal and kept it a secret all her life – a vital detail in the story of Albert Einstein that still remains shrouded in mystery.

With Hans Albert's authority, Michelmore cited this unexplained incident as the root of later trouble in the marriage. He gave it as the cause of a bleak introspection which engulfed Mileva with ever increasing frequency as the years passed. The implication seems to be that Mileva had opposed the decision to give away their daughter, and blamed Einstein for pushing her to acquiesce in it. Another possibility is that she agreed to the decision more readily, but was then overwhelmed by feelings of guilt.

In either case, this would go some way to explaining the melancholy so persistently ascribed to Mileva. In old age, Einstein described her as distrusting, taciturn and given to depression – attributing this to a schizophrenic background on her mother's side. His diagnosis should be treated with extreme caution, and may reflect his desire to disassociate himself from the mental problems of his younger son. But variations on the theme recur in Einstein biographies. Carl Seelig, drawing on Einstein's own comments, wrote that Mileva's 'dreamy, ponderous nature often curdled her life and her studies.' Her contemporaries, he added, found her 'gloomy, laconic and distrustful'. Einstein's admirer Philipp Frank remarked that Mileva 'did not have the ability to get into intimate and pleasant contact with her environment', adding that there was something 'blunt and stern' about her. By this account there was always a clear contrast between Mileva's 'harsh and self-denying' personality and Einstein's care-free cheerfulness, which Frank believed often left her uneasy.

It is true that the love-letters suggest a moodiness in Mileva long before Lieserl was conceived, but, in these early years at least, the differences between her and Einstein were fewer than Frank supposed. The young Einstein admitted to being 'full of whims' himself, and was constantly swinging between high moods and low. A man who felt cut off from humanity by an invisible wall was hardly in 'intimate and pleasant contact' with his own environment. And as for harshness and self-denial, we need only recall his talk of devoting his life to the 'strict angels' of science. Mileva's reaction to their early misfortunes was often pessimistic, with a suggestion that the world was out to punish her. Equally, there were moments when she showed great optimism in the face of her troubles, taking strength from her hopes for happiness in love. If she did slip deeper into despair as time went by, it is not enough to blame this on a character flaw, unconnected with her relationship to Einstein. The trauma of giving up her daughter would appear to have been crucial.

This does not explain everything, however. Michelmore wrote that Mileva stayed with Einstein because she 'knew that her love for the man was strong enough to survive'. For several years after Lieserl's birth their relationship endured, and even flourished. Only by returning to these events can we see how other tensions began to accumulate, with ultimately disastrous consequences.

In February 1902 Einstein's appointment to the Patent Office was still four months away, but he had already given up his teaching post at Schaffhausen and moved to Berne. He told Mileva that he would happily have suffered another two years working for Dr Nüesch, if only that could have guaranteed her recovery after Lieserl's birth. In fact it gave him great pleasure to abandon his outraged employer midway through the school year, and he bragged to a friend that he had 'sailed away from N[üesch] with spectacular effect'. He installed himself in Berne at comfortable digs, of which he drew a pseudo-scientific diagram for Mileva, carefully noting the precise position of everything from the bed to the chamber-pot. The ancient city appealed to him, particularly the four miles of street arcades that allowed him to stroll from one end of town to the other without getting wet in the rain. In order to earn some money, he placed an advert in the local newspaper, offering private tuition in mathematics and physics ('trial lessons free').

Among the respondents was Maurice Solovine, an ebullient Romanian studying at Berne University, who was eager to be initiated into what he saw as 'the mysteries of physics'. Solovine later recalled the thunderous 'Come in!' that answered his knock at Einstein's door, and the extraordinary brilliance of the eyes that stared at him from the apartment's gloomy interior, which smelt of coffee and pipe-smoke. He found an instant rapport with Einstein, and their first discussion lasted two hours, with another thirty minutes in the street before they parted. 'I admired his extraordinarily penetrating mind and his astonishing mastery of physical problems,' said Solovine. 'He was not a brilliant speaker and he did not make use of vivid images. He explained things in a slow and even voice, but in a remarkably clear way.' Einstein's sessions with him were soon ranging across a broad range of scientific topics, with forays into the philosophy of Plato, Hume and John Stuart Mill. Later the two men were joined by Conrad Habicht, who had known Einstein when they were neighbours at Schaffhausen. A bank director's son who had studied mathematics and physics at Munich and Berlin, he was now completing his studies in Berne.

Einstein's lessons did not bring in much money, and he used to joke that he could earn more by busking with his violin. Far more important to him was the pleasure he found in the company of Solovine and Habicht. The young men formed the intellectual equivalent of the Three Musketeers, and constituted themselves with mock formality as 'the Olympia Academy'. Einstein's charisma and intelligence made him the natural leader. A Latin dedication worked up by his fellow members hailed him as 'expert in the noble arts . . . a man with the greatest peace of mind and family virtue . . . infallible high priest of the church of the poor in spirit'. He presided over their meetings as 'President of the Academy', revelling in an atmosphere of mutual admiration and rather priggish high spirits. The three friends are shown together in a splendid photograph, all sporting moustaches, wing-collars, and bow-ties. On the left was Habicht – dapper, bespectacled and self-possessed, his dark hair neatly parted on the right, a cigar held elegantly in his lap. In the middle perched a smirking Solovine, dressed in a light three-piece suit similar to Habicht's, but looking dishevelled and swarthy. And on the right was Einstein, more darkly clad than the others, with a handkerchief neatly displayed in his breast pocket, gazing thoughtfully into the middle distance. The creation of the Academy gave him another private world, cut off from dreary philistine life, in much the same way that he had built his own dreamworld with Mileva. Almost half a century later, in 1948, Einstein reminisced to Solovine that the Academy was 'far less childish than those respectable ones which I later got to know'.

Einstein always maintained that a general overview of physics could be more valuable than specialist knowledge. He sharpened his ideas on the others' wits, and gained fresh insights from their joint study. Among the scientists they read was Ernst Mach, whose 'incorruptible scepticism and independence' particularly inspired Einstein. The three friends debated together like undergraduates, irritating Einstein's neighbours with loud and boisterous arguments that lasted late into the night. According to Solovine, they enjoyed eclectic meals of sausage, Gruyère cheese, fruit, honey and cups of tea. They also sustained themselves with draughts of Turkish coffee and hard-boiled eggs. Einstein's enthusiasm for food was immortalized in a cartoon by Solovine, showing his curly-haired bust under a decorative arch of sausages. Once Habicht and Solovine celebrated his birthday by buying him caviar, expecting a rapturous reaction. 'When Einstein ate something out of the ordinary he would become ecstatic and would praise it in extravagant terms,' Solovine recalled. Unfortunately the President of the Academy became so absorbed in explaining Galileo's principle of inertia that he gobbled down all his expensive treat without a thought. 'So that was caviar,' he said, when his astonished friends finally spoke up. 'Well, if you offer gourmet foods to peasants like me, you know they won't appreciate it.'

Many of the Academy's discussions took place on long walks. Einstein and Solovine would often leave at six in the morning to trek the eighteen miles from Berne to Thun, a lakeside town considered among the most picturesque in Switzerland. There they would while away the afternoon together before returning by train in the evening. Music recitals provided another common pleasure, since Berne was a stopover for many distinguished musicians on European tours. On one occasion Solovine skipped a discussion session, due to take place at his own lodgings, to hear a celebrated Czech quartet. He left a note of apology with his landlady – claiming 'urgent business' – and a peace offering of four hard-boiled eggs. After polishing these off, Einstein and Habicht took revenge on his betrayal by smoking furiously and piling all Solovine's furniture and crockery on his bed. Solovine hated tobacco and was 'almost overwhelmed' by the suffocating fug that greeted his return. 'I opened the window wide,' he remembered, 'and began to remove from the bed the mound of things that reached almost to the ceiling.'

Habicht and Solovine were not the only companions that Einstein found in Berne. Lucien Chavan, an electrical technician from Lausanne, was another applicant for private lessons who became a long-time friend. Einstein was also reunited with Hans Frösch, a medical student at the University of Berne who had been one of his closest classmates at the Aargau cantonal school. These hearty male friendships posed an obvious threat to his exclusive intimacy with Mileva, who voiced concern that he was forgetting her while she remained with her family after Lieserl's birth. Einstein rushed to reassure her, although there was a hint of equivocation in his words. 'Don't be jealous of Habicht and Frösch – what are they compared with you! I long for you each day – but I don't show it because it's not manly . . . But nevertheless, it's true that it's very nice here. But I'd certainly rather be with you in a provincial backwater than without you in Berne . . .'

But . . . but . . . but. Einstein's pleasure in his new surroundings made it hard to maintain the idea that he and Mileva stood alone against a hostile world. Nevertheless, he did his best. In the summer he reported that he and a crowd of friends were off on a hike to the Beatenberg, a peak near Thun. His merry spirits were obvious, but he assured Mileva that he would be even happier when his companions left after the weekend. 'I'd rather be going with you up to the Beatenberg than with a group of men – I'm a man myself, after all,' he wrote. 'When I'm not with you, I think about you with such tenderness as you can hardly imagine; this in spite of the fact that I'm a bad boy when I'm with you.'

Einstein's appointment at the Patent Office finally came through on 16 June 1902, when he was elected technical expert, third class, for a trial period only. He had been warned by an existing employee that the work was very dull, and that his position could hardly be more menial, but now Mileva could come to join him at last, and it was a matter of pride that neither cared about others' opinions. His eight-hour working day was spent perched on a stool, poring over technical data to discover what was unique in each invention submitted for patent protection. Sometimes he portrayed this as his 'cobbler's job' – an undemanding routine that left his mind free to focus on science. Soon after starting, however, he assured one friend that the work was 'uncommonly varied and makes you think a lot'. It required an ability to see to the heart of a problem, in what were often vague and muddled applications. The objects under analysis were mundane – from engineering gadgets to typewriters – but Einstein always found charm in everyday technology. In later years he took out several patents – some joint and some individual – on devices he had helped to design himself, including a noiseless household refrigerator and a new type of hearing-aid. It is an interest that can be traced back to his childhood, his uncle's expertise in electrotechnology and his father's business. Haller, the Patent Office director, was 'more severe than my father' but inspired in Einstein a similar affection.

In the autumn of 1902, Hermann Einstein fell fatally ill. His health had buckled under the burden of his repeated business failures, and he was suffering from heart disease. His son returned to be with him in Milan, but there was no hope. Hermann died alone on 10 October, after asking his family to leave the room when he felt his strength ebbing away. The moment haunted Einstein with guilt for the rest of his life. According to Helen Dukas and Banesh Hoffmann, who both knew him well, he was left with a 'shattering sense of loss'. In a jointly written biography, they described him as 'dazed and uncomprehending . . . overwhelmed by a feeling of desolation, asking himself repeatedly why his father should have died rather than he'. They also quoted Einstein's own comment that his father's death was the deepest shock he had ever experienced.

No small part of the blow was the responsibility Einstein now felt for his mother, who had inherited Hermann's debts with no income to pay them. Einstein drew on his own meagre finances to support her, and the remaining years of her life were ones of unwelcome dependency. Pauline took refuge with her dead husband's chief creditors, her sister Fanny and brother-in-law Rudolf, in the town of Hechingen, in Germany. She stayed with the couple – the parents of Einstein's second wife – for the best part of a decade, moving with them to Berlin in 1910. The following year she left to become housekeeper for a widowed merchant at Heilbronn, in the Neckar valley, before moving back to Berlin in around 1914 to manage the domestic affairs of her widowed brother Jakob. Her own misfortunes did nothing to soften her feelings towards Mileva and may have made her more eager than ever to find vicarious fulfilment in her son's career.

On his deathbed, Hermann Einstein finally gave his permission for his son's marriage to Mileva. The banns were published that December in Berne, Zurich and Novi Sad, and the ceremony took place in Berne County Hall on 6 January 1903. It was a quiet, rather perfunctory affair. The two witnesses were Solovine and Habicht, and it appears that the only celebration was a meal that evening in a local restaurant. There was no honeymoon, and by one account the couple returned to their new marital home to find that Einstein had locked himself out. This was a fitting echo of their student days in Zurich, where his landlady was woken at all hours by the shout, 'It's Einstein, I've forgotten my key again.' The wedding invitation gave the couple's address as Tillierstrasse 18, on the right bank of the Aare, where Einstein registered with the civic authorities four days after the ceremony. By October they had moved to the second-floor flat at Kramgasse 49 that is now preserved as a small Einstein museum. The building stands in the medieval heart of Berne between two of the city's eleven extravagantly carved fountains, and a few hundred yards from its famous clock tower. Here relativity was born.

Both partners gave good reports of married life, although there were telling differences in emphasis. Towards the end of January 1903 Einstein wrote to Michele Besso, 'Now I'm an honourably married man, and lead a very nice, comfortable life with my wife. She takes care of everything, cooks well and is always happy.' This reads like a testimonial to a housekeeper rather than a soul mate, and the stress on Mileva's cheerfulness suggests a certain relief that the cloud caused by the Lieserl affair had temporarily passed. Nevertheless, Einstein was still immensely fond of his bride and, as will become clear, it seems she still shared closely in his intellectual life.

For her part Mileva told Helene Savić, 'I am, if possible, even more attached to my dear treasure than I already was in the Zurich days. He is my only companion and society and I am happiest when he is beside me.' Her utter dependence on Einstein was unmistakable, and it is hard not to see something sad in her instinctive recourse to their student days for a paradigm of happiness. This same letter suggests that the fate of Lieserl was still uppermost in Mileva's mind, since she asked about the chance of finding teaching jobs for her and Einstein in Belgrade. As Jürgen Renn and Robert Schulmann have remarked, this might have allowed the couple to raise the child themselves. The inquiry came to naught, however, and when Mileva returned to check on Lieserl's progress that autumn she discovered she was pregnant once again.

A postcard sent from Budapest, where she presumably halted in transit, mentioned what may well have been morning sickness. A few weeks later Einstein wrote to say that he was 'not the least bit angry' that his poor Dollie was 'hatching a new chick'. He added, 'In fact, I'm happy about it and had already given some thought to whether I shouldn't see to it that you get a new Lieserl.' This was also the letter in which Einstein reacted to news of Lieserl's scarlet fever. His comment that he had 'already given some thought' to providing Mileva with a replacement child suggests that adoption was agreed before the disease took hold, and was not a reaction to its effects. Whether Einstein had truly been contemplating a second child is very debatable – the second pregnancy was clearly unplanned, and equally clearly he had kept any thoughts on the subject to himself. His letter ended with an appeal for Mileva to come home soon. 'Three and a half weeks have already passed and a good little wife shouldn't leave her husband alone any longer. Things don't yet look nearly so bad at home as you think. You'll be able to clean up in short order.'

Hans Albert, their first son, was born on 14 May 1904. It was only then, according to Mileva's biographer Dord Krstić, that her parents fully accepted the marriage. Krstić repeats a probably apocryphal story that Miloš Marić travelled to Berne to present his son-in-law with a bank book worth 100,000 Austro-Hungarian crowns. Einstein is said to have rejected this handsome sum – the equivalent of about 25,000 dollars at the time, says Krstić – with a moving speech explaining that he had married Mileva for love, not money. Sadly there is no evidence beyond hearsay for either the offer or the heroic refusal.

Solovine recalled that Mileva often attended sessions of the Olympia Academy and listened attentively to its discussions, but without intervening. Perhaps Mileva preferred to discuss the issues with Einstein afterwards, when they were alone together. There is, however, good evidence that she felt at ease in the Academy's company. Solovine and Habicht were among the few people 'who conquered Mileva's wayward heart,' according to the biographer Carl Seelig. Einstein used to tease her by launching into risqué stories in front of their guests. 'Have I told you the joke about the old whore ...' he would start off, knowing that Mileva would instantly leap in with a reproving 'Albert!' On one occasion, Habicht was approached by a tradesman who sold tin plates engraved with the buyer's name and title. Habicht had him write 'Albert Ritter von Steissbein, President of the Olympia Academy', and fixed the result at the door of Einstein's apartment. 'Ritter von Steissbein' might loosely be translated as 'Knight of the Backside'. The addition of '-bein' to 'Steiss' turns it from the German for buttocks into 'coccyx', but also carries an indecorous suggestion of *Scheissbein*, or shit-leg. According to Solovine, Einstein and Mileva 'laughed so much they thought they would die', and the name recurs elsewhere. Einstein sent an almost illegible postcard to Habicht that read, 'Totally drunk – unfortunately both under the table. Your servant Steissbein and Wife.'

After performing well at a civil-service examination, Einstein was elevated from probationary to permanent status at the Patent Office in September 1904. Around this time, and at Einstein's urging, Michele Besso took a job there too. He was to be present during the dramatic flowering of Einstein's genius in the following months. Einstein found work in the Patent Office dull compared with his own scientific studies, but his walks home with Besso gave him the opportunity to discuss his own ideas in physics and philosophy. His friend, like Mileva in her student days, was enlisted into Einstein's personal research. The Besso and Einstein families became almost inseparable, with Mileva forming a close friendship with Anna Besso.

The year of 1905 was to be Einstein's *annus mirabilis*, in which he produced three separate articles that shook the foundations of science. The papers were sent off at intervals of less than two months, and it is often remarked that they seem to cover dazzlingly disparate subjects. But several scholars have pointed out that common threads exist. Professor Jürgen Renn stresses that each is based on a 'particulate' view of the world, understanding phenomena in terms of minute bodies: atoms, molecules, electrons and chunks of energy. Each of the papers also marks the final consequence of a long chain of work by masters of classical physics – Boltzmann, Planck and Lorentz. From his letters, it is clear that Einstein avidly devoured their ideas. However, he had sufficient distance from their way of thinking to interpret their research from a new perspective – and to appreciate its revolutionary implications. Their work was like delicious fruit that was ripe for picking.

Einstein's papers share a cavalier artistry that was quite alien to conventional scientific discourse, with its plodding progression from experimental results to explanatory theory. Einstein preferred to begin by voicing his dissatisfaction with conventional wisdom, pointing to ideas that were inelegant or out of harmony. As Gerald Holton has put it, his objections were ones that others might dismiss as being of a predominantly aesthetic nature. 'He then proposes a principle of great generality. He shows that it helps remove, as one of the deduced consequences, his initial dissatisfaction. And at the end of each paper, he proposes a small number of predictions that should be experimentally verifiable, although the test may be difficult.' It was an approach quite different from that of any other scientist of his day, and the rewards it earned him were breathtaking.

When describing each paper to Habicht, Einstein chose to call the first 'very revolutionary'. It was sent to *Annalen der Physik* on 17 March, three days after his twenty-sixth birthday, and was published in June. Among other things, it offered an explanation of the photo-electric effect, which Einstein had written about so rapturously to Mileva after she discovered her first pregnancy. Experiments had shown that electrons were ejected from certain metal surfaces when the surfaces were struck by light. Surprisingly, however, the speed with which the electrons emerged varied with the colour of the light rather than its intensity. The brightest red light, for example, forced out electrons with less speed than a dim blue light. This odd behaviour could not be explained until Einstein suggested that the energy associated with the light beam came in microscopic particles, which he called light quanta. As the brightness of the light increased, more quanta rained down on the metal and more electrons were blasted out. But the speed with which they emerged increased only when the quanta grew bigger, as the light moved to a higher fre-quency and changed in colour to the blue end of the spectrum. Below a certain size of quantum, said Einstein, the electrons were not deliv-ered enough energy to escape from the metal at all.

This was indeed revolutionary. Quanta were implied in the research of the leading German physicist Max Planck to explain the way that hot bodies emit radiation, like a poker glowing with red light. But it was Einstein who had the vision to see the far-reaching consequences of Planck's work. His explanation met with scepticism, because it was still generally believed that light consisted of waves. Einstein was returning in part to Newton's idea of light as a stream of particles, long since dropped because waves were better at explaining such effects as interference and diffraction. Yet even as Einstein talked of light quanta – or photons, as they were later called – he also referred to light as having a frequency, an essential part of wave theory. He was confronting science with what has become a famous paradox: that light has the properties of both waves and particles. This was the work for which Einstein was awarded his belated Nobel prize in 1922, but the apparent conflict at its heart always made him uneasy. Near the end of his life he wrote to Michele Besso that he still had no clear idea what light quanta were. 'Nowadays every Tom, Dick and Harry thinks he knows it,' said Einstein, 'but he is mistaken.'

The next great paper was received by *Annalen der Physik* on 11 May and published in July. Its subject was Brownian motion, named after the Scottish naturalist Robert Brown. As early as 1827 Brown had used a microscope to observe the random zigzag motion exhibited in water by tiny particles such as fragments of pollen grains. What puzzled Brown was that this motion did not arise from currents in the fluid, or from evaporation, or from any other discernible cause. More than seventy-five years later, Einstein gave his answer: the tiny particles were buffeted about by the invisible molecules that made up the water around them. As C. P. Snow put it, 'This was like a conjuring trick, easy when explained.'

Until then a minority of physicists still doubted the physical reality of atoms and molecules, and some, such as Ernst Mach, remained stubbornly unconvinced even after Einstein's flash of insight. Even to a pioneer of atomism such as Ludwig Boltzmann, the concept was primarily a mathematical tool. However, Boltzmann's efforts prepared the ground for Einstein's work, which gave atoms a physical meaning and provided the nearest that could be expected to a direct proof of molecular reality. What is astonishing is that Einstein had arrived at his explanation before he even knew that Brownian motion existed. He recalled in his autobiographical notes, 'I discovered that, according to atomistic theory, there would have to be a movement of suspended microscopic particles open to observation, without knowing that observations concerning Brownian motion were already long familiar.' It was his friend Besso who pointed out how well-known the phenomenon was, and told him its name.

The greatest paper of all, on relativity, was received on 30 June and published on 26 September. It contained no references, implying that Einstein had reached his conclusions in isolation, by pure thought. We know that he was widely read, however, so the lack of attribution does more to confirm the picture of an amateur scientist cut off from the research establishment. Einstein either was unaware of the need to give credit where it was due or believed that the previous work was so well-known – and that he had moved so far beyond it – that footling attributions were unnecessary.

As we have mentioned, the relativity paper dealt with Einstein's concern about an anomaly between explanations of motors and dynamos. Jürgen Renn argues that, to develop a theory that gave a consistent account of the phenomena underlying both devices, Einstein adopted an atomistic view of electricity. If electricity was seen as consisting of a stream of electrons, then these ostensibly different electromagnetic effects could be explained in terms of relative motion. This was implicit mathematically in the work of the great physicist Hendrik Lorentz, although Einstein rejected the idea of the ether, which was a key aspect of Lorentz's work. 'Einstein once again picked up a theory that was already lying around and gave it new physical meaning,' said Renn. 'He turned existing ideas upside down.'

Thousands of popular explanations of Einstein's work have been put forward, with endless repetition of examples based on flashing lights, stopwatches and speeding trains. We do not intend to cover this ground again. In essence, the underlying problem was to reconcile Newton's laws of motion with the theory of electromagnetism produced by the Scotsman James Clerk Maxwell in the 1870s. Just as this lay at the root of the motor/dynamo anomaly, so it also underlay the puzzle that Einstein began to address at the age of sixteen, when he wondered what it would be like to move with the speed of light. Travel at such speeds is allowed by Newton's laws but wreaks unfortunate consequences on Maxwell's picture of light. If we regard a light wave as a series of electromagnetic oscillations – a regular pattern of peaks and troughs – then we can see that an observer moving alongside with the same speed would be tied to a particular trough or peak and would no longer experience the oscillation. In other words, the light beam would no longer exist for the observer supposedly travelling with it.

There was a deeper problem. According to Newton's laws, there is no such thing as a state of absolute rest or absolute motion. If you measure the speed of a car, for instance, it could be relative to the ground, relative to the moon, or relative to some distant galaxy. But at first sight this principle is inconsistent with Maxwell's prescription of an absolute value for the speed of light (186,000 miles per second).

What Einstein did was to accept both apparently contradictory principles, take them as fundamental postulates, and remove the contradiction by taking apart the idea of speed: the distance something travels in a given time. In order to keep the speed of light constant – irrespective of the speed of the observer relative to the source of the light – Einstein had to distort time and distance, producing effects which do great violence to common sense.

For example, Einstein's approach meant accepting that a ruler would seem to contract if it moved relative to an observer. At about 90 per cent of the speed of light it would appear to shrink to half its length when stationary, contracting more rapidly the closer it approached the sacred speed. If it could match the speed of light it would shrink to nothing, although this would be impossible, because relativity also shows that its mass would then be infinitely large, providing an infinite obstacle to motion. A person holding the ruler would not notice these amazing changes: its proper length never changes, only its appearance to an observer moving relative to it. Even the observer would not notice any change at the vastly slower speeds encountered in normal life.

The distortion of time is even more startling, since it seems to threaten our grip on reality. Einstein predicted that a moving clock would appear to tick more slowly than one at rest. This eventually prompted a Viennese newspaper to announce, 'The Minute in Danger, A Sensation of Mathematical Science.' We think that by looking at a clock we are putting an objective label on time, fixing a single 'now' that is occurring simultaneously throughout the cosmos, but Einstein showed that simultaneity is also relative to your point of view.

Almost as an afterthought, Einstein submitted another short article to *Annalen der Physik* in September 1905 on the relationship between mass and energy. He showed that when a body releases energy in the form of radiation its mass decreases by a proportionate amount. This is a remarkable deduction, since it means that all energy has mass. But its true importance did not become clear until two years later, when Einstein announced that the reverse is also true: that all mass has energy. The formula with which he captured this relationship, $E = mc^2$ (in which E stands for energy, m for mass and c for the speed of light), has become one of the most famous ever written. If c is expressed in metres per second, c^2 is a huge number: a nine followed by sixteen zeros. In other words, a vast amount of energy can be extracted from only a tiny amount of mass – such as the loss in mass that occurs when the nuclei of heavy atoms like plutonium and uranium fall apart. Einstein called this the most important consequence of his relativity theory, and the atom bomb was to provide the most dramatic vindication of its truth.

What credit, if any, can Mileva take for the theory of relativity? Great claims have been made on her behalf, and from several directions. 'Her intellect lives in those lines,' according to her Serbian biographer Desanka Trbuhović-Gjurić. 'Her part was not small,' says Dord Krstić, a Serbian physicist who has researched Mileva's life for more than thirty years. 'There is reason to believe that hers may have been the primary contribution,' says Dr Evan Harris Walker, one of Mileva's chief advocates, from the Walker Cancer Research Institute at Edgewood, Maryland. If these claims are true, then Einstein's failure to acknowledge Mileva's help was an act of intellectual fraud. They are truly astonishing allegations – and caused a sensation when first brought to public attention in 1990, at the annual meeting of the American Association for the Advancement of Science, in New Orleans.

Mileva's case was put forward by Dr Walker, supported by the linguist Senta Troemel-Ploetz. Against them stood Professor John Stachel, with whom Dr Walker had already clashed in the American journal *Physics Today*. Their confrontation in New Orleans was heated, with Walker recalling a hostile atmosphere of 'shouting and screaming'. Professor Stachel, as the editor of the first volume of Einstein's papers, stood by his published judgement that no hard evidence of collaboration existed. He accused Dr Walker of appearing to be 'a fantasist, who judges reality on the basis of his own desires'. Walker later recalled that some of the opposition thought that he 'was trying to tear down Einstein because he was Jewish.' He added, 'I had no interest or motive of that sort.' Walker stuck to his charge that Stachel was distorting historical facts. He repeated his belief that the 'basic capricious ideas that were the turning points of relativity' came from Mileva, while Einstein provided only 'the overall formalism of the theory'. His ally Troemel-Ploetz stated, 'It was quite normal for men to appropriate women's work and take credit for them. Einstein was a very normal man.'

This was strong meat, and the debate claimed headlines across the world – in London *The Times* reported 'Mrs Einstein's claim to fame, relatively speaking' on its front page. However, only limited attention was paid to the evidence deployed by each side.

Professor Stachel, for one, does not deny that men have often passed off women's efforts as their own. He cites the example of the German astronomer Maria Winkelmann, whose husband initially claimed the credit when she discovered a comet in 1702. The French writer Colette was forced by her husband to publish some of her early novels under his name, and several pieces performed as his own by Felix Mendelssohn were the work of his sister Fanny. All that Stachel doubts is that sufficient evidence presently exists to say that Mileva suffered in the same way. There would certainly have been nothing outlandish in Mileva and Einstein presenting a paper as co-authors. A ready precedent existed in the work of Marie and Pierre Curie, whose collaboration after their marriage in 1895 led to the discovery of two new elements, radium and polonium. The very term 'radioactivity' was introduced in one of their joint papers in 1898, and in 1903 they were jointly awarded the Nobel prize for physics with Henri Becquerel. The London astronomer William Huggins and his wife Margaret (who both shared Einstein's passion for the violin) published an extensive series of papers together between 1889 and 1905. William was always listed as the senior author and initially wrote in the first person singular, but he soon moved to the plural in recognition of his wife's contribution. Another example of marital cooperation is provided by the Viennese physicist Paul Ehrenfest and his wife Tatyana, who, like Marie Curie, became friends of Einstein and Mileva. The Ehrenfests' joint publications included an influential study of statistical mechanics, completed five years after the relativity paper, which included passing references to Einstein's own early work on the subject.

The case for Mileva's authorship was first put forward in her biography by Trbuhović-Gjurić, *Im Schatten Albert Einsteins*. This first appeared in Serbian in 1969 but gained a wider readership only when the German edition was published in 1983, after the author's death. The book contains many fascinating hints, but relies heavily on hearsay. Around 1905, for example, Einstein is alleged to have told Mileva's father, 'Everything that I have created and attained I owe to Mileva. She is my genial inspiration, my guardian angel against mistakes in life and even more in science. Without her I would never have begun my work nor finished it.' These lines certainly have the same tone as much that the young Einstein wrote in his love-letters (of which Trbuhović-Gjurić had no knowledge). But we have already seen that these letters are suggestive less of the intellectual relationship between Einstein and Mileva than of their emotional relationship. And unlike the letters – straight from Einstein's pen – these other comments come to us fourth-hand from Mileva's student friend Milana Bota.

In an interview with a Belgrade journalist in 1929, Bota claimed to have been told by Mileva of her role in relativity five or six years earlier. She said that Mileva found the subject painful, as if it hurt to recall 'her most beautiful hours', or as if she was reluctant to slight Einstein's reputation. Trbuhović-Gjurić repeated many such comments from Mileva's relatives and acquaintances, and they do suggest that a belief in her scientific role was quite widespread in these circles. But did this belief have any basis in fact? Milana Bota was not a disinterested party: her account reflects her great affection for Mileva, and perhaps also her lingering resentment against Einstein ('the German, whom I hate'). We must also be wary of a more general tendency for home-town folklore to exaggerate the claims of local heroes and heroines. This was evidently at work in Trbuhović-Gjurić herself, who wrote of her pride in Mileva as 'our great Serbian woman'.

One reason why these claims have gained currency is Einstein's own failure to provide a clear and consistent explanation of relativity's origins. Not only did his paper contain no references, but he contradicted himself in later accounts of the influences on his work. It remains unclear, for example, how much he was stimulated by the so-called Michelson–Morley experiment of 1887. This tested the speed of light to see if it was changed by the relative movement of the ether (the medium which supposedly carried light waves); it found that light had exactly the same speed in all conditions. A speech that Einstein gave in Japan in 1922 suggested that this 'unaccountable result' was his 'first route' to relativity, but a letter that he wrote a year before his death maintained that it played 'no decisive role'.

Mileva's supporters have sought to complete the picture. Evan Harris Walker has suggested that the result was brought to Einstein's attention by Mileva, and that 'she therefore was as capable of discovering the principles of relativity as her husband'. However, there is no evidence to support either Walker's premiss or his deduction – but there is a concrete suggestion that the converse may be true. In a detailed rebuttal of Walker's claims, Stachel has pointed out that Einstein wrote to Mileva in 1899 that he had read a scientific paper in which the experiment was discussed with twelve other ether experiments. He described the whole paper as 'very interesting' but gave no sign that Michelson–Morley had special significance for him (ten of the experiments listed by the paper also had negative results). Stachel derides the idea that the experiment was a magic key to relativity: if this was so, he says, every scientist who read of it should have beaten Einstein to his discovery.

Dr Walker's argument suggests that Einstein, in later life, deliberately played down the importance of Michelson–Morley in order to hide his debt to Mileva. But Einstein's inconsistency is more likely to be evidence of his unreliable memory and his own uncertainty about how his ideas crystallized. He also had a habit of tailoring his words to each new audience, and of readjusting anecdotes for dramatic effect. Such arguments would fall away, of course, if it could be shown that Mileva signed the relativity paper as co-author. This was alleged by Desanka Trbuhović-Gjurić. She claimed that the Russian physicist Abram F. Joffe recalled that all three of the epoch-making articles of 1905 were signed 'Einstein-Marić'. Joffe, she alleged, saw the originals while working as an assistant to Wilhelm Röntgen, the discoverer of X-rays, who reviewed papers for *Annalen der Physik* before publication. This claim has been taken up by Evan Harris Walker, who has located an article in a 1955 Soviet physics journal where Joffe states that the author of the 1905 papers was 'Einstein-Marity'. Dr Walker has placed great stress on the use of 'Marity', the Hungarianized spelling of Mileva's Serbian surname, claiming that all biographical sources call her 'Marić'. He argues, 'Only if Joffe had actually seen the manuscript, as reported, with her name written by her on it, would he have remembered the name in the form "Marity". This is a singular piece of evidence that, indeed, Mileva Marić co-authored the theory of relativity.'

Since Joffe died in 1960, it is impossible to question him about his sources and text. However, there is at least one well-known Einstein biography, published the year before Joffe's article, that refers to 'Marity'. Moreover, the comments located by Dr Walker do not support the gloss that he gives them. What Joffe wrote was that the author of the papers was 'a hitherto-unknown functionary of the Patent Office in Berne, Einstein-Marity', adding in brackets, 'Marity – the family name of his wife, which according to Swiss custom is added to the husband's family name'. It is clear that Joffe took 'Einstein-Marity' to refer to Einstein alone: after all, Mileva was not 'a hitherto-unknown functionary' at the Patent Office. Walker believes that Joffe's explanation of the joint name is mistaken, but this itself would be important only if there were firm evidence that Joffe saw it on the manuscript. No claim to that effect has been found in either this article or any other by Joffe. Indeed, it is very unlikely that his master, Röntgen, was in a position to show it to him. Röntgen was an experimentalist, not a theorist, and would have been an odd choice to review the relativity paper before publication. This is likely to have been done by Max Planck or the editor of *Annalen*, Paul Drude. And, as John Stachel asks, 'If Röntgen read the paper even before it was published in 1905, why did he wait until 1906 to ask Einstein for a reprint of it?'

Conversely, the claims for Mileva cannot entirely be disproved, because the crucial evidence does not survive. In 1943 Einstein was asked to put the manuscript of the original relativity paper up for auction, in aid of the American war effort. He was unable to do so, revealing that he had discarded it after publication. Conspiracy theorists can make of this what they choose, but it is likely that he simply used the manuscript as scrap paper on which to scrawl more calculations. He wrote it out again for the auction, under his secretary's dictation, pausing only to ask if this was really what he had written. 'I could have said that more simply,' he told her.

By pressing Mileva's case too far, her supporters help obscure the grounds for believing that she did play a role in the birth of relativity – not as the senior partner, or even as an important creative force, but as a loyal helper and supporter to whom Einstein was genuinely in debt. Einstein once said that he would be happy living and working in a lighthouse, so little did he depend on other people. In fact, he relied on co-workers throughout his research career. Many of these have recounted his need to talk through his ideas, even if only by delivering a monologue to their willing ears. It seems entirely plausible that Mileva helped to provide such an audience as Einstein grappled with relativity, not least because much of his work was necessarily done at home. There are entertaining accounts of him snatching spare moments at the Patent Office for his own work, thrusting the papers into his desk if he heard approaching footsteps. His sister recounted that his superior turned a blind eye to Einstein's extracurricular studies; nevertheless, they were mainly conducted out of hours.

The broadening of Einstein's circle since their marriage had begun to reduce his dependence on Mileva, but it was only later that this became a serious problem between them. In April 1904, he can still be found signing a letter to Grossman 'from Albert and his student'. He was gossiping happily about physics in letters to Mileva as late as 1908. Professor Gerald Holton, a world authority on the genesis of relativity, says, 'From the beginning, they always read books together. Einstein is a man who needs books and he needs someone to talk with . . . There is no doubt that they talked a lot about his ongoing work.' Dr Peter Bergmann, who worked with Einstein from 1936 to 1941, makes a similar point. 'When people collaborate in theoretical physics, it is impossible to assign quantities of collaboration to each person – to say one contributed 40 per cent and the other 60 per cent. But it seems very clear from the letters – which are of course fragmentary – that Einstein felt he was greatly aided by the way he discussed this subject with his fiancée and later wife.'

There is also reason to think that Mileva was still performing the function of scientific amanuensis that she had taken on as a student, hunting down research material for Einstein and checking facts. Mileva's biographer Dord Krstić envisages husband and wife working together late into the night, by the light of a paraffin lamp. He believes that Mileva studied with Einstein 'quietly, modestly, and never in public view'. It has been widely reported that Einstein told friends, 'My wife does my mathematics.' Very probably the words are apocryphal – perhaps they were a joke. But this is also the story passed down to Paul Einstein, Mileva's great-grandson who lives in Hawaii. The most striking and well-balanced testimony comes from Hans Albert, through the mediation of his interviewer Peter Michelmore. According to Michelmore's account of the final breakthrough on relativity:

> Mileva helped him [Einstein] solve certain mathematical problems, but nobody could assist with the creative work, the flow of fresh ideas . . . The transfer of the broad concept of the theory to its logical mathematical progression on paper took five weeks of sapping work. When it was over, Einstein's body buckled and he went to bed for two weeks. Mileva checked the article again and again, then mailed it. 'It's a very beautiful piece of work,' she told her husband.

Even though this account is at best third-hand, it almost certainly reflects what Mileva told her son. It appears that she made much less of her own role than her latter-day champions: it was Einstein alone who provided the ideas, and Einstein alone who composed the paper and drove himself to exhaustion in the process. Nevertheless, she helped to solve 'certain' problems, checked for slip-ups, and proofread.

The important thing is not to push these hints too far. This can only be done by exaggerating three things: Einstein's own mathematical failings, Mileva's mathematical prowess, and the importance of mathematics to the relativity paper. It is true that Einstein's teacher Hermann Minkowski thought him a 'lazy dog' who was not interested in mathematics at all. Einstein admitted neglecting the subject 'to a certain extent' as a student, and felt that he lacked an intuitive sense of what was most important in it. But his Polytechnic marks in mathematical subjects were better than Mileva's: in the theory of functions, for example, he scored 11 out of 12 in his final exam against her mere 5. Most important of all, Jürgen Renn points out that the algebra in Einstein's 1905 paper on relativity is not especially sophisticated. 'If he had needed help with that kind of mathematics, he

would have ended there,' says Renn. He adds that it was not even the mathematics that was new – having been developed to a great extent by Lorentz – but Einstein's interpretation of it. Any suggestion that Einstein was secretly incapable of understanding his own work would be bizarre. Did any of his peers harbour a doubt that Einstein lacked the necessary intellectual calibre to develop relativity? Certainly not, says the physicist Abraham Pais, who knew Einstein during the last nine years of his life and has meticulously studied the development of his ideas. 'What more do you want? Mermaids?'

The evidence suggests that if anyone else played a creative role in Einstein's development of relativity, it was Besso, not Mileva. Besso's role was emphasized by Einstein during the speech he delivered in Japan in 1922. He recalled approaching 'a friend of mine in Berne' to discuss his misgivings about the invariance of the speed of light. He had wasted almost a year in 'fruitless considerations' on the problem, but talking to Besso brought a breakthrough. 'Trying a lot of discussions with him, I could suddenly comprehend the matter,' he said. 'Next day I visited him again and said to him without greeting: "Thank you. I've completely solved the problem." ' Five weeks after this flash of insight, he said, the theory of special relativity was complete. There is no suggestion that Besso provided the crucial idea that time was not absolute, but somehow their debate had been the catalyst that Einstein needed.

His own formulation was that his friend acted as a 'sounding-board' – the best in Europe. It is a metaphor that now recurs in almost every account of their relationship, but it is a misleading one that Besso himself rejected. Literally speaking, a sounding-board is a screen placed behind a speaker or musician to reflect the sound with greater power towards the audience. Its function is not to bring the sound into sharper focus for the performer himself, in the way that Besso helped to concentrate Einstein's ideas. In any case, Besso was no mere echo – there is firm evidence that he made an active contribution to Einstein's intellectual development. Besides discussing Brownian motion with his friend, it was Besso who around 1897 first recommended that he study the works of Ernst Mach. Besso also drew on his own studies at the Polytechnic to give Einstein valuable insights into applied thermodynamics. It is clearly because he did not

passively echo Einstein's ideas that he was able to help with relativity. The 'pettiness' that Einstein complained of in him – his readiness to challenge detail, to demand complete clarity in explanation – helped his friend to see that only a radical solution would work. Einstein gave the answers, but Besso seems to have asked him the right questions.

Einstein gave a revealing picture of Besso's talents in a letter he wrote in 1926 to the director of the Patent Office in an attempt to prevent his friend's dismissal. In his appeal, which would prove to be successful, Einstein said that Besso's strength lay in his 'out of the ordinary intelligence' and that his weakness was 'his truly insufficient spirit of decision'. Einstein continued:

> Everyone at the Patent Office knows that one can get advice from Besso on the difficult cases; he understands with extreme rapidity both the technical and the legal aspects of each patent application, and he willingly helps his colleagues to arrive at a quick disposal of the case in question, because it is he, in a manner of speaking, who provides the illumination and the other person will-power or the necessary spirit of decision.

Just as Besso disliked the 'sounding-board' metaphor, so Mileva's defenders have rejected it on her behalf. In fact, however, it may be applied to her with rather greater accuracy than to Besso. What a sounding-board provides is an echo that merges so completely with the original sound that it is not heard in its own right. To achieve this effect, the sounding-board must stand close to the source of the sound it reflects. Even during the years of their courtship, we have no evidence of Mileva challenging Einstein's ideas as Besso did. She was without doubt a key confidante, but she seems to have been largely uncritical in her responses. Many of her letters are lost, but those that survive are telling – particularly her reply to Einstein's first known discussion of relativistic themes in the summer of 1899. Mileva's answer combined loving banter with observations on the weather and a request for advice on her impending examinations. Indeed, as Professor Stachel has remarked, she commented on almost everything Einstein had written except the science. The evidence suggests that Mileva's contribution to relativity was not primarily intellectual: it

was emotional. Even her help with mathematics may best be seen in this light: its most likely value for Einstein was as reassurance, a comforting fail-safe.

As a young man without credentials, Einstein attacked the wisdom of the greatest names in science. Despite his faith in the power of his own mind, he was not ready to challenge the establishment alone. He needed an ally, not to fight at his side but to cheer him on to victory. He required 'a lot of emotional resources', to quote Jürgen Renn, and it was Mileva who helped to provide them. The mental landscape of most young students is dominated by received wisdom and established ideas; the limit of their ambition is to find what Professor Renn calls 'an ecological niche left by the big masters'. Entire careers flourish in such specialist niches but never escape them, since all their basic assumptions rain in from outside. Not so with Einstein. It is as if Mileva's love, and her absolute faith in his ability, created for him a kind of microclimate: a self-sustaining environment in which he could refine his scientific vision free of outside dogma. To muster the courage for his chosen mission, he needed someone to affirm his worth and the rightness of his aims. One such ally was as good as a hundred if his private world was tightly enough defined. Mileva was ready to define that world as including them alone.

6

Starved For Love

FAR from earning Einstein instant acclaim, the papers of 1905 were at first largely ignored in the scientific community. According to his sister, Einstein had expected sharp opposition and immediate criticism of the relativity theory. Instead there was an icy silence from most quarters, and he was badly disappointed. The major exception was the response of the highly influential Max Planck. Without him, Einstein's work might have waited far longer for recognition. Planck began lecturing on the theory that winter, firing the imagination of his assistant Max von Laue, who was one of the first scientists to pay a call on the unknown author in Berne. Von Laue found Einstein's appearance so unprepossessing when he first arrived at the Patent Office that he let the young man walk past him ('I could not believe he could be the father of the relativity theory'). He was equally unimpressed when Einstein gave him one of his cheap cigars, and he surreptitiously threw it into the river as they crossed a bridge. An early proponent of relativity, von Laue would underline why it took time to gain acceptance by confessing as an old man that it took even him decades to master all its implications.

This initial interest marked the modest beginning of the end of Einstein's scientific isolation. The number of converts grew as word passed round, with one Polish professor declaring to a colleague, 'A new Copernicus is born.' The future Nobel prizewinner Max Born of Germany found Einstein's reasoning 'a revelation', and Hermann Minkowski — the former professor in Zurich who remembered Einstein as a 'lazy dog' — emerged as another powerful ally. Yet most physicists remained unconvinced, uninterested or unaware. In July 1907, two years after Einstein had written his paper, Planck wrote to him that supporters of relativity were only 'a modest-sized crowd'.

His new admirers were taken aback by the shabby domesticity in which the 'new Copernicus' subsisted. Jakob Laub, a pupil of Minkowski and another early pilgrim to Berne, found Einstein kneeling in front of the oven in his chilly flat, poking the fire. Physics remained something that he squeezed in between the demands of job and family. He described himself in early 1907 as a 'venerable federal ink-shitter', who rode his scientific hobby-horse and played violin within 'the narrow boundaries' fixed by his two-year-old son. The previous year Mileva had made clear to Helene Savić how hard it was to survive on his paltry salary. Looking forward to a visit by her friend, she wondered whether 'our poor purse will stand the strain'.

Little Hans Albert was increasingly central to Mileva's life. Her love for him had grown as his personality began to take shape, and she took a proud delight in the 'unbelievable questions' with which he now tested his parents. 'Our boy is such a droll fellow,' she told Savić, 'and we often have to suppress our laughter in order to stay serious when he has one of his roguish ideas.' Despite this tenderness, Mileva seemed to yearn for a scientific rigour in child-rearing. 'Do you follow your own certain principles which are untried by other people or do you follow proven principles?' she asked her friend. 'I have looked in vain for relevant literature, which would really offer something. Perhaps you could give me your advice.' It was an oddly revealing request. Whereas Einstein exploited 'relevant literature' on his own terms, it appears that Mileva's intelligence was rather more pedantic. She liked to have guidance, and to follow authority.

Mileva reported that Einstein spent his free time at home playing with his son, but added that his administrative work and scientific papers were 'piling up in an alarming manner'. As the years passed, and her husband's workload grew, her alarm would increase. Mileva pined for the old student days in Zurich. She asked whether Savić believed she and Einstein had changed much over the years, adding, 'I often have the feeling I am sitting in a certain small room in Zurich, enjoying my most beautiful days . . . I often think of you as you were when I knew you then, and seldom as I know you now. Don't you think this is strange?'

It was in 1907 that Einstein had what he called 'the happiest thought of my life'. In his own words, 'I was sitting in a chair in the

Patent Office at Berne when all of a sudden a thought occurred to me: "If a person falls freely he will not feel his own weight." I was startled. This simple thought made a deep impression on me. It impelled me toward a theory of gravitation.' The September 1905 paper is now described as 'the special theory of relativity' because it cannot adequately deal with questions of acceleration. Einstein's happy thought now revealed to him that gravity and acceleration are directly equivalent. For the falling man, the force of acceleration matches that of gravity so precisely that his sensation of weight is cancelled out. Einstein now knew that extending relativity to cover acceleration would also provide a new theory of gravity to replace that of Newton. Another eight years of strenuous endeavour were needed to develop his flash of inspiration into a finished theory, but without it relativity would have remained incomplete.

Not all Einstein's attention was focused on relativity in these years, and he also became increasingly concerned with the nature of radiation – in particular, the particulate description of light used by quantum theory. One of his more minor but intriguing projects was a method of measuring small quantities of electricity. The 'Maschinchen' or 'little machine' he designed for this purpose has since been claimed as the work of Mileva, who is said to have collaborated in its construction with Conrad Habicht's brother, Paul. According to Trbuhović-Gjurić, the long time the project took can be ascribed in part to Mileva's distraction by household chores and in part to her thoroughness and perfectionism. The machine was described in a paper written by the Habicht brothers and patented under the name Einstein-Habicht, but this is cited as another example of Mileva being denied her due. Indeed, it is alleged that one of the brothers asked why she did not insist on her own name being included. 'What for?' she is said to have replied. 'We are both only One Stone [Ein Stein].'

The trouble with this anecdote is that it has no reliable provenance: the main source for it is Trbuhović-Gjurić. A fleeting hint that Mileva helped is given in Carl Seelig's biography of Einstein, but his source is unknown. Crucially, Mileva's suggested role is not borne out by the letters that survive from this period. The 'little machine' is mentioned repeatedly in Einstein's correspondence with Paul Habicht, and others, without the smallest suggestion that Mileva was involved. The one letter surviving from Einstein to Mileva in 1908, when work on the machine was intense, contains no mention of it. Nor does Mileva appear to have described her alleged involvement to Helene Savić. All in all, the claims made for her seem as unsatisfactory as the machine itself. Tiresomely complicated, and apt to malfunction, it never achieved popularity.

In June 1907 Einstein made a new attempt to secure an academic position, this time as a *Privatdozent*, or unsalaried lecturer, at Berne University. At first he still met with frustration. His relativity paper, offered as part of his application, was declared incomprehensible by the professor of experimental physics. Einstein also failed to meet the requirement of submitting a hitherto unpublished article, or '*Habilitationsschrift*'. His application was rejected, and he began looking for jobs teaching mathematics. But then came a postcard from his old adviser and doctoral supervisor Professor Alfred Kleiner, who had watched his progress and now wanted Einstein to join him as a professor at the University of Zurich. As a first step, Kleiner urged him to have another attempt at becoming a *Privatdozent* in Berne. This time he met all the requirements, and in 1908 he became a member of the academic community for the first time. It was hardly an exalted role, however, and it had to be juggled with his continuing work at the Patent Office. Einstein was forced to lecture at odd hours, reconciling himself to an audience of just three friends for one 7.00 a.m. session that summer. His sister, who was studying Romance languages at Berne, would occasionally drop in to provide moral support. Sometimes his audience shrank to a single pupil.

The signs are that Einstein and his wife were still good friends in 1908. At Easter, Mileva took Hans Albert to visit her family in Vojvodina, leaving her husband behind in Berne. Einstein wrote to her much as he had done in their student days, sharing with her his latest scientific enthusiasms. He told Mileva with excitement of a flaw he suspected in relativistic work by Minkowski, and of an experimental test for relativity being carried out at Würzburg University in Germany. She was also given news of the books he had ordered – one on the kinetic theory of gases, another a collection of humorous classics. All this was amiably mixed with loving gossip, including a typical warning that the flat was 'already very dirty' without her guiding hand. 'I am writing cabbages and turnips, but what does it matter?' remarked Einstein, amid a jumble of ideas that suggested easy intimacy.

But there was now an important difference from the early days, for Einstein had begun his first formal scientific collaboration. Early in 1908 he had started working with Jakob Laub, the mathematician who was the first person to publish work with him as a co-author. There was an ambivalence in his comments on Laub that recalled earlier letters, when Besso was first joining him in scientific debate. Then Einstein had seemed anxious to reassure Mileva by covering his praise for Besso with a coating of disparagement. Now Laub got much the same treatment. Einstein told his wife that they worked together 'a great deal', had just been for a long walk together, and even ate all their meals together. Yet he added, 'In spite of Laub I do not like loneliness at all. I wait lovingly for your return.' Einstein wrote that Laub was 'a quite nice chap – although very ambitious, almost rapacious. But he does these calculations which I would not find time to do and that is good.'

The appearance of a happy marriage was still there that summer, in the cheerful holiday postcards the couple sent to friends. Hans Albert accompanied his parents on a visit to Mürren, above the beautiful and precipitous Lauterbrunnen valley, and to the nearby hamlet of Isenfluh, with its dramatic views of the Jungfrau mountain. At this point in his life, Einstein seemed to share with Mileva a passion for Switzerland's rugged scenery: the previous summer was spent hiking in the Bernese Oberland. Later his tastes were very different, and his secretary Helen Dukas wrote in 1952 that he disliked mountains because they got in the way of his view. Instead he loved the earth's wastes, the sea and the prairie, anything vast and unending to the gaze. Perhaps mountains reminded him of his student days with Mileva and bitter-sweet memories of their trip to the Splügen pass. The adult Hans Albert once said that 'even the sight of a mountain' depressed his father, and remarked how odd this was 'with his Swiss background'. He also suggested that one of the reasons Einstein loved boating was 'the wide vistas of water, the distances he can see'. Einstein seemed in later life to share with Shelley the sad charm of desolate places, 'where we taste/ The pleasure of believing what we see/ Is boundless, as we wish our souls to be.'

One consequence of Einstein's growing reputation was a fresh opportunity in the spring of 1909. Zurich University created a new position – associate professor of theoretical physics – and he was chosen to fill it, after being proposed by Professor Kleiner. One of the most touching stories about Einstein tells how another candidate, Friedrich Adler, apparently stood down in his favour despite being offered the chair first. This thin, pale young man was the son of the founder of the Austrian Social Democratic Party, and a person of principle. He is said to have stepped aside after declaring that his talents did not bear 'even the slightest comparison to Einstein's'. The two men became friends and neighbours, but the story gains its greatest poignancy from the extraordinary events of Adler's later life. In 1916, driven on by pacifist and socialist opposition to the First World War, he shot dead the prime minister of Austria. He was sentenced to death but then had this commuted to only eighteen months in prison.

The story of Adler's self-sacrifice in 1909 was told by Philipp Frank, who no doubt heard it from Einstein's own lips. But a more interesting account exists in a letter that Einstein wrote to Michele Besso, several months after the assassination, discussing a petition they planned to make on Adler's behalf. With a decency typical of his best instincts, Einstein was ready for his name to be used in any way that would save his former friend from execution. Equally typical, however, was the astringent description he gave to Besso of Adler's character. On the one hand, he wanted the petition to stress how good-hearted and unselfish Adler had been in former years. On the other, 'for information', he wanted Besso to know that Adler was unbalanced: an intellectually sterile and obstinate dreamer, whose appetite for self-sacrifice had a heavy touch of masochism, and who was almost suicidal in his eagerness for martyrdom. It was in this context that he recounted the story of 1909 – to demonstrate not Adler's nobility, but his craziness. The truth seems to be that Adler was at best ambivalent about whether he wanted the Zurich post. Professor Robert Schulmann, who has studied Adler's letters to his father, also believes that Adler knew he was really second choice. Kleiner had dangled the appointment in front of him, almost as an insurance, while hoping to snatch it back later for Einstein, whom he considered 'among the most important theoretical physicists'. Adler felt resentful, it seems, and withdrew to avoid humiliation.

Whatever the reasons for Adler's decision, Einstein's appointment was made in spite of the anti-Semitism that was widespread in Europe at the start of the century. In a final faculty report on his suitability for the post, his future colleagues remarked on the 'disagreeable qualities' common among Jews. These, they noted, included 'all kinds of unpleasant peculiarities of character, such as intrusiveness, impudence and a shopkeeper's mentality in the perception of their academic position'. Happily for Einstein, the faculty did not think it was dignified to adopt anti-Semitism as a matter of policy. The vote in his favour – ten ayes, one abstention – was made in secret in March. Einstein was appointed on 7 May and handed in his resignation to the Patent Office on 6 July 1909.

A couple of days later, Einstein received more confirmation of his growing prestige. Along with Marie Curie, Ernest Solvay and Wilhelm Ostwald (whom Hermann Einstein had begged to help his son in 1901) he was awarded an honorary doctorate by the University of Geneva, to celebrate the three hundred and fiftieth anniversary of its foundation by Calvin. Einstein almost failed to attend the ceremony, having thrown the invitation away. He thought the elegant sheet of paper carrying a Latin inscription was 'impersonal and of little interest'.

His appointment to Zurich was reported in the local papers, where it was noticed by a certain Anna Meyer-Schmid. This was the same Anna Schmid to whom Einstein had composed an affectionate poem a decade earlier, while staying at the Hotel Paradise in Mettmenstetten. The now married Anna sent Einstein a card to congratulate him on his appointment, and in May 1909 received a warm reply in which he reminisced about their brief encounter. Although the letter was short, his tone was powerfully nostalgic and sentimental. He pronounced himself 'immeasurably' pleased to hear from her, promising that he recalled their 'lovely weeks' together even more fondly than she did. 'I wish you from the heart all possible luck,' he wrote, 'and can well imagine that you have become an excellent, happy woman, just as you were then a lovely and happy girl.' Einstein assured Anna that he

remained the same 'simple fellow' as before: all that had changed was
the passing of their youth, 'the enchanted time which sees heaven full
of bass violins every day'. Whatever may have been intended, the
effect was of a man sighing after lost passion. Nor was this diminished by the extreme brevity — and shoulder-shrugging ruefulness — of
his one comment about Mileva: 'Miss Marić really did become my
wife.'

Einstein urged Anna to visit him in Zurich, giving as his address the
physics institute where he was due to start work in October. It seems
that she wrote back almost immediately, but this time her greetings
were intercepted by Mileva. The effect was electric. Mileva suspected
an affair and wrote to Anna's husband, vigorously protesting about
the 'inappropriate' correspondence. Her manner suggested that Einstein's outrage was as great as her own; she claimed that he had
returned Anna's letter with a note saying he did not understand it.
Two weeks later, however, Einstein wrote to Herr Meyer that Mileva
had acted without his knowledge. He insisted that Anna's behaviour
had been totally honourable, and that his wife had been blinded
by jealousy. His embarrassment and anger were plain, despite an
acceptance that he was partly to blame. He apologized for his 'careless behaviour' and conceded that he had answered Anna's first card
'too heartily, thus re-awakening sympathy which existed between us'.
But he insisted that his intentions had been innocent, and promised
that his relationship with her would go no further.

It was a humbling experience for Einstein, and he brooded on it.
Five months later he told Besso that his 'spiritual equilibrium, lost on
account of M[ileva]' had not returned. The following April found him
apologizing to his mother for his 'bad humour', and asking her not to
worry about it. There was no good in taking one's depression and
anger out on others, he added: 'One must force it down one's gullet
alone.' Even after four decades, his bitterness endured. In a letter to
the Meyers' daughter, written in July 1951, when both Anna and
Mileva were dead, Einstein returned with relish to the theme of his
first wife's jealousy. He argued that it had been a pathological flaw,
and was typical in a woman of such 'uncommon ugliness'.

Professor John Stachel says this remark was the first to shock him
as he worked through Einstein's papers after his appointment as their

editor. Its viciousness is undiminished by the agreement of other observers on Mileva's charmless appearance in later years. One called her face 'hard and settled as though it were a plaster cast', while another spoke of it as 'harsh, almost coarse'. If such comments are hard to reconcile with photographs of Mileva as a student, or around the time of her wedding, then perhaps that is the point. Though never a beauty, it seems that in those early days she had a radiance, a glowing purpose, that could give her real prettiness. If anything reduced her to 'uncommon ugliness' it was the extinction of that spark as her marriage collapsed.

Of Mileva's jealousy there is plenty of evidence. Hans Albert admitted it, and said, 'She was a typical Slav, capable of strong negative feelings, and once hurt she could not forgive.' However, this jealousy was always implicit in the fierce devotion that Einstein had previously prized in her. The possessiveness he found so suffocating amounted to the same uncompromising commitment that he found sustaining as a student. By encouraging Mileva to believe that they stood alone, united against a world of philistines, he had made it inevitable that fraternization with people outside their magic circle would appear as betrayal. In any event, the letter he wrote to Anna Meyer-Schmid would have made most wives uneasy. Einstein had managed to provoke Mileva into exactly the clinging behaviour he found most uncongenial; in turn, this made him back away even more, provoking her to cling still tighter.

The Meyer-Schmid affair must have symbolized for Mileva the way that Einstein's attention was increasingly directed away from her into other directions: his work, his male friends, his scientific colleagues, and now even this woman from his past. Her unease can only have been heightened by her husband's growing eminence within his profession, which drew him away into ever more distinguished circles while Mileva remained tied to their home. In September 1909 Einstein travelled to Salzburg to deliver his first paper to a scientific conference. He confided to a colleague that he had never met a real physicist until he was thirty: now he was to perform before some of the most distinguished practitioners in his field. As if to stress his new distance from his wife, and his desire to escape the claustrophobic atmosphere of home, he departed for the conference several weeks before it began. Mileva was left behind with Hans Albert, contemplating their impending move to Zurich with churning emotions. She wrote to Helene Savić of the seven years that she had spent with Einstein in Berne – 'so many beautiful and, I must say, also bitter and difficult days'. Mileva boasted to Savić that Einstein was now counted 'among the leading German-speaking physicists' and had become 'frightfully courted'. But her pride was mixed with fear for the future. 'I am very happy about his success, which he has really earned,' she wrote. 'I only hope and wish that fame does not exert a detrimental influence on his human side.'

The two best accounts of Einstein's return to Zurich – one by his friend Philipp Frank, the other by his pupil David Reichinstein – suggest that his success gave him a new self-confidence, far tougher and more durable than the brittle bravado of his student days. At last he was fully established as a physicist, and for the first time he knew that his voice was being heard. 'As a result of his great scientific discoveries, Einstein had already acquired a profound inner feeling of security,' wrote Philipp Frank. 'The pressure that had often burdened his youth was gone ... the problems of daily life did not appear important.' In even stronger terms, Reichinstein wrote of a 'Messiah-feeling' unfolding with this new sense of vocation. According to him, 'Einstein's soul took wing' in these years. 'Increasing success supplied his soul with a feeling of superiority ... The sensation of insecurity, his feeling of not being equal to the struggle of life disappeared.' Reichinstein found this exuberance overpowering, and his account contains dark hints that Einstein's arrogance bordered on hubris. Frank, while rather less critical, makes it equally clear that Einstein's self-possession made him uneasy company. He seemed to have difficulty in taking everyday matters seriously, and his social manner swung between childlike cheerfulness and apparent cynicism.

It was not that Einstein had been transformed, but that his old sense of separateness had gained a new intensity. This was enough to make Mileva seem increasingly superfluous to his happiness, but not enough to make him entirely self-sufficient. Frank remarked on the paradoxes of Einstein's behaviour. Here was a man who could seemingly sympathize 'deeply and passionately with the fate of every stranger', yet on closer contact 'immediately withdrew into his shell'.

Clearly there were limits to his inner security: indeed, it was by imposing those limits that he remained secure. He still seemed to care for his wife enough to observe such small conventions as buying her a Christmas present – even if he left it to the last moment. A postcard survives from 17 December 1909 in which he begged Habicht to rush him the title and publisher of a music book, containing the tunes of old dances, that he had selected as his gift.

Mileva's worries were added to by her strong sense of isolation: she had few friends to whom she could turn for commiseration. Helene Savić, for example, appears not to have been entirely sympathetic. It seems likely that her deeper affection may have been for Einstein, making Mileva as much a rival as a friend. In a letter to Savić soon after the move to Zurich, Mileva adopted a tone of gentle reproach as she returned to the subject of her husband's remoteness. The hint it contains of Savić's spite recalls how Savić had mocked Mileva with Einstein's mother in the summer of 1900. Mileva wrote,

> You see, with such fame, not much time remains for his wife. I read a certain maliciousness between the lines when you wrote that I must be jealous of science, but what can be done, the pearls are given to one, to the other the case . . . I often ask myself . . . whether I am not rather a person who feels a great deal and passionately, fights a great deal and also suffers because of that, and out of pride or perhaps shyness puts on a haughty and superior air until he himself believes it to be genuine. And I must ask you, even if the latter were the case, and my innermost soul stood less proudly, even then could you love me? You see I am very starved for love and would be so overjoyed to hear a yes that I almost believe wicked science is guilty, and I gladly accept the laughter over it . . .

Mileva's description of herself as 'starved for love' mirrors comments made many years later by her elder son. Hans Albert was taking issue with Philipp Frank's description of his mother's supposedly harsh character. 'Stern? Severe? This is not, I believe, really correct,' he said. 'A person who had gone through all kinds of mishaps and so on, but not really severe. I would say able to give . . . and in need of love.

That means somebody not essentially based on intellect.' Hans Albert's closeness to his mother had intensified as the marriage began to decline. In her letter to Helene Savić, Mileva remarked that the timing of her son's birthday meant that his admission to school was likely to be delayed. 'Then he will stay for another year for his mama,' she added. 'We are actually inseparable and cling terribly to each other.'

It was around this point, with the marriage apparently at such a very low ebb, that Mileva conceived her second son. Whether or not the pregnancy was planned is unknown, but it provided Mileva with another focus for the love to which her husband seemed increasingly indifferent. Eduard Einstein was born on 28 July 1910. His parents called him 'Tete' (also rendered as 'Tetel', 'Tede', and 'Tedel'), a nickname derived from Hans Albert's pronunciation of the Serbian word for child ('dete'). They referred to the two boys as 'the little bears'. Einstein wrote to tell his friends that 'the stork has brought us a healthy little boy', and seemed suitably cheerful. However, the extra burden on his marriage was considerable. Einstein's salary was no more than he had received in the Patent Office. As he once joked, 'In my relativity theory I set up a clock at every point in space, but in reality I find it difficult to provide even one clock in my room.'

There was also the burden on his time and patience, but in this respect Einstein was striking resilient. Hans Albert recalled:

I don't believe he showed any particular interest in my brother and me while we were mere infants. But, according to my mother, he was a fine baby sitter. When she was busy around the house, father would put aside his work and watch over us for hours, bouncing us on his knee. I remember he would tell us stories – and he often played his violin in an effort to keep us quiet. But I also recall my mother saying that even the loudest baby-crying didn't seem to disturb father. He could go on with his work completely impervious to noise.

One of Hans Albert's earliest memories was of his father making him a cable car out of matchboxes and string. 'I remember that that was one of the nicest toys I had at the time and it worked.'

Einstein's first Ph.D. pupil, Hans Tanner, recalled visiting him at his apartment:

> He was sitting in his study in front of a heap of papers covered with mathematical formulae. Writing with his right hand and holding his younger son in his left, he kept replying to questions from his elder son Albert who was playing with his bricks. With the words: 'Wait a minute, I've nearly finished,' he gave me the children to look after for a few moments and went on working. It gave me a glimpse into his immense powers of concentration.

There is a strikingly similar description of domestic turmoil chez Einstein by David Reichinstein. This account belies suggestions that Mileva was a lazy housewife: instead it suggests frenetic activity. Reichinstein wrote of finding the door to the flat thrown open, letting in air to dry the freshly scrubbed floor and the washing hung up in the hall. 'I entered Einstein's room; calmly philosophic he was with one hand rocking the bassinet in which the child was lying (his wife was at work in the kitchen). In his mouth Einstein had a bad, a very bad cigar, and in his other hand an open book. The stove was smoking horribly. How in the world could he bear it!'

On one occasion, so Reichinstein reported, Einstein was overcome by the stove's fumes after lying down on a couch to sleep. His life was saved due to a chance visit by his friend Heinrich Zangger, a professor of medicine at Zurich University, who threw open the windows and revived him. This was not the last time that Einstein would be in debt to Zangger, a tall and sharp-featured farmer's son of tremendous energy and wide intellectual interests. He had first met Einstein in 1905 to discuss Brownian motion, and gradually came to act as a personal and professional confidant. Einstein praised him for his sensitivity and pyschological insight, and for what he described as Zangger's paternal influence. His friend's humanity and dynamism were both well demonstrated in 1906, when he saved the lives of more than a hundred men trapped after a mine disaster at Courrières in France. Rescuers had been ready to give up, but he was convinced that survivors could still be found and he managed to have the digging continue. Zangger was one of Einstein's most loyal helpers when his marriage eventually broke apart.

During these earlier years, Einstein found a means of escape from domestic pressures in the company of his students, with whom he would discuss physics long into the evening. Hans Tanner remembered staying with him until closing time in a café on Zurich's Bellevueplatz, before being hauled back to Einstein's apartment to help check for errors in an article by Planck. Reichinstein remembered Einstein absenting himself from one café session with the excuse that it was washing-day and he had to mind the children. Mostly, however, the contact between Einstein and Mileva appears to have been increasingly fleeting. On a trip to the theatre, he would arrive straight from work and expect to find her waiting with his supper – two sandwiches – to be bolted down in the interval. Musical evenings with friends served only to underline their apartness. 'Since there are rather many musical occasions in our house, we really have very little time that we can pass in privacy and tranquillity,' Mileva told Helene Savić in a letter of early 1911. She boasted to her friend that she never failed to attend Einstein's public lectures, which may suggest that she wanted to keep an eye on him in the wake of the Anna Meyer-Schmid episode. Mileva's remaining interest in science was still being kept alive by her husband's work, and his lectures gave her the increasingly rare pleasure of sitting and listening to his voice – as his 'little student'.

Mileva recognized in herself a dangerous tendency to live in the past, particularly her days at the Federal Polytechnic School. It seemed to her, she told Helene Savić, that 'we women cling much longer to the memory of that remarkable period called youth, and involuntarily would like things to remain that way'. Men, she believed, were able to 'accommodate themselves better to the present moment'. The irony is that it was Einstein himself who had promised a marriage in which they would remain perpetual students. His own accommodation with the present was quite fragile, and had been easily disturbed by Anna Meyer-Schmid. When she contacted him again in 1926, he wrote of 'the beautiful time of our youth' rising 'out of the trap-door once again'. While Mileva was able to recognize what power the past held over her, he had merely stowed his memories under the floorboards.

Some descriptions of Einstein in this period sound more like those of a bachelor student than of a married man. Reichinstein recalled how together they attended a lecture on psychoanalysis, given by one of Einstein's co-workers, 'Mr Y.' The audience was made up mainly of young men and women 'who had come to be enlightened about questions of love and their effects on the subconscious'. Einstein showed little interest but afterwards joined Reichinstein and the lecturer in a café, where their group included two sisters 'of rare beauty and charm' – Slavs like Mileva who had come to Zurich to study science. As the lecturer continued to expound his ideas, attempting to prove their scientific basis, Reichinstein noticed that Einstein 'evidently had greater interest in living eyes than in the psychoanalytic problems of his friend'. His account continues:

> Y. had not yet perceived the change which had come about in Einstein's attention, and was continuing with his proofs. Suddenly he noticed the direction of Einstein's glances and perceived at the same time that Einstein had not listened to a word of his explanations. Y. indignantly threw a book on the table and said: 'Why professor, if you were in love you would believe that more important than your quantum theories.' Einstein replied in a gentle, somewhat embarrassed voice: 'No, ladies and gentlemen, my quantum theories are really of great importance to me.' Einstein threw me a glance as if he needed my confirmation that he was right.

If Reichinstein caught this encounter correctly, it hardly suggests that other interests were absent from Einstein's mind. It also confirms the impression that Mileva had some justification in her jealousy over Anna Meyer-Schmid.

Further pressure was placed on the Einsteins' increasingly fragile relationship by another move, this time far more dramatic than the switch from Berne to Zurich. In the spring of 1910 – less than six months after he had assumed his Zurich position – Einstein revealed to his mother that he had been offered a better salary by a larger university. The call had come from the German University in Prague, where he would take up his appointment in the spring of 1911.

Moving to Prague was one upheaval too many for Mileva. It had been one thing to live a bohemian life with Einstein in the snug surroundings of Berne and Zurich; it was quite another to do so in the capital of Bohemia itself, amid the brooding atmosphere of its spires, domes and golden cupolas. This was a step as daunting in its way as the one she had taken fifteen years earlier when she left Hungary to start a new life in Switzerland. Then she had been a young student, driven on by academic ambition. Now she was a married woman in her mid-thirties, with two young children in tow. The move was being made for the sake of her husband's career alone. It was a gamble in which she had no special stake.

Even Einstein had his doubts. Like Mileva, he enjoyed living in Zurich. He liked its unstuffy atmosphere, its beautiful setting by the lake, and the proximity of so many friends for music-making and debate. Above all, his work was going well: during eighteen months in the city, he produced eleven scientific papers. It was not even as if Prague was at the cutting edge of theoretical physics, and to this day it remains puzzling why Einstein went there. Mileva told Helene Savić that her husband accepted the call 'after ample reflection because of material advantages', but this is hardly a full explanation. It is true that he was to become a full professor for the first time, and the higher salary must have been welcome for a man with a growing family – money mattered much more to Einstein than is often supposed. But he also had every prospect of promotion if he stayed put. He had ruffled a few faculty feathers with his self-willed ways, but a pay rise in the summer of 1910 suggested greater things to come. It was granted after a student petition was raised, pleading for Einstein to be kept at Zurich.

Yet all the considerations that made Zurich such an agreeable place to stay were also reasons for a restless man to leave. Ten years earlier, Einstein had written to Mileva in exasperation at the ignorant complacency of the physicists he met at the Winterthur Technikum. 'Would I too become so lazy intellectually if I were ever doing well?' he wondered. 'I don't think so, but the danger seems to be great indeed.' Moving to a new intellectual environment was one way of heading off that danger. There was intense competition for the post in Prague, but his main rival, Gustav Jaumann, a professor at the Technical Institute in Brno, eventually withdrew in a huff, sneering that the German University's interest in Einstein showed that it preferred mere modernity to merit. Mileva, who felt more at home in Zurich than anywhere else, reluctantly gave the move her blessing.

Had she known how dismal life would be in Prague, she might have put up more of a fight. The city was an unfriendly place, shot through by tension between the native Czechs and their overlords from the Habsburg empire. Academia provided no refuge from what amounted to a nineteenth-century system of apartheid. There was one university reserved for the Czechs, another for the German-speaking minority, and each camp had its own hermetically sealed social system. Professors from the two institutions might never meet except at a foreign congress, and when they returned they would ignore each other once more. Adding to the unease was the presence of a large Jewish community, whose former ghetto had been formally incorporated into the city in 1850. Anti-Semitism had a long history among the Czechs, and the prejudices that would later coalesce as Nazism were already a growing influence on the German community. Einstein and Mileva were doomed to be odd ones out in this mixed-up city.

Hans Albert and Einstein's stepson-in-law Dimitri Marianoff both gained the impression from Einstein that he had liked Prague very much. His letters at the time suggest otherwise, although he seemed happy enough when he took up his appointment at the start of April. He wrote to friends that he was working comfortably in his 'splendid institute', praised the magnificent library, and declared that his new position as director of the Institute of Theoretical Physics gave him 'much joy'. There is a suggestion that they were forced to leave their first lodgings because the neighbours complained about Eduard's crying, but they then set up home in a three-room flat in the Smichov quarter, on the left bank of the Vltava river. The apartment stood on the mezzanine floor of a newly built block in the art-noveau style. It had electric lights, and Einstein's increased income meant that Mileva could now have a live-in maid to help her. But these comforts were only small compensations for a pervasive dirt and squalor in depressing contrast to spick-and-span Switzerland.

One problem was fleas. Einstein may have unwittingly introduced them to the flat when he bought a second-hand mattress. The maid's room was infested, and he once found his body covered in bugs after spending just a few minutes there to extinguish a fire. The only way to get rid of them was to take a bath – itself a rather unpleasant business in Prague. The water used for washing and house-cleaning was a sinister brown liquid straight from the river, which left behind a black sludge in the basins. For cooking there were slightly cleaner supplies from a fountain in the street, but Einstein complained to his friend Lucien Chavan in Berne that only boiled water was safe for drinking. Typhoid was an ever-present threat in these conditions; the fleas also prompted fears about bubonic plague. Adding to the depressing mood were the city's sooty air and oppressive summer heat.

In later life, Einstein would make a joke of Prague's hardships. 'The filthier a nation is, the tougher it is,' he said. He boasted to Besso in May 1911 that his sons were 'of really robust health, which is rare for city children'. In fact, the family was troubled by sickness throughout the stay in Prague, with one visitor considering Einstein 'seriously ill'. This can only have added to the pressure upon Mileva, who was very lonely. Never an expert at getting on with strangers, she had little chance of striking up a rapport with the other professors and their wives. Their conversation was full of jibes against her fellow Slavs, and a world away from the liberal attitudes of Zurich. Philipp Frank, her husband's successor at the German University, told how two professors saw a house sign hanging dangerously over the pavement. 'It doesn't matter much,' said one, 'since it is extremely probable that when it falls it will strike a Czech.' Einstein's closest colleague at work was Czech by birth, but had been raised and educated amid Germans. Now he would refuse to buy postcards unless they were printed exclusively in German, and he picked fights on the subject with Czech postal clerks. When Einstein asked an institute servant where he could buy some blankets, he was directed to a shop run by a Czech. But as soon as his predecessor, Ferdinand Lippich, found this out, he sent a maid over to ask that the purchase be made at a German shop instead. 'The animosity between Germans and Czechs seems considerable,' Einstein remarked.

His first impression of the local people (and one which suggests a great tolerance of dumplings) was that they were excellent cooks; many even had a certain charm. Within a couple of months, though, he was complaining that they seemed alien and had no natural humanity. They were soulless, 'without any goodwill towards their fellow men'. Looking around him, Einstein saw a divided society with snobbish luxury and creeping misery side by side on the streets. Most of the population were unfriendly to Germans and could not speak his language. He pleaded with Besso to relieve the couple's isolation by coming to 'pitch his wigwam' in Prague. 'How one could use a man of your intelligence and good nature here!'

Einstein soon found that his academic post had its drawbacks too. Although he had been engaged specifically as a professor of theoretical physics, he immediately found that he must also involve himself in what he called 'experimental adventures'. Humdrum tinkering in the laboratory was not his forte (he was always pleasantly surprised when something went right, Hans Albert recalled) and denied him time for thinking. His students seemed less industrious and intelligent than in Switzerland, and Einstein was disconcerted by their grievous lack of interest in 'my beautiful subject'. He had been warned about this by Anton Lampa, one of the committee that had proposed him for the job. Einstein refused to believe it: he was sure he would find 'an echo from this forest' if only he called out clearly enough. He had been disappointed, and only one man and half a dozen 'half-usable' women regularly took part in his seminars. Prague's isolation from the mainstream of European physics meant that his colleagues were ill-equipped to discuss his work. In addition, there was too much bureaucracy. He joked about having to apply 'to the exalted Viceroy for the sanction of cleaning expenses'. The 'pen and ink shitting' was endless, he said.

The red tape had tripped him up from the first, when he offended his prospective employers by professing no religion. Officialdom was satisfied only after he declared himself a Jew, with suitable solemnity. Then this great hater of formality found that he had to buy an ornate uniform in which to swear allegiance to the imperial authorities. It consisted of a three-cornered feather-trimmed hat, a coat and trousers with gold bands, a thick black overcoat and a sword. His usual attire was so casual that once, when he arrived for a reception at a luxurious Prague hotel, he was mistaken for the man sent to repair the lights. Every day, as he walked to work, he had to grit his teeth as the Institute's porter – reeking of alcohol – bowed and scraped in obsequious greeting. The people of Prague, he observed, were 'an odd mixture of pomposity and servility'.

Einstein shrank from all this, but his reaction was no longer to find common cause against the world with Mileva. What friends he found, he seems to have kept to himself. Marianoff wrote:

> He loved sitting under the trees in the gardens of the cafés on the Moldau River with his confreres, drinking their 'white coffee' and beer. Mileva was a mathematician too. She wanted to join in these talks, but she was left at home with her children and she became more silent and more discontented every day . . . Mileva's fiery disposition resented the fact that she was never taken into Einstein's full confidence in the working out of his problems.

A chilling portrait of Einstein appears in a historical novel by his Prague contemporary Max Brod. Brod is known today as the man who saved Franz Kafka's novels for posterity, by defying his friend's dying wish for his unpublished manuscripts to be burnt. But he was also a writer himself, and a member of Prague's intellectual élite. He met Einstein at the home of Berta Fanta, wife of the owner of the 'Unicornis' pharmacy and a lover of science and philosophy, who held open house every Tuesday for the city's Jewish intellectuals. The relatively unknown Kafka would sit tongue-tied in a corner on the rare occasions that he appeared at these evenings. Einstein, in contrast, took a vigorous part as the group's discussions ranged from Kant to Hegel. His cool indifference to conventional wisdom made a deep impression on those around him. Brod, who often accompanied Einstein on piano as he played Mozart violin sonatas, sketched a picture of Einstein in *Tycho Brahe's Path to God*.

The real-life Brahe was appointed court mathematician at Prague in 1599, but died two years later after drinking too much at a feast. He earned his place in history by laying the basis of modern precision astronomy, and was helped in his observations by his sister, Sophia. Max Brod cast Einstein in the guise of Brahe's colleague and successor

Johannes Kepler, one of the greatest names of science. Kepler was a somewhat unsavoury individual – professing a 'dog-like horror of baths' – and had a depressive and ill-tempered wife, Barbara. His triumph was to lay down the laws of planetary motion, showing that orbits are elliptical rather than the circular paths that had been conventional wisdom since the time of the Greeks.

In his novel, Brod gave Kepler an eerie tranquillity that Einstein's friends immediately recognized. Here was a scientist utterly devoted to his studies, and who found in that devotion an impregnable defence against 'the aberrations of feeling', like a ballad character who has sold his heart to the devil for a bullet-proof coat of mail. Describing his 'almost superhuman' detachment, Brod wrote, 'There was something incomprehensible in its absence of emotion, like a breath from a distant region of ice . . . He had no heart and therefore had nothing to fear from the world. He was not capable of emotion or love.' As he described this unnatural calm, Brod had the more passionate Tycho Brahe contemplate Kepler and groan, 'A spotless angel! But is he really? Is he not rather atrocious in his lack of sympathy?' At another point Tycho confronts Kepler and tells him, 'You really serve, not truth, but only yourself; that is to say, your own purity and inviolateness.'

An embarrassed Brod later insisted that, although he had taken Einstein as his model for Kepler, he had had no intention of suggesting that Einstein shared such heartlessness: only the same intolerance of received opinion. Einstein's friends expressed no such qualifications, and the physical chemist Walther Nernst read the book and told him, 'You are this Kepler.' In his biography of Einstein, Philipp Frank quoted Brod at length to illuminate Einstein's personality. He described Einstein's aversion to intimacy as 'a trait that has always left him a lonely person among his students, his colleagues, his friends, and his family'.

Einstein himself was well aware of his growing isolation from the everyday world. For much of his time in Prague he was lost among the *Alice in Wonderland* paradoxes of quantum theory. His university office overlooked the gardens of Bohemia's mental asylum, and he jokingly compared himself to the lunatics ambling about below him. 'Those are the madmen who do not occupy themselves with the quantum theory,' he told Frank. But Einstein was not mad, and he was not wandering about aimlessly. He had made progress, particularly towards understanding gravity.

Four years earlier Einstein had decided that gravity could bend light rays. This remains a startling idea: a shaft of sunlight does not seem substantial enough to feel gravity's tug. But, since light carries energy (allowing the sun to heat the earth), $E = mc^2$ shows it must also have mass. Therefore, like everything else with mass, it must come under gravity's sway. In 1907 Einstein had believed the effect was too small to be noticeable. Now he was convinced that it could be detected experimentally, by checking whether light from the stars was distorted as it passed the sun. He calculated the amount of deflection to expect, and in June 1911 appealed to astronomers to verify his findings.

To some extent Einstein was rediscovering ideas from the past that may have appeared in the popular science books he devoured as a youth. In the second edition of his great work *Opticks* in 1717, Newton had himself posed the question 'Do not bodies act upon light at a distance?' – but had left it unanswered. Unknown to Einstein, his own reply was anticipated as early as 1801 by a German astronomer called Johann Georg von Soldner, who came up with almost exactly the same figure for deflection by the sun. Later the Nazi Philipp Lenard had von Soldner's paper reprinted in an attempt to show that a nineteenth-century Aryan had beaten the twentieth-century Jew, but the 1911 result was simply a staging-post on Einstein's journey. He realized four years later that he had given only half the correct deflection, because space itself was 'bent' as well.

Einstein was now in ever-greater demand, and Mileva spent much of the autumn of 1911 alone. In September her husband was in Karlsruhe for a major conference; in October he gave a series of lectures to secondary-school teachers in Zurich. But by far his most important engagement was around the start of November, which found him at Brussels for a meeting of Europe's leading physicists organized by Ernest Solvay, a wealthy industrial chemist. Einstein grumbled that this Solvay Congress – the first of many – was a 'witches' sabbath' and interrupted his work. However, it placed him on equal terms with some of the greatest figures of twentieth-century science. Besides Marie Curie and Max Planck, he was mixing with Ernest Rutherford, the man who unlocked the secrets of the atom, Hendrik Lorentz, the Dutch physicist whose work set the stage for relativity, and Henri Poincaré, a legend among mathematicians. Einstein built friendships with two of these giants that cast particularly strong light on his own character. One was Lorentz, with whom he would be unsuccessfully nominated to share the Nobel prize in 1912. Einstein had begun a correspondence with Lorentz on radiation theory in March 1909. As early as May of that year he wrote, 'I admire this man like no other, I would even say I love him.' They met for the first time in February 1911, when Einstein and Mileva stayed with the Lorentz family while he delivered a lecture at Leiden. In an effusive thank-you letter, Einstein wrote of his host radiating such kindness that it blotted out his inner feeling that he was unworthy of it. Later he returned from Brussels with a renewed adoration, reporting that Lorentz had presided over the Solvay meeting with 'incomparable tact and unbelievable virtuosity'.

Abraham Pais has described Lorentz as a father figure for Einstein, and there seems no reason to demur. He was the older of the two by a quarter of a century, calm and dignified with a neat white beard. Lorentz had a way of enveloping those around him in a warm feeling of sympathy. For Einstein, whose work touched so intimately on his own, this warmth was especially strong. A mutual friend recalled seeing Lorentz pose a problem for Einstein to solve, then sit back smiling 'exactly the way a father looks at a particularly beloved son – full of secure knowledge that the youngster will crack the nut he has given him, but eager to see how'.

As Pais points out, Lorentz spent almost his entire life within the comfortable bounds of the Dutch upper-middle class. There was a stability and serenity to his existence that his peripatetic admirer rather envied. That much was clear in Einstein's graveside address after Lorentz's death in 1928, when he spoke of a life 'ordered like a work of art down to the smallest detail'. Lorentz had made the compromise between scientific striving and philistine comforts that he himself found so elusive. It was a compromise that Einstein's father had attempted too, albeit in a far more modest and bumbling way. Einstein's description of Hermann ('exceedingly kind, mild and wise') certainly finds an echo in his graveside tribute to the 'never-failing kindness' and 'intuitive understanding' of Lorentz. 'Everyone followed him gladly,' Einstein said, 'for they felt that he never set out to dominate but always simply to be of use.'

Einstein's other noteworthy encounter was with Marie Curie, for whom the Congress came at a time of great personal discomfiture. Newspaper reports, based on stolen letters, were bawling to the world that she was having an adulterous affair with the Frenchman Paul Langevin. Rumour had it that the couple were about to elope, and Curie faced humiliation. Since the death of her husband Pierre in 1906, under the wheels of a horse-drawn wagon, her public image had been that of a loyal widow. Now she was pilloried as a scarlet woman, and there was an international scandal. Einstein, to whom the subject of adultery was soon to be of more than academic interest, looked on with wry amusement and a contempt for the prurient outcry. 'The penny dreadful story hawked in the papers is nonsense,' he told a friend. Einstein argued that it was already well-known that Langevin wanted to divorce his wife: if he and Curie were in love, then so be it. It was a robust view that Einstein would live up to in his own later life, and Curie's vilification in the press can only have hardened his resolve to keep such matters out of the headlines.

But perhaps most revealing was his attitude to Curie as a woman. He found it hard to believe that Langevin could be romantically involved with her. He had seen the couple together with Langevin's wife and detected no special tension. More importantly, Curie was too plain. 'She has a sparky intelligence,' Einstein wrote, 'but despite her passionate nature is not attractive enough to be dangerous to anybody.'

Endearingly, some accounts have suggested that Mileva went along to the Congress and was able to share her husband's glory. In fact, he left her at home. A plaintive letter from Mileva at the start of October suggests how she regarded their separation during these months. 'It must have been very interesting in Karlsruhe,' she wrote. 'I would like to have been there and listened a little, and seen all these fine people . . . It is such an eternity since we saw each other, I wonder if you will recognize me.' She still signed herself as 'Dolly' – or to be precise, '*deine alten D*' (your old D) – and called Einstein by a new pet name, 'Babu'. His own cards, addressed '*Liebes weiberl*' (Dear Wifey) and signed 'Ba', still showed flashes of genuine affection. At 1.00 a.m., travelling in a sweaty train carriage to Brussels, he experienced 'an inner fit of tenderness' on finding that Mileva had packed him some apples and ham as a snack for the journey. Food remained the surest way to Einstein's heart, and in such foolish moments their old love glimmered.

At the end of the year, Einstein learned that his jilted sweetheart Marie Winteler had married. 'With that a dark point in my life diminishes,' he told Besso. Another twist of fate had provided an unwelcome reminder of the past for Mileva. Einstein's letters to Besso indicate that the couple's live-in maid, Fanni, gave birth to an illegitimate child, and they were drawn into unsuccessful attempts to find the baby a home. In September 1911, they agreed to let Fanni keep the youngster with her in their flat, with Einstein telling Besso that it would eventually go to its grandmother. The echo of her own predicament nine years earlier cannot have been lost on Mileva.

Her retreat into the background of Einstein's life is illustrated by an account by Paul Ehrenfest of a visit to Prague in February 1912. Ehrenfest was a brilliant physicist, whom Einstein described as the best teacher of the subject he had ever met. However, he was a deeply unhappy man, haunted by self-doubt and the feeling that he was unequal to the tasks he had set himself. He was devoted to his wife and collaborator, Tatyana, and was eventually to commit suicide after a partial estrangement from her. In the same fit of despair, he shot and blinded his retarded younger son. Although Ehrenfest was always among Einstein's more volatile friends, the relationship was one of his closest. They began corresponding in the spring of 1911, and he invited the Austrian to stay at the Prague apartment when he was travelling around Europe in search of a job. The two men hit it off instantly: when they were not chattering excitedly about science, they played Brahms, with Einstein on violin and Ehrenfest on piano.

Ehrenfest kept a meticulous diary of his life, to the extent of drawing sketches of people who happened to sit opposite him on trains, or recording that he arrived at Prague's Franz-Josef Bahnhof at precisely 2.50 p.m. But, in the characteristically full description of his 'awfully happy' stay with the Einsteins, Mileva's name hardly appears. She was at her husband's side when, cigar in mouth, he met Ehrenfest at the station. She was there again to say goodbye when their guest left a week later. But that, more or less, is that. Ehrenfest's biographer has described how, after collecting their guest from his train, the Einsteins took him to a coffee-house. While Mileva was present, the conversation was confined to small talk about Prague, Zurich and Vienna. Only when she left to go home did it burst into life, with the two men launching into an animated discussion of statistical mechanics.

The visitor took a particularly strong liking to young Hans Albert, chatting and joking with him in the lulls between scientific debate. Ehrenfest called him a 'liebes liebes Buberl' (dear dear boy) and sat next to him at mealtimes. He also took him on an outing to see a museum, and walked by his side on a Sunday-afternoon stroll while Einstein pushed Eduard's pram. Hans Albert had withstood the rigours of Prague better than the rest of the family. 'He loves going to school, is improving well with his piano lessons and delights in asking interesting questions of his papa about physics, mathematics and nature,' wrote Mileva.

But there was also a lonely and sombre side to the little boy's character. He had developed the habit of dawdling by the river on his way back from school, peering into a lock to see the water surging through. The elemental power of the torrent transfixed him, and he would stay watching it for so long that an anxious Mileva scolded his late return. This was the start of a fascination with water that was to inform Hans Albert's work on hydraulics. He could lose himself in the great forces that carve out rivers, just as his father claimed to do in the forces that shape the cosmos. As to whether his dawdling was also a way to delay going home, one can only speculate. But Hans Albert recalled that it was around this time that he began to feel the growing friction between his parents.

He told his second wife that the discord became obvious after his eighth birthday, in May 1912. His choice of date is fascinating, as we now know that this is when his father had just renewed contact with the woman who would become his second wife: his cousin Elsa. No biography has presented a satisfactory account of Elsa's role in the disintegration of Einstein's first marriage, the blame for which is usually borne by Mileva alone. The secrecy that has surrounded Einstein's liaison with his cousin is a tribute both to his skill at covering his tracks and to the devotion he inspired in the people around him. Those who knew the truth ensured that it stayed hidden for decades.

7

I Must Love Somebody

ELSA was judged prettier than Mileva by those who knew them both, and with her blue eyes, blonde hair and substantial figure – the latter partly due to a weakness for chocolates – she might have passed in her prime as a Valkyrie in an amateur production of Wagner. However, there was an inescapable aura of absurdity about her. There are many mocking anecdotes concerning her short-sightedness, for example, and it is alleged that she once mistook the table decorations at a banquet for salad, and began to cut up an orchid on her plate. Vanity led her to favour a lorgnette rather than spectacles, and Einstein's unkempt hair has been ascribed in part to her attempts to act as his barber, raising the eyeglass intermittently to check on progress.

Not that her own hair was very tidy – a wild coiffure was one of many family characteristics that Elsa and Einstein had in common. Photographs show them with the same ripe nose, the same plunging brow and the same uncompromising chin. As the years passed by, their similarity grew to the point where in many photographs the addition to Elsa of a painted-in moustache would render the pair indistinguishable. A rabbi who visited them sixteen years after their eventual marriage wrote, 'The resemblance of Mrs Einstein to her husband was extraordinary. She, too, was short and stocky, and her hair was worn like his, in wavy locks, but was not quite as grey as his. She even wore clothes similar to her husband's – a sweater and slacks.'

This deep-seated likeness was one reason why Einstein felt at home in Elsa's company. Life with Mileva had meant a schism from his family; now that the marriage had turned sour, he turned back to it for warmth and reassurance. After all, he and Elsa were related twice over. Her father, Rudolf, was a first cousin of Einstein's father, and her mother, Fanny, was a sister of Einstein's mother. It was Rudolf who had been Hermann's main creditor when his businesses failed. And it was with Rudolf and Fanny that Pauline went to stay following Hermann's death in 1902, not leaving until she took up her house-keeping job at Heilbronn in 1911.

Elsa was born in 1876 in Hechingen, a small Swabian town to which many of the family traced their roots, and which Einstein regarded as a kind of spiritual home (his dedication as a member of the Olympia Academy in 1903 was addressed to 'The Man of Hechingen'). She shared with him the same Swabian dialect, the same fund of proverbial sayings, even many of the same memories. Her family made frequent visits to Munich when Einstein was growing up there, and they often played together. They were taken on the same Sunday outings, even enjoying their first artistic experience together at the Munich Opera (she sat in the orchestra while he was in a gallery). Later Elsa claimed that she fell in love with her cousin even as a child, because of the beautiful way he played Mozart on the violin.

Like Einstein, Elsa had married outside the family in her early twenties. Her husband was a textile merchant of Swabian origin named Max Löwenthal, with whom she had two daughters, Ilse and Margot. A son was born in 1903 but did not survive. Biographies of Einstein often describe Elsa as a widow, but in fact she divorced her husband on 11 May 1908, after they had spent some twelve years together. She subsequently moved with her daughters into an apartment above her parents in Haberlandstrasse, Berlin.

The reasons for the divorce remain unclear, save for dark hints that Max Löwenthal was a bad lot who dissipated their money. Its effect was to leave Elsa eager for a new relationship, not least to provide security for her daughters, to whom she was devoted. Both girls were slightly built and emotionally delicate. Dimitri Marianoff, who later married Margot, wrote that his bride possessed 'that shyness pussy cats have who rarely leave their mother's side'. Almost every account of Elsa stresses her motherly qualities, and to Marianoff they were all too acute. 'Her maternal instinct was abnormal, reaching into all the channels of her children's lives. It was the instrument that swayed and directed them,' he said. Marianoff's marriage to Margot was as much a failure as Elsa's to Löwenthal, and one reason was that Margot never cut free from her family.

Many descriptions present Elsa as little better than an amiable simpleton, but this is unfair. For one thing, she was not always amiable. When crossed, she could be a fierce and determined antagonist, and she proved an aggressive defender of her second husband's privacy. In addition, despite a total ignorance of science, she was not without intellectual pretensions. Her library was well-stocked with German and European literature, and in 1913 and 1914 she participated in public poetry readings, reciting work by Heinrich Heine, among others. Although one review remarked unfavourably on her dramatic range, it also conceded that she earned great applause from her audience. Elsa gave elocution lessons to help pay for her children's education, and was a talented mimic. However limited her vision, both mental and ocular, she possessed sensitivity and wit.

It remains true that her main interests were domestic. Elsa enjoyed taking care of people: cooking for them, fussing over them, making them feel at home. She enjoyed instilling the Swabian *Gemütlichkeit* that both she and her cousin had enjoyed as children, with its snug material comforts and unsophisticated warmth. For Einstein, these attractions were irresistible. The bourgeois south-German certainties that he had found so 'philistine' as a love-struck young rebel now promised a place of refuge.

Contact was resumed when he visited Berlin in the last week of Easter 1912. His ostensible purpose was to talk shop with fellow scientists, but much of his free time was spent with Elsa and her family. Mutual affection between the couple appears to have rekindled almost instantly, and it is clear that Einstein spoke at length about his unhappiness at home. Elsa was a sympathetic audience, and took little convincing that Mileva was the villain of the piece. Einstein felt at ease with her: he even liked it when she laughed at him, in her 'delightful way'. Together they made an outing to the Wannsee area on the south-west edge of Berlin, where the river Havel forms a series of hauntingly beautiful lakes. The surrounding woodland of oak, birch and pine is dotted with castles and romantic retreats, and has long been a favourite haunt for lovers. Einstein wrote of his 'blissful' memories from the trip, and the landscape's quiet, melancholy charm became special to him. 'I grew very fond of you during those few days – I can hardly say it,' he wrote to Elsa a week after returning to Prague.

It has to be said that Elsa was not the only one of Einstein's female relatives to catch his eye. It appears that, either during this trip or some time earlier, he had also flirted with her younger sister, Paula. In his letter, he took the opportunity to reassure Elsa that she alone was the object of his desire and that her sister had only irritated him. 'I cannot understand how I could have ever liked her. In reality, it is very simple. She was young, a girl, and welcoming. That was enough. What remains is a pleasant fantasy.'

Elsa was to have further experience of her cousin's wandering gaze, but for the moment this was enough to satisfy her. Einstein's letter, in reply to one that she dispatched soon after his departure from Berlin, was the start of a secret correspondence that spanned almost two years. Anxious to evade Mileva's suspicions, Elsa wrote to his place of work rather than his home and made him promise to destroy all her letters. However, she carefully preserved his replies. Tied with a ribbon, the earliest carried a cover note calling them 'especially beautiful letters from the best years'. Their existence clearly became known to Marianoff, who wrote, 'His letters to her, if ever published, will take their place among the love letters of the world.' Copies eventually reached the Einstein papers project, and they have now been published by Princeton University Press.

Einstein's first message, on 30 April 1912, was a nervous declaration of love for his cousin. It began on the subject of his mother. He had discovered that Pauline was thinking of moving back to Berlin, acting as housekeeper for her brother Jacob and sister-in-law Julie Koch. This was the same Aunt Julie whom Einstein had once described as a 'veritable monster of arrogance', and he could now forsee 'very fatal' consequences if she were to become his mother's employer. 'It is dangerous to be so completely dependent upon one's relatives,' he told Elsa.

His cousin shared an insider's perspective on the family tensions that Einstein found so oppressive. Living above one's parents is not an easy situation, and Einstein observed that Elsa was 'closely watched'.

She also shared his ambivalence towards his mother, with whom there had been ample opportunity for friction while Pauline was staying with Rudolph and Fanny. It was to this fund of sympathy that Einstein now appealed as he discussed his discovery of his mother's plans:

> Naturally, I do not tell my mother about the bad things I learned. It would bring her nothing but depressing shame, and one does not change for the better at her age. I suffered terribly in the past because I was quite unable to love her. If I look at the bad relationship between my wife and Maja or my mother, so I must say with regret that all three of them seem to me very unsympathetic, unfortunately! But I must love somebody or it is a wretched existence. And this 'somebody' is you; there is nothing that you can do about it. I do not ask your permission. I reign supremely in the shadow-realm of my imagination, or at least I imagine it so.

Einstein ended this remarkable letter by bridling at a suggestion from Elsa that he was under Mileva's thumb. Having poured out his resentment against his wife's nagging, it seems that he nevertheless found it a little unnerving to see the picture reflected so clearly. He admitted having the appearance of a hen-pecked husband, but insisted that he only gave way to Mileva 'out of pity'. He told Elsa, 'I assure you with conviction that I think of myself as a completely worthy member of the opposite sex. Perhaps there will be an opportunity to convince you of this some time.'

The prospect of an affair with Elsa both excited Einstein and appalled him. Having announced his love for her so forcibly, he wrote again a week later to draw back from what he had proposed:

> I cannot tell you how sorry I feel for you and how much I wish I could be someone for you. But there would only be confusion and misfortune if we were to give in to our mutual attraction. You know this only too well. But you must never think of me as a disappointment. I like you and have shown it to you honestly. Do not put me in the same drawer as my mother, I implore you.

Einstein's concern about Elsa's opinion of him was very strong –

his final paragraph opened with the words 'Think of me with fond memories and not with bitterness.' Again, however, the tone was of a man dictating affection on his own terms.

Einstein placed great stress on how much he was suffering – 'much more than you', he assured Elsa. Both lacked a sympathetic partner, he implied, but only he was still encumbered by an unpleasant one. In an apparent reference to his mounting sexual frustration, he described the pain of being 'unable to love, really to love' a woman whom he was only allowed to look at on occasional visits. He wrote of having to fight again and again to avoid falling victim to bitter moods. Nevertheless, he would 'capitulate to the unavoidable in order to prevent something more disagreeable'.

A fortnight later, Einstein steeled himself to announce that he was writing to Elsa for the last time. He urged her to take the same decision on her own side, warning, 'I have the feeling that nothing good will come of it, not for the two of us and not for others if we were to get close to each other.' He was still anxious for her good opinions, and added, 'You know that when I speak like this, I am not hard or lack feeling, but do it because I carry my cross without hope, like you.' This was not the last time that he would refer to Mileva as the cross he had to bear, Christ-like, along the road of self-sacrifice. But the disingenuousness of his words – or perhaps the depth of his self-deception – was clear at the close. Einstein urged Elsa to remember that she had 'a cousin who has a heart for you' and in whom she could always confide. And to facilitate such confidences, he promised to send her a new address at which she could continue to contact him.

As this suggests, Einstein and Mileva were on the move once again. His growing prestige had meant that attempts to woo him from Prague started almost as soon as he arrived. Overtures from the University of Utrecht were made in August 1911, soon followed by others from Berlin, Vienna and Leiden. One reason for Einstein's trip to Berlin at Easter 1912 had been to investigate a possible research appointment there. An offer was made but he declined it, underlining that there were limits to his desire to be at Elsa's side. Conscience alone should have dictated his decision, however, since he had already committed himself elsewhere. On 30 January – two and a half months before his visit to Berlin – he had been appointed on a ten-year contract as professor of theoretical physics at the Swiss Federal Poly-technical School, to start that October.

Negotiations for the appointment had begun the previous September, when his friend Heinrich Zangger – acting as middle-man for his Zurich colleagues – visited Einstein in Prague. He was also urged to return by Marcel Grossmann, now head of the Polytechnic's mathematics and physics section. There was a nice irony for Einstein in being courted by the Alma Mater that had rejected him as a graduate: he would even be able to improve the out-dated syllabus he had once found so frustrating. 'Hallelujah!' he wrote to his friend Alfred Stern after receiving confirmation of the appointment, which he added had brought great joy to all the household – 'we old people and both little bears'.

Einstein joked that he felt like a homing pigeon flying back to its loft, but according to Philipp Frank – who succeeded him at Prague – he secretly had reservations about stepping back into his past. This is borne out by his persistence in considering other options such as Berlin, long after the matter was supposedly sealed. Frank believed he allowed himself to be swayed towards Zurich by Mileva, who yearned for her adopted city. She told Besso that she could hardly feel homesick for Prague after such mixed experiences there, and would have been very reluctant to settle in another strange city. If Frank is right, this must have been one of the last times her husband ever deferred to her, but it is not impossible. Einstein was a great ditherer when faced with practical choices, and liked where possible to leave them to others. This was reflected in his desperate attempts to juggle the competing offers. He felt particularly guilty at letting down his friend and idol Lorentz, who backed the invitation from Utrecht and then raised the suggestion that Einstein succeed him at Leiden. After rejecting the first offer, Einstein wrote to him, 'with a heavy heart, as one who has done a kind of injustice to his father'.

The Einsteins returned to Zurich in August 1912, moving into an apartment at Hofstrasse 116. Hans Albert suggested that his father mark the event by parading through the streets in his ceremonial Prague uniform. According to Philipp Frank, he agreed, smiling, 'At worst people will think I'm a Brazilian admiral.' There was every reason for him to be in good humour as he returned in triumph to the city of his student courtship. And if ever there was a possibility of his marriage rekindling its lost spark, it was in these benign surroundings. Hans Albert recalled that his father seemed light-hearted and full of energy during this period, whistling happily as he went around the house. He liked to play with the children when he returned from the Polytechnic in late afternoon, and so long as his work went uninterrupted he was 'a riot'. However, this work was now testing Einstein more than ever before. He later told Elsa that during the winter months of 1912–13 he worked harder than at any other time in his life. As he wrote to his cousin, his subject was 'an heroic continuation of the relativity theory together with a gravitation theory'.

In 1908, Einstein's former teacher Hermann Minkowski had repackaged relativity in a neater mathematical form that dealt with space and time as an inseparable whole, called 'space-time'. The next step was to find a new language to describe this four-dimensional landscape. Einstein turned for guidance to the same friend whose lecture notes he had cribbed years before as a student. 'Grossmann, you must help me, or else I'll go crazy,' he said, immediately after returning to Zurich. Marcel Grossmann acted as his machete-wielding guide through the jungles of non-Euclidean geometry. This is dense and forbidding territory where space is curved so that parallel lines do not exist and the three angles of a triangle do not add up to 180 degrees. It was not uncharted, however. Much of the pioneering work was nearly a century old by the time Einstein showed an interest, thanks to the efforts of pure mathematicians who were interested in abstract spaces of arbitrary dimension and curvature. Now Einstein was to endow their work with profound physical significance.

To extend his special theory to deal with gravity, Einstein needed a mathematical tool that would allow him to deal with this exotic geometry. In 1913, he and Grossmann published a paper in which they began this programme, using what is called tensor calculus. Einstein's 1913 paper was marred by what they later saw as conceptual flaws, but came tantalizingly close to the finished theory of general relativity that he presented three years later. He was gaining a new respect for mathematics, and had never found science more difficult. 'Compared with this problem, the original relativity is child's play,' he wrote at the start of his labours with Grossmann.

The intensity of this work seems to have left Einstein with less energy than ever to devote to his marriage. Moreover, his collaboration with Grossmann was another unpleasant reminder to Mileva of her displacement as his scientific aide. Such spare time as Einstein enjoyed, he rarely spent alone with her. Hans Albert remembered his father lazing in bed on his own in the mornings, and in the evenings plunging himself back into a busy round of music-making. His most frequent host was Adolf Hurwitz, professor of mathematics at the Polytechnic, with whom he would play Handel, Corelli and Schumann (Mileva's favourite). Einstein would take his family round to the Hurwitz home on Sunday afternoons, arriving on the doorstep with the sardonic greeting, 'Here comes the whole Einstein hen house.'

Hurwitz's daughter Lisbeth, who became a lasting friend of Mileva, noticed that Einstein's wife was often silent and gloomy. She was suffering rheumatic pains in her legs that made walking difficult, and during the icy winter she would arrive at the Hurwitz house looking scared and clinging tight to her husband for support. Mileva hoped for better health as the days grew warmer, and she spoke of visiting a therapeutic mud-bath come summer. But a reference to 'my big Albert' in a letter dated 12 March 1913 suggests that her problems were not confined to poor health. 'Albert has devoted himself completely to physics and it seems that he has little time if any for the family,' Mileva told Helene Savić. It was as if he lived for his physics problems alone, she said.

Two days after this letter was written, Lisbeth Hurwitz noted in her diary that Einstein had excused himself from their usual music evening with a vague reference to 'family matters'. The following day Lisbeth and her mother visited Mileva and found her face badly swollen. It seems that Lisbeth may have been suggesting that Mileva had been beaten. Einstein was a powerful man and, for what it is worth, Hans Albert recalled that when he misbehaved his father 'beat me up'. An innocent explanation presents itself in a note Einstein sent on the day of Lisbeth's visit, answering an invitation to visit his friend Professor Alfred Stern. He explained that he was writing in Mileva's stead since she was 'somewhat ill' through toothache. Of course, this may simply have been a convenient lie: the marriage seems to have decayed so badly, and Einstein seems to have had so much difficulty in understanding his emotions, that the more unpleasant explanation remains plausible. It is known that Einstein's divorce papers – which remain under seal in Jerusalem – refer to violence within the marriage.

The implications of Lisbeth's report are particularly striking when one remembers the date on which Lisbeth visited Mileva: 14 March 1913 was Einstein's thirty-fourth birthday. It also happens to be the day to which one can trace the resumption of his correspondence with Elsa. She had made the first move, apparently by sending him birthday greetings, and it may be that these had come to Mileva's attention and provoked an unpleasant scene.

As if to ensure that Einstein responded, Elsa had asked him to recommend a book on relativity for the layman, and to send her a photograph of himself. Einstein held back from promising to visit her in Berlin – pleading pressure of work – but pronounced himself touched that she had thought of him. 'If your ways ever lead to Zurich we will take a beautiful walk (without my unfortunately so-jealous wife),' he promised. Another letter, nine days later, pressed Elsa with renewed force to visit him in Switzerland. Once again there was a disparaging reference to Mileva. 'I would give something if I could spend a few days with you but without . . . my cross,' he wrote. Einstein was exhausted by what he described to Ehrenfest as his 'literally superhuman efforts' on general relativity and told Elsa, 'Now I must have a little peace otherwise I will rapidly go to pieces.'

The world was reluctant to leave Einstein be, and in July 1913 he became the target of another academic poaching expedition. Max Planck and Walther Nernst descended on Zurich, with wives in tow, to offer him a job in Berlin. He would become a member of the grand Prussian Academy of Sciences, would take a chair at Berlin University, and would become director of the yet to be established Kaiser Wilhelm Institute for Physics. All this would be accompanied by a specially generous salary and complete freedom to devote his time to research, with no teaching. It was an extraordinarily sumptuous deal for a man so young, but Einstein asked for time to think. He promised that he would give his decision when the visitors returned from an outing to see the local sights. Ever the showman, he added that he would signal assent by waving a white cloth when they met again at Zurich railway station. The little drama was acted out, and the Germans returned home triumphant.

Einstein had good reasons to surrender. Berlin was a physics powerhouse, where he could work alongside scientists of world stature. In addition, he was eager to escape the burden of teaching: that summer in Zurich he had five hours of lectures to give each week, a two-hour seminar and duties as a student supervisor. He told Lorentz that he could not resist 'the temptation to accept a position which frees me of all obligations so that I can devote myself freely to thinking'. To Ehrenfest he described the new post as 'this odd sinecure', saying that he accepted it, 'because it got on my nerves to give courses'. His only apparent reservation was a slight uncertainty that he could live up to expectations. The Germans were treating him like a prize hen, he told another friend, but he was not sure 'whether I shall ever really lay another egg'.

There were other reasons for Einstein's nervousness. He had a profound detestation of much that he felt Germany to stand for: authoritarianism, conformity, intellectual and spiritual rigidity. That was why he had been so glad to abandon his schooling in Munich and follow his family to Italy. That was one reason why he had given up German nationality while still a teenager. Now he was proposing to return, not merely to Germany, but to the very capital of all things Prussian. He was surrendering to the forces from which he had once fled – and, not coincidentally, moving back into the ambit of his family.

When Philipp Frank published his biography of Einstein in 1948, it is almost certain that he knew nothing of the correspondence with Elsa. Nevertheless, he showed no doubt that her presence sweetened the pill of Einstein's return to Germany. Frank wrote, 'Einstein remembered that his cousin Elsa as a young girl had often been in Munich and had impressed him as a friendly, happy person. The prospect of being able to enjoy the pleasant company of this cousin in Berlin made him think of the Prussian capital more favourably.' These words troubled Einstein's more recent biographer, Ronald Clark. He was ready to accept that the source of the information was Einstein himself, but not that his subject had sufficient guile to be planning a new liaison before his first marriage had ended. Frank's account also conflicts with the assumption made by the majority of biographers that Einstein was guided in all his actions by science alone. But it is supported by a letter that Einstein sent to Zangger in 1915, referring to 'the loving care of a female cousin who in fact drew me to Berlin'.

Like so many of Einstein's comments, this must be read with caution. It was written at a time when Einstein wanted to win Zangger's sympathy for Elsa, and to stress the depth of his affection for her, in order to excuse his behaviour towards Mileva. To assume that Elsa's presence was the main reason for his move to Berlin would be as wrong as to think that she played no part. What Elsa provided, with her promise of love and sympathy, was a countervailing force to those aspects of Berlin that Einstein found repellent. Thanks to her, he would return to an environment where the oppressive and the comforting were in uneasy balance. In that respect, it would be a real homecoming.

Within days of receiving the offer, he dispatched three excited letters to Elsa celebrating their impending reunion. Einstein stressed the 'colossal honour' that the appointment represented, and the scientific freedom it would give him. But his main theme was 'the beautiful times' the couple would now spend together. 'I am not required to read lectures there but am completely free to do what I want to do,' he told her. 'And one of the main things that I want to do is to see you often, to run around with you and to chat with you.'

Unsurprisingly, his enthusiasm for Berlin was not shared by Mileva. Quite apart from a natural reluctance to leave her beloved Zurich once again, and to subject the lives of her children to renewed disruption, she had few illusions about the prejudice Slavs encountered in Germany, and fewer still about the hostility she would face from her in-laws. Einstein showed scant sympathy, and even some sign of enjoying her distress. That August he wrote to Elsa that, 'My wife goes there with very mixed feelings because she is afraid of the relatives, probably most afraid of you (with good reason, hopefully). But you can enjoy yourself with me without the need of hurting her. Something which she does not possess, you will not be able to take.'

Although at first he wrote of moving that autumn, Einstein then told Elsa that he could not bring himself to leave the Polytechnic so abruptly. He decided instead to stay in Zurich until the spring of 1914. This teased out the agony for Mileva, but allowed him time to gather his strength for the challenges ahead. In August 1913 the couple took a long-discussed walking holiday through the mountains of eastern Switzerland, crossing the Maloja pass down to Lake Como in Italy. It was a route filled with sad echoes of their romantic journey twelve years earlier, north from the same lake across the Splügen pass, when Lieserl was conceived. This time, however, they were not alone. Besides Hans Albert, the party included Marie Curie and her two daughters, Irene and Eve.

Plans for the joint holiday had been made that March, when Einstein and Mileva had briefly stayed with Curie while he delivered a lecture in Paris. The couple were dazzled by the sophisticated French capital – even for Einstein, such visits remained a novelty – and felt indebted to their hostess for guiding them through a hectic tour. As Ronald Clark has suggested, their thank-you notes reflect the social embarrassment of two innocents abroad. Einstein begged Curie's forgiveness in case his 'rough ways' had caused her any embarrassment, while Mileva apologized for bungling her goodbyes. 'Our parting occurred so quickly the other evening, that I was not able properly to take my leave of you before I found we were sitting alone in the train,' she wrote. The invitation to Switzerland expressed the couple's gratitude for Curie's kindness, with Mileva hoping that Irene would prove a congenial playmate for Hans Albert.

Eduard was ill when the day of departure arrived, forcing Mileva to stay behind until he was well enough to be left with friends. Her temporary absence did nothing to mar Einstein's pleasure, since it was Curie's company alone that interested him. Hans Albert recalled his father musing with her on the deep wells left by Ice Age glaciers, and Curie challenging him to name all the peaks on the horizon. Eve Curie recalled the youngsters running on ahead as the two scientists chatted, then laughing when Einstein stopped and seized her mother's arm, exclaiming that he wanted to know what happened to passengers in a falling lift. He was, as ever, thinking about the problem of gravitation.

There is no doubting the mutual respect between Curie and Einstein. It was partly thanks to her personal reference – praising 'the clearness of his mind, the shrewdness with which he marshalled his facts and the depth of his knowledge' – that he had won his professorship in Zurich. Later he would look back on a 'sublime and unclouded' relationship with her, spanning twenty years. But these words, written after Curie's death in 1934, obscured an ambivalence in his feelings.

Einstein praised in Curie exactly those uncompromising qualities that others have seen as defining his own greatness: 'Her strength, her purity of will, her austerity towards herself, her objectivity, her incorruptible judgment . . . an abiding sense for the asperities and inequalities of society'. But he admitted that these same virtues gave her a 'severe outward aspect' that was 'easily misinterpreted by those who were not close to her'. Even her intimates, he implied, were unnerved by her 'curious severity'. Writing to Elsa, immediately after his walking holiday, he was considerably more blunt. 'Madame Curie is very intelligent but has the soul of a herring, which means that she is poor when it comes to the art of joy and pain,' he told his cousin. Her main expression of feeling was grumbling, he added, and her daughter Irene was 'even worse – like a grenadier'.

This little outburst seems partly designed to reassure Elsa that his sympathies remained with her – despite prolonged exposure to another woman – and follows a promise that he would have missed 'all the holidays in the world' to be with her instead. In that respect, it recalls his similar snide remarks, for Mileva's benefit, on Besso and Laub. But there was definitely something about Curie that repelled him, even as he warmed to her intellectually. He referred to it again, some years after his marriage to Elsa, in one of the most revealing conversations he ever had.

This was with Esther Salaman, a young Jewish woman who came under his spell while studying in Berlin, and who once glumly suggested to him that she lacked the creativity for theoretical physics. In a voice that always felt to Salaman as if it came from a long way off, Einstein replied, 'Very few women are creative. I should not have sent a daughter of mine to study physics. I'm glad my wife doesn't know any science; my first wife did.' Surely, responded Salaman, Marie

Curie was creative. 'We spent some holidays with the Curies,' said Einstein. 'Madame Curie never heard the birds sing.'

It is striking that this condemnation of Curie's emotional blinkers sat beside an emphatic restatement of Einstein's similarly restricted vision. 'I'm not much with people, and I'm not a family man,' he told Salaman. 'I want my peace. I want to know how God created the world.' Having attacked indifference to birdsong, Einstein was boasting of his own indifference to humanity. Salaman sensed that the calm certainty of his self-description was deceptive. When he spoke to her, as patiently as if he were talking to a child, she caught a glimmer of a man drawn towards emotional engagement but deeply nervous of it. 'His voice was a protection of his inner self rather than an expression of it,' she remembered. 'He felt kindly towards people, but not intimate with them, not even sure of them.'

Einstein had discovered in Curie a woman with an emotional austerity matching that which he affected himself, and he did not like it. His words to Salaman implied that science could never be a proper pursuit for women. The majority were doomed to frustrating failure, while those that succeeded did so at the cost of everything in them that was charming. This makes his bitter reference to the scientific background of 'my first wife' especially intriguing. It has been cited by one biographer as evidence that Mileva was 'mentally importunate', weighing down her husband with demands to share in his work. But the context suggests something more: that Einstein believed it almost inevitable for science to turn women sour.

A sham of unity still survived in September 1913, as the Einsteins took their children to visit Mileva's parents near Novi Sad. Hans Albert retained vivid memories of this stay, which was not to be repeated. The rural calm of the Marić summer home – patrolled by cats and chickens, and backing on to a garden full of fruit and vegetables – deeply impressed him. When a thunderstorm shattered the intense heat, and local children waded happily in the overflowing gutters, he longed to join them but was forbidden from doing so, much to his chagrin, in case it aggravated an ear infection from which he was suffering. But this visit was memorable for another reason. On the Sunday that their parents were due to leave for Vienna, where

Einstein was delivering a lecture, Hans Albert and Eduard were baptized as Orthodox Christians.

The elder boy never forgot the beautiful singing in church, just as the priest in charge never forgot how three-year-old Eduard did his best to disrupt proceedings by running around in excitement. It remains unclear whether Einstein was present at the ceremony, gave his permission for it, or even knew that it was taking place. Indeed, until the discovery of a locally postmarked letter, relaying his movements to Zangger, it had been assumed that Mileva and her sons had gone to Novi Sad without him. They returned to Zurich separately, and his only recorded comment on the baptism was to say it was a matter of indifference to him, but had made his in-laws happy. Mileva was as sceptical of her own religious traditions as her husband was of his, but, as the marriage fell apart, she was binding the children to her side of the family.

After his lecture in Vienna on 23 September, Einstein set off alone to visit 'a few relatives in Germany', as he put it in his letter to Zangger. This trip included Heilbronn, Ulm and Berlin, where he had a chance to see Elsa. He had been promising her this rendezvous since spring, assuring her that they would 'give each other a lot of pleasure'. His first letter afterwards suggested a man transformed.

> I am back in Zurich now, but I am not the same as before. I now have someone of whom I can think with untroubled delight and whom I can live for. Even if I had not felt that way already, your letter which awaited me here would have told me so. Both of us will have each other, something we were missing so badly, and give each other equilibrium and a happy outlook on the world.

Einstein now referred to Elsa's offspring as 'my stepchildren', anticipating events in the same jocular way in which he had described Pauline Einstein as 'the mother-in-law' during his courtship of Mileva. Equally reminiscent was his letter's disorderly high-spirits, and his apologies for its lack of coherence. 'Excuse the salad which I put before you,' he wrote, 'but you are now my comrade and all is dished up by me warts and all.'

During their days together in Berlin, Elsa had showered her cousin with all the motherly love at her disposal. Both took a particular delight in his greedy consumption of her home cooking, which became a recurring theme in their correspondence. 'What gave me most pleasure in your letter was your confession that you enjoyed cooking the mushrooms for me and still remember it fondly,' he wrote in mid-October. 'How much I like this and how gratefully I accept it from you!' Elsa posted him packets of goose scratchings – tasty morsels of crackling – and he assured her that this moved him far more than any beautiful poem she might care to recite for him. 'I know what the psychologists would make of that but I am not ashamed,' he declared. Too much high-mindedness was depressing, and he was sure that Elsa would not despise 'the primitive part of the character' such tastes revealed.

Equally motherly were Elsa's attempts to improve his personal hygiene. During his stay she gave him a hairbrush, which he referred to as 'the bristly girlfriend', and instructions to pay more attention to his appearance. Like a proud child mastering a new challenge, he subsequently issued frequent bulletins on his progress. 'Hairbrush is used regularly, also remaining ablutions are being carried out rigorously,' he assured her in November. Once again there was an echo of his student days with Mileva, to whom he had reported his triumphs at shaving in much the same manner. Elsa's concern for him, and the affectionate nagging that embodied it, were initially gratifying. He pronounced himself happy to submit to her 'amiable mastery' in all things, even declaring in one letter that it did him good to be told off. Otherwise, he said, it would seem that everyone regarded him 'as a saint and a shell-less egg, neither of which I am, thank God'.

However, there were signs that Einstein would soon find Elsa's attentions as suffocating as those of either Mileva or his mother. Even before his stay with her, he had jibbed at his cousin's homilies on healthy living. He declared that he intended to die with the minimum of medical help, having sinned 'just as my wicked soul desires' with a diet of smoking, hard work and indiscriminate eating. He would go walking only if there was pleasant company ('therefore seldom, unfortunately') and sleep only when he felt like it. As for personal grooming, there were limits to his patience. Although ready to comb his hair (or at least to pretend he was doing so), he drew the line at brushing his teeth, citing 'scientific considerations'. Pig bristles could drill through diamonds, he said, so how could his teeth withstand them? By the end of the year, he was telling Elsa that he did not feel true to himself in all this titivation. It was the first step towards 'Berlinering' – his own word for the process of becoming a stuffed-shirt German of the kind he most detested.

Berliners seemed to him the epitome of philistinism. In one virulent passage, he wrote to Elsa, 'What a contrast when these people meet the English and the French. How crude and rough they are. Vanity without genuine self-reliance. Civilization (beautifully cleaned teeth, elegant tie, well-ironed tailcoat, immaculate suit) but no personal culture ('rough in speech, movements, voice, feelings'). Einstein made clear to Elsa that he would resist all attempts to be poured into this mould. 'If I appear to be so unappetizing then find yourself a friend who is more to your female taste,' he warned her grimly, signing off 'with a powerful swear word' as 'your honest, dirty Albert'. This letter and the following one featured pointed jokes about kissing her hand from a 'disinfecting and sterilizing distance'. He called himself 'the incorrigible dung finch'.

Einstein told Elsa that his slovenly manners were a useful way of discouraging fools who might otherwise disturb his peace. Just as he had done with Mileva, he held out to his cousin the suggestion that she alone was a free spirit worthy to share his world. 'How nice it would be if the two of us could live together in a little gypsy house-hold,' he wrote in one letter. This echo of his student 'household' with Mileva carries with it the old yearning to combine domestic comforts and bohemian freedoms. Of course, there could be no pretence here of a shared scientific mission. The best Einstein could manage was a half-hearted attempt to equate his studies with Elsa's literary recitals. In this respect they were both 'travelling folk . . . chosen from the swarm of philistines to dance on the tight-rope'. While he rode his physics hobby-horses, he suggested, she could 'sit proudly on the little horse of the poets'.

This was an impossible pose to maintain. Not only was Einstein basically uninterested in Elsa's recitals, he distrusted her pleasure in public performance. He warned her against 'insatiable and painful ambition', and nagged her to find a more worthwhile occupation, such as charity work. The fact remains that he attempted – however fleetingly – to dignify their relationship with the language of like-minded intellectuals standing apart from everyday life. If this gloss was spurious with Elsa, there may be renewed grounds to suspect it had been a little bogus with Mileva. What Einstein most often admitted to wanting from his cousin was a simple sympathy – 'somebody with whom I can chat in a human fashion and to whom I can mean something personally'. Given such love, he told her, 'I cease to belong to the "disinherited" '.

As Elsa entered more deeply into Einstein's life, her strained relations with his mother became increasingly troublesome. He called their quarrel 'the dangerous adventure' and was greatly relieved when his cousin took steps to end it. She persuaded him to take a peace offering of sweets when he visited his mother on the way home from Berlin. He reported the recipient to be full of remorse and equally eager to make friends, even suggesting that she was encouraging their romance. 'My mother consoled me, saying that I will soon be near you, without my prompting her about it in any way,' he told Elsa. The truth was that an underlying antipathy remained between the women, and Einstein's letters suggest that this suited him. His advice to Elsa was to treat his mother with all possible reserve, and strictly avoid confiding in her. He wrote that his mother deserved 'the slightly unpleasant situation' of having to accept Elsa's forgiveness.

Mileva did not ask Einstein about his cousin when he returned to Zurich. He thought that he could detect a glimmer of suspicion – perhaps at the way his personal appearance had started to improve – although this may have indicated only his own feelings of guilt. He told Elsa that 'she does not underestimate the importance that you have for me'. But it is still unclear, at this stage, to what degree Mileva regarded Elsa as a special threat distinct from her in-laws in general. 'She is now thinking day and night how she can protect herself from your persecutions,' Einstein told Elsa at the end of the year. But there is no evidence that Mileva believed her husband was about to be stolen from her, battered though their marriage was. Einstein described the 'icy silence' between them as 'more loathsome than ever', but had no plans to leave her. Instead he intended to pursue his affair while remaining her husband, and even then had no intention of flouting marital convention too openly. He remarked to Elsa how agreeable it would be to take her, rather than Mileva, on a lecture trip to France he planned for 1914. 'But the order is always to pretend,' he said. 'Only when we are born and when we die are we permitted to act in an honest way.'

Elsa had taken his talk of forming a gypsy household rather more literally. But when she pressed him to show his hand, at the start of December 1913, Einstein's reply was uncompromising. 'Do you believe it is easy to get divorced if one has no evidence of the fault of the other person?' he asked. He added that there was nothing that could convince a court of law that his marriage had broken down – even though he suggested that this was only due to Mileva's cunning. He told Elsa that he treated his wife as an employee, had his own bedroom, and avoided being alone with her. 'I can quite well stand this form of "living together",' he said. 'I fail to understand why you are so terribly offended by it.'

One suspects that he understood full well. His subsequent letters attacked Mileva with renewed vehemence, as if to prove to Elsa where his loyalties lay. He described his wife as 'an unfriendly, humourless creature who herself has nothing from life and who undermines others' joy of living through her mere presence'. She was 'the sourest sourpot there has ever been', a plagued individual who gave their home the atmosphere of a cemetery. By nature 'unpleasant and mistrustful', she felt persecuted if given the same treatment in return. Einstein said that he shuddered even to think of seeing Mileva and Elsa in the same room.

Yet running through these attacks was a grudging recognition of the reasons for Mileva's despair. 'Up till now she had, so to speak, nothing whatever to do with other people – all except poor me!' Now Mileva was faced with a life surrounded by the Einstein family, and her husband admitted this was not an entirely pleasant prospect. In December 1913, as the move drew nearer, he wrote:

My wife howls unceasingly about Berlin and her fear of my relatives. She feels persecuted and fears that her last quiet minute arrives at the end of March. Well, there is some truth in it. My mother is of a good disposition, on the whole, but a true devil as mother-in-law. When she is with us then everything is filled with dynamite.

For some time, Mileva and his mother had tiptoed around each other's sensibilities in what Einstein described as 'an egg-shell dance, not really graceful but comical'. Now there was open warfare once more, because his mother had bypassed Mileva and sent Christmas presents to the children via his sister Maja. Tears were shed, the games were returned, and Mileva declared that neither she nor the children would have anything to do with her mother-in-law again. Nor did they, it seems. Einstein remarked laconically that he would be beside himself over the affair, if only he could be bothered.

Nevertheless, he agreed with his wife's decision, and commented to Elsa that his mother was 'very perfidious in her hatred'. He added:

No wonder that under such circumstances love flourishes towards science, which raises me up from the valley of tears into the quiet atmosphere, impersonal and without swearing and yammering. But I hope that you will fetch me down a little, even if not with the curry-comb and toothbrush, if I may ask you so, but with a friendly glance and cosy chatter.

As the move to Berlin neared, and his life became ever more fraught, Einstein applied himself to science with renewed intensity. His letters to Elsa during the first two months of 1914 were brief and apologetic. He was busy with 'really big things', working hard on an extension of his theory of gravitation in the face of tough criticisms from the likes of Planck and von Laue. 'I think seriously day and night about the deepening of things which I have found out gradually during the last two years and which mean an incredible advance in fundamental problems of physics,' he said. After such weighty work he did not feel in the mood for loving chatter, 'in the same way someone can't play the violin if he has just been working with a large hammer.' But he promised Elsa that he still looked forward to their reunion, and the chance to set down the burden of physics and walk with her again through the Berlin woods. He dreamed of recapturing not only their trip to the Wannsee two years earlier, but the idealized delights of their childhood. 'We will revive all our memories from our earliest days and forget everything evil which happened in between.'

It was Mileva who travelled to Berlin after Christmas to arrange the family's new accommodation. Einstein remarked how enjoyable he found her absence, joking that this proved his marriage could still bring him pleasure. However, he had been dreading what new collisions might occur between his wife and his family, and suggested that she avoided all contact with them. 'The less personal friction the better,' he told Elsa. In the event, the visit passed off without undue incident.

Mileva stayed with Fritz Haber, one of the leading scientists in Berlin and director of the Kaiser Wilhelm Institute of Physical Chemistry and Electrochemistry. Haber was a small, dapper man with a great dome of a bald head and an enormous pince-nez. He was painfully short-sighted, like Elsa, and once caused great merriment on a visit to Einstein by pouring tea into the sugar bowl and preparing to drink it. Haber was a Jew who, unlike Einstein, went out of his way to conform to the conventions of German society. He combined an outward arrogance with a rather less obvious tenderness of heart, and was another of those who were to help Einstein during his divorce. He had begun to correspond with Einstein on scientific matters while the latter was in Prague, and had been instrumental in bringing him to Berlin. He now helped Mileva to find a suitable flat, and became very fond of her.

On her return, Einstein reported that Mileva suspected 'a certain danger' in Elsa, who somewhat disingenuously had offered to help her in the home-hunting. However, Einstein said that he now refused to discuss his relatives with his wife at all. They both left Zurich in late March, although they did not travel to Germany together. Einstein set off to visit his uncle Caesar Koch in Antwerp, followed by Ehrenfest and Lorentz in Leiden. Mileva took the children for a holiday at Locarno, on doctor's orders so that Eduard could recover from a fresh crop of illnesses. The boy had managed simultaneous attacks of flu, whooping cough and inflammation of the middle ear. This had its good side, Einstein coolly observed, since it delayed his wife's arrival in Berlin, leaving him alone with Elsa. As the day of their reunion approached, he excitedly told Elsa that they would have fourteen days together: 'Hallelujah . . . I will come alive anew.' Early in April he wrote to Ehrenfest, 'It is pleasant here in Berlin . . . my relations here give me great joy, especially a female cousin of my age to whom I am attached by a long friendship.'

After Mileva arrived in mid-April, the couple at first kept up some semblance of normal married life. Normal, that is, by Einstein's standards. On one occasion, friends arrived for dinner to find only Mileva at home. Her husband's whereabouts remained a mystery until eventually the telephone rang: he had been waiting for over an hour at the Dahlem underground station, mistakenly believing that he had arranged to meet his guests there. Einstein's spirits were high. 'Life here is better than I anticipated,' he wrote to Professor Hurwitz at the start of May. He was having to observe 'a certain discipline . . . as regards clothes etc.', in order not to upset his straight-laced colleagues. But on the whole, he noted with evident surprise, the Germans were 'quite human'.

This was not Mileva's opinion. Ehrenfest, who spent a week with the couple in May, found her unhappy and already pining for Switzerland. The terrors of Berlin had evidently lived up to her worst imaginings, and her misery communicated itself to her elder son. 'Mileva went about her housekeeping gloomily,' wrote Hans Albert's interviewer Peter Michelmore. 'She did not have any friends in Berlin. She hated the city at first sight.' Hans Albert shared her unhappiness, despite the avuncular attentions of Ehrenfest, who took him to the zoo and for walks in the park. The boy chafed against the discipline and rote-learning at his new school, in a manner reminiscent of his father.

In the summer of 1914, when the school term ended, Mileva took her sons back to Zurich. Hans Albert believed they were going for a holiday and would return to Germany in September. In fact, it was the beginning of the end of his parents' marriage. Mileva never returned to her husband's side.

In later life, Hans Albert was at a loss to explain what had happened. He recognized the changes that had taken place in his parents' relationship, particularly the extinguishing of all Mileva's scientific ambitions. However, he dismissed the suggestion that this was the reason why the couple had parted. In his own words,

Why the separation came is something that was never quite clear to me. Trying to reconstruct it all afterwards, particularly from some of his own utterances, it seems that he had the impression that the family was taking a bit too much of his time, and that he had the duty to concentrate completely on his work. Personally, I do not believe that he ever achieved that, because in the family he actually had more time than when he had to look after himself and fight all the outside world alone.

And how did Mileva take the separation, Hans Albert was asked. 'Very hard,' he said.

Einstein wept after he had seen off Mileva's train; Haber had to support him as he walked home from the railway station. Einstein's friend Janos Plesch later insisted that he was 'born close to the water', and that tears came easily to his eyes when he heard of other people's misfortunes. But it was rare indeed for him to weep on his own account. It is too easy to say (as some have) that Einstein was crying solely for the loss of his children, rather than for the loss of his wife. This was a very emphatic punctuation point in his life. One era within it was ending; another, laden with uncertainties, was about to begin. However bitter his feelings towards Mileva had become, Einstein must have been haunted by the times when their future together had seemed the one point of hope in his existence: the times when he had told her that, 'Without you, my life is no life.'

8

An Amputated Limb

THE First World War started on Mileva's home frontier, following years of growing tension between Serbia and Austria-Hungary. Einstein had commented on the worsening situation in a note to Helene Savić in December 1912, adding, 'I think, however, that this sabre-rattling has little meaning.' Eighteen months later Archduke Ferdinand of Austria was assassinated in Sarajevo by a Serbian student, and in July 1914, after an aggressive Austrian ultimatum to Serbia, the two countries went to war. Russia, Serbia's main ally, quickly moved to defend its interests, the network of alliances across Europe drew in the other great powers, and a local conflict developed into a world war. More than four years of slaughter began.

These were the years in which Einstein emerged as a vocal pacifist, ready to risk a measure of public odium for his beliefs. He stood apart when ninety-three leading intellectuals put their names to a manifesto defending German war aims. Instead, he and some others signed a rival 'Manifesto for Europeans' advocating international cooperation. He also joined a pacifist political party, the League of the New Fatherland, and secretly gave his support to anti-war campaigners in Switzerland and Holland. However, sincere though this stand was, it had its limits. Einstein carried on working in a post that was financed by ardent militarists, and stayed friendly with colleagues such as Haber and Nernst who were pioneering chemical weapons. In private he was ready to attribute the war to German brutishness, but in public he was less provocative, and blamed the aggressive nature of humanity.

Einstein lacked the optimism, the faith that his fellow man could be redeemed, necessary to sustain a personal crusade against the war. 'Europe, in her madness, has now started something incredible,' he told Ehrenfest. 'At such a time we see the wretched species of beast we belong to. I am going on quietly with my peaceful meditations, and feel only a mixture of pity and disgust.' The war tended to appear in his letters as something distant, vague and irrelevant. 'Apart from the general misery that one experiences mainly through the newspapers, I lead a happy, extraordinarily tranquil life,' he wrote in the spring of 1915, as poison gas drifted over Ypres and thousands died on the Eastern Front. Einstein boasted of his 'conscious disengagement' from the war, and remarked that it was possible to live quite cosily, regarding the rest of humanity with the detachment of an attendant in a lunatic asylum.

Mileva and the children had found temporary lodgings in a Zurich boarding-house. Looking back as an adult, Hans Albert recalled, 'That was probably the worst time, because then nobody knew what the future would bring – whether this was just a temporary condition or whether the marriage would end finally.' Einstein told his wife that the most he would offer her in Berlin was loveless coexistence. He found the thought of a friendly relationship with her quite impossible after all that had happened. 'It shall be a loyal and business-like relationship. All personal things must be kept to a minimum,' he said. Evidently Einstein set out a series of rules that Mileva would have to obey if they were to share a home again. In general terms he wanted her to stay out of his way and to speak when spoken to. Whatever the details, the ultimate effect would have been to leave him free to live his own life.

Although the precise contents of these conditions are unknown, since sensitive correspondence from this period remains under seal, letters we have had access to make clear that Einstein had set them and that they were not negotiable. He told Mileva to think his proposal over and deliver a clear answer, without any ands, ifs or buts, so that he knew exactly where he stood. Mileva refused to comply, and stalemate ensued. 'I don't expect to ask you for a divorce but only desire that you stay in Switzerland with the children,' Einstein wrote in July 1914. 'All I ask of you is that you send me news of my beloved' boys every two weeks. I send them heart-felt kisses.'

This tenderness was not reciprocated by ten-year-old Hans Albert, who made no reply to his father's increasingly plaintive greetings.

Einstein accused Mileva of intercepting his messages and turning the boy against him. Her protestations of innocence were met with a new ultimatum. She could read what he wrote to the children, but was not to discuss it with them. Nor was she to read, discuss or influence Hans Albert's replies, even to the extent of reminding him to write. If these orders were followed, she could be certain that Einstein would not make trouble. But if anything in Hans Albert's letters seemed 'suggested', Einstein would sever all contact with the children forthwith.

This was a desperate threat, since to carry it out would have hurt Einstein deeply. He saw no reason why – as he put it – his inability to live with Mileva should affect his relationship with the children. The fear that she was poisoning their opinions of him preyed on his mind. He could now see in Hans Albert many glimmers of his own younger self, and in letter after letter he tried to engage the boy's sympathies. There was constant encouragement for Hans Albert's piano lessons ('You cannot believe how much joy you can make for yourself and your friends with music'), backed up by anecdotes about his own 'completely unmusical' father. Einstein was also eager to encourage Hans Albert's love of boating ('I should tell you that was also my greatest passion when I was your age'). Above all, he kept probing to discover his son's intellectual interests to see if they resembled his own. 'I am very happy that you enjoy geometry,' he wrote. 'That was one of my favourite pastimes . . . I would really enjoy teaching you, but unfortunately that's not possible.' At the start of 1915, Einstein told his son, 'In a few years you will also be ready to practise the art of thinking. It is very good when one can do that.'

Einstein sent money from Berlin to meet his family's expenses, but Mileva complained that it was not enough. Bills went unpaid, and she would creep past her landlady to avoid being asked for overdue rent. Although too proud to ask her father for help, she was eventually reduced to approaching one of her friends for a loan. She also supplemented her income by setting up as a private tutor, giving lessons in mathematics and on the piano. The Hurwitz family lent her music scores, and she also borrowed an introductory text on Italian, apparently hoping to teach beginners despite having no prior knowledge of the language.

Einstein insisted that he was being as generous as circumstances allowed. 'I would have sent you more money, but I didn't have any left myself,' he told Mileva in September 1914. 'I myself am living very simply, almost shabbily. In this manner we will be able to set aside something for the children.' That autumn he packed up and dispatched his family's remaining belongings, together with much of the furniture from their flat. In December he promised to send Mileva a yearly maintenance of 5,600 Reichsmarks, in quarterly instalments. Brushing aside any objections, he added, 'I do not wish to be bothered by any more trifling matters. I have kept nothing except the bare essentials for a room to sleep and work in.'

The unpleasant truth for Einstein was that marriage at a distance was in some ways more onerous than within four walls. Mileva's need for his support was now more explicit, not less, and at the same time she had gained new dominance over his children. Einstein's querulous replies to her letters suggest a man thrown on the defensive. 'If I had known you twelve years ago as I know you now,' he wrote, 'I would have judged my responsibilities towards you quite differently.'

By the end of 1914 it was clear to the couple's friends that the marriage had collapsed. Mileva left her boarding-house and rented a flat on Voltastrasse, close to the Polytechnic. There she put up a Christmas tree and invited over the Hurwitz family to celebrate the new year. The visitors were treated to tea, cakes and stoic assurances that Einstein would continue to care for her. He posted games to his children as presents, but spent Christmas in Berlin as the guest of Professor Nernst, talking physics and playing Beethoven on the violin.

Einstein established himself in a bachelor apartment around the corner from Elsa, and was now free to see his cousin as often – or as little – as he liked. The arrangement was very much to his taste: close enough for comfort, but not yet close enough to seem cramping. 'In my personal relations I have never been so serene and happy as now,' he told Zangger in July 1915. He added that he was living 'a completely secluded life but not a lonely one', thanks to his cousin's loving care. That summer he and Elsa holidayed together on the Baltic island of Rügen, one of Germany's remotest outposts. There Einstein enjoyed what he described as the most restful time of his entire adult life, lost in contemplation of the vast and lonely sea. Many years later he joked to his younger son that people were like the ocean: sometimes smooth and friendly, at others stormy and full of malice. The important thing to remember was that they too were mostly made of water.

Unpleasant emotion posed less of a threat to Einstein whenever he could play this trick of reducing it from the human to the coldly objective. The letter in which he boasted to Zangger of his serenity showed the same process at work. He depicted Mileva as a cold-blooded schemer, plotting dispassionately to frustrate his access to the children. Einstein had won her permission to take Hans Albert on a mountain hike at the start of July, only to receive a last-minute note from his son refusing to go. While unable to disguise his irritation, and certain that his wife was to blame, Einstein piously observed how petty this seemed when set against the unreasoning hatreds of war. 'So long as one is young, one admires lively emotion and despises cold calculation,' he told Zangger. 'But today I think the derailments that stem from blind emotion bring much more painful misfortune than can the most heartless schemer.'

The hiking holiday was postponed until September, when Einstein also visited the French pacifist Romain Rolland in Geneva. According to Hans Albert's recollections, he and his father travelled as far as southern Germany, staying in wayside inns and even fitting in some boating on the Danube. But Einstein gave only evasive answers when the youngster asked if he would be taking the family back to Berlin. 'I want you educated in Switzerland,' he said, then changed the subject. The following month Einstein complained about the 'unloving tone' of his son's latest letter. 'I will not visit you again until you request it,' he said.

It remains remarkable how diligently Einstein strove to keep contact with his sons during 1915, for this was the year in which his scientific labours reached their fiercest intensity. As he struggled to complete the extension of relativity, he increasingly cut himself off from the outside world. Letters were far less likely to be answered than to be impaled on a large meat hook and later burnt. The work was most intense in mid to late November, when Einstein wrote to almost no one. The sole exceptions – aside from David Hilbert, a German mathematician whose work on gravity ran remarkably close to his own – appear to have been Mileva and Hans Albert. A note from Einstein to his wife on 15 November indicated a truce between the couple. 'Your letter sincerely pleased me,' he wrote, 'for I can see from it that you are not trying to hinder or thwart my relationship with the boys. I can tell you that as far as I am concerned, that relationship is the most important of my personal life.'

Three days later came a breakthrough. Einstein revealed to the world that he could now explain an astronomical puzzle – a variation in the orbit of Mercury around the sun that had perplexed scientists since it was first reported in 1859. The unexplained effect, which Einstein had been aware of since 1907, provided the acid test for his ideas. Success showed that, after eight years of groping for the truth about gravity, he had discovered new fundamental principles that were better at describing the universe than their existing rivals. His latter-day colleague Abraham Pais has described this as possibly the strongest emotional experience of Einstein's life. It was certainly a rapturous one. Einstein reported having had heart palpitations and feeling as if something inside him had snapped. 'I was beside myself with ecstasy for days,' he told Ehrenfest.

The facts are simple enough. Each orbit, there is a tiny change in Mercury's perihelion: the point at which it passes closest to the sun before sweeping out again on its massive elliptical circuit. Taking into account the gravitational tugs of the other planets, Newton's laws did not predict the full extent of this deviation. Some astronomers ascribed it to the gravity of an undiscovered planet, provisionally named Vulcan. But all attempts to find Vulcan failed, as did all attempts to embellish Newton's formulae with special hypotheses. The beauty of Einstein's new theory of gravity was that his equations produced the right result with no fixing and no flummery. Not only that, they also showed him how and why he had previously under-estimated the bending of light by the sun.

After a few final days of frenzied work, the full structure of the general theory of relativity was in place. Einstein showed that gravity was not a force from one body acting on another, but a property of space-time itself. Massive objects create distortions in the space-time around them, and these four-dimensional curves act as pathways for smaller objects to follow, rather as a ball bearing follows the line of least resistance over a bumpy two-dimensional plain. For most people this curved space-time is tricky to visualize, and it is best not to try. Einstein had produced a theory that untangled the fabric of the universe, but which tied lesser men's brains in knots.

His exertions left him exhausted. In December 1915 Einstein wrote to Besso that he was 'satisfied but rather done in'. The wartime hysteria in Berlin was oppressive, and he admitted to Ehrenfest that 'Every fibre of my body itches to get away from here.' He toyed with making another trip to Switzerland, but then announced that he was too tired to face the likely delays at the frontier. Instead, he promised Hans Albert that he would pay a visit at Easter the following year – 'even if I have to camp out at the border until they let me cross'.

Hans Albert's growing maturity tantalized Einstein. This man who had been so fond of his own father, but so frustrated by his intellectual shortcomings, yearned to act as mentor to his own son. 'Albert is now reaching the age where spending time with me can mean so much to him,' he told Mileva. 'You can safely let him stay with me from time to time. Your relationship with him will suffer no damage ... my influence is limited to the intellectual and aesthetic.' As Einstein knew, the thought of either of their sons visiting Berlin and coming into the clutches of his family terrified Mileva. All his promises that he would keep his sons safely away from his relations did nothing to reassure her, and Einstein complained that she was forcing him to beg for the right to see his children. The visit at Easter took on ominous significance.

Einstein urged Hans Albert to practise a piece for piano and violin so that they could play together when he arrived. In a letter brimming with affection, he told his son that he had been 'doing a lot of interesting things lately' and was eager for the time when they could discuss them. That might have to wait a few years, he admitted, but meanwhile there were plenty of other things for them to share. He told his son about 'a strange experience' he had recently enjoyed at a small party attended by a palm-reader. 'She looked at my hand and told me things about myself that were correct, even though she had never met me before,' he wrote. 'Isn't that peculiar?' According to one later account, Einstein did believe 'to some extent' in such unlikely phenomena, even in telepathy. Frieda Bucky, wife of a doctor friend, Gustav Bucky, reported that he felt it was natural for one human being to 'pick up vibrations' from another. To be incapable of this was to have the skin of an elephant.

Perhaps a fortune-teller could have warned Einstein how disastrous his Easter visit would be, and how much his own insensitivity was to blame. In February 1916 he had stunned Mileva with the following announcement: 'I hereby apply to you to change our well-tested separation to a divorce.' His letter moved smoothly on to give friendly advice about dosing the children with calcium chloride to protect their teeth and bones. Einstein appears to have overlooked that Mileva was still in love with him, and had not lost hope that her marriage could be salvaged. Separation was arduous enough, but had been mitigated by Einstein's assurance that he had no desire to divorce. Now this last prop was being kicked away.

Einstein would later suggest that his hand had been forced by Elsa and her family. He told Mileva to put herself in his shoes for a change, and recognize the pressure he was under. Rumours were circulating about Elsa's lifestyle, he said, and were causing particular suffering to her elder daughter, Ilse. The girl had reached marriageable age, and the whispers were handicapping her prospects. Could not Mileva understand how heavily this weighed upon him? All he wished to do was to set things straight by a formal marriage.

Given such grim portents, the Easter visit began remarkably well. The two boys met their father so 'politely and willingly' that Einstein wrote Mileva a thank-you note. He praised the way she was bringing the children up ('I could not wish for anything better') and thanked her for not alienating them from him. Within days, however, all had changed utterly. Einstein wanted to take Hans Albert away for another mountain hike, and it appears that this produced a ferocious exchange with Mileva. Perhaps, in her fear and insecurity, she suspected her husband of plotting their son's removal. The result was Einstein's angry departure. Hans Albert was once again bitterly hostile, and stopped replying to his letters. Einstein told Besso that he had made an irrevocable decision not to see his wife again, and added, 'I would have been broken physically and mentally if I had not finally found the energy to keep her away from me and out of my eyes and ears.'

The misery was simply too much for Mileva. Something gave way, and soon after Einstein's departure it was she who suffered a physical and mental collapse. The crisis lasted several months and was severe enough to raise fears for her life. Some accounts suggest that Mileva suffered a series of heart attacks, but details of her illness remain frustratingly elusive. Such scrappy hints as survive – particularly in letters by Besso and Zangger, who both attended her – would seem consistent with both physical disease and extreme anxiety and depression. Mileva's doctors were unable to provide any treatment, other than telling her to lie motionless and avoid excitement. She was unable to care for her children, and they were taken in temporarily by Helene Savić, who had fled war-torn Serbia and was living near Lausanne.

Einstein's first reaction was that his wife was shamming in order to prevent their divorce. He told Besso that she would use any means to achieve her will, and added, 'You have no idea of the natural cunning of such a woman.' Einstein claimed that at first, after hearing Mileva's condition, he had been ready to return to Zurich despite his 'bad experience' at Easter. But mature reflection had persuaded him otherwise, since his wife would demand to see him and his presence was unlikely to be sedative. Her illness might be genuine, but he suspected that Besso and Zangger were two kindly men being led by the nose. As the child who had been burned in the past, Einstein wrote, it was he who best knew the dangers of this fire.

These opinions were shared by Einstein's mother, who wrote to Elsa that Mileva was only ill when it suited her, adding that 'by far the largest part was simulated.' Her only uncertainty was as to why her son did not take the chance to look after the children himself. Besso, however, was reproachful. This dear-hearted man never wavered in his affection for Einstein, but he was always ready to act as his conscience, even if the task was uncomfortable. Now he wrote that, far from being a case of hypochondria, Mileva's suffering had been clear in her appearance for a long time. Rather than letting herself go, she had burdened herself with too much work as she struggled to support the children. With exquisite tact, but great firmness, Besso rebuffed Einstein's attacks on Mileva's character. We were all sinners, he reminded his friend, and deserved a more balanced judgement than Einstein was offering. Otherwise, said Besso, we would all go to hell.

Einstein retreated in the face of this disapproval, but only to take up a new offensive position. In blithe contradiction of his previous letter, he assured Besso that he did not believe that Mileva's ills were simulated. He now held them to be 'purely nervous' and typical of the weaker sex. Warming to his theme, he outlined his broader views on relations between men and women:

> Dear Michele!
> We men are lamentable, dependent creatures. I admit this with
> joy to everyone. But compared with these women, each one of
> us is a king; because he stands tolerably well on his own two
> feet, without always waiting for something outside himself to
> cling to. The others, though, are always waiting until someone
> comes along to be put at their disposal. If that doesn't happen,
> they simply collapse.

He did not stop there, but launched a strident justification of his decision to demand a divorce. Did his behaviour really look so horrible in Besso's eyes? Who could have endured spending the rest of his life with such an odious smell stuck up his nose? Not Einstein – and if that meant God would send him to hell, so be it.

His sensitivity to Besso's reproaches emerged most clearly at the close of his tirade. Einstein noted sadly that a postscript to Besso's last letter had addressed him with the formal German '*Sie*' rather than the familiar '*du*'. He assumed this was a deliberate rebuke, and his tone was deeply hurt:

> Dear Michele!
> For 20 years we have understood each other well. And now I
> see an anger against me arise in you, on account of a female
> who is none of your concern. Fight it! She would not be worth
> it if she were a hundred thousand times in the right!

No sooner was this letter sent, however, than Einstein made a shaming discovery. The offending postscript had not been written by Besso at all, but by his wife, Anna, from whom the formal address was perfectly in order. An apologetic postcard was on its way the same

Pauline Einstein, 1858–1920 (*AIP Emilo Segre Visual Archives*)

Albert Einstein in 1896 (*Eidgenossische Technische Hochschule Zurich*)

Mileva Marić in 1896 (*Schweizerische Landesbibliothek, Bern*)

Einstein in 1912 (*Eidgenossische Technische Hochschule Zurich*)

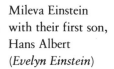

Mileva Einstein
with their first son,
Hans Albert
(*Evelyn Einstein*)

Wedding portrait of
Mileva Marić and
Albert Einstein, 1903
(*Evelyn Einstein*)

Mileva and her sons Eduard and Hans Albert in 1914 (*Hebrew
University of Jerusalem*)

Einstein's study in Berne (*Schweizerische Landesbibliothek, Bern*)

Albert Einstein and his second wife Elsa in 1921 (*AIP Emilo Segre Visual Archives*)

Einstein's summer house in Caputh, outside Berlin. (*Roger Highfield*)

Interior of Einstein's summer house in Caputh. The main living room. (*Roger Highfield*)

Interior of Einstein's summer house in Caputh. View of the kitchen, where the maid overheard rows over Einstein's affairs. (*Roger Highfield*)

Einstein in the early
1940s (*Pictorial Press
Limited*)

Einstein's biographer
Carl Seelig and
Eduard Einstein
(*Eidgenossische
Technische
Hochschule Zurich*)

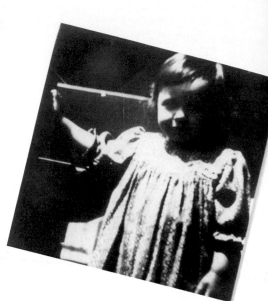

Probably the best known picture of Einstein (*Pictorial Press Limited*)

Could this be Einstein's illegitimate daughter, Lieserl? The photograph comes from a collection of Einstein family snapshots. (*Evelyn Einstein*)

(*Sunday Daily Telegraph*)

Einstein scholar Robert Schulmann (*Roger Highfield*)

Einstein scholar John Stachel
(*Roger Highfield*)

Albert Einstein at the Eighth American Scientific Congress in 1940 (*Daily Telegraph*) evening, with the wry sign-off, 'That this should happen to a scientist!'

This was not the last time that Anna Besso would stir his emotions: her sympathies for Mileva were rather too clear. On the one hand, Einstein was grateful for the news that she regularly sent him of his children. He was also happy to be coddled and pampered by her when visiting Zurich. He would joke about the restorative powers of the 'Sanatorium Anna', and jokingly called her 'my foster mother'. But if she dared to move beyond the role of motherly nursemaid, fireworks followed. One sharp exchange (sadly missing from the published Einstein–Besso correspondence) left Einstein complaining that 'never before has anyone been so impudent to me, and I hope nobody will be so in future.'

Einstein asked Besso to keep him informed of Mileva's illness, but eagerly seized on any suggestion that this irritating problem might soon go away. 'Your silence reassures me,' he wrote to Besso at the start of August, 'hopefully everything in Zurich is on the way to improvement.' Even brisker was his attitude a fortnight later. Einstein had convinced himself that Mileva was suffering from tuberculous meningitis, a potentially fatal infection of the brain membranes. 'It pleases me that my wife is slowly getting better,' he wrote. 'But certainly if it is brain tuberculosis, as is apparently likely, a quick end would be better than long suffering.'

These brief lines came sandwiched between banalities about a lost address and a cancelled trip to Holland. Einstein's tone was business-like and unyielding, making clear that he would not waste any tears over his wife's demise. Mileva failed to die, however. Instead her illness dragged on inconclusively, with frequent spells in hospital. At home her bed was set on a balcony, where she lay day and night staring out at the roofs of Zurich and the surrounding mountains. Sometimes she was strong enough to look after her children again, directing household affairs with a calm hand and even conducting Hans Albert's music lessons. At other times Professor Zangger and his wife were forced to intervene. The unpredictable mood was captured by a letter from Besso to Einstein at the start of December. For five weeks all had gone well, he reported, but then 'the attacks' had returned. Besso put the blame on a letter that Hans Albert had received from his father. The boy had refused to show the contents to Mileva, who promptly went into fits.

Before this relapse, Einstein had made another tactical withdrawal. 'From now on I will not bother her with the divorce,' he had told Besso in September. 'The battle on the subject with my relatives is finished. I have learned to resist tears.' He had learned no such thing, of course, but for the moment Mileva's distress was more troublesome to him than Elsa's. If his wife was attempting emotional blackmail, then Einstein was ready to give in for a quiet life. The following month he repeated his pledge. 'I will see to it that she suffers no more disturbance on my account. As to a divorce, I have definitely renounced it.'

The fact that Mileva's agony continued suggests that blackmail was not her object. Einstein told Helene Savić that Mileva's plight caused him pain, but not enough to change his feelings for her. 'In spite of this interest, she is and will forever remain for me an amputated limb,' he wrote. 'I will never again become close to her. I will finish my days far from her, feeling this is absolutely necessary.'

Einstein was well aware that his harsh attitude disturbed people. From the earliest days of the separation, he had realized the importance of good public relations. Writing to Zangger in May 1915, he had stressed that leaving Mileva was a matter of survival. He wanted his friend to understand this, he said, 'so that you are not tricked by appearances into getting a darker picture of me than I deserve'. Now, slightly over a year later, he thanked Savić for not condemning him on the strength of appearances 'like the majority of my acquaintances'. He added with regret that his children did not understand the way he had acted and felt a deep anger against him. The outlook seemed bleak. 'I find, although it is painful, that it is better for them if their father does not see them any more. I will be satisfied if they grow up to be useful and esteemed men.'

The renewed hostility of Hans Albert caused Einstein especial pain. 'I think his disposition towards me has stepped below freezing point,' he told Besso. 'In his place, at his age and in the present circumstances, I would probably have reacted in the same way.' Einstein encouraged Besso to act as a proxy father for the boy, but his friend's position was uncomfortable. His close contact with Einstein made

Mileva wary of him, so much so that his mere presence seemed to make her condition worse. Fear of upsetting her inhibited him from drawing too close to Hans Albert, for whom he felt great love.

Einstein continued to write to his son, and eventually succeeded in eliciting a response. 'Don't be frightened when you and Tete are alone,' he told him. 'Even though I am not with you, you still have a father who loves you above all else, who always thinks about you and who will always take care of you.' By the end of 1916, Einstein was talking openly about moving his son to Berlin. He knew that this would confirm his wife's worst fears, and at first made some attempt to sound conciliatory. 'There can be absolutely no question that I will take Albert away against Miza's will,' he told Besso. 'I am no tyrant after all.'

Einstein knew that his energies would be sorely tested by looking after a child, but his desire to shape his elder son's future was over-powering. 'I am greatly occupied with the idea of removing Albert from school and teaching him myself,' he told Besso in March 1917 – adding, 'I think I could give the boy a lot, not just intellectually. Do you think that my wife would understand?' He also considered paying for his son to stay with his sister Maja in Lucerne. The small matter of Mileva's consent rapidly dwindled in importance. In late May he would only promise, with ominous emphasis, that 'nothing will occur *unless necessary* that would make my wife unhappier than she already is.' Three days later he was unequivocal: 'In these circumstances no consideration should be taken for my wife, but only what commends itself for the boy.'

Einstein's feelings for his younger son were considerably murkier. Eduard had learned to read unusually early, and could soon recite long passages from memory with absolute recall. He was enjoying newspapers by the time he entered primary school, and moved on with little delay to the delights of Goethe and Schiller. His gifts were extraordinary, but Einstein was more perturbed than proud. He showed early concern that his son's appetite for knowledge was out of control, urging him not to become a bookworm and to save some things for when he grew up. Einstein felt far more at home with Hans Albert, a bright but not brilliant pupil whose progress at school more closely resembled his own. To him, Einstein could offer gentle reproof on spelling errors or sympathy on the trials of Latin, with reassurance that good grades were not all-important.

It was not only Eduard's intelligence that disconcerted his father. He was an openly emotional child, sometimes radiantly cheerful but also prone to nervousness and impatience. Zangger described him as 'a delicate little chap' with shy, girlish manners that were 'completely un-Einstein-like'. Again, the contrast with his elder brother was pronounced. Hans Albert had learned to bury his feelings so well that classmates called him '*Steinli*' – Little Stone. In a poem written for a later school reunion, one contemporary described him as 'the most impassive man of the century', hiding behind a broad smile and never losing his composure. Einstein admitted that Hans Albert had 'an undeniable tendency to a certain taciturnity', but did not find it unsympathetic. Eduard's sensitivity worried him far more.

It seemed to Einstein that the problem was made worse by Mileva's indulgence of the boy's continual ill health. Besides running the gamut of normal childhood sickness, Eduard was troubled by persistent headaches and pains in his ears. Einstein, with his characteristic horror of illness, interpreted this as hypochondria. And by the time Eduard was six and a half, his father felt convinced that he was mentally disturbed.

It was a brutal judgement on a child so young, but Einstein showed a passionate conviction in it. In December 1916 he wrote to Besso, 'I'm pleased that everything goes well with my poor little one, but I'm not making any illusions for myself. One must be able to look reality in the eye, even when it is this hard.' He expanded on this unhappy hint the following March. It seemed impossible that Eduard would ever grow into a normal adult, he said. With a striking echo of his attitude towards Mileva a few months earlier, he even seemed to wish his son dead. 'Who knows if it would not have been better if he had left the world before he had really known this life.'

In an extraordinary passage, Einstein went on as if to hold himself responsible for Eduard's infirmity. 'I am to blame for him and I reproach myself, for the first time in my life. In everything else I took things lightly or felt myself not truly responsible,' he wrote. Einstein explained that he believed his son's condition to be hereditary, and connected to scrofula – tuberculosis of the lymph nodes – in Mileva.

He had seen glandular swellings on his wife's body at the time of Eduard's conception, he said, but had known nothing about the disease and had not realized their importance. 'Now the calamity is there, as was inevitable. The solution is to endure it and not moan. One looks after the sick and takes comfort in the healthy.'

Despite his outward show of self-accusation, Einstein's argument placed great stress on his own helpless ignorance. Its main thrust was to pin the blame for the problem on Mileva, not himself. The whole matter of Eduard's condition filled him with distaste, and he left it to his friends to seek a solution. Professor Zangger suggested that Eduard be sent for an extended stay at a children's sanatorium in the Swiss mountain resort of Arosa. Einstein agreed, but could not resist observing that he preferred the child-rearing style of the ancient Spartans. He became increasingly irritated by the cost of his son's care, and increasingly suspicious that medical mollycoddling would do more harm than good. With thinly veiled sarcasm, he wrote to Mileva that he hoped the boy's long stay at high altitude would not make him too sensitive to unclean city air. 'Tete must come back; I cannot raise the money,' he told Besso in November 1917. 'I don't believe in the new medical magic of X-rays. I have reached the point where only diagnoses *post mortem* inspire my confidence.'

The following month Einstein told Zangger that modern medicine was a disease infecting humanity. He did not want his son to spend his childhood 'in a kind of disinfection machine'. The irony was that earlier that year he had suffered a serious health crisis of his own – a physical and nervous collapse that uncomfortably recalled Mileva's. Besides the emotional strain of the separation, he had also severely overworked himself: instead of resting after his triumphs with general relativity, he had produced ten scientific papers in 1916, plus a book explaining relativity to a wider audience. Adding to this were the strains of life in wartime Berlin, and the long-standing stomach trouble he ascribed to his student days in Zurich. The burden was simply too great.

Severe pain gripped his body, and he lost fifty-six pounds in two months. At first he feared that he had cancer, then his doctor diagnosed gallstones, prescribing spa treatment and a strict diet. The ever-helpful Zangger helped to procure the necessary foods, and Einstein's

Berlin relatives supplemented his supplies through their contacts in southern Germany. His doctor urged him to take a cure at Tarasp, a spa in Switzerland's lower Engadine valley, but Einstein showed the same scepticism as he did towards Eduard's treatment in Arosa. 'I find it hard to summon the necessary superstition,' he grumbled, and he chose the cheaper option of visiting his relatives in Lucerne. In time the diagnosis shifted to a stomach ulcer, but it was several years before his recovery was complete. While bedridden, he was visited by Hedwig Born, wife of the physicist Max Born. She asked him whether he feared death. 'Why should I?' he replied. 'I feel such solidarity with all living people that it is a matter of indifference to me where the individual begins and where he ceases.'

A primary effect of this illness was to bring Einstein even more closely under the maternal influence of Elsa. He moved to an apartment next to his cousin's in the summer of 1917, taking care to give Besso the impression that it was all her idea. He praised Elsa's home cooking for helping him to regain lost weight, and took full advantage of the comforts provided by her family's wealth and contacts. Philipp Frank recalled visiting Einstein during the war, and being invited to dinner at Elsa's father's home. When Frank politely demurred, saying that an unexpected guest would be unwelcome in a time of shortages, Einstein replied, 'You need have no scruples. On the contrary, my uncle has more food than the per capita average of the population. If you eat at his table you are furthering the cause of social justice.'

It was on this occasion that Frank first met Elsa. Praising Einstein's scientific talents, she cited as evidence his skill at opening the exotic assortment of tin cans that provided much of their food. While others in Berlin went hungry, her resourcefulness also ensured that Einstein still had fresh eggs and butter every day. In the darkest days of the war she procured the services of painters and locksmiths by bribing them all with 'well-filled sandwiches'. Even Einstein's passion for smoking could still be indulged, thanks to the gift of a hundred rare cigars. That was 'a unique occurrence in these times', Elsa wrote to Pauline Einstein, and caused him childlike joy.

There is nothing to suggest that Einstein was now madly in love with his cousin. Indeed, to the extent that we can trust his own words, passion was something he wished to avoid. He likened himself to a blob of oil floating on the water, perfectly self-contained. 'I have come to know the mutability of all human relations,' he told Zangger, 'and learned to isolate myself from heat and cold so that the temperature balance is fairly well assured.' In one letter around this time – the precise date is uncertain – he assured Mileva that he now had no intention of giving up his bachelor lifestyle 'which has revealed itself as an indescribable blessing to me'. But Elsa's motherly care had its price. She was determined to have Einstein as her husband, and early in 1918 he bowed to her demands and again asked his wife for a divorce. According to family legend, he promised Mileva that he would 'always remain true to you – in my way'.

The divorce demand hit Mileva at a time of renewed vulnerability. Towards the end of 1917, her younger sister Zorka had arrived in Zurich to lend support during her continuing convalescence. But Zorka herself swiftly showed signs of depressive mental illness, and Zangger reported in February 1918 that she would have to be cared for in an asylum. A later letter indicates that Zorka was lodged at the Burghölzli psychiatric clinic in Zurich, where Eduard too would eventually be consigned. Adding to Mileva's distress was the news that her brother, Miloš, had been captured by the Russians while serving as a medical orderly in the Austrian army. Broken-hearted, and worn out by long months of suffering, she could resist no further. Negotiations for the divorce settlement began.

One outsider drawn into the divorce process was Einstein's Berlin colleague Fritz Haber. Haber had every reason to feel especially moved by the affair: his own disastrous first marriage bore many parallels to Einstein's. Like Mileva, his bride was a fellow scientist – Clara Immerwahr, the first woman to receive a doctorate in chemistry from the University of Breslau. Like Mileva she was quiet and unassuming, with a lisp that accentuated her natural shyness. She was also a woman of ideas. When Haber published a major work on gases, in 1905, he dedicated it to his wife for her 'silent cooperation'. They had worked together at home, each at their own desk, with Clara painstakingly checking and calculating Haber's data.

Soon, however, all went sour. Haber was every bit as inconsiderate a husband as Einstein – quite capable of setting off alone on a train journey, forgetting that he had left Clara outside the ticket office. The pressures of looking after their son (born in 1902, a year after their marriage) also took their toll. In the words of Haber's biographer, Clara became less spirited and perhaps less brilliant. Depression took hold and she allowed herself – like Mileva – to become stout, untidy and unattractive. 'Where once similar backgrounds and similar interests had fostered deep attachment, a lethargic tolerance developed, and the marriage slowly began to disintegrate.' The ending was sudden and tragic. Clara Haber was disgusted by her husband's work developing poison gas for the German forces. When he went to the Eastern Front to supervise operations personally, she killed herself.

Advising Einstein on his divorce may have allowed Haber to lay some of these ghosts to rest. He may also have felt some responsibility for having helped bring Einstein to Berlin, thus precipitating the separation. It seems that he made strenuous efforts to reconcile the couple, but eventually he admitted defeat. Thereafter, so Hans Albert told Ronald Clark, he set about securing Mileva 'the best deal possible'. Also active on Mileva's behalf – as ever – was the tireless Besso, who served where necessary as an intermediary. In May 1918, Einstein was moved to say that his wife was behaving 'very nicely' and that a 'thoroughly friendly' tone had developed between them. 'I realize that I spoilt things a lot previously by being too vehement and severe,' he admitted.

The most sensitive part of the divorce was the financial settlement. By his own account, in May 1917, Einstein's yearly income after tax was about 13,000 Reichsmarks. From that total, he said, he was sending 7,000 Marks in regular instalments to his wife and about 600 to support his mother. When various 'irregular payments' to Zurich were added, Einstein said, his savings were in danger of being exhausted, leaving nothing to provide for his children's future. He claimed in January 1918 to have sent a total of 12,000 Marks to Mileva during the previous year – nearly his entire take-home pay. Zangger had been deputed to meet bills in Zurich on his behalf, but the arrangement had left Einstein increasingly restive. 'I will give Zangger what he laid out for me last year,' he wrote, 'but I will not put up with people incessantly organizing me like a little boy . . . it's a question of a screw without end.'

The trump card that Einstein played was the Nobel prize for physics. If his wife agreed to an uncontested divorce, the money from the prize would safeguard the future of her and the children for ever. If she did not, then she would not see a penny more than the 6,000 Swiss francs he had decided was a reasonable annual maintenance. Rather than wanting to acknowledge Mileva's contribution to relativity, as some have claimed, Einstein offered the prize proceeds to Mileva simply as the best way to obtain a divorce. Paid in Swedish kronor, the prize would be worth about 32,000 dollars or 180,000 Swiss francs to Mileva and would provide a hedge against the plummeting value of the German currency used for his previous payments. But there remained one problem: Einstein had not yet won the Nobel prize.

The Nobel committee that picked the laureates was notoriously conservative and was reluctant to award the prize for relativity because the theory was still controversial, lacking sufficient experimental confirmation. As it turned out, Einstein did not receive his prize until 1922. Even then, it was actually the prize for 1921, which had been held over from the previous year, and was not in recognition of relativity. Ironically, he was honoured for his work on the photoelectric effect – the theory whose implications he would feel ill at ease with for the rest of his life.

It is a striking confirmation of Einstein's sublime self-belief that he felt sure in 1918 that the Nobel prize – and its money – were bound to come his way eventually. By the same token, it says a lot for Mileva's enduring faith in him that she believed it too. However, Einstein had first been nominated for the prize of 1910, and his name had been put forward every year thereafter save two. As they wrangled over the divorce, he and Mileva could never be absolutely sure that his huge contribution would be recognised by the Nobel committee – but both must have suspected that it could be only a matter of time. In the meantime, Einstein undertook to send Mileva regular alimony payments.

Einstein received a copy of the divorce papers early in July. He laughed the matter off in a letter to Besso, comparing himself to Till Eulenspiegel, the peasant rogue from German folklore who meets such a sticky end in Richard Strauss's symphonic poem. But the strain on him was considerable, and the following month he dreamt he had cut his throat with a shaving-knife. The immediate cause of his nightmare was the offer of an academic chair in Zurich, to be shared between the University and the Polytechnic. The initiative had come from Zangger, for whom it offered a last-ditch opportunity to bring his friend back to the children. It provoked Einstein into much breast-beating, and he admitted to being very tempted, but the answer was still no. The avowed hater of the Germans now said that he was bound to his colleagues in Berlin by unbreakable ties of affection and moral obligation. Finally he decided 'to do something that I normally absolutely hate' – come to a compromise. He would retain his base in Berlin, but would return to Zurich for a few weeks each year to give lecture courses. That way he had an excuse to see Hans Albert regularly and would avoid the 'great personal problems' of living in the same city as Mileva.

Einstein was obliged to admit in his legal submissions that he had committed adultery. There were also references to fierce fights between him and his wife, which had made their continued marriage intolerable. He told Besso that the divorce was entertaining all those who knew what was going on, and he felt exasperated by the need to shift documents back and forth between Zurich and Berlin. There were some compensations, however. A document from December 1918 shows Einstein acknowledging receipt of a portfolio of shares (in a distillers and the Bosnia-Herzegovina railway) from Elsa's father. It seems likely that this gift had been delayed deliberately until after the divorce contract had been agreed. The note stipulated that, in the event of Einstein's death, the shares would be returned to Elsa's estate. Nothing would go to Mileva.

The divorce decree was issued on 14 February 1919, and after a modest interval Einstein and Elsa were married on 2 June. The ceremony took place in a Berlin register office, and the celebrations were as inauspiciously low-key as those for Einstein's marriage to Mileva. Within months, however, Einstein's life was to be transformed.

9

The Holy One

THROUGHOUT all his years with Mileva, Einstein was unknown outside physics. Within a few months of his divorce and remarriage, however, he was celebrated across the world. People who had only the haziest understanding of his discoveries held him in awe. He became the first superstar of science.

He owed his sudden fame to the headline writers of newspapers in England and America. 'Revolution in science, New theory of the universe, Newtonian ideas overthrown,' thundered *The Times* in London on 7 November 1919. 'Lights all askew in the heavens, Men of science more or less agog . . . Einstein theory triumphs,' announced the *New York Times* two days later. Their reports revealed the findings of two British expeditions earlier that year to observe a solar eclipse. Scientists based at Sobral, in northern Brazil, and on the island of Principe, off the west coast of Africa, had witnessed the bending of starlight predicted by Einstein in his general theory. The results caused a sensation when announced in London at the rooms of the Royal Society, whose president hailed relativity as perhaps the most momentous product of human thought.

Abraham Pais has called this 'the birth of the Einstein legend'. It hardly mattered that no one at the London meeting could give a clear non-mathematical statement of the new ideas: a world exhausted by war was eager for distractions, and relativity became a public sensation. Warped space and the bending of light provided instantly beguiling slogans, however obscure their detail. Suddenly the mysteries of the heavens – mysteries that held a magic for anyone who had gazed up at the night sky – seemed to have been unlocked. Einstein's strange new order, in which little was what it had seemed, captured the disturbed mood of the times. Yet it was also a triumph of human logic, a vindication of rationality after the war's senseless barbarism. Einstein was not the only man for whom science could provide an escape from the dark and irrational.

Once the story broke, reporters rushed to meet the man behind it. They could not believe their luck. Instead of some stereotypical grey academic they found a wild-haired eccentric with rumpled charm and a mocking sense of humour. Einstein was good copy, and soon his opinions were being sought at every opportunity and on every subject. 'They all want articles, statements, photographs etc.,' he wrote at Christmas 1919. 'The thing reminds one of the story of the emperor's new clothes, but it is a harmless piece of folly.' He soon felt that he was like Midas, but, instead of gold, everything he touched turned into a fuss in the newspapers.

Einstein became a media sage, courted the world over. During the next decade he made visits to Scandinavia, the United States, Japan, the Middle East, the Far East, South America and the United Kingdom, where the London Palladium asked him to put on his own three-week show and the daughter of his host, Lord Haldane, fainted on meeting him. During a trip to Geneva, he was mobbed by young girls, one of whom tried to snip off a lock of his hair. Babies, cigars, telescopes and towers were named after him, and a daily torrent of letters began to arrive. They continued for the rest of his life: letters from well-wishers, religious cranks, spongers begging for money, pressure groups seeking endorsements, children wanting help with their homework – even, eventually, from a little girl asking, 'Do you exist?'

Elsa set out to shield her new husband from this frenzy of public curiosity. She became a mixture of a general manager and a watchdog, organizing Einstein's social schedule and warning away unwelcome visitors. Barring the door, and peering suspiciously through her lorgnette, she would inspect each new arrival from head to foot then brusquely demand their business. Her bark could be fearsome, and one regular guest compared her to Cerberus, the three-headed hound guarding the entrance of hell. 'Don't be put off by Frau Einstein,' her husband told a physics researcher who asked to visit him. 'She's there to protect me.'

Their home at Haberlandstrasse lay on a peaceful tree-lined street in Berlin's Bavarian Quarter. At least one visitor felt that the buildings were 'uniformly ugly', but the interior of their apartment at number five radiated unpretentious comfort. In an echo of Einstein's childhood nickname, the main salon was known as the Biedermeier room, after the solidly reassuring style of its heavy wooden furniture. It was dominated by a grand piano on which Einstein kept his violin case, and led out to a balcony that was rarely used but drew in floods of sunlight. There was a gloomily intimate dining-room with a massive sideboard filling the length of one wall, and a library with books stacked to the ceiling. Pictures adorned the walls, porcelain filled the shelves, and goldfish swam in a bowl on the window-sill. There was little originality to the furnishings, but no shortage of the cosiness that Elsa so prized.

For Einstein it was like a return to his childhood. Descriptions of the flat evoke what his son-in-law called 'the well-to-do philistine atmosphere' in which Einstein had grown up. Now, as then, there was neither poverty nor wealth but solid bourgeois comfort. Now, as then, this answered Einstein's need for domestic security while also providing something satisfying to kick against. Philipp Frank felt that his friend remained a 'foreigner' in his new surroundings – 'a bohemian guest in a middle-class home'. The truth is that Einstein was in his element. The mark of a foreigner is that he has to adapt to the customs of his hosts, but it was Elsa and her children who bent to the whims of Einstein.

One of Elsa's first tasks was to tend the deathbed of the woman whose role she was taking over in many ways. A few years earlier, Einstein's mother had undergone surgery for abdominal cancer. The disease returned in 1918, and by the end of the following year it was clear that she was terminally ill. She asked to be with her son, and at the start of 1920 arrived to spend her last months in his new marital home. Einstein set up a bed for her in his study, and reported to Zangger, 'she clings to life but still looks good.' Morphine helped to ease Pauline's agonies, but loosened her grip on reality. Her mind began to wander. As Einstein had told Besso, it was a dismal affair. Almost apologetically, he admitted that it left him too agitated to attend to his work.

Pauline's ambition had been one of the sharpest spurs to her son's development. He had eagerly told her of his successes, posting off a press cutting in May 1919 'for the further nourishment of Mama's anyhow already considerable mother's pride'. His first reaction on learning of the crucial eclipse results had been to send her a postcard, passing on the 'joyous news'. Now her last illness sapped his energies. He told Max Born in a letter at the end of January 1920 that Pauline was 'in a hopeless condition and suffering unspeakably', adding that it seemed that many months would pass before she was finally released. Far from making his usual boasts of indifference to human cares, he voiced envy of Born's better ability to rise above them.

All this has diminished still further my already faltering desire to achieve great things. Now you are quite different. Your little clan has its own difficulties to deal with . . . And you, Max, are giving lectures on relativity to save the institute from penury, and writing papers as if you were a single young man living in splendid isolation in his own specially heated apartment, with none of the worries of a *paterfamilias* nagging you. How do you do it?

Pauline Einstein died in February 1920, rather sooner than her son had expected. He told Zangger of the 'terrible torments' she had suffered, and went on: 'We are all quite exhausted . . . One feels down to the bones what blood ties mean . . . One stands here as if in front of a wall, unable to build a picture of the future.' A year or so earlier, he had assured his friend Erwin Freundlich that there was no one whose death would disturb him. Now Freundlich's wife, Käthe, was secretly glad to see the hollowness of his boast exposed. 'For Einstein wept, like other men,' she said, 'and I knew that he could really care for someone.' The following month, Einstein wrote to console Hedwig Born after her mother had died of influenza. 'I know what it means to see one's mother suffer the agony of death and be unable to help,' he told her. 'There is no consolation.'

Einstein's feelings for his mother had not suddenly lost their old ambivalence, however. Dr Janos Plesch, who attended Pauline on her deathbed and became a close friend of her son, believed that he was saddened but not heartbroken by her plight. It seems that Plesch detected the hostility and resentment that lingered on and made it hard for Einstein to mourn his mother's passing without reservation.

When Einstein's prickly Aunt Julie died in 1914, he had admitted to Elsa, 'I don't really feel any pain about that, God forgive me.' Now he felt pain, but it was almost certainly combined with the same guilty sense of antipathy. These mixed emotions can only have made the death more disturbing, particularly since its timing carried such rich symbolism. Just as Einstein's first marriage began in the shadow of his father's death, so his second was beginning with the loss of his mother. Fate seemed to be telling him that intimacy carried a fatal price.

Although he had told Hedwig Born there was no comfort in such a situation, Einstein did offer some. 'The old, who have died, live on in the young ones,' his note to her continued. 'Don't you feel this now in your bereavement when you look at your children?' Einstein's relationship to his sons was of central importance to his emotional life in the years after his mother's death, but remarriage had also given him two daughters, who had taken the name Einstein by legal decree even before he became their stepfather. Einstein treated them with affection, even love, but it did not strike observers as the love of a father. After all, thanks to Elsa's parentage, they were also his second cousins.

Ilse, her mother's favourite, was a delicately attractive young woman who kept sophisticated company and dressed in the latest fashions. In 1924 she married Rudolf Kayser, the editor of Germany's foremost literary magazine, and moved with him into a modishly furnished house where they played host to Berlin's smart set. She continued to visit her old home, but Einstein spent far more time in the company of her younger sister. Margot was a frail and nervous individual, plainer and less sociable than Ilse, who remained living at home even after her marriage in 1930 to Dimitri Marianoff. Margot and Einstein grew extremely close, and he encouraged her developing career as a sculptor. According to Marianoff, she was so shy that 'many times' she would hide under a table when caught unawares by her stepfather's guests. Einstein would then cover her with the tablecloth, and she would not emerge until the visitors left. Other evidence suggests this was not simply shyness, but a strange possessiveness. Margot could be openly jealous of people who kept Einstein in conversation too long, showing a fire quite out of keeping with her usual bashfulness. She vigorously nagged her stepfather in private on everything from his slovenly dress to his bad manners, and often subjected him to amiable mockery. This bossy affection irresistibly recalls that of her mother for the same man. In later years, it was Margot more often than Elsa who accompanied Einstein on public appearances.

Einstein's grim mood after his mother's death found an echo in the general misery of postwar Germany, although he told Zangger that his Berlin colleagues were far more agreeable since defeat had punctured their complacency. 'Misfortune suits humanity incomparably better than success,' he said. But Einstein was a convenient target for the bitterness that swept the country in the wake of its humiliation. A hate-campaign arose against him, feeding off anti-Semitism, the resentment of professional rivals, and hostility about his stand against the war. There were disturbances in February 1920 during a lecture he gave at the University of Berlin, and in August a mass meeting was held in the city's largest concert hall with the sole purpose of discrediting his ideas. The meeting was sponsored by a new organization calling itself the Study Group of German Natural Philosophers, whose number included Mileva's former lecturer Philipp Lenard. Einstein tagged them the Anti-Relativity Company. With typical bloody-mindedness he went along to watch their performance from a box seat, and laughed and clapped as he was vilified from the stage.

Einstein told his friends that the experience was very amusing, but his unadmitted rage spewed forth in an article he wrote for a local newspaper. Heaping scorn on his critics, whom he conceded were not worthy of a reply, he taunted that they would never have spoken up had he been 'a German national, with or without swastika'. It was a justifiably bitter reaction, but one that publicly exposed the limits of his cool self-sufficiency. This caused surprise and embarrassment to many of his friends. The Ehrenfests found his reaction a vulgar echo of the attacks – proof that 'these damned pigs' had touched Einstein's soul. 'That people can still disappoint and irritate you to the point where it affects your peace of mind just does not fit my image of you, which I keep on the private altar of my heart,' wrote Hedwig Born. Einstein, she recalled, had spoken of withdrawing to the 'secluded temple of science' from the rough and tumble of ordinary life. 'So if the filthy waters of the world are now lapping at the steps of your temple, shut the door and laugh. Just say, "After all, I have not entered the temple in vain." Don't get angry. Go on being the holy one in the temple . . .' It was advice that Einstein would try to follow for the rest of his life. But, as he admitted to the Borns, 'Everyone has to sacrifice at the altar of stupidity from time to time, to please the Deity and the human race.'

Einstein's home life was arranged to allow no more intimacy than he required, and he and Elsa had separate bedrooms at opposite corners of the apartment. Her own explanation for this was that he snored 'unbelievably loudly' and was impossible to sleep with. If Einstein left his room at night, his most likely destination was the kitchen, where he would improvise on the violin and enjoy the echoing acoustics of the tiled walls. A daytime refuge was constructed for him in the attic. His stepson-in-law Rudolf Kayser remarked on the 'puritanical simplicity' of this little turret, but recognized that comfort was not the point: it permitted 'complete retirement and, therefore, independence'. The maid was allowed to dust the books once a week, when Einstein was out, but Elsa was barred from entering. She felt rather hurt, wrote Plesch, 'but Einstein was adamant . . . it was the independence that mattered.'

Plesch portrayed his friend as a man 'fanatically insistent' on independence, to the extent of rejecting the corporative 'we' of marriage. No one, least of all Elsa, was to have the right to speak for him. It was as if he simply failed to grasp the meaning of the first person plural, said Plesch, who wrote that the only time he saw Einstein furious was when Elsa let the word 'we' slip from her lips. The man who filled his letters to Mileva with references to the work 'we' would complete, and the life 'we' would lead, now forbade his second wife ever to use the word on their common behalf. 'Speak of you or me but never of us,' he snapped. The importance of the point is borne out by a snatch of verse found among Einstein's papers:

> I feel ill at ease with that little word 'We'.
> No man is at one with another, you see.
> Behind all agreement lies something amiss.
> All seeming accord cloaks a lurking abyss.

Einstein spoke with the same voice in a splendidly guarded endorsement of a biography written of him in 1931 by Rudolf Kayser, and dedicated to Elsa. The book, he conceded, was 'as good as might be expected of one who is perforce himself, and who can no more be another than I can'. Yet in the same introduction he warned that 'what has perhaps been overlooked is the irrational, the inconsistent, the droll, even the insane' which nature implanted in every individual.

Elsa was rarely heard to call him by his first name. She would refer to 'my husband' or 'my old one', or sometimes to 'the Professor'. But often she would simply use his surname, saying 'Einstein wants this' or 'Einstein needs that'. Despite this distance, however, he depended on her utterly. Elsa even gave Einstein pocket-money, knowing that if trusted with any large sum he was likely to give it away impulsively, as easily to a transparent swindler as to a genuinely deserving cause. Plesch's portrait suggests some helpless baby, reliant on mother at every turn:

> As his mind knows no limits so his body follows no set rules: he sleeps until he is wakened; he stays awake until he is told to go to bed; he will go hungry until he is given something to eat; and then he eats until he is stopped. I can remember his consuming between five and ten pounds of strawberries at a sitting on more than one occasion ... As Einstein never seems to feel the ordinary impulses to eat, etc., he has to be looked after like a child. He was very lucky in his second wife.

It was as if Einstein was happiest living in a trance, content for others to guide him around the obstacles of daily life. According to Marianoff, a typical meal would begin with Elsa summoning him from his work by increasingly peremptory calls. Einstein would appear with a gaze of fixed absorption, muttering protests under his breath, then move to the table like a sleep-walker. He would sit at his soup bowl, moving the spoon back and forth to his mouth with a rhythmical and mechanical motion, shaking his head vaguely when conversation was directed his way. The food set before him would be consumed without question or comment. It was as if his mind was far away in space and had not yet returned to his body. In the meantime, that body was entirely under Elsa's care.

Elsa described how Einstein sometimes restlessly roamed the apartment, lost in thought, oblivious to her existence. He would wander off to his study, come back, absently finger the piano, jot down some notes, then wander off to his study again. She would make herself scarce, but only after setting out some food for him to eat when the spell broke. Her husband was like a boy lost in a dreamworld, sauntering out into the rain without a coat or hat, then returning to stand aimlessly on the staircase. Plesch told how Elsa once opened her husband's suitcase after a foreign trip and was surprised to find the contents arranged with exquisite neatness and care. Rightly detecting a woman's hand at work, she demanded to know who had been looking after him so lovingly in her absence. Einstein looked a little embarrassed, then admitted that the hand at work was her own. He had not bothered to open the case since Elsa had packed it for him before departure.

Life was not easy for Elsa, who became the butt of much snide criticism in Berlin. She was dismissed as intellectually unworthy to be Einstein's companion. She was accused of stopping fellow scientists from visiting him, in favour of celebrities from politics and the arts. She was said to be glorying in her husband's fame without appreciating his inner worth. It was all rather unfair. Philipp Frank wrote, 'The people about her were always inclined to look very critically at her and, as a compensation for the respect that they reluctantly paid her husband, to unload upon her all the reproaches they would have liked to bring against him.'

Elsa never pretended to understand relativity, and told questioners, 'It is not necessary for my happiness.' But this was not the whole story. Her friend Antonina Vallentin suggested that Elsa felt irritated, even slightly humiliated, by the foolish impression that her ignorance created. Vallentin wrote, 'Elsa's quick intelligence would have certainly let her glimpse the world in which her husband lived, but she abstained, deliberately, and Einstein has always been grateful to her for having left this line of demarcation between them.' This rather exaggerates Elsa's mental acuity, but probably holds a grain of truth. The intellectual gap between Einstein and his second wife suited him better than it suited her.

Vallentin also hinted that Elsa was blithely exploited by Einstein in his dealings with the outside world. It was he who gave the command to repel unwelcome boarders, but she who was left alone to fend off the blows. Like a knowingly winsome child, he could rely on his charm and apparent naïvety to excuse his own boorishness. And, whenever he chose, he could overrule his wife by unexpectedly extending an interview or accepting an invitation. There were indeed many visits to Haberlandstrasse by celebrities outside science, from Charlie Chaplin to Heinrich and Thomas Mann, but these would not have been tolerated unless they gave satisfaction to Einstein, and any innocent pleasure that Elsa derived was made up for in unease. Vallentin was at pains to stress that Elsa was in many ways a shy woman, and that, unlike Einstein's shyness, her own bore 'no compensatory feeling of self-satisfaction'. Plesch was equally emphatic, writing, 'She kept herself in the background as far as possible, and never willingly took any of the limelight.'

Elsa tended to be blamed for Einstein's own ambivalence towards life as a celebrity. He genuinely disliked constant media attention, and treated fame's trappings with contempt. Formal social dinners, for example, were dismissed as 'feeding time at the zoo'. Yet fame became addictive in its way. Hans Albert called his father a bit of a ham, and many years later described taking a trip with him through the backwaters of America, where Einstein went completely unrecognized. At first this amused Einstein greatly, but then he began to show an irritable disappointment. He enjoyed having an audience, even if only to complain about it, and his harsh words on the subject may reflect a certain guilt about this secret satisfaction.

Such ambivalence was highlighted by one of his earliest brushes with a biographer, Alexander Moszkowski. Einstein granted the writer a number of interviews, which were then collected as a book in 1921. It was a small piece of self-indulgence by a man who enjoyed holding court and passing opinions. But Einstein's friends were appalled, since his enemies in the Anti-Relativity Company had already accused him of being a self-publicist. They were quick to blame Elsa, convinced that her love of publicity was leading astray her unworldly husband, and sought to intervene. Hedwig Born fired off a letter ordering Einstein to cancel his permission for publication ('and what's more at once and by registered letter'). She explained:

If I did not know you well, I certainly would not concede innocent motives to any other human being given these circumstances. I would put it down to vanity. The book will constitute
your moral death sentence for all but four or five of your friends.
It could subsequently be the best confirmation of the accusation
of self-advertisement . . . Please, dear friend, quickly relieve our
worries . . . I shall never talk to anyone about this business, for I
have heard enough how much you dislike it when women
meddle in your affairs. 'Women are there to cook and nothing
else'; but it sometimes happens that they boil over . . .

This was a pun on the German for cooking ('*kochen*') and boiling
over ('*über-kochen*'). Whatever illusions Hedwig Born retained about
Einstein's lack of vanity, she had none concerning his attitude
towards the opposite sex.

Her husband Max joined in the attack, with the same manner of
someone acting *in loco parentis*. He apologized for his officious tone
but told Einstein, 'You do not understand this, in these matters you
are a little child. We all love you, and you must obey judicious people
(not your wife).' Einstein's reply was characteristic. 'The whole affair
is a matter of indifference to me, as is all the commotion, and the
opinion of each and every human being,' he wrote. 'Therefore
nothing can happen to me.' It is revealing that he nevertheless promised to suppress the book, which appeared despite his efforts under
the title *Einstein the Searcher*. It clearly irritated him when Hans
Albert bought a copy in Zurich. Einstein urged him to swap it for
something else, and to check with Papa before obtaining 'something
like that' in future: 'I was unable to prevent its publication, and it has
caused me a lot of grief.'

One of the most interesting passages in the book concerned the
education of women. The author gamely remarked that Einstein's
opinions were 'tolerant, and yet did not suggest . . . a champion of the
cause.'

'As in all other directions,' Einstein said, 'so in that of science the
way should be made easy for women. Yet it must not be taken
amiss if I regard the possible results with a certain amount of
scepticism. I am referring to certain obstacles in woman's organ-

ization which we must regard as given by Nature, and which forbid us from applying the same standard of expectation to women as to men.'

According to Moszkowski, Einstein believed that high achievements in science were beyond women's grasp. He would accept Marie Curie only as a 'brilliant exception, more of which may occur without refuting the statute of sexual organization.' At one point he burst out, 'It is conceivable that Nature may have created a sex without brains!'

Moszkowski called this a grotesque remark, which was in no way to be taken literally. It was intended, he said, as 'an amusing exaggeration' of Einstein's belief that physical differences between the sexes were matched on the mental plane. The soul of woman had a refinement of which man was not capable, but scientific genius depended on 'a preponderance of brain substance'. Thus, wrote Moszkowski, it was no more possible to imagine a female Galileo or Kepler than it was a female Michelangelo. The only comfort was that 'although a woman could not create the differential calculus, it was she that created Leibniz; similarly she produced Kant if not the *Critique of Pure Reason*.' There is reason to think that this accurately reflected Einstein's opinions. In a letter to one admirer, he remarked that the study of mathematics 'almost always takes its revenge on women', due to their inability to withstand the necessary exertions. Hedwig Born recalled that he once announced that 'where you females are concerned, your production centre is not situated in the brain.' He showed little enthusiasm for sexual equality, and wrote to his son Eduard that only women of a masculine disposition campaigned for women's rights.

It is ironic that, as he attacked the scientific talents of women, his own work was becoming increasingly sterile. It was after the First World War that Einstein turned to the quest for a so-called unified field theory, a single set of equations that would marry the laws of gravity and electromagnetism. These were then believed to be the two fundamental forces in nature, so a theory explaining both would solve all nature's puzzles. The project appealed irresistibly to Einstein's yearning for order and harmony, and its colossal ambition was in keeping with his view of his own exalted mission. His imagination was fired in 1918 by the German-born mathematician Hermann Weyl, who suggested extending general relativity to treat electromagnetism – like gravity – as an aspect of the geometry of the universe. Although Einstein pounced on a flaw in the plan, he found it aesthetically appealing. In 1922 he produced his first paper on the subject. Years of work followed, but Einstein's scientific instinct was no longer as strong as it had been. He also ignored emerging evidence that gravity and electromagnetism were not nature's only forces after all, since other interactions were at work within the atom. Even today, those who venerate Einstein's achievements at the forefront of the effort to unite nature's fundamental forces are baffled by his quixotic approach.

As his fiftieth birthday approached in 1929, reports circulated that Einstein was on the verge of a great discovery. The public clamoured for details, and when his latest paper emerged it was printed in full by the *New York Herald Tribune*. In London, it was displayed in the window of Selfridges department store and drew large crowds. All this was a tribute to the power of Einstein's name, but in fact the paper's thirty-three equations were meaningless to the layman and solved only a few preliminary problems of fiendish technical complexity. In the 1930s, Einstein continued his pursuit of unification with his assistant Walther Mayer and then Peter Bergmann and Valentin Bargmann. As a sad measure of the excitement elicited by this venture, only a small minority of theoretical physicists worked on the problem internationally. One of the great men of science, Wolfgang Pauli, made a withering remark on how Einstein's tenacity and inventiveness guaranteed a new unification theory each year. 'It is psychologically interesting that for some time the current theory is usually considered by its author to be the "definitive solution".'

Einstein's determination to follow his own road, which had led to such success in the past, was now taking him down a dead end. He showed the same heroic folly in his refusal to accept the new challenge of quantum mechanics. Indeed, one reason for his interest in a unified field theory was that he thought it would help to eliminate the quantum paradoxes that he himself had helped to reveal. In 1924, the Frenchman Louis de Broglie turned round Einstein's work on the photoelectric effect from 1905. Just as Einstein had suggested that light 'waves' could also be treated as particles, so de Broglie suggested that 'particles' such as electrons could also be treated as waves. Then the German Werner Heisenberg showed that uncertainty was an essential feature of this sub-atomic world, because the 'particles' did not possess distinct properties of momentum and position. You could say where one was, or how quickly it was moving, but not both at the same time. This was not some technical problem, but an irreducible fact of nature. It was a world that could be described only in terms of probabilities. One of the key concepts of quantum mechanics is the 'wavefunction' – the quantity that is used to calculate the probability of a particular sub-atomic event occurring. According to the so-called Copenhagen interpretation of quantum theory, there are in general a vast number of possible outcomes until the very moment that the wavefunction is 'collapsed' by an act of observation or measurement. The most famous illustration of this idea is the 'cat paradox' devised by Erwin Schrödinger, which implies that a cat can be both alive and dead at the same time.

Einstein fought grimly against this lack of certainty ('God does not play dice' was his famous riposte), and held a long debate with the Danish quantum expert Niels Bohr. Ironically, his persistent objections helped the new theory by forcing its proponents to clarify it. But his opposition pushed him ever further to the fringes of science, as younger thinkers without his inhibitions moved to the centre. Abraham Pais has written that Einstein's peers experienced 'a sense of loss, of being abandoned in battle by a venerated leader'. Ehrenfest was so upset that once, as he admitted that Bohr was right and his beloved friend Einstein was wrong, tears streamed down his face.

As his dominance of science waned, Einstein found distractions in public life and his deep-rooted passion for idealistic politics. The rise of overt anti-Semitism encouraged him to stand up for Zionism, the drive for a Jewish homeland. In 1921 he had joined Chaim Weizmann, later the first president of Israel, on a fund-raising trip to America. Two years later he made a visit to Palestine, and became the first person to be given the freedom of Tel Aviv. Einstein also showed support for the Communist regime in Moscow, and helped to found an organization calling itself the Association of Friends of the New Russia. Marianoff reported that he was particularly impressed when told by Margot that the Soviet system had eliminated prostitution.

His views were less naïve than has sometimes been claimed, but were often impractical, and his commitment to action was at best intermittent. In 1922 he joined a Committee of Intellectual Co-operation set up by the League of Nations. He resigned almost immediately, rejoined, but never took much part in proceedings and finally quit for good in 1931.

One reason for his first resignation was the assassination by right-wingers of Germany's foreign minister, Walther Rathenau, a Jewish acquaintance of Einstein's and a fellow internationalist. The murder deeply disturbed Einstein, and was another sign of the poisonous mood taking hold of the country. This even tainted an attempt by the city of Berlin to honour him with the gift of a summer house on the banks of the Havel river. The scheme became mired in a mixture of incompetence and legal problems, and was then attacked by local extremists determined to do Einstein down. Finally, in the summer of 1929, he bought a plot of land at the village of Caputh, near Berlin, and built his own house on it.

Einstein's sister, Maja, stayed at the house in the autumn of 1930 and wrote to a friend that it was 'furnished with all the chicanery of modern times, yet with a lot of taste'. It was of simple design and contained items of furniture from Haberlandstrasse. The rooms were of modest size, except for the living-room overlooking the garden. Einstein and Elsa had separate bedrooms, his doubling as a study that was as sacrosanct as was his little turret in Berlin. The interior of the house was of rich dark wood, relieved by the chequerboard tiled floor of the entrance hall. There was a sun terrace where Einstein's stepdaughters liked to lounge, but his own favourite spot was a shady overhang on the north side.

The cabin's situation was 'simply wonderful,' according to Maja: from a slightly raised perch in a forest, it commanded a view across the lake and 'rolling landscape all around'. Solitary walks in the woods gave Einstein 'indescribable joy', and rich friends had already clubbed together to buy him a beautiful mahogany boat that he kept in Plesch's boat-house on the Havel.

In his little boat, Einstein could be alone. He could also enjoy the company of a close friend or member of the family, leaving visitors – and Elsa – far behind. Maja described how she spent much of her time sailing with him that autumn. It was the most beautiful part of her visit to Caputh, she said: sometimes brother and sister talked a great deal, sometimes they were silent. Maja said she was happy that they were together and so was he. Einstein told Eduard that the time he spent sailing was 'majestic without compare', but his mood during these trips was not always tranquil, as one visitor found after joining him on the water with Hans Albert. 'Every time his son made what he thought was a mistake in the sailing of the boat, Einstein would burst out about the educational system of the gymnasia – how inefficient it was, and how it was responsible for all the mistakes men make in later life.'

The architect who designed the summer house, Konrad Wachsmann, developed a close relationship with Einstein and Elsa. His recollections, recently published in German, reveal that the marriage was by then under considerable strain. There were frequent rows, even talk of separation, and the reason was always the same. Women were drawn to the world-famous professor like iron filings to a magnet, says Wachsmann, and Einstein responded with open eagerness to their attentions. A series of liaisons developed, some of them casual, a few of them intimate, all deeply wounding to the pride of his betrayed wife. Einstein provoked Elsa into the same jealous furies that he had complained of in Mileva. His wife would refuse to speak to him for days on end, except on the most necessary matters, and would go about their apartment with a fixed and icy smile.

Einstein in turn would retreat even further into himself, or flee to the home of a male friend such as Plesch or Max Planck. Finally his anger would erupt against what he called this 'childish' behaviour by his wife, and there would be threats of departure on both sides. Marianoff described how he and Margot witnessed one such outburst as Elsa and Einstein walked into the room where they were sitting. 'He was aroused and shouting like a lion, and let me tell you, when Albert's voice was raised in anger, one heard it in every corner of the house.'

It was a problem that had been developing for some time. The international sensation caused by relativity had only added to Einstein's charisma. Everywhere he went he would be the centre of attention – particularly female attention. An unaccountable passion for science arose in women to whom the subject was normally soporific. Each would demand a personal explanation of relativity, with the attendant opportunity to hear the great man's voice and feel his eyes upon them. A witness at one Frankfurt dinner party described how Einstein joined in a performance of some chamber music, only to find himself surrounded by besotted female admirers, all competing to cover him with praise. One was so overwhelmed that she left convinced that he was a spiritualist, since he believed 'in the fourth dimension'.

Up to a point, Elsa regarded this interest with amused tolerance. An insider's view is provided by Marianoff, who described in detail how social hostesses pursued their famous prey.

> Many of them were very beautiful, and nearly all of them wanted more from Einstein than was indicated in their very formal approach. Some managed with the stratagem of war generals to meet him; others did so openly. One woman, on being presented to him, turned to Elsa, frankly, and said: 'May I speak to Professor Einstein for a few minutes?' – a quite open declaration that she wished to see him alone. Elsa tactfully replied, 'Of course, you may,' and smiled knowingly at him. He smiled back, because both of them understood the motive behind the request. Her tact and delicate instinct were masterly in handling instances such as this, but some were unavoidable, and many times were accompanied by an atmosphere of distaste . . .
>
> Many women tried to come into his life. Some wrote letters recalling to him a brief transitory meeting; others brought flowers and left them with a note and their addresses. We, of the household, understood these to be only the worthless emphases of fame. They reminded me of the stragglers of a romantic period, who followed the leader of a brilliant and dazzling army.

According to Marianoff, these approaches left Einstein largely unmoved, since there were 'no dark fires in his blood' and his 'healthy love of the physical' was confined to walking and sailing. But there is plenty of evidence to the contrary, not least the curious affair of Grete Markstein, the Berlin actress who claimed to be Einstein's daughter.

Even though this allegation was false, it appears that her relationship with him was far more intimate than he cared to admit.

Abraham Pais has referred to letters written by Einstein in the early 1920s 'showing that for several years he had a strong attachment to a younger woman'. According to Pais, the letters expressed emotions 'for which, perhaps, he had no energy to spare in his marriages'. The romance ended late in 1924, 'when he wrote to her that he had to seek in the stars what was denied to him on earth.' But Pais remains convinced that Einstein had experienced a profound attraction, 'more emotionally felt' than his relationship with Mileva. The relevant letters are inaccessible, and Pais does not reveal the identity of the woman. However, there is reason to believe that she was one of Einstein's earliest secretaries, Betty Neumann, the niece of a close friend of Einstein, Dr Hans Mühsam. Indirect evidence comes from letters by Elsa showing that Einstein fell out badly with his friend, who had previously visited him almost daily and had been one of his closest confidants.

Chaim Weizmann's wife, Vera, who accompanied Einstein and her husband on their trip to America in 1921, described him as 'gay and flirtatious'. Elsa told Mrs Weizmann that she did not mind Einstein making eyes at her, since intellectual women did not seriously attract him. Instead he was drawn 'out of pity' to women who did physical work. Much the same point was made by Janos Plesch, who described his friend as a man with a strong sex drive, eagerly taking full advantage of the charms with which nature equipped him. 'In the choice of his love-partners he was not too discriminating,' wrote Plesch, 'but was more drawn to the robust child of nature than the subtle society woman.' By way of example, he recounted an incident where Einstein became enraptured by the sight of a girl kneading bread. Elsa sensed trouble, and stepped in smartly to keep the two of them apart. Plesch passed on his observations to his son, Peter, who puts the matter even more bluntly: 'Einstein loved women, and the commoner and sweatier and smellier they were, the better he liked them.'

Marianoff believed that physical beauty never mattered much to Einstein, and he echoed Elsa's point about an attraction based on pity. In his opinion, all the women who succeeded in becoming

Einstein's friends were very homely. 'This peculiar fact was commented on by his intimates. Personally, I always felt that Einstein was
attracted towards the ugliness of women only because of his large
compassion.' By other accounts, this 'large compassion' extended
further than Marianoff thought, and was just as likely to be aroused
by the beautiful as by the plain. Einstein told one acquaintance that
the sight of a pretty young woman made him sad, since it reminded
him of the short span human beings were allotted on earth. Herta
Waldow, who served as his live-in maid from 1927 to 1932, said, 'He
liked beautiful women, and they in turn adored him.'

Waldow had first-hand experience of Einstein's cavalier attitude
towards his own sexuality, since he had a disconcerting habit of
leaving his dressing-gown undone as he wandered out of the bathroom. Nor was this immodesty reserved for indoors. Once he sprang
up from lounging in the sun to greet her female cousin, only for the
robe he was wearing to fall away and reveal his nakedness. Einstein
was unabashed by the young woman's blushes. 'How long have you
been married?' he demanded. Ten years, came the reply. 'How many
children have you got?' Three, said the cousin. 'And still you go red?'
he mocked.

The tension caused by Einstein's girlfriends was obvious to
Waldow, who came to know some of them well. One of her
employer's most regular escorts to concerts and the opera was Toni
Mendel, a wealthy and elegant Jewish widow. She cultivated Elsa
with gifts of chocolate creams, although Waldow felt that her 'close
friendship' with Einstein was only grudgingly tolerated by his wife.
Frau Mendel would collect Einstein for their outings in her chauffeur-
driven car and also buy their tickets for the night's show. But Einstein
still depended on Elsa to dole out his pocket-money, and there were
angry scenes when he demanded funds to pay for his companion's
incidental expenses. Einstein made frequent overnight visits to the
luxurious Mendel villa on the Wannsee, playing the piano in the
music room at great volume until six o'clock in the morning. It was a
friendship that survived when both parties were driven out of Germany by the Nazis, with Einstein living in Princeton and Frau Mendel
in Ontario. Herta also observed frequent visits by Estella Katzenellen-

bogen, the rich and elegant owner of a florist business, who transported Einstein about Berlin in her expensive limousine.

Then there was a blonde Austrian, Margarete Lebach, who became a weekly visitor to Einstein's summer house in 1931. She too brought edible offerings for Elsa – vanilla pastries that she baked herself. Einstein celebrated their delicate flavour in verse, writing that they made 'the little angels sing'. Frau Lebach enjoyed great liberty in his company, as Waldow has explained:

> When she came, Frau Professor would always go into Berlin to do some errands or other business. She always went off into the city early in the morning and only came back late in the evening. She left the field clear, so to speak. The Austrian woman was younger than Frau Professor, and was very attractive, lively, and liked to laugh a lot just like the Professor.

The couple's relationship was an open secret among local people, who would see them sailing together on the Havel. But vanilla pastries can buy only limited wifely sufferance. Waldow overheard a passionate argument about the Austrian interloper between Elsa and her daughters. Einstein was away, and the maid listened through the wooden walls of the summer house as the girls told their mother she must either put up with the relationship or seek a separation. They spoke of Einstein merely by his first name, rather than their usual and more affectionate 'Father Albert'. Elsa was in tears, but made her decision. The trips into Berlin continued.

It was this kind of humiliation that drove Elsa into fits of jealous rage. Once, after a sailing trip at Caputh, Einstein forgot to bring back from the boat some clothes that needed washing. His conscientious assistant Walther Mayer volunteered to fetch them, and brought back a bundle that Elsa took away to sort out. Shortly afterwards, Einstein was summoned inside and the couple's guests overheard a sharp exchange of words. It emerged that Mayer's bundle included an elegant and very low-cut bathing-dress, which he had wrongly assumed to be Margot's. Konrad Wachsmann, who recounted the story, added that the outfit belonged to 'a good acquaintance' of Einstein, and that Elsa became 'monstrously worked up'. Without naming the woman, he went on:

Her appearances in Caputh brought vexation with her every time, above all because the people in the village chatted about it. Truth to say, I understood the anger of Elsa Einstein, which I was very sorry about, because everything in Caputh was always poisoned for a few days after the visits of this beautiful woman.

Einstein joked that he preferred 'silent vice to ostentatious virtue', but there was little that was furtive about his affairs. Either they were conducted in open view, or easy clues were left for Elsa to discover. Another incident, recounted by Marianoff, gives the impression that Einstein was eager for his wife to know what he was up to:

While at Caputh I was out with him on his boat. After he attended to the big sails, and after it was running smoothly, he settled down with his hands on the rudder to the steering of it. We discussed different subjects idly, and finally the conversation turned on an incident that had been bothering Elsa to the extent of involving her health. It was a delicate matter, one that should have been sent into oblivion for all concerned. I said to him: 'Don't ever discuss this with Elsa again, Albert. It troubles her.'

Einstein nodded his head energetically in acquiescence. On our return to the house, we had no sooner stepped across the threshold of the door when, exactly like a small boy who had something on his mind that must be told to mother, he blurted out, in a tumble of sentences, the whole story that only a minute before he had decided to be silent about. I was amazed and speechless
. . .

Marianoff reported that he later reproached Einstein, saying how wounded Elsa had been by his confession. At first Einstein did not reply, and continued walking, but then he said slowly, 'We do things, but we do not know why we do them.'

As he grew older, Einstein had begun to express some very bitter feelings towards the opposite sex. One anecdote tells how he felt that a woman was tormenting 'a great artist' that he knew in Berlin, destroying the man's peace of mind and independence. While discussing some example of her shrewishness, Einstein declared, 'You know that is a creature I could kill in cold blood. I'd like to put a rope

around her neck and tighten it until her tongue lolled out.' To empha-
size his words, he made the appropriate gestures with his hands.

Einstein was also voicing deep misgivings about the institution of
holy matrimony. He told Plesch that it must have been invented 'by
an unimaginative pig', and once declared to Konrad Wachsmann that
it was 'slavery in a cultural garment'. The young architect would
listen patiently as Einstein argued that marriage was incompatible
with human nature. He claimed that 95 per cent of all men, and
probably as many women, were not monogamous by nature and
would prefer to enjoy a number of partners. It seemed to him that
marriage made people treat each other as articles of property and no
longer as free human beings.

The subject became a personal favourite, to which he returned
often during the remaining years of his life. 'Marriage is the unsuccessful attempt to make something lasting out of an incident,' he told
one friend. Asked on another occasion whether it was permissible for
Jews to marry non-Jews, he replied with a laugh, 'It's dangerous – but
then *all* marriages are dangerous.' Another questioner wanted to
know whether the real reason he smoked his pipe was for the pleasure
of cleaning and filling it, which he did incessantly. Einstein responded,
'My aim lies in smoking, but as a result things tend to get clogged up,
I'm afraid. Life, too, is like smoking, especially marriage.'

Wachsmann believed that Einstein's extra-marital liaisons were
'almost without exception' platonic, but was painfully aware of the
effect they had on Elsa. 'She probably suspected more than knew that
she had only borrowed this husband, and that every day she could
lose him again. The thought that she was leading her marriage on
credit must have hung over her like a Damoclean sword.' Elsa's private letters suggest that she sought as far as possible to block the
subject of infidelity from her mind. A genius of her husband's kind
would never be irreproachable in every respect, she wrote in 1929.
Where nature gave extravagantly, nature took away extravagantly.
Any attempt to analyse Einstein would result in unpleasantness: he
had to be taken as a wonderful, utterly exhausting whole.

In 1928 Einstein met the woman who was eventually to replace
Elsa as his mothering protector, Helen Dukas. Their encounter stem-
med from a physical collapse that he suffered while staying at the

Swiss mountain resort of Zuoz, when the strain of carrying a heavy suitcase proved too much for the body that Einstein had treated with cheery contempt for half a century. He was diagnosed as suffering from an enlarged heart, and remained bedridden for four months after his return to Berlin. It was Elsa who sought out an assistant to help him work while recuperating. Dukas was recommended by her elder sister Rosa, the executive secretary of the Jewish Orphan Organization, of which Elsa was honorary president. They enjoyed a special rapport because Elsa knew Dukas's mother and grandmother from Hechingen, their mutual home town. Dukas was out of work, after losing her post at a small publishing firm when it went into liquidation. She reported for duty on Friday 13 April, full of apprehension, but was put at ease when ushered into the invalid's bedroom. Einstein was at his most self-deprecatingly charming. 'When he looked up and saw me, he stretched his hand towards me and said smiling: "Here lies an old corpse." '

Dukas was a tall, slender and outwardly austere young woman, whose diffidence concealed a tough and sometimes sardonic personality. Although highly intelligent, she went to work for Einstein only after being assured that she would not need to understand physics. If asked to explain relativity, she would sometimes offer an explanation that he personally devised for her: an hour sitting with a pretty girl passes like a minute, but a minute sitting on a hot stove seems like an hour. Dukas admitted that she never lost a certain shyness in Einstein's presence, but she was soon treated as one of the family, sitting down to meals at Haberlandstrasse and joining the excursions to Caputh. 'That is Miss Dukas, my faithful helper,' Einstein said as he introduced her to the architect Wachsmann. 'Without her nobody would know that I was still alive, because she writes all my letters for me.' Dukas became fiercely loyal to her employer: she was liable to attack as 'dung' any biography that dared shed light on Einstein's personal life, and she saw newsmen as her 'natural enemies'. Wachsmann had an early taste of her protectiveness when he telephoned the apartment at the time of Einstein's fiftieth birthday. Dukas answered and admitted after some probing that the professor had gone away to escape the media fuss. He was hiding at Plesch's country estate at Gatow, but Dukas resolutely refused to let the location slip. 'That is not known to us,' she snapped – adding tartly, 'And if it was, I wouldn't tell you anyhow without express instructions.'

Not all outside pressures were so easy to resist. The Wall Street crash of October 1929 plunged the world into an unprecedented recession, and brought mass unemployment to the already failing German economy. This was the cue for Hitler's Nazi Party to begin its move towards power, winning nearly a fifth of the seats in the Reichstag elections of 1930. There was fighting on the streets between Nazis and Communists, and the liberal Weimar Republic set up in 1919 began to disintegrate. Hitler promised to make Germany great again, blaming the country's ills on decadent democrats and money-grubbing Jews. Einstein was once more the bigots' whipping-boy, with Philipp Lenard again leading attacks on 'Jewish physics' and 'its most prominent representative, the pure-blooded Jew, Albert Einstein'. The Nazis became the Reichstag's largest single party in July 1932, and were supported by powerful business interests. Einstein knew that his days in Germany were numbered, and began to consider ways of escape.

America beckoned. Einstein and Elsa spent the winters of 1930–1 and 1931–2 loosely based at the California Institute of Technology in Pasadena. The first of these visits attracted immense publicity, and Einstein's liner was met at New York by a crush of fifty journalists whose antics he likened to a Punch and Judy show. Besides parrying some particularly inane questions ('Will you define the Fourth Dimension in a single word?' asked one optimistic reporter), he also condemned Hitler for 'living on the empty stomach of Germany'. Einstein enraged his more conservative admirers by suggesting later during his stay that wars would be impossible if only two per cent of people had the courage to refuse military service. But mostly he was greeted with adulation, and was even given the title 'Great Relative' on a visit to an Indian Reservation at the Grand Canyon, where he posed smirking in a head-dress and carrying a pipe of peace.

On his second visit to Pasadena he held discussions with the educationalist Abraham Flexner, who was planning to create a new research centre with five million dollars provided by Jewish philanthropists. The Institute for Advanced Study in Princeton, as this became, might have been designed expressly to meet Einstein's needs.

Flexner referred to it as a haven where great scholars could work 'without being carried off in the maelstrom of the immediate'. He met Einstein again in the spring of 1932, while both were in Oxford, and directly offered him a place at the new Institute. Further talks followed in Germany, on the verandah at Caputh, and the invitation was accepted. Typically it was left to Elsa to sort out her husband's salary, after he suggested what seemed to Flexner the ludicrously low sum of 3,000 dollars a year. She agreed a more satisfactory 15,000 dollars, with the understanding that Einstein would start work a year later.

In December 1932, the Einsteins set off for America once again. It was intended only as another temporary visit, but they were never to return to Germany. Einstein sensed that this was the end. As they left Caputh he told Elsa, 'Turn around. You will never see it again.' The Nazis came to power in January 1933, when the senile President Hindenburg reluctantly appointed Hitler as chancellor. In March, the Brownshirt thugs of the Sturmabteilung raided the house at Caputh, hoping to find arms hidden by Communists. They discovered nothing more threatening than a bread-knife, but the message to Einstein was clear. On his return to Europe, he sent his resignation to the Prussian Academy and started to make arrangements for emigration.

Einstein set up a temporary home at the Villa Savoyarde in Le Coq sur Mer, a bathing-resort on the Belgian coast, in the spring of 1933. He was convinced the Nazis had the 'whip hand in Berlin' and were rearming. 'If they are given another year or two, the world will have another fine experience at the hands of the Germans,' he warned. Reports circulated that the Nazis had put a price on his head, and he was placed under armed guard. Elsa was at her most redoubtable and told a reporter from the Reuter agency, 'We have nothing to do with politics. A savant should be left in peace.' Even at this difficult hour, however, it appears that her private humiliation continued. Micha Battsek, Einstein's godson, recalls staying at Le Coq at the time with his parents, Karl and Rose, who were old friends of Einstein. The six-year-old Micha was fed chocolates by Helen Dukas, while his father tricked journalists by presenting himself in the guise of Einstein, whom he slightly resembled. But Battsek also vividly remembers the presence of a beautiful Viennese in her early forties. This was Margarete Lebach, the same woman who had caused Elsa so much heartache in Berlin. 'She was a very nice-looking lady who was a very close friend of Einstein's and who many years later my mother and father more or less implied was rather more than that,' says Battsek, who has no memories of seeing Elsa in Belgium at all. Lebach, a friend of the Battsek family, died in Vienna in 1938, after the Nazis denied her cancer surgery.

Einstein, Elsa and Helen Dukas set sail for a new life in the United States in October 1933. Rudolf Kayser emigrated to Holland, while Ilse took refuge with Margot and Marianoff in Paris. The transition was not an entirely easy one. Einstein had told his friend Besso almost a decade before that America was a land that made him appreciate Europe: though people there were freer of prejudice, he thought them dull and superficial. After his arrival, he described Princeton as a small, quiet and pretty place where the professors thought they were clever and the students played football and shouted all the time. He had a particularly jaundiced view of American women, which had been stimulated when a group calling itself the Woman Patriot Corporation opposed his application for a visitor's visa in 1932, claiming that he was a dangerous left-wing subversive. His reply was a masterpiece of misogynist scorn:

> Never before have I experienced from the fair sex such energetic rejection of all advances; or if I have, then certainly never from so many at once. But are they not right, these vigilant lady citizens? Why should one open one's doors to a man who devours hard-boiled capitalists with as much appetite and gusto as the Cretan Minotaur used to devour luscious Greek maidens, and who on top of that is so wicked as to reject every kind of war, except the unavoidable war with one's own wife? Therefore give heed to your clever and patriotic womenfolk and remember that the Capitol of mighty Rome was also once saved by the cackling of its faithful geese.

On his very first trip to the United States, he had faced great indignation for allegedly calling American men 'the toy dogs of the women, who spend the money in the most unmeasurable, illimitable way and wrap themselves in a fog of extravagance'. This appears to have been a mistranslation of a misquotation. Nevertheless, it had a sufficiently Einsteinian ring to cause him endless embarrassment.

Einstein's married life in America spanned just three years. It followed the same pattern as before, as an encounter in the winter of 1933 suggested. Husband and wife were described by Churchill Eisenhart, then a student at Princeton University, after they ate as guests of his parents. 'During dinner, Professor Einstein returned again and again to how well his wife took care of him. Finally, my mother interjected: "Prof Einstein, your wife seems to do absolutely everything for you. Just exactly what do you do for her?" With a twinkle in his eye, he replied at once: "I give her my understanding." ' Einstein's biographer Ronald Clark has described the confessional friendship that the couple both established with Leon Watters, a wealthy Jewish biochemist. Watters later wrote that Einstein 'found little time to fulfil the duties expected of a husband.' While able to enjoy the travels and honours that came with his success, Elsa nevertheless 'missed the sympathy and tenderness which she craved, and found herself much alone in these respects.' Speaking of his wife, Einstein told Watters that women were like delicate scientific instruments, and difficult to handle. After Watters's own marriage, Elsa wrote to him, 'I think that you are the most considerate, loving husband. How gladly would I send Albert to you to be taught.'

Her husband's limitations were painfully exposed in May 1934, when Elsa received news from Paris that Ilse was mortally ill. Though his affection for his stepdaughter remained, Einstein refused all pleas to return to her. Elsa set sail alone, arriving to find an emaciated figure on the brink of death. Ilse was suffering from tuberculosis, but according to Marianoff had resisted conventional treatment in the belief that the problem was essentially psychological. Despite Elsa's entreaties, she had preferred to put her faith in psychoanalysis. Margot cared for her sister devotedly, showing hidden reserves of strength, but could not prevent the inevitable. In Marianoff's opinion, the death broke Elsa's spirit, ageing her almost beyond recognition. Her friend Antonina Vallentin wrote, 'She had the courage to resume the thread of life, desolate as she was . . . But she was always aware of her irreparable loss, it was like a wound that refused to heal.'

Elsa went back to America, accompanied by Margot, with her

daughter's ashes hidden under her clothing inside a cushion to avoid the attentions of Customs officers. Her own death was not long delayed. The first symptom, a swelling of the eye, was noticed when she and Einstein moved into what became his last home – 112 Mercer Street, Princeton – in the autumn of 1935. At first it was put down to the strain of the move, but by Christmas she was hospitalized with heart and kidney problems. At her own insistence she was brought home, under orders to remain completely immobile. With one eye closed, and her hand trembling uncontrollably, she struggled to write to Vallentin of her continuing pride in Einstein's success. 'He himself believes his latest work to be the best he has ever done,' she reported. Elsa said that her husband was deeply upset by her illness, and wandered about like a lost soul. 'I never thought he loved me so much. And that comforts me.'

The Polish physicist Leopold Infeld, who had begun to collaborate with Einstein, stated that Einstein gave his wife 'the greatest care and sympathy'. But Infeld also remembered that Einstein 'remained serene and worked constantly'. An even stronger picture of his power of detachment was painted by Peter Bergmann, another of his collaborators. They worked together as Elsa was dying next door. The anguished cries that came out unnerved Bergmann, but Einstein was totally absorbed in his work. Bergmann believed that this demonstrated not so much Einstein's powers of concentration as his wish to escape: 'He would otherwise have been overwhelmed.'

Elsa died on 20 December 1936. Einstein had no interest in spending the customary seven days in mourning, according to Marianoff, and calmly issued the order 'Bury her.' Within a matter of days, Einstein had returned to his post at the Institute for Advanced Study. Infeld noted his sallow complexion but could not bring himself to utter the usual platitudes of condolence: 'We discussed a serious difficulty in our scientific problem as though nothing had happened.' Einstein wrote to Max Born, 'I have settled down splendidly here: I hibernate like a bear in its cave and really feel more at home than ever before in all my varied existence. This bearishness has been accentuated still further by the death of my mate, who was more attached to human beings than I.' Two weeks after Elsa's death, he also wrote to Hans Albert. His bereavement, he said, was the latest in a series of events that seemed designed to make his life difficult. 'But as long as I am able to work I must not and will not complain, because work is the only thing which gives substance to life.'

10

The Searcher's Burden

DESPITE their divorce, neither Einstein nor Mileva had been able to let go of the other. Their lives remained untidily knotted together throughout Einstein's second marriage and beyond it. He later claimed that Mileva developed an attitude after their divorce that was reminiscent of Medea – the jealous foreign-born wife of Jason in Greek mythology, who responded to her husband's desertion by killing their children and his new wife and father-in-law. Einstein complained that it was thanks to Mileva that a shadow had fallen across him and his sons. The impact of this tragedy had remained with him, he said, undiminished in later life. It was 'most possible' that these sad circumstances had driven him to immerse himself in work.

Letters between the couple tell a different story, and they often show mutual respect and even renewed affection. No sooner had Einstein married Elsa than he returned to Zurich to discuss the children's future. He spent the summer of 1919 mostly apart from his new wife, preferring to take the boys on a trip to Lake Constance before escorting Eduard to Arosa for further convalescence. Shortly afterwards, he wrote to Mileva demanding that she leave Switzerland and come to live in Germany 'as soon as possible'. Having researched the matter on holiday, he recommended Constance as a new home. The schools there were excellent, he said, and he would be happy to help Mileva hunt for a house. Variations on this scheme preoccupied him for the following two years. In December 1919 he wanted Mileva to live at Durlach, near Karlsruhe, where a distant cousin of his ('an excellent man') ran a school. Later he began to extol the attractions of Darmstadt, further north along the Rhine valley, where there was a fine technical college.

The main reason for these demands was the catastrophic inflation beginning to engulf postwar Germany, and the accompanying collapse of its currency. In 1914 it took just over four Marks to buy an American dollar, but by July 1919 it was fourteen Marks and rising. At the end of 1922 the figure would be over 7,000 and by December 1923 a single dollar would cost 4,200,000 million Marks. These were the days in which German children used stacks of worthless banknotes as building blocks in their games, and shops closed for lunch with one set of prices then reopened with another. It was obvious at an early stage to Einstein that he would have problems meeting his agreed alimony, and Mileva's transfer to German soil would have sidestepped what he called 'the insurmountable exchange-rate wall'. As he faced the prospect of caring for his dying mother, he told Besso that it would be 'an immense relief' if the move took place. He stressed to Mileva that she would live more comfortably, and that his sons would see more of him if they were in the same country. Only gradually did he accept that she refused to be shifted. Even then, Einstein continued to press for Hans Albert to come to Germany to complete his education.

Mileva was now living in an apartment at Gloriastrasse 59, still on the Zurichberg. Einstein assured his friend Maurice Solovine that she was in good health, but it appears she was still spending frequent periods in hospital. More than ever, her children were the focus of her life. The uncertainty of the maintenance payments forced her to live frugally and sew the family's clothes herself. She was tireless in her efforts to find a cure for Eduard's ill health, and travelled with him to a specialist hospital on the North Sea island of Föhr. It may be this trip to which she was referring in a letter to a friend in Belgrade, quoted by one of her Serbian biographers but of uncertain date. This voiced Mileva's fears that Eduard was likely to lose his hearing, and described how an arduous voyage to the German coast had failed to secure any relief. Food was extremely scarce, and they returned after three weeks more exhausted than when they set out. The letter also touched on Mileva's own persistent illness, including her weak heart. 'It has got a little better but demands a lot of care from me,' she wrote. 'I generally play the heroine, so long as I can, but then there comes a time when I have to surrender . . . then every illness, even an insignificant one, is a great disturbance.'

Friction continued over Einstein's desire for his children to visit him in Berlin. He told Mileva in 1920 that it was 'simply ridiculous' to forbid trips by Hans Albert, since at sixteen the boy was almost a grown adult. With the assurance of a man who was master in his new household, Einstein insisted that Elsa would stay hidden and that he and Hans Albert could even have their meals alone. 'But such things are absurdities,' he told his ex-wife. 'One shouldn't have to make such an issue out of things just because of you females.'

Despite these disagreements, it is clear that Mileva allowed Einstein considerable access to the boys. A letter he sent to Besso in July 1920 mentions plans for an autumn holiday with them in his native Swabia, near Sigmaringen. The summer of 1921 saw a trip to Wustrow on the Baltic coast, with sailing top of the agenda. In a gracious letter afterwards, Einstein offered his thanks to Mileva for the 'lovely days' he had enjoyed. Once again, he was especially grateful that his sons had not been induced to be hostile towards him. Later that year, Einstein took Hans Albert off to Italy. They stayed in Florence (where Einstein sent Besso a postcard of the Palazzo Vecchio) and in Bologna (where he gave a lecture in his faltering Italian). Eduard was deemed too young to join the excursion, but was consoled by the gift of a silver watch that his father had owned since his student days. The boy proudly showed off the gift to visitors, but was allowed by Mileva to wear it only on Sundays.

When Einstein returned from Italy, he stayed at Mileva's apartment. Besso was instructed to contact him at 'Mitza's address', and it was there that the Hurwitz family found their old friend when they arrived for an evening of music and conversation on 30 October. Einstein appears to have been in an ebullient mood, discussing his experiences of America and its growing obsession with the automobile. He had assured his sons in an earlier letter that there was no question of Mileva having to absent herself when he came to Zurich. His decision to share her roof was faintly scandalous, but he repeated it on subsequent visits. Ronald Clark has told how in 1929, while attending a Zionist Congress in Zurich, Einstein enjoyed shocking the English statesman Sir John Simon by boasting, 'I am staying with my first wife.' Elsa Einstein disliked the arrangement, not because she suspected impropriety but because of the gossip it might engender.

According to Konrad Wachsmann, the Caputh architect, this objection left Einstein cold. His principle was '*Dem Reinen ist alles rein, dem Schwein ist alles schwein*' – an untranslatable play on words, to the effect that a pig sees smut where the pure see purity.

The potential for gossip was in any case limited. Wachsmann has stated that Mileva's existence was largely unknown in Berlin, so that nobody outside Einstein's immediate circle realized that Elsa was his second wife. The corollary was that almost no one knew that he had two sons, or that Ilse and Margot were only his stepchildren. This was sometimes deeply painful for Mileva. She was particularly hurt in 1922 by a newspaper picture caption publicly identifying Ilse as Einstein's daughter. At the time, Einstein was again on holiday with his sons on the Baltic coast, this time at the old Hanseatic port of Lübeck. He showed only limited sympathy for Mileva's worries and told her that he had no influence on the newspapers, joking that, if he had been concerned by the malice of the media and other people, he would have been dead and buried long before.

There was similar widespread ignorance about the fate of the Nobel prize money. Einstein received news of his honour in November 1922 as he sailed with Elsa to make a speaking tour of Japan. The money was transferred to Mileva in the following year, but this was kept secret even from Einstein's closest friends. Lorentz, for example, wrote confidently to him that the 'material side' of the prize would 'ease the cares' of his daily life. In fact it was used to buy three houses for Mileva in Zurich: one to live in, the other two as investments. She made her home at Huttenstrasse 62, a five-storey house on the Zurichberg. There she lived until her death.

It was and remains a quietly elegant building, on a tranquil and leafy side-street in the city's academic heartland. The welcoming mood was set by the Latin greeting '*Salve*' set in stone above the entrance. Stained glass and metalwork in the art-nouveau style adorned the doors and balconies, while the ceilings featured ornate plasterwork in a rose design. This same rose emblem stood out on the steep walls towering above the city and the Zurichsee beyond. From her third-floor apartment, Mileva commanded a sweeping panorama and could look down on the Polytechnic where she and Einstein had first met.

Einstein made a personal inspection before approving her purchase, in a high-speed visit witnessed by Georg Busch, later one of the elder statesmen of Swiss physics but then a fifteen-year-old schoolboy who dreamed of becoming an electrochemist. His parents had moved into the house as its first owners in 1909, but were forced to sell by the worldwide recession. 'I was doing some experiments in the bathroom,' recalled the eighty-four-year-old Professor Busch. 'All of a sudden the door opened, Einstein's well-known head appeared for a few seconds, and he said "Oh, chemistry goes on here!" Then off he went.'

The Busch family continued to live in the house for three years as Mileva's tenants. Professor Busch remembered her as a 'very friendly and motherly' woman, who spoke slowly with a low, warm voice that had a distinct East European accent. She seemed prematurely old to his young eyes: rather unattractive, limping and badly dressed. Yet, when he was sent to deliver the family's rent, he was struck by her kindness and sharp intelligence. No words were wasted in her conversation. 'She spoke very distinctly and expressed herself very precisely,' he remembered. 'She wasn't just talking.'

Once Mileva asked Busch what he had it in mind to do when he left school. He told her that he planned to study physics, and she made a reply that would stay with him always. 'Oh, physics?' she said. 'That is very beautiful, but very hard. One can't know whether one will turn out to be Einstein.' The words were spoken softly, with a smile, and Professor Busch had no doubt that they showed a real esteem for her former husband. This was reflected in Mileva's decision to keep the name that already meant so much around the world. After the divorce she reverted initially to her maiden name, but then she sought special leave to call herself Mileva Einstein once more. Permission was granted by a decree of the cantonal government of Zurich on 24 December 1924.

Einstein's letters around this time show a genuine rapprochement with his ex-wife, as if the handing over of the Nobel prize money had cleared the air between them. He returned from a lecture tour of South America in 1925 bearing a basket of cactuses as a present for Mileva, as well as a collection of Brazilian butterflies for his sons. Mileva had given up opposition to the boys visiting Berlin, and now received a cordial invitation to accompany Eduard and stay at

Haberlandstrasse herself. Einstein wrote of his eagerness to resume friendly relations, pointing out encouragingly that other divorced couples seemed to get along perfectly well. The alternative reminded him of the way in which he had broken from Marie Winteler in his youth. 'But that does not bear thinking about,' he added.

Mileva visited him in Berlin several times during subsequent years, but drew the line at staying as Elsa's guest. She entered the apartment only for short visits, sometimes lodging at night with Fritz Haber, and was always at her most reserved. Herta Waldow, the maid, recalled her as an unattractive 'foreign type' who arrived alone, without the children, and left again after talking amiably with her hosts for an hour or two. Konrad Wachsmann, who also encountered her, depicted Mileva as an inhibited and monosyllabic figure, waiting in uneasy silence with Elsa for her former husband to appear. 'But when Einstein came into the drawing-room, her eyes suddenly shone and the atmosphere became brighter.'

Concern for the children underpinned the couple's improved relations. In June 1925 he told his 'dear Mileva' that he was only too glad to discuss her concerns about their sons. In a touching admission, he called them the best part of his inner life, one that would live on once the clockwork of his body had run its course. Einstein told her that he could well imagine her worries about their future, since the apple never falls far from the tree. However, their encounters remained at best bitter-sweet. Hans Albert revealed that he and his brother never established an easy relationship with Einstein, even though they were keenly aware of his love for them. 'While it was there it was very strong,' Hans Albert said. 'He needed to be loved himself. But almost the instant you felt the contact, he would push you away. He would not let himself go. He would turn off his emotion like a tap.'

The separation and its aftermath had affected Hans Albert deeply, and left him with a lifelong horror of divorce. 'He was rather repressed and I think rather damaged by the whole experience,' recalled his daughter, Evelyn.

Once I remember a discussion about children and childhood. I was saying that childhood was a time for learning and playing and getting one's self straight. He said, 'No. Childhood is not a time to have fun.' I remember being just hit in the face by that. Pretty much it was like 'I had a rotten childhood and I am going to make darn sure that every child I have around is going to too.'

Hans Albert had been only twelve when his mother suffered her breakdown after Einstein's divorce demand in 1916. Evelyn felt that he remained bitter about being forced to shoulder the burdens of adulthood prematurely. 'He was expected to act as the man of the house,' she said. 'If there was a faucet to fix, a light-bulb to replace, a banister to mend, then he would have to do it. I think he resented it.' In 1917 Einstein praised the way that his son had 'behaved like an adult man' and had given Mileva 'real support'. Like a hell-fire preacher, he told Hans Albert that it was through suffering and injustice – not pleasure and comfort – that a person truly developed. His own path had been strewn with thorns rather than roses, he said – adding, 'Have Mama tell you about the early days sometime.'

The young man who emerged from this ordeal closely resembled his father. He was of the same height and stocky build, and possessed the same knack of appearing somewhat rumpled in whatever clothes he was wearing. Even their handwriting was almost impossible to tell apart – a source of confusion over the years, since both would sign letters as 'Albert'. But the antagonism that Einstein had already detected did not disappear. During their holiday at Lübeck in 1922, he reported 'an unpleasant and touchy scene' with his eldest son. He told Mileva that it eventually emerged that the reason for the outburst was that Hans Albert did not want to act as their mediator. The following year he revealed that his eldest son had sent him a letter showing 'mistrust, lack of respect and a crude disposition to me'. Appealing for sympathy to Eduard, Einstein wrote that he felt bad about the way he had been rejected but said that no father would tolerate such treatment. He would not stand for it, and was quite prepared to estrange his eldest son, no matter the personal suffering that the collapse of their relationship would cause.

No permanent schism took place, but there was continual squabbling. Hans Albert was the first of the children to visit Berlin, and was openly resentful towards Elsa. This greatly embarrassed Einstein, who warned him that he would not be welcome unless he was more polite. Einstein was genuinely grateful when his son's behaviour moderated. He wrote that even if Elsa did get on one's nerves sometimes, and was a bit dim, she did excel at being kind-hearted.

Hans Albert's two most sustained pieces of defiance were his choice of career and his choice of bride. He announced as a teenager that he wished to study engineering, a practical rather than theoretical branch of science. This was a bitter disappointment to Einstein – the supreme theorist, despite his own interest in technology – and his attempts to hide his feelings only served to accentuate them. 'I am pleased that Albert has a strong interest in a particular subject,' he told Mileva in 1918. 'What he is interested in isn't really important, even if it is, alas, engineering. One cannot expect one's children to inherit a mind.' There was the same mixed message in a letter he sent to Heinrich Zangger around the same time. He declared that Albert has already begun to take pleasure in thinking, 'strange to say, over technical questions'. But in the long run he said that any intellectual activity pleased him, even if it was philistine. He mused that perhaps one day Hans Albert would realize that practical pursuits are superfluous. After all, he told Zangger, he too was once destined to be an engineer—but the thought of having to expend his inventive spirit on the pragmatic objectives of industry, sweating in pursuit of some target or profit, was utterly unbearable: 'Thought is an end in itself, like music!'

Einstein told Zangger that if he had no immediate problem to reflect on he would work anew on long-familiar mathematical theorems for the sheer pleasure they gave him. Why, was the unwritten question, could his son not be the same?

Hans Albert reiterated his ambitions when Einstein visited Zurich after his marriage in 1919. A colourful description of their meeting – and Mileva's response to it – was provided by Peter Michelmore, based on interviews with Hans Albert and subsequently given his approval.

Hans Albert was hostile to his father. Now a husky boy of fifteen and fiercely independent, he told his father he had definitely made up his mind to be an engineer, although he knew that Einstein wanted him to follow a more 'purely scientific' career.

'I think it's a disgusting idea,' Einstein said.

'I'm still going to be an engineer,' the boy insisted.

Einstein strode away saying that he never wanted to see his older son again. Mileva waited until he had cooled down and later brought the two together again. She kept telling both boys that Einstein was still their father and wanted their love and respect. He was a strange man in many ways, she explained, but he was good and kind. Mileva knew that for all his bluff, Albert could be hurt in personal matters – and hurt deeply.

As Einstein had hinted in his letter to Zangger, the disagreement was a neat inversion of his own conflict with his father at around the same age. Like Einstein, Hans Albert was stubborn enough to stay true to his vocation, without ever entirely shaking off his father's shadow. He followed the steps of both his parents to enter the Swiss Federal Polytechnical School in 1922, earning a civil-engineering degree in 1927. Then he spent four years working in Germany's Ruhr valley for the Dortmund Steel Company. Around 1930 Hans Albert flirted with the idea of becoming a patent examiner – and thus returning to his father's path – but instead returned to the Polytechnic in 1931 as a research assistant in the hydraulics laboratory. Most of his work was to do with rivers. 'Rivers don't like to be changed around,' he once said. 'They fight back.'

After his initial distress abated, Einstein began to take pride in his son's achievements. 'My Albert has become a sound, strong chap,' he wrote to Besso at the start of 1924. 'Grossmann wrote to me that he has scored the best exam of all his comrades. He is a total picture of a man, a first-rate sailor, unpretentious and dependable.' Einstein even insisted that he was rather relieved that his son had rejected physics, and thus avoided such frustrations as seeking a unified field theory. 'Science is a difficult profession. Sometimes I am glad that you have chosen a practical métier, where one does not have to look for a four-leafed clover,' he told Hans Albert in March 1924. This became a persistent theme in his letters – but not a very convincing one. Einstein believed that only difficult work was worthwhile. 'I have little patience with scientists who take a board of wood, look for its thinnest part, and drill a great number of holes where drilling is easy,' he said.

Hans Albert always had a ready answer when asked why he had not pursued physics. 'When someone else has picked up all the good shells from a beach,' he said, 'you go to another beach.' He publicly insisted that Einstein had 'never sought to impose his will' on either himself or his brother. Even if this had been true regarding his career, however, it was quite untrue regarding his marriage. Hans Albert met Frieda Knecht while living with his mother on Gloriastrasse in Zurich. Their families had apartments in the same house, and Frieda became one of the few people to penetrate Hans Albert's stony reserve. She was nine years his senior – a plain and rather short woman of four feet eleven inches, with a blunt manner but a sharp mind. Her similarity to Mileva was pronounced, and fittingly the romance developed as Hans Albert studied at the Polytechnic. In 1925 he announced his intention to wed, and was greeted by thunderous paternal outrage. In the words of Evelyn Einstein, 'Albert had such a hell of a time with his parents over his own marriage that you would think he would have had the sense not to interfere with his sons. But no. When my father went to marry my mother there was explosion after explosion.'

Einstein's objections to Frieda closely followed those that his own parents made against Mileva: namely, that she was a scheming older woman and of unhealthy stock. According to Einstein, Frieda's diminutive height was evidence of dwarfism that could be passed on to any future offspring. He believed her mother to be unbalanced (in fact, she suffered from an overactive thyroid) and that this hereditary taint could be passed down to his prospective grandchildren. No doubt these fears were informed by his own confused feelings towards the sickly Eduard: perhaps surprisingly, Mileva seems to have shared them. She discussed her concern with Einstein even before their son's announcement, and at first he reassured her, confident that Hans Albert did not yet feel tied. When the truth became clear, it strengthened the new *détente* between the couple as they united in opposition to the proposed wedding. In a series of letters to his ex-wife, Einstein bemoaned Hans Albert's stubbornness and alluded darkly to the

Book of Exodus, with its warning that the sins of the fathers would be visited on the children, unto the third and fourth generation. 'It would be a crime to bring such children into the world,' he told Mileva.

Einstein believed that part of the problem was his son's inhibitions with respect to the opposite sex. He suggested that Hans Albert be sent to a pretty forty-year-old woman of his acquaintance for unspecified remedial instruction. More delicately, he attempted to influence his son through a mutual friend in Zurich, Hermann Anschütz-Kaempfe. He also wrote to Hans Albert directly, and urged Mileva to assist in doing everything possible 'to prevent a disaster'. Eventually he was forced to admit defeat, complaining that Hans Albert was too naïve to see how firmly he was under Frieda's thumb. His manner remained grudging in the extreme. He implored his son to agree not to have a child with Knecht and said that only firm compliance would see him come to terms with their decision to wed. However, Einstein's letter in early 1927 made it clear that he would still bitterly regret the marriage, even if it remained childless, adding insouciantly that of course, no third person had a right to get involved in such matters: they could only offer the benefit of experience, if wanted.

Hans Albert married Frieda on 7 May 1927 in Dortmund. He never revealed the full extent of his father's opposition, but he dropped heavy hints to his interviewer Peter Michelmore. Michelmore's toned-down account makes no reference to Einstein's preoccupation with hereditary defects, but presents the episode as evidence of his antipathy towards marriage in general. Einstein's advice to his son on the eve of the ceremony was to cancel it, since he would only get separated later and it was not worth all the trouble. This was also a reason that he gave for not having children, since they would make the inevitable divorce more complicated. When a child did arrive, in 1930, Einstein grumbled to Hans Albert, 'I don't understand it. I don't think you're my son.'

This dreaded arrival was a boy, whose parents named him Bernard Caesar. 'We decided there were enough A's in the family so we started with B's,' Hans Albert once explained. Einstein had greeted news of the pregnancy with Eeyore-like gloom — 'Fate will now take its course, tragic as it is,' he told Mileva — but his fears proved entirely without foundation. Bernard, or 'Hadi' as he became known to his family, was a healthy child and emerged as a favourite of his grand-father, inheriting Einstein's violin. Einstein even came to admit that Hans Albert's marriage was very happy, and had made his son more cheerful and open. Maja Einstein, who met Frieda for the first time in 1934, found her 'much better than her reputation which came to me from my brother and sister-in-law . . . rather ugly, small and uncer-emonious, but intelligent, modest, tactful'. She added that early mar-riages to ugly older women seemed an inherited evil in her family, 'stemming from the father, whose aversion against his daughter-in-law may derive from a quite deep-seated psychological abyss'.

Einstein's differences with Hans Albert temporarily inclined him more favourably towards Eduard. Despite their outward differences, so he told Mileva in January 1926, he now saw that his younger son was the one he more closely resembled in character. It is certainly true that many of Eduard's contemporaries believed that it was he who inherited his father's spark. Hans Albert's daughter Evelyn recalled, 'He was definitely a genius. Next to Tete, my father was just a plod-der.' But Einstein's feelings were never simple, and his attitude towards Eduard had a measure of ambivalence remarkable even in him.

Eduard proved an outstandingly able pupil after entering secondary school in the spring of 1923, but was easily bored by lessons. Instead, his energies were spent composing aphorisms and poems, in which he lampooned friends and teachers with a sharp wit and precocious elegance of expression. Many of these efforts appeared in class maga-zines, one of which also described the fourteen-year-old Eduard delivering a classroom lecture on the history of astronomy 'in a clear and intelligent manner, in exemplary German'. This performance provoked stormy applause, but the report had one small complaint. 'Disappointing', it said, 'that amongst the great men such as Kepler, Newton etc., he did not also mention Einstein.'

Eduard's contemporaries were well aware of his father's fame, but believed him to be unburdened by it. They knew him as a mild, quizzical and sometimes dreamy boy, but an apparently well-balanced one, unusual only in his intelligence and the quickness of his ironic repartee. He showed no real enthusiasm for mathematics or physics and mostly devoted himself to literature and the arts. Music was another of Eduard's talents, and he was a fluent pianist with an early taste for Chopin and the Bavarian composer Max Reger. Eduard's emotions were less transparent than they had been in his early childhood, and a schoolmate who visited him at home was astonished by his spirited playing. It revealed a passion usually hidden by mocking scepticism. At the keyboard, Eduard seemed another person altogether.

As if to prove his worthiness to be Einstein's son, Eduard was desperately eager to engage his father intellectually. He wrote to him frequently, discussing his favourite composers and philosophers with boyish exuberance, and offering samples of his own writings for paternal approval. Einstein praised his enthusiasm and at first the same quality infected his replies, which ranged happily from music ('I don't think it's right that you should despise the Haydn sonatas, you scoundrel') to philosophy ('I like what you write about Schopenhauer. I too find the splendid style is worth far more than the actual contents'). As time passed, however, Einstein showed signs of being overwhelmed by his son's relentless self-assertion. Eduard complained of a tetchiness in his replies, and was not entirely reassured by Einstein's effusive denials, in which he insisted that he was 'as happy as a baby with its bottle' when he read his son's letters, 'because I can see that you are racking your brains about the principal things in life'.

The rest of the family received a far more equivocal message. Einstein repeatedly told Mileva how much he liked Eduard, but also wished aloud that he were less pretentious. He wrote to Hans Albert that his younger brother was a nice boy, but that his letters were 'completely impersonal' and his interests superficial. 'Drilling holes through thick pieces of wood is certainly not his passion, but there must be fellows who take pleasure in God's creation – perhaps that is the purpose of the latter. After all, our goals are merely soap bubbles.'

Eduard's 'impersonal' letters were in fact charged with deep feeling. He approached his father on the intellectual plain partly because they had never established any easy emotional communication. But what he wrote, even if occasionally overwrought, was not aridly pretentious. It was in art and culture that Eduard had found a way to express his passions, much as the young Einstein had done in religion and then physics. The tragedy was that father and son spoke separate languages, save for their common devotion to music. In Eduard's eyes, it was Einstein's letters that seemed impersonal. He later wrote to a sympathetic friend, 'In my schooldays I often sent my father rather rapturous letters, and several times got worried afterwards because he was of a cooler disposition. I only learned a lot later how much he treasured them.'

Einstein's bearing towards his younger son was bound to confuse him. After initially praising Eduard's aphorisms, he then suggested that they were copied from another author. The idea – though deeply wounding to Eduard – took hold within the family. Hans Albert later stated that his younger brother's abilities were purely reproductive, and that for all his voracious reading and photographic memory he had no creative talent, and could only parrot the ideas of others. This is a view repudiated by his brother's classmates, one of whom has published a collection of Eduard's literary juvenilia, all of it original and much of it both moving and witty. The charm of his aphorisms may be lost in translation, but many of the more melancholy ones seem to touch directly upon their young creator's life.

He who stretches out his arms too longingly will always be repulsed.

Nothing is worse for man than to meet someone beside whom his existence and all his efforts are worthless.

The worst destiny is to have no destiny, and also to be the destiny of no one else.

Taken as a whole, Eduard's writings went far beyond the maudlin jottings of a typical adolescent. But Einstein disliked his son being introspective just as much as he disliked him being impersonal. He warned Eduard with studied light-heartedness against taking himself too seriously and quipped that we are all two-legged animals descended from the apes – the heavy burden of atavistic instincts we have inherited is the very stuff of life.

Einstein continued to believe that Mileva over-mothered Eduard. He wanted him to leave home and make his own way in the world, perhaps by visiting England to learn the language. In Einstein's view, this was the only way to jolt Eduard out of his dreamy affectations, and he urged Mileva to set aside her personal feelings on the matter. He pressed his case with great force, perhaps supplied in part by memories of his own mother's long shadow. There is no doubt that Mileva's bond with Eduard was extremely close, but it is unclear whether her protectiveness was a cause of his emotional delicacy or a reaction to it. Very likely, it was something of both.

A picture of mother and son in the late 1920s can be built up from the memories of Maja Schucan and Waltrud Kappeler, who each went to Mileva as a teenager for private lessons in mathematics. Frau Kappeler recalled her as a kind but very correct tutor, rather melancholy, and much older in appearance than most women in their early fifties. Mileva 'dressed like a mouse', disliked bright sunlight, and frequently complained of headaches. Frau Kappeler found her somewhat intimidating, but this was not the impression left with Frau Schucan, who enjoyed her lessons and found Mileva both welcoming and sympathetic.

> The drawing-room at Huttenstrasse was cosy, the furniture dark, the windows high, and also rather dark curtains. I always sat next to Frau Einstein at the table in the middle of the room, and with great patience and conspicuous clarity she taught me the basics of algebra and mathematics, and helped me to solve my school exercises. She had a motherly manner, and everything that had seemed complicated became simple under her guidance. Things went better at school for me straight away.

Both pupils knew of Mileva's illustrious connection, and Frau Schucan remembers addressing her as 'Frau Professor Einstein'. In the rare moments when Mileva spoke of her own life, she told Frau Schucan 'that she had always worked together with her husband'. But neither of the girls gained any impression that Mileva claimed to be the unrecognized author of relativity. Nor did she show any sign of bitterness towards her former husband.

Both girls found that Eduard was the centre of attention in the household. Frau Schucan recalled that Mileva would always call in her son after their tutorials ended. She would ask him to play on the piano before standing by, smiling, as she plied the youngsters with tea and biscuits. Eduard was two years older than Frau Schucan, but she had heard of his intellectual gifts – and especially his talent as a writer – through a mutual friend. She asked him to show her his poems, and was delighted when he proceeded to compose one on the spot. They met frequently at parties and dances, and soon she had fallen in love. Eduard was by no means conventionally attractive, having very bad teeth and little talent at dancing (he tended to tread on his partner's feet), but that did not matter. 'He was not like the others, and that fascinated me,' said Frau Schucan.

Though Eduard showed great fondness for his admirer, her love was unrequited. In 1929 he went to study medicine at Zurich University (just as Mileva had done before transferring to the Polytechnic) with the object of becoming a psychiatrist. Eduard displayed the same passion for psychology that his mother had shown in her youth, and had begun expounding the theories of Sigmund Freud to his friends at around the age of fifteen. One unnamed classmate later wrote, 'Once, on a hike, he described to me the nature of schizophrenia. Did he already suspect that he was in danger from this flank? That would be terrible.' In a sense, psychology was a natural meeting-point between Eduard's beloved humanities and his father's exact science. Nevertheless, it was not a vocation of which Einstein approved. He told Eduard that he had read Freud's writings but was unconverted, and believed his methods dubious – even fraudulent. Einstein had met Freud in Berlin, and corresponded with him on peace and disarmament. In 1936, however, Freud would remark to him, 'I always knew that you admired me only "out of politeness" and that you are convinced by very few of my assertions.'

To Eduard, in contrast, Freud was 'one of the greatest geniuses', who in a few words could express deep truths that repaid hours of reflection. He had a picture of his hero above his bed, looking particularly grumpy. Tragically, Eduard was doomed to be a patient rather than a practitioner of the psychoanalytic art. Early on at university, he suffered a traumatic depression from which he never recovered. He plunged into a mood of listless apathy, shunning his friends, cutting his classes. He spent his days alone at home in his book-filled room.

Frau Kappeler, whose lessons with Mileva took place during Eduard's earliest days as a student, saw little to suggest his growing despair. Often Mileva would ask him to conduct the tutorials in her place, pleading a headache, and he did so with aplomb. A different side emerged when Eduard accompanied his pupil and some of her friends on an excursion from Zurich. He had shown that he was attracted to her, but reacted with unexpected intensity when another youth approached her to make conversation. 'I remember that at this moment his eyes went black, he looked so excited, and I was a bit afraid,' said Frau Kappeler. 'He looked so strange.' Frau Schucan recalls being similarly unnerved when she returned to visit Eduard shortly before her final school exams. He admitted that all was not well, and said that he was attempting 'self-analysis' on Freudian lines. 'This struck me as rather sinister,' said Frau Schucan, who persuaded Eduard to leave his room and walk with her through the evening streets. 'The moon shone and Teddy seemed at once near and endlessly far away. In his eyes was something frightening, strange.'

The immediate trigger of Eduard's breakdown was a failed romance: in keeping with family tradition, he had become involved with an older woman. According to his contemporary Eduard Rübel, this was a mature medical student who mothered Eduard and with whom he became besotted. Some reports say that she was married. Einstein seems to have been aware of the affair, and in an undated letter he warned Eduard to leave his older girlfriend – she was too cunning for him – and find a harmless plaything instead. Another note warned, 'Being occupied with the opposite sex is as delightful as it is necessary, but it must not become one of the main tenors of life, otherwise the person is lost . . .'

The best cure that Einstein could offer for melancholy was hard work. 'How beneficial a job would be for you,' he told Eduard. 'Even a genius like Schopenhauer was crushed through unemployment.' He told his son that life was like a bicycle, since a man could keep his balance only if he kept moving. 'In one respect you should be pleased about the symptoms of your illness,' he added with cheery detachment. 'One cannot learn anything so well as by experiencing it one's self. Therefore, if you are able to overcome this matter, you will have the prospect of becoming a really good doctor of the soul.'

Advice like this did little to improve Eduard's mood. In the summer of 1930 his letters to his father became hysterical and vituperative. According to Antonina Vallentin, who would have heard of them from Elsa, they were 'incoherent, pathetic and unhinged' – rambling diatribes in which 'the desire to affirm a weak personality through grand language alternated with outbursts of despair.' By Hans Albert's account, his brother accused Einstein of abandoning him and casting a shadow over his life. Eduard announced that he hated his father.

Einstein returned to Zurich to talk his son round, but without success. Later in the same year, according to one of Mileva's Serbian biographers, Eduard lost all self-control and threatened to throw himself from the window of his third-floor bedroom. Mileva is said to have held him back, despite his greater size and strength, before calling for medical help. The same source says that Mileva then travelled to Berlin to fetch her ex-husband, arriving in November 1930 on the day that Elsa's younger daughter, Margot, was marrying Dimitri Marianoff. The latter reported seeing Mileva as he and his bride – accompanied by Einstein – emerged from the register office in the Schöneberg district. 'I would not have noticed her, except that she looked at us with such an intensely burning gaze that it impressed me,' Marianoff wrote. 'Margot said under her breath, "It is Mileva" . . . We never knew then or afterward why she was there.'

The content of Mileva's subsequent discussions with Einstein is not known. However, his letters indicate that he returned again to Zurich before his second visit to America in December 1930. He likened himself to a nomad who had pitched camp in his former home and told Hans Albert that the most beautiful part of his stay was making music with Tetel and 'the hot-blooded baroness'. Whether this was a satirical reference to Mileva is unclear. What remains striking is the suggestion that, after all that had happened, music still allowed father and son to find peace together. Antonina Vallentin described how she witnessed Eduard's inner turmoil when she saw him play the piano on a visit to Berlin.

He had an absorbed look on his face, as though, like his father, he was divorced from his surroundings while playing. But I also caught a glimpse in it of a far-away expression, irreparably sad.

In the boy's relationship with his father there was passionate admiration, mingled with unexpected rebellion, which was like a secret resentment.

Peter Michelmore, after talking to Hans Albert, also wrote of Eduard's 'intense and contradictory feelings towards his father – feelings of love, even worship, curiously mixed with a sense of rejection and personal inadequacy'. It seems that as they performed together in Zurich, on piano and violin, Eduard could disentangle these emotions, and literally be in harmony with Einstein – for so long as the music lasted, at least.

Mileva attempted to care for Eduard at home, and in the early summer of 1932 he was well enough to visit Einstein's sister Maja in Italy. He arrived at her door virtually unannounced, clutching a small suitcase, and stayed eight days. Much of this time he spent sitting at the baby grand piano that Einstein had bought for her, playing Mozart 'with the greatest accuracy and soberness'. Soon after his return to Zurich, however, his condition deteriorated. In late 1932 Eduard was admitted for the first of many stays at the Burghölzli mental institution, where he was treated for schizophrenia.

It was at the Burghölzli that Carl Jung had served his psychiatric apprenticeship, and he claimed that it was then an institution with oppressively narrow horizons, where the human personality of the patient was ignored. This judgement was harsh, for by the standards of its age the clinic was relatively progressive. The very concept of schizophrenia was outlined in 1908 by its then director, Eugen Bleuler, whose son Manfred was in charge for much of Eduard's time there. Equally, however, Bleuler's definition of schizophrenia was very broad. Today a case such as Eduard's might be diagnosed differently, and would almost certainly not involve institutional treatment. His first admission came as modern therapies were replacing the forced baths and mechanical restraints of the past, but the new methods were thought by some to be profoundly flawed; their benefits for Eduard are debatable.

Eduard was subjected to insulin therapy, which was common at the time. The aim of this was to induce a coma lasting perhaps two hours, during which the brain could supposedly regenerate. Some patients emerged from unconsciousness with a new-found calmness, but others experienced no significant effect. Still others never awoke at all, or suffered lasting brain damage. In a letter of November 1940, Einstein referred to this approach having utterly failed in Eduard's case.

There is also evidence that Eduard was subjected to electro-convulsive therapy, in which seizures are induced by applying electric shocks to the head. No clear explanation of why this should be therapeutic has ever been provided, although some experts still insist that it is the optimal treatment for severe depression. According to his second wife, Hans Albert once remarked that shock treatment had 'ruined' his brother. Conditions were certainly primitive when it was introduced at Burghölzli and other institutions from the late 1930s. Patients were fully conscious and charges of up to thirty milliamps would be administered, without the benefit of muscle relaxants, producing convulsions so severe that bones would be broken and dislocated. Some patients suffered heart attacks and some died of suffocation: the prospect of enduring the treatment inspired terror.

Today the Burghölzli is a welcoming and well-run place. Living conditions in Eduard's time were harsh, however, and overcrowding was endemic on the dark and gloomy wards. The majority of patients were allowed little freedom, and even in the reforming 1930s staff would routinely refer to them as 'convicts' and 'inmates'. It is likely that Eduard was spared the worst indignities, since Einstein appears to have paid for him to be cared for in the elite first-class section, where a limited number of patients were granted private rooms, their own plushly-furnished lounge and a private dining-room. Many also had private nurses, and were excused from work in the clinic's grounds and workshops. The arrangement was very discreet, and most of those in the main third-class category were unaware that first class existed.

Eduard wrote to Frau Schucan from the Burghölzli in December 1932, thanking her for some poems she had sent him. He showed no self-pity, and assured her that his condition was quite tolerable. He devoted most of his short message to wishing her well and apologizing for any unhappiness he had caused her. The extent of his decline was evident only in his handwriting, once fluid and elegant but now a smudged and scratched scrawl. In another letter to her he wrote, 'Sometimes my head aches for hours on end like an inflamed tooth. You must not think that I am going through all this ordeal in order to get wisdom. It would be utterly silly to want to become wise by force. I wish for nothing more than to be passably contented. Sometimes I feel like the man in Hermann Hesse's beautiful story "Iris", who plunged himself too deeply into his own past and never found the way back.'

Einstein told his son not to worry about his 'monastery-like treatment'. He made a clumsy attempt at comfort by telling Eduard about a friend in Pasadena – perhaps apocryphal – who had entered an institution because of depression, only to remain there because he believed there was no place better for a man working with his brain. Einstein continued to show great distrust of psychoanalysis, telling Eduard that people who began it seemed unable to extricate themselves. He asked his son to visit him in Berlin – adding, 'I have the feeling that nobody but I can do you good in these circumstances.' Elsa told her friend Vallentin that Einstein was deeply affected by his son's plight. 'This sorrow is eating up Albert,' she wrote. 'He finds it difficult to cope with it, more difficult than he would care to admit. He has always aimed at being invulnerable to everything that concerned him personally. He really is so, much more than any other man I know. But this has hit him very hard.' Einstein even agreed that when his son visited, he could teach him some psychoanalysis, in line with Eduard's hope that his father also undergo self-examination. However, this bid to understand his son was marred by a flash of astonishing superciliousness: Einstein said he would try to keep a straight face while carrying out Eduard's wishes.

Einstein's attitude dismayed his faithful ally Michele Besso, who had undergone psychoanalysis himself in the mid-1920s after losing faith in his abilities at work. Besso was now on the brink of his sixtieth birthday, and his white hair and beard had begun to give him the look of an Old Testament prophet, as impressive as Einstein himself. His letters were increasingly rambling, but he had lost none of his old powers of empathy. In September 1932 he wrote a long and touching appeal to his 'dear, good and old friend', urging Einstein to

give Eduard greater help and understanding. With all his characteristic tact and delicacy, Besso stressed how his own son, Vero, had
become a unifying force in his life and had reconciled him to the
strains within his own marriage. He stressed his bonds with Einstein –
from the days in Bern when he felt 'pure joy' seeing his friend's genius
at work, through to the days of the separation, when Besso felt that
his attempts at reconciliation had only hastened the divorce. He
described how an 'impartial' acquaintance, after seeing a photograph
of Einstein with one of his stepdaughters, had remarked, 'I thought he
had a son; one never sees a picture of his sons.' And yet here was
Eduard – clever and sympathetic, however burdened and withdrawn
– in desperate need of his father's guiding hand.

Besso could anticipate Einstein's response to these proddings, and
offered his own disarming summary of how it might run:

> What can I do about it? Everyone must come to terms with one's
> self. I had to and still do. What do you know, white-haired child,
> of the searcher's burden, and the burdens that people try to put
> on me from all sides? Help if you can, otherwise reconcile your-
> self, just as others have to reconcile themselves.

And yet, wrote Besso – and yet. He begged Einstein to take Eduard
with him on his foreign travels, to spend six months with his son so
that they could work out their differences. Then he would see Eduard's life from the inside, and realize what they had in common.

Einstein did not immediately reply, and Besso feared that he had
overstepped the limits of their intimacy. He wrote again, this time
enclosing a 'delightful' exchange of letters between Eduard and himself, intended to move Einstein's heart. He noted that in his letter to
Eduard he had amended a reference to 'your mighty father' in order
not to upset the youth further. He had urged Eduard to visit Einstein
in Berlin – telling him, 'We old people all need youngsters more than
we think.'

Einstein replied on 17 October 1932, assuring Besso that he had
not taken offence but showing a certain defensiveness. He reiterated
his view that Eduard's problem was hereditary, and that external
influences played little part. He also told Besso that he had invited
Eduard to visit him in Princeton the following year. However sincere

this was, Einstein's plans became unravelled with the advent of Nazi power three months later. It was now he who needed help, and one offer came from an unexpected quarter. When Mileva heard that he was unable to return to his home in Berlin, she offered him and Elsa the temporary use of her own apartment in Zurich. The invitation surprised and delighted Einstein, even though he declined to accept it.

From his chosen refuge in Belgium, Einstein returned briefly to Switzerland in May 1933. This required him to delay a trip to England, where he was a visiting research Student of Christ Church, Oxford. He wrote to his host, Professor Frederick Lindemann, explaining that his younger son was seriously ill. 'I should never have a quiet moment in England,' he added. 'You are not a father yourself, but I know you will certainly understand.' Nothing is known of his hurried journey to Zurich, or the hours he spent in the company of his family, but a photograph survives from their last encounter showing father and son – wearing suits – sitting uneasily side by side in a well-furnished room. Einstein holds a violin and bow, gazing sadly to the left. His son, legs folded away from his father, looks down at a manuscript with an intense, almost pained, expression.

In June 1933, Einstein wrote to promise Mileva his continuing financial and moral support. He again urged that work of some kind would be the best cure for Eduard, suggesting that he could write a thesis and prove to his sceptical father the truth of Freud's beliefs. Four months later he set sail for America and left Europe for good. Mileva and her troubled son were never to see him again.

Mileva brought Eduard back home as often as she could, and Einstein paid for him to attend specialists in Switzerland and Vienna. Hans Albert claimed that these included Freud himself, but there is no other evidence of it. Eduard's knowledge of psychiatry made him very hard to treat, since he could anticipate the usual tests and avenues of questioning. Brief hopes that one Viennese doctor had cured him were later denounced by Einstein as a gruesome swindle. In 1934 Eduard again visited Maja Einstein in Italy, this time accompanied by a male nurse who never left his side. She was devastated by the change since their meeting two years earlier: Eduard was fat and bloated, almost unrecognizable. 'There also hangs over him a leaden melancholy, which makes it even sadder when his old sunny smile very seldom flashes like lightning across his face and disappears. Thank God his nurse is here. I could not have managed him on my own. He suffers terribly, poor, poor boy!'

Maja wrote of her strong bond with Eduard and how she had spent much of his stay in tears, tormented by the tantalizing glimpses he gave of his old lively intelligence. Michele Besso painted a similar picture in 1937, after visiting Mileva's apartment. There he saw Eduard at the piano, performing Handel and Bach with both power and tenderness. But Besso remarked on his corpulence and his reluctance to see his friends, claiming that Eduard had not left the house for a year. Einstein's son entertained him with brilliant discourses on psychology, but the words came slowly from his lips, like notes from an old organ one had to play with one's fists.

When Besso's academic links with Zurich were severed in 1938, such visits were no longer possible. In the same year, Hans Albert resigned his job at the Swiss Federal Polytechnical School and emigrated with his family to America. His father had invited him over for an extended visit in 1937, following Elsa's death. Press photographers recorded their meeting at the docks in New Jersey – the two men rather reluctantly posed together, with Hans Albert lighting his father's pipe. Einstein refused to give an interview, telling reporters, 'After all, private life is private life.' He provided his son with money and encouragement for a permanent move, and Hans Albert found work in South Carolina as a hydraulics researcher with the Department of Agriculture, where he stayed until joining the University of California at Berkeley in 1947. In the year of his emigration, his second son, Klaus, died of diphtheria at the age of six. His father wrote to him, 'The deepest sorrow that loving parents can experience has come upon you.'

It pleased Einstein greatly to have his son settled in the same country, even though they were to meet only intermittently. For Mileva, however, Hans Albert's departure added to a growing isolation. Her father had suffered a fatal stroke in February 1920. Her mother had died on New Year's Day in 1935, at the age of eighty-eight. Now, in the same year as Hans Albert's emigration, came news of the death of her sister. Zorka Marić's treatment at the Burghölzli had proved as unsuccessful as Eduard's, and she had soon returned to live in Novi Sad with her parents. Her behaviour remained decidedly erratic: she regarded human beings with almost universal detestation, and showed affection only towards animals. When her father sold his farm, shortly before he died, he rather unwisely hid the proceeds in an unused stove. Zorka promptly burnt the notes to ashes. She took to drink after the loss of her mother, but lived on alone at the family home, surrounded by dozens of cats. Her body was found only several days after she died, lying on the straw-covered kitchen floor as her cats padded around unconcerned.

This left only Mileva's brother Miloš unaccounted for. His fate after his capture during the First World War had remained a mystery, and in 1935 he too was formally declared dead. In fact, however, his Russian captors had allowed him to pursue his work as a doctor. Amid the turmoil of the Communist revolution and its aftermath, Miloš carved out a successful career as a professor of histology. He worked first in the city of Dnepropetrovsk and later in Saratov, where he died in 1944. Colleagues and students respected him for his astonishing memory and erudition, combined with an unusual ability to explain complicated problems briefly and clearly. He shared with Mileva a shy and taciturn manner; but, while the life of his talented eldest sister had turned to tragedy, his own had found distinction and fulfilment.

II

All an Illusion

As Mileva watched Eduard sink further into wretchedness, and the world lurched once more towards war, Einstein hid himself amid the academic calm of Princeton. He described it as an island, a refuge where 'the chaotic voices of human strife barely penetrate'. In this small American university town, he claimed to enjoy 'that solitude which only life among people with an utterly different past and attitude towards life can afford'.

These comments are a little misleading. Einstein had the company of a loyal entourage within his home, whose past and attitude towards life could hardly have been more similar to his own. It was their presence that made his 'solitude' endurable, however reluctant he was to acknowledge it. Nevertheless, both comments were typical of Einstein's later years. They come from letters he wrote to Queen Elizabeth of Belgium, with whom he had struck up an unusual friendship before his departure from Europe. They had met in 1929, when she invited him for the first of several visits to her palace, and Einstein became a prolific and outspoken correspondent to the woman he addressed simply as 'Dear Queen'. She and her husband, King Albert, were the most modest and unaffected of royals. Einstein was particularly pleased when he stopped unexpectedly for lunch with them in 1931, and shared a simple meal of spinach, fried egg and potatoes, without a servant in sight. Despite such informality, he remained a commoner and they remained royalty, and this inescapable barrier – the reassuring absurdity of the relationship, and the certainty that it could go only so far – was an important reason why Einstein so enjoyed such contact so much.

His letters to Elizabeth have been cited as among his most intimate, but one of their great themes was Einstein's insistence on his indifference to intimacy. One of his most characteristic messages came in March 1936, during Elsa's last illness. It was written at the instigation of a mutual friend, who urged Einstein to comfort Elizabeth (now Queen Mother) when she fell into prolonged despair following the deaths of her husband and daughter-in-law. Einstein began by describing how the first spring sunshine had jolted him 'from the dreamlike trance into which people like myself fall when immersed in scientific work'. He urged Elizabeth to take heart from the new life unfolding around them, with its hint of 'something eternal that lies beyond the reach of the hand of fate and of all human delusions'. But his central passage went as follows:

> Have you read the Maxims of La Rochefoucauld? They seem quite acerbic and gloomy, but by their objectivization of human and all-too-human nature they bring a strange feeling of liberation. In La Rochefoucauld we see a man who succeeded in liberating himself, even though it had not been easy for him to be rid of the heavy burden of passions that Nature had dealt him for his passage through life. It would be nicest to read him with people whose little boat has gone through many storms . . .

Einstein might have been writing to himself rather than to Elizabeth. He made it clear that he was now unavailable for a joint perusal of La Rochefoucauld's work, owing to 'the great water' of the Atlantic, which he had no intention of crossing again. Not for nothing had Einstein boasted, in a letter to Elizabeth immediately after her husband's death, that his European friends called him 'the great stone face'.

Einstein was appalled by Hitler's ascendancy in Europe, but was still reluctant to allow such matters to invade his private world. In the summer of 1939 he wrote to Elizabeth in terms strikingly similar to those he had used to Ehrenfest during the First World War. He boasted that 'except for the newspapers and the countless letters, I would hardly be aware that I live in a time when human inadequacy and cruelty are achieving frightful proportions.' The year before he had written to Michele Besso with black cynicism, ridiculing his friend for believing that England would stand up against the Nazis. Not entirely without reason, Einstein suspected the English prime minister, Chamberlain, of being ready to sacrifice eastern Europe in the hope that Hitler would occupy himself with attacking Russia. His own response was to wash his hands of the whole sorry affair. 'I no longer care a straw for Europe's future . . . I wouldn't want to live if I did not have my work . . . In all events, it's good that one is already old and doesn't have to reckon on a long future personally.'

This self-protective indifference was belied by Einstein's enthusiasm for Hitler's defeat. He had now jettisoned his old pacifism, and whole-heartedly supported the crushing of the Nazis by force. Organized power could be defeated only by organized power, he said – 'much as I regret this'. He took up US citizenship in October 1940, just over a year after the declaration of war by Britain and France. He called for 'the German bloodhounds' to be stopped at all costs and regarded his former compatriots as moral degenerates. In the summer of 1942 he wrote, 'Due to their wretched traditions the Germans are such a badly messed-up people that it will be very difficult to remedy the situation by sensible, not to speak of humane, means. I keep hoping that at the end of the war, with God's benevolent help, they will largely kill each other off.' Einstein took practical steps to hasten this end. In the later stages of the war, he helped the US Navy on a part-time basis, carrying out theoretical work on explosions for a consultant's fee of twenty-five dollars a day. He also encouraged Hans Albert to carry out 'war work', and his son became an employee of the Army Corps of Engineers.

Einstein subsequently denied having worked for the military in any way. In the words of his biographer Ronald Clark, 'he was human enough to push to the back of his mind the unpleasant facts he did not wish to acknowledge.' This reticence is connected with the responsibility that Einstein felt for encouraging the development of atomic weapons, having sent a letter to President Roosevelt in 1939 that set out the military implications of nuclear fission. Einstein was largely speaking on behalf of colleagues who had helped to draft the letter for him, and he had only a vague idea of the technological challenges and the form an atom bomb might take (warning that it would probably be too heavy to carry in an aeroplane). It is also clear that other, less celebrated, interventions were far more important than Einstein's in stimulating US atomic research. Nevertheless, Einstein later expressed his regret at having played any part in aiding the destruction of Hiroshima and Nagasaki. Hans Albert came to realize that his family name was linked for ever with the horrors of nuclear warfare. Some years after Einstein's death, he was on a lecture visit to Lahore when a man leapt forward, seized his tie and began to shake him. 'Your father was responsible for the atom bomb, and now you have to pay for it,' the attacker raved, apparently ready to exact revenge on the spot. He was dragged off by a group of academics and students, but it was a terrifying moment.

At the time the bombs were dropped, Einstein's reaction was the bleakest possible understatement. News of the attack on Hiroshima reached him while he was staying at Saranac Lake in New York's Adirondack Mountains. On 6 August 1945, Einstein was resting after lunch when Helen Dukas heard on the radio that a new kind of bomb had been dropped on Japan. She told him as he came down to tea, and his only reply was '*Oh, Weh*' – 'Alas.'

Dukas was now constantly at her employer's side, living with him at Mercer Street as cook, housekeeper and general factotum. Her workload was overwhelming, and the telephone in her room rang day and night. Her devotion to Einstein during the Princeton years was absolute, and her hostility to inquiring outsiders – even family – became legendary. She had an outlook not unlike that of Chico, a wirehaired terrier who joined the household in the early 1940s and tried to bite chunks from postmen delivering Einstein's mail. Dukas thought nothing of running from the house in a dirty apron to save Einstein from a mob of reporters, shouting 'Professor Einstein, they are newsmen, don't talk, don't talk.' When the press was clamouring for a photo call and press conference on Einstein's seventy-fifth birthday, in 1954, her orders to his colleagues at the Institute for Advanced Study were simple: 'Tell them to jump in the lake.' Perhaps it would be better, they tactfully suggested, to say, 'No statement will be given.'

In later years Dukas would even screen letters from Einstein's family to prevent him being disturbed. His granddaughter Evelyn recalled, 'Sometimes she would make the decision that Albert was too busy to either read or answer a letter from me. So she would read it and answer it, which always offended me.' Mark Darby, the archivist at the Institute for Advanced Study, was struck by Dukas's insistent presence when he inspected the Institute's collection of pictures of Einstein. 'I noticed she had a way of getting herself into every photograph . . . You can see her eyes right in the camera. She just felt like she owned the guy.'

Dukas was so much a part of Einstein's life that at least one young visitor thought she was Einstein's wife. It has even been suggested that she and Einstein had an affair. Peter A. Bucky, the son of Einstein's friend and doctor Gustav Bucky, has claimed that Hans Albert suspected such a liaison and privately alluded to it on several occasions. However, Dukas herself admitted that Einstein usually showed no more affection for her than if she were a table or a chair. Bucky's credibility is also weakened by his parallel suggestion that Dukas was the long-lost Lieserl, adopted under another name and returned to Einstein's side through unexplained coincidence and subterfuge. The truth seems to have been simpler: Dukas was a woman in need of someone to revere, and Einstein was a man in need of a devotee. However, there is no clearer evidence of their bond than Einstein's will, drawn up in 1950 and witnessed by – among others – Kurt Gödel, one of the greatest logicians ever to have lived. Dukas was left not only Einstein's books and personal effects but 20,000 dollars – 5,000 dollars more than Eduard, and twice as much as Hans Albert. More importantly, the net income from royalties and copyright fees on all Einstein's papers and literary works was hers for so long as she lived. As the *New York Times* commented, 'In his will, Einstein left Miss Dukas his most valued possessions.'

Of course, Einstein had long since proved that he preferred female company in the plural to the singular. Dukas was only one of a triumvirate of women who lived with him at Mercer Street. His stepdaughter Margot (also awarded 20,000 dollars in the will) had positioned herself closer to Einstein than either of his sons. Her husband, Marianoff, had initially joined her in the United States, but they separated in the summer of 1934. She and Dukas took the American oath of allegiance alongside Einstein in 1940. In the words of one perceptive commentator, Margot grew 'so much like Einstein in attitude and outlook that it was difficult to think of them as linked only by collateral lines on the family tree'. Her adoration of her stepfather sometimes bordered on absurdity. In Margot's eyes, Einstein did not just go boating but 'sailed like Odysseus' – an heroic figure 'so natural and strong' that he seemed to her like an elemental force, 'a piece of nature'. The sentimental side to Margot's character seems to have appealed to Einstein, who once remarked, 'When Margot speaks, you see flowers growing.' The house was filled with examples of her sculpture, and they were frequent walking companions.

The third member of Einstein's female trio was his sister Maja. He had invited her to live with him in 1939 after anti-Semitic laws were introduced in Italy by Mussolini. Her husband, Paul Winteler – to whom her marriage was not always easy – remained in Europe, moving in with his brother-in-law Michele Besso in Geneva. Maja wanted to return to the man she called 'Paulus Rex', or King Paul, and was endlessly homesick for Florence. But the war and persistent ill health meant that she was not to see Europe again. Maja took comfort in the love of her brother, who showed her an unstinting tenderness and care that neither of his wives had enjoyed. All traces of the tension that had existed in earlier years – when Einstein teased his sister, and privately ranked her among the philistines – had disappeared since his second marriage and their mother's death. She wrote how brother and sister were now closer together than ever before.

Maja's physical resemblance to Einstein was now greater even than Elsa's had been. The wildly radiating strands of her silver hair bore out her family nickname, 'Sun', although Maja wrote that her brother's endless kindness meant that 'he has more right to such a "shining" name than I have.' Towards the end of her life, Maja sent her relatives in Geneva a photograph of herself on the porch at Mercer Street: she reported with glee that only her husband was sure it was not of Einstein. Even the sound of Maja's voice, and the sceptical simplicity with which she framed each statement, carried an unmistakable echo of her brother.

At first Maja feared that Einstein's circle in America saw her merely as an adjunct to him, and were friendly 'only because one strokes the dog to flatter the master'. But she took pride in being the first person to whom Einstein would confide his thoughts, including those on science. Her brother respected her intelligence, even though she was ill-equipped to discuss abstruse physics. He retained the need for an admiring audience to hear him think aloud. One of Einstein's collaborators, Ernst Straus, said, 'Since she was a very good listener, he liked to explain his newest ideas to her. He did not feel that he understood something until he himself had understood it in these simple and basic terms.' The warmth underpinning their relationship shines out from one of Einstein's gentler jokes at Maja's expense. She was a vegetarian, but had an overwhelming passion for hot dogs. Einstein attempted to solve her dilemma by decreeing that, in Maja's case, a hot dog could be classed as a vegetable.

The most touching evidence of his affection came after Maja suffered a stroke in 1946 and became bedridden, with Margot acting as her nurse. Einstein would read to his sister each evening from works by their favourite authors. 'Every day I look forward to this hour and have the satisfaction of seeing that he too looks forward to it,' she wrote to a friend in a faltering hand. 'He dislikes it very much if he has to give up these evenings when he has important visitors.'

One other figure – a man this time – was of central importance to Einstein's Princeton years. Dr Otto Nathan had been among Einstein's first visitors when he and Elsa moved to America in 1933, volunteering to help them settle in. A fellow German, he too had fled the country of his birth to escape the Nazis. Nathan was a distinguished economist who had served as an adviser to the Weimar Republic, and was a delegate to the World Economic Conference at Geneva in 1927. He went to Princeton to teach at the University, but he rapidly made himself indispensable to Einstein as a business adviser and fixer. One bond between them was their radical outlook on politics – indeed, during the 1950s Nathan had difficulty obtaining a passport from the US State Department. He suffered badly during the McCarthy inquisition into communism, and became a target of the House Un-American Activities Committee. These experiences only served to toughen still further his stern and suspicious personality. An ascetic man, who neither smoked nor drank and rarely indulged in jokes, Nathan showed an unswerving loyalty to Einstein that lasted long after the latter's death, being Dukas's closest friend and ally for almost half a century.

The elderly Einstein provided a rich source of anecdotes for his American hosts. It was commonplace to see him on the streets of

Princeton, strolling to the Institute or the nearby Marquand Park – stories tell of a car driver who ran into a tree after recognizing him, and of the awed hush that descended on any physics seminar where Einstein appeared. He got on particularly well with animals and small children. One eight-year-old girl tried to bribe Einstein with fudge to do her homework. He politely declined to help, but did compensate her with some biscuits. When it rained, he would comfort the family tomcat with the words, 'I know what's wrong, my dear, but I really don't know how to turn it off.' Along with the whimsy, however, was that broad seam of cynicism. On one occasion, Margot was concerned about her parakeet – it seemed rather glum – and asked Einstein and his assistant if it was pining for a mate. 'All of that is an illusion,' said Einstein. 'Having a mate is an illusion.'

It was a remark that would not have surprised Mileva. During her last years in Switzerland, she was a drably dressed figure and increasingly frail. Yet she still possessed an indefinable presence, according to fellow countryman and Nobel chemistry laureate Vladimir Prelog, who lived across the street. Among his neighbours he noticed 'an old lady, whom we often saw from our balcony coming in and out of the house, who was different from the others – in a certain way "eminent". Later we learned that she was Mileva Einstein-Marić. Although I could speak to her in our common mother tongue, I did not dare to contact her, because I was afraid that she might be approached too often by people asking questions about her ex-husband.'

Hans Albert's daughter Evelyn found her grandmother bad-tempered and moody when she was taken to visit her as a little girl. Mileva would talk about the five-year-old as though she were not in the room. 'To Mileva, I was "that alien child" because I was born in America,' recalled Evelyn. The dry and prickly side to Mileva's character found a rather obvious symbol in the extensive cactus collection she compiled – presumably including the specimens that Einstein had brought her from South America. Evelyn felt that she cared for little else, but other reports are more sympathetic. Maria Grendelmeier, who moved into the house at Huttenstrasse in 1942 with her husband Josef, remembers Mileva's unfeigned joy when the Grendelmeiers' first son was born the following year. Mileva kept a Siamese cat on which she lavished indulgent affection, and she planted black-berry bushes in the garden that still produce fruit today.

As the years passed, Mileva found Eduard's stays at home a heavy burden. His illness was clear to neighbours such as Frau Grendelme-ier, who recalls Eduard as a 'friendly but incalculable' young man with a 'love–hate' relationship with his mother. When her first son was born, he told her with suave authority, 'Frau Grendelmeier, when you need to know anything medical about the baby, just call.' But his charm and apparent self-assurance could evaporate in spasms of wild excitement, which often coincided with the stifling Föhn wind that blows sporadically from the Alps. Mostly these outbursts were harm-less, although unsettling. Eduard would hammer tunelessly and at great volume on the piano, or hurl pictures and other objects out of the windows. He would jump out at neighbours from the darkness on the stairs, or scandalize his mother by answering the door with no trousers on.

But there was also a sense of real danger. On at least one occasion, Frau Grendelmeier heard that Eduard had attacked his mother and made as if to strangle her. Similar reports of violence were passed down through Hans Albert's side of the family. When these outbursts occurred, Mileva's last resort was to telephone the Burghölzli so that Eduard could be taken back into care. Frau Grendelmeier remembers a yellow car pulling up outside in the small hours to take him away.

Eduard continued to write his philosophical aphorisms, and a sym-pathetic doctor sent examples to Einstein in America, without at first revealing the author's identity. It seems unlikely that Einstein had no inkling of what was afoot, but he told Besso that their clarity and precision had stood out among all the many letters he continually received. 'It is a thousand pities for the boy that he must pass his life without hope of a normal existence,' Einstein wrote. 'Since the insulin therapy has finally failed, I look for nothing more from medical help. I place very little store by this fraternity, and think it better on the whole to let Nature run its course.' In a letter to Eduard, evidently sent at around the same time, Einstein told his son what had hap-pened and urged him to keep writing. 'In the end,' he said, 'nothing gives more joy and satisfaction than that which one wrests from oneself in the best form one can achieve. I feel this particularly now that my life is almost over.'

In the latter half of the 1940s Mileva's health began a precipitous decline, and she is believed to have suffered a number of small strokes. On one occasion she broke her leg, apparently while battling through icy streets to visit Eduard at the Burghölzli. Passers-by are reported to have found her lying unconscious on the road to the clinic, a frail and anonymous old woman whose strength had finally given out. She was taken to hospital but made only a partial recovery, sensing that her death was near and terrified about what the future would hold for her son. Her mind suffered as much as her body. One account of her last months describes her undergoing orthopaedic treatment during the early part of 1947, convinced that the white walls of her sickroom were the swirling snow of a blizzard, through which she was fighting in vain to reach her son.

This traumatic period saw Mileva's relations with Einstein slide back into enmity and mistrust. Tension had been gathering since the end of the 1930s, when Mileva began to be overwhelmed by the cost of Eduard's care. She ran into severe financial problems, which resulted in the forced sale of two of the three houses she had bought with the Nobel prize money. In order to prevent the additional loss of her home at Huttenstrasse, Mileva agreed that Einstein should take over ownership in 1939 through a specially created company in New York. By his own account, Mileva retained power of attorney over the house and kept what rental income was not required for the continuing mortgage payments. Einstein also made regular cash transfers to Switzerland to safeguard her and Eduard's livelihood, with additional payments to meet building repairs, taxes and other contingencies.

Now, as his former wife neared her end, Einstein decided on drastic action. He made arrangements to sell the house at Huttenstrasse to generate capital for Eduard's subsequent care by a guardian. 'When the house has been sold and Tetel has a reliable guardian, and Mileva is no longer with us, I will be able to go to my grave with peace of mind,' he wrote in July 1947. A buyer was found, and that autumn the deal went through in the face of Mileva's helpless opposition. There was no danger of her being evicted from her apartment, but the psychological blow was devastating. Einstein was acting almost as if she were already dead, and it was clear that Eduard would then spend the rest of his life in a stranger's home. Mileva was distraught, and seized the most obvious weapon of retaliation available. Since she had retained power of attorney over the house, the proceeds from the sale were first handed over to her. Einstein expected their immediate transfer to America, but Mileva kept them. Einstein's letters were ignored, and she would not even reveal how much the sale had raised.

Einstein sought help from Dr Karl Zürcher, a Swiss attorney and son of his old friend Emil Zürcher who had handled the couple's divorce papers and befriended Mileva. In December 1947 he begged the lawyer to make Mileva 'do her duty' and hand the money over. He warned that he would write Eduard out of his will if she did not comply. Harsh though this was, Einstein insisted he had no choice if he hoped to leave anything to his other beneficiaries. The following month he pressed his case again, setting out in detail the financial assistance he had given his former wife since their divorce. 'I know that Frau Mileva has always made out that I neglected her,' he observed. The same tone appeared in a letter to Hans Albert in the summer of 1948, expressing exasperation that the amount and location of the money was still unknown. 'Perhaps she has hidden it in the form of cash or it has simply been stolen ... Everything is possible due to her taciturn and mistrusting nature.'

By this time, Mileva's life was draining away. It appears that she had suffered another stroke at the end of May, paralysing her left side, after Eduard began to ransack the apartment in search of some imaginary missing object. She was cared for at a clinic a short drive from her home, where visitors such as Lisbeth Hurwitz found her distracted and confused. Staff confiscated her bedside bell after she rang repeatedly for assistance, without what they deemed sufficient cause. She spoke of wanting to join Eduard as a patient at the Burgh-ölzli, then lapsed into semi-unconsciousness and lay muttering the words 'No, no'. Death came to the seventy-three-year-old on 4 August 1948. Frau Grendelmeier, who sought to visit her but was turned away, says, 'She died alone. She died quite alone.'

It was an austerely fitting end to a life clouded by broken promises and disappointed hopes. Eduard appeared dazed, Frau Grendelmeier recalls. He seems never to have spoken of his mother again.

Mileva was buried in Zurich's Nordheim cemetery, where her grave has since vanished in the course of reorganization. Her death notice in the local papers carried no mention of her former husband: the passing to eternal rest of 'our beloved mother, Mileva Einstein-Marity' was recorded in the names of Albert and Frieda Einstein-Knecht of Berkeley, California, and Eduard Einstein, for whom no address was given. Frieda travelled to Zurich to sort out Mileva's effects and help clear her apartment, as did Otto Nathan.

According to Helen Dukas, a hoard of 85,000 Swiss francs was found hidden under Mileva's mattress. This was presumably the missing money from the house sale. Dukas regarded its discovery as final proof of Mileva's madness and badness, and she felt humiliated on Einstein's behalf, since Mileva had been cared for during her last illness under the provisions of Swiss poor laws. Years later, Dukas remained violently sensitive to enduring rumours that Einstein had left his ex-wife to die a pauper. 'This is how legends arise, and one also sees how quick people always are to believe the negative,' she wrote in December 1956, after hearing of comments made by a doctor involved in Mileva's care. Dukas returned to the subject in November 1957, still protesting against the injustice to Einstein's memory, and bemoaning the doctor's gullibility. 'He must surely have seen that he was dealing with a poor lunatic,' she wrote.

It was in the year of Mileva's death that Einstein discovered his own fatal illness. For some time he had suffered from frequent attacks of nausea that began with a mumbling and a gurgling in his stomach then grew into unbearably sharp pains in the upper abdomen. The discomfort would spread to between the shoulder blades and culminate in diarrhoea or vomiting. In the autumn of 1948, a growth in his abdomen was diagnosed. An operation carried out in December by Dr Rudolf Nissen at the Jewish Hospital in Brooklyn revealed an aneurysm in the abdominal aorta, a ballooning of the main artery from the heart. About eighteen months later it was found that the aneurism was enlarging under the pressure of blood flowing through the weakened area. Helen Dukas said that from that moment 'the sword of Damocles' hung over Einstein and his entourage. His own mortality was underlined by the death of Maja in June 1951. Einstein had confided in Hans Albert that her predicament in the last years of her life was so miserable that it might have been better if the stroke in 1946 had killed her outright.

Eduard was now in the hands of a guardian, Dr Heinrich Meili, who around the start of 1950 placed him in the care of a pastor in the village of Uitikon, prettily positioned on the hillside above Zurich. The pastor, Hans Freimüller, had a grounding in psychoanalysis and combined evangelism with providing therapy for disturbed young men. He has recalled his first meeting with Eduard, a paunchy and nervous forty-year-old with fascinating eyes. 'Their languid brilliance was irradiated with a wondrous luminosity which could not be interpreted other than as an expression of goodness which looks for protection,' the pastor wrote. Among Eduard's few possessions were some yellowed music books, left over from his student days, and at first it was through this medium alone that he seemed able to communicate. Pastor Freimüller remembered, 'During the first weeks, Mr Einstein's interest was almost exclusively piano playing. Occasionally one feared the strings would break from such ferocious playing.' Gradually, Eduard's shyness receded as he got to know the pastor's three young sons, whom he entertained with poems and jokes. He gave concerts for children from the church youth group, who had befriended him on visits to the vicarage, and he began to be accepted into the village community. The pastor's wife arranged for him to take a job writing addresses on envelopes for a local firm. Eduard was visibly pleased to be earning a little money and having independence.

Among the villagers in Uitikon was one of Eduard's best friends from school, Peter Herzog, by then a married schoolteacher. His widow, Nora, recalled his shock at seeing the sad figure Eduard had become, so utterly changed from the boy whose intelligence seemed to frighten his teachers, and for whom all his peers had expected a magnificent career. Eduard visited their home, but Herr Herzog felt unable to make real contact with his guest, who could talk of little but his fear and uncertainty about the future. Perhaps these fears would have abated had Eduard been allowed to stay in Pastor Freimüller's enlightened care. After only a year, however, he was removed by his guardian to live with a lawyer's widow in the Zurich suburb of Höngg. She gave him affection and understanding, but Freimüller's attempts to draw him back into normal life were at an end. Even today, the pastor remembers it was 'a very painful parting'.

Einstein would have had almost no contact with Eduard in these years had it not been for one of his biographers, Carl Seelig. This kind-hearted man, who lived in Zurich, cultivated Einstein's friend-ship by the novel stratagem of sending him a constant supply of dried soups. These were to Einstein what lime tea and madeleines were to Proust, reviving nostalgic images of former times. He thanked Seelig profusely for 'furnishing me and my nose with a totally Swiss environ-ment'. The protective Dukas was also won over, telling Seelig that the soups were 'manna from heaven' given the dietary problems created by Einstein's illness. The resulting intimacy served both parties: Seelig gained greater access to Einstein's secrets than any other writer, but felt so much a part of the family that he kept most of the details to himself.

The mentally ill had a fascination for Seelig, who arranged a meet-ing with Eduard in early 1952. Einstein gave this his blessing, adding that though his son's condition was 'relatively mild' there was no hope of his ever taking up a career. 'There must be intense emotional inhibitions there, the nature of which are inaccessible to laymen at least,' Einstein wrote. Seelig dined with Eduard in a restaurant next to the Fraumünster church on the banks of the Limmat in Zurich, and found him eager to talk. One of his anecdotes was of visiting Einstein in Berlin and looking through a telescope on the apartment's balcony – ostensibly at the moon, but also with great enthusiasm into the houses opposite. Soon, however, it became clear to Seelig that there were many large gaps in Eduard's memory. He was particularly astonished that Eduard could say nothing at all about his paternal grandparents. Einstein later blamed this on the 'unbridgeable' enmity between Mileva and his mother – his father had, of course, died before Eduard's birth – and explained that there were 'no personal contacts of any sort' between the two sides of the family. Neverthe-less, it seemed to Seelig that his son's ignorance was symptomatic of something wider. As Eduard sat chain-smoking and bestubbled, racking his brains to dredge up details from the early years, Seelig told him not to torment himself about events he had been too young to recall. No, came the smiling reply, this interested him. With Seelig's help, he could now get to know his family for the first time.

It was in Seelig's interest to play on this theme, to encourage Einstein to pass on biographical information. But he also had a deep and genuine compassion for Eduard. 'The face of your son has something tormented and brooding, but also a serene smile and a trustfulness that are speedily charming,' he told Einstein. They continued to meet, visiting the theatre and chatting together on walks with Seelig's Dalmatian dog. After only a few weeks, Seelig offered to act as Eduard's guardian. Einstein appeared moved, but politely declined the offer and explained that the post was already filled. This is very sad, since it was clear around this time that Eduard wished to break away from the wardship of Dr Meili, whom he apparently found unsympathetic. Seelig became his closest friend, staying loyal even after Einstein's death.

Seelig kept Einstein informed on changes in his son's condition, but all letters had first to go through the hands of Dukas. In 1952 she admitted being tempted to keep a particularly distressing bulletin to herself, passing it on to her employer only after consultation with Margot. Even then, she took care to give her own gloss on the contents before allowing Einstein to read it. This was what Americans called 'cushioning', she told Seelig. Two years later, Dukas announced that she and Nathan had decided to hold back any bad news about Eduard to avoid Einstein being distressed. It is likely that they were accurately anticipating their master's wishes. In January 1954, Einstein wrote to Seelig to explain why he had severed all contact with his son. 'You have probably already wondered about the fact that I do not exchange letters with Teddy,' he said. 'It is based on an inhibition that I am not fully capable of analyzing. But it has to do with my belief that I would awaken painful feelings of various kinds if I entered into his vision in any way.'

The year of 1954 saw Hans Albert's fiftieth birthday. His differences with his father remained unresolved, and they met only seldom. Hans Albert told one interviewer that his famous name brought constant problems with telephone operators, post office clerks and suspicious traffic policemen. People would stare him in the eye and say,

'Impossible, Einstein has no son.' When the same interviewer asked him to pose by a bust of Einstein, which he passed regularly at the Berkeley university library, Hans Albert was reluctant. 'Do you know what it is to have your father a statue?' he asked. Hans Albert gave this interview only after obtaining the written consent of his father (it seems he had expected it not to be granted) and he stressed his pride in Einstein's achievements. But he also admitted how uncomfortable it was to sense strangers staring at him like an oddity, or to notice the furtive scrutiny of fellow academics as they secretly made unflattering intellectual comparisons. 'It has a tendency to make a son completely lose his own identity,' he said.

Hans Albert once remarked that he had led an absolutely quiet life. 'From school I went into my first job and I was never without a job since then. All I did all my life is work.' It was this stern dedication that Einstein praised in a letter to mark his elder son's half century. He reminisced a little about Hans Albert's childhood, and an occasion on which the boy commandeered his razor to whittle wood, leaving it looking like a saw. He also recalled Hans Albert's childish corruption of the German word for curtain – '*Vorhang*' became '*Voio-Voio*' – which the boy then applied to anything grand but insubstantial, whether smoke from the fireplace or empty conversation. This appealed to Einstein's vein of cynicism, and he now applauded his son for having ignored the showy and the superficial by devoting himself to hydraulics.

It is a joy for me to have a son who has inherited the main traits of my personality: the ability to rise above mere existence by sacrificing one's self through the years for an impersonal goal. This is the best, indeed the only thing through which we can make ourselves independent from personal fate and other human beings.

Einstein went on to tell his son that they shared the same restless mental inquisitiveness, combined with the same dislike for studying academic literature. It was their shared vice, he said, but a heroic way to live. His letter ended, 'Continue as you have done up to now. Keep up your humour, be good to people but take no notice of their words and deeds. Your father.'

When Hans Albert's second wife wrote a memoir of her husband, she quoted from this letter, but only in a heavily edited form that omitted its bleaker remarks. She also overlooked a detail that rankled enough for her husband to mention it to a BBC journalist. Hans Albert said that Einstein had never managed to remember his son's birthdays. He confirmed that he had received 'a very nice letter' when he was fifty, 'but the very first sentence was, "Unfortunately, I have to admit that I didn't think about it, but your wife wrote me."'

Einstein's praise for Hans Albert came as his own work was slipping ever more out of touch with current research. His views, particularly his dogged opposition to quantum theory, had turned him from a creative individual who was ahead of his time into a loner on the scientific sidelines. Einstein told Leopold Infeld that his colleagues thought him more of a historic relic than an active scientist. Infeld later wrote, 'It was distressing to see Einstein's isolation and aloofness from the main stream of physics. On several occasions this man, probably the greatest physicist in the world, said to me in Princeton: "Physicists consider me an old fool, but I am convinced that the future development of physics will depart from the present road."'

The quest for a satisfactory unified field theory continued unabated. When Einstein seemed to be on the right track, he would declare, 'This is so simple God could not have passed it up.' However, all his efforts were fundamentally misconceived, according to the physicist who later came to live in his house on Mercer Street, Frank Wilczek. 'Einstein was trying to solve the problems of his youth, which had become obsolete,' Wilczek said. 'They really were clearly misguided, and no one starting from an awareness of the experimental realities of the time would have undertaken that programme . . . It was never ever remotely plausible that the richness of structure that we see around us and the laws of quantum mechanics could emerge just from unifying gravity and electromagnetism.' Einstein outlined his ideas on unification in a new appendix for the third edition of his book *The Meaning of Relativity*, in 1949. It became a worldwide media event – mainly because of its coincidence with his seventieth birthday. The *New York Times* printed a page of his manuscript under the headline 'New Einstein theory gives a master key to the universe.' In Britain, the *Daily Telegraph* printed the four equations that 'set out the heart of the theory'. Einstein asked Dukas to tell reporters to come back in twenty years, and grumbled to Hans Albert that the publicity was unwarranted and tasteless. 'It is an imbecility to put something like that before the public, quite apart from the fact that only a very small minority will understand,' he told his son.

The fuss was a tribute to Einstein's grip on the popular imagination. The manager of the Institute for Advanced Study recollected how he had to act as a behind-the-scenes minder 'to help protect him from hero worshippers and cranks who in their own peculiar way were every bit as resourceful as bobby soxers in full chase of some current idol of show business'. The public, he said, looked on Einstein

> not only as the greatest of mathematicians, but as a statesman, philosopher, an oracle, and a symbol – and for good measure an authority on subjects as far removed as art, astrology and (on one occasion) old bones. They attempted to reach him by telephone at any hour of the day or night. They deluged him with mail. And they sought him out in person, arriving at the institute by bus, train, automobile and plane. Given half a chance they would sniff along the institute corridors like bloodhounds attempting to uncover his study which, as a matter of fact, was concealed behind two thin, unmarked, oak doors at one end of the ground floor.

Einstein had done nothing to diminish public curiosity by his involvement in politics, which was never greater than after the Second World War. He wrote an open letter to the United Nations calling for the formation of a world government, dedicated to the ending of war and empowered to interfere in individual states to stop the oppression of minorities. It was Einstein's oft-repeated view that this was the only way to control nuclear weapons. He was a constant critic of Cold War attitudes, both in written articles and in radio broadcasts, and he advocated better relations with the Soviet Union when this was decidedly a minority cause. During the McCarthy era, when many critics attacked him as an enemy of America, he supported the kind of non-violent civil disobedience pioneered by Gandhi. Conscientious objectors found an ally in Einstein, as did academics fighting for freedom of thought. He was also a vocal friend and supporter of Israel, though politely turning down an offer to succeed Chaim Weizmann as the country's second president.

In the starkest contrast, his hatred for all things German continued unabated. He made it clear that he wished to have nothing more to do with the country of his birth, whose inhabitants he blamed indiscriminately for the massacre of the Jews under Hitler. The intellectuals had behaved as badly as the mob, he said, only excepting a handful of his closest colleagues. He had come to believe that the Germans were the cruellest race on the earth, with the mentality of gangsters, and claimed to see no sign of remorse for their years of mass murder. It was a deep and unmitigated loathing, which disturbed many of those who knew him. But Einstein did not waver. As his life drew to a close, he resolutely turned his back on the land that had helped to shape him.

Another link to the past was broken on 15 March 1955, the day after Einstein's seventy-sixth birthday, with the death of Michele Besso. His Patent Office comrade, go-between with Mileva and life-long confidant was two months short of eighty-two. We referred in our first chapter to the moving letter of condolence that Einstein wrote to Besso's son Vero and sister Bice, envying his friend's marital happiness. As Einstein put it, 'The gift of leading a harmonious life is rarely joined to such keen intelligence.' He had made an equally telling comment to Bice a few years earlier, when she asked why Besso had never made any great intellectual discoveries like his own. The reply was recorded by Bice's son-in-law in an article for the *New Yorker*. 'Aber Frau Bice,' said Einstein laughing, 'this is a very good sign. Michele is a humanist, a universal spirit, too interested in too many things to become a monomaniac. Only a monomaniac gets what we commonly refer to as results.'

Einstein later told Besso that he had meant what he said, but urged his friend not to worry about it. 'A butterfly is not a mole; but that is not something any butterfly should regret.'

Less than a month later, on Tuesday 12 April 1955, Einstein paid his last visit to the Institute for Advanced Study. His assistant Bruria Kaufman asked him if everything was comfortable. Einstein replied to her, smiling, 'Everything is comfortable. But I am not.' He had an intense pain in his groin, which he had not experienced before, and at home the next day he complained of tiredness and loss of appetite. He lay down to sleep in the early afternoon, but at about 3.30 p.m. Dukas heard him running into the bathroom, where he collapsed. Dukas had already sent out two warning messages to Einstein's personal physician, Dr Guy Dean, and now summoned him to come immediately. Dukas was at Einstein's side throughout the ensuing consultation, at which two other doctors were also present, and even helped Dr Dean to take an electrocardiogram. That night, which Einstein passed with the help of morphine, she made herself a bed in his study. Dukas was concerned that her bedroom would be too far away to help if he deteriorated further. She insisted – in spite of his objections – that she be nearby. His body was now badly dehydrated, and it was Dukas who fed him ice cubes and mineral water by spoon.

The next day, a group of doctors, including Dr Gustav Bucky and a specialist aortic surgeon from New York, deliberated on his condition. Perhaps the bleeding from his aneurysm could be halted with surgery. Einstein listened patiently, but protested that such intervention was tasteless: 'I want to go when I want.' He asked if the death he was facing would be a horrible one. The compassionate but honest Dr Dean said it might last a minute or it might last weeks, there was no way of knowing. Einstein's humour had not deserted him, however: he told Helen Dukas, 'I can die without the help of the doctors.'

By the Saturday morning, Einstein was heavily jaundiced and in immense pain from internal bleeding. He was unable to lift his head from the pillow. Throughout his ordeal, he had often rejected painkilling injections and reproached Dukas for fussing around him. Now he finally agreed to enter hospital, after being told that Dukas could no longer cope with his care. Soon after arrival at Princeton Hospital, he phoned her to ask for his spectacles. The following day he asked for the unfinished draft of a speech and his most recent calculations on unified field theory. As death approached, he motioned to his heart and told Otto Nathan he felt close to success with his ideas. He had once said, 'If I knew that I should have to die in three hours it would impress me very little. I should think how best to use the last three hours, then quietly order my papers and lie peacefully down.'

Hans Albert had not been summoned until the Friday evening –
more than forty-eight hours after his father had collapsed – when he
received a telephone call from Margot. He caught the first plane from
California and arrived on the Saturday morning. Einstein seemed
pleased to see his son, and spent Sunday afternoon chatting with
him about science. Later they were joined by Otto Nathan, and the
conversation switched to politics, with Einstein dilating on the dangers of allowing Germany to become a military power again. Hans
Albert thought that, given a little more opportunity, he might be able
to talk his father round to seeking more specialized care at a hospital
in New York. But time had run out. In the small hours of the following morning, Einstein's nurse, Alberta Rozsel, noticed he had difficulty breathing. Another nurse came to help her, then left, and Rozsel
heard Einstein mumble something in German that she could not
understand. They were his last words. Shortly afterwards, at 1.15
a.m., he gave two deep breaths and died.

The news was made public at 8 a.m. An obituary cartoon captured
the world's reaction: it showed the earth spinning among the other
planets of the cosmos, half its side covered by a massive plaque saying
'Albert Einstein lived here.' However, the first tributes had hardly
appeared before Einstein's mortal remains had been hastily disposed
of. At 2 p.m. on the same day the body was taken to a funeral home in
Princeton. Ninety minutes later it was removed to the Ewing Crema-
torium in Trenton, where twelve of those closest to Einstein – including Nathan, Dukas and Hans Albert – held the briefest of ceremonies.
Nathan read a few lines from Goethe's eulogy to Schiller, then the
body was immediately cremated. Einstein's ashes were scattered at a
spot that remains undisclosed, in order to deter latter-day pilgrims,
but which is believed to have been a river not far away.

However, that was not the entire end. Earlier that morning an
autopsy had been performed by Dr Thomas Harvey, who removed
Einstein's brain and preserved it for analysis. This is a macabre story,
but worth telling. A few months before his death, Einstein had written
to Seelig that he liked the idea of donating his body to medical
science. But he added that he had not left any explicit instructions on
the matter, since he feared it would appear a theatrical gesture. The
removal of the brain was entirely on the doctor's own initiative. Dr

Harvey did not know the feelings of the family on the matter: 'I just knew we had permission to do an autopsy, and I assumed that we were going to study the brain.' Einstein's family only got to know of it from a report in the *New York Times* the next day, after one of Harvey's colleagues spoke to a reporter.

'The family suffered, I think immeasurably, when Thomas Harvey whipped the brain out of Einstein at the autopsy and did not even tell the family he was going to do that,' commented one doctor who has since carried out studies on the tissue. 'It was an obvious and very good idea, but it is astounding he did that without just one phone call, saying, "Look I have got your grandfather's body here. Don't you think we should take the brain out?" And to have done it and then thought about it afterwards was really appalling.' Even Otto Nathan, who witnessed the dissection of Einstein's body, had not realized what was going on, but he contacted Harvey and gave the decision his retrospective approval. The doctor assumed that Nathan was acting with Hans Albert's authority, but had no direct dealings with Einstein's son.

Before removing Einstein's brain, Dr Harvey had pumped the preservative formalin into it through the arterial system. Parts of the organ still survive today: some of them are suspended in formalin, but the majority of the brain was cut into fine sections and embedded in an impervious but transparent material called celoidin that allows microscopic examination. The subsequent analysis has produced fascinating results. Dr Marian Diamond, a professor of integrated biology at Berkeley, reported in the journal *Experimental Neurology* that Einstein's brain differed significantly from the norm. Previous research had found that rats placed in a highly stimulating environment – with plenty of companions, and a varied array of ladders, swings and tunnels to explore – showed significant brain changes. In particular, they had more of the glial cells that surround and support neurons, the nerve cells in the brain that process and transmit information. Similar work has been performed with cats and monkeys, and the number of glial cells seems to be a key indicator of how a more developed brain has larger, more interconnected, nerve cells. Dr Diamond said she discovered that – compared with a database of eleven 'normal' male human brains – Einstein's brain had more glial cells per neuron. Whether he was born this way, or whether he had benefited from the stimulus of his environment, it is impossible to say.

The field of molecular biology that has developed since Einstein's death enables the remains of his brain to be subjected to genetic analysis. Each cell of his brain tissue, like all other cells in the body, contains Einstein's entire genetic complement. So, for example, a molecular biologist at the University of Medicine and Dentistry of New Jersey, Dr Charles Boyd, has used some of Einstein's brain as a source of DNA to investigate whether Einstein's fatal aneurysm was caused by a mutation in one of the genes responsible for the formation of blood vessels. He said the existence of the brain 'offers a unique opportunity to do such genetic studies of the heritability of aneurysms in the Einstein family.'

If alive today, perhaps Einstein would have been comforted by the thought that his genetic bequest could be used to test his conviction that attributes are passed from generation to generation. His genes may well be cloned so that they can be spliced and analysed in perpetuity. There will be a strong temptation for medical researchers to use this blueprint in the hunt for genetic factors that influence intelligence. One Californian company has even expressed interest in a commercial venture to sell momentoes containing Einstein's DNA, multiplied to a visible white smudge by gene-amplification technology and packaged with a photograph. The preservation of Einstein's brain has ensured that there remains a genetic monument to the man who never wanted a memorial.

This is just the kind of ghoulish posthumous interest in Einstein that Nathan had feared. 'I feel the less that is published about his illness and the developments that led to his death, the better it is,' he told Carl Seelig. 'I cannot see why the public should have an interest in those details, or why we should satisfy that interest if it should exist.' This did not deter Einstein's doctor and friend from the Berlin days, Janos Plesch, who was one of the last to see him in Princeton Hospital. As soon as he heard a radio bulletin giving news of the death, Plesch sat down and started to write a letter to his son Peter. Dated 18 April 1955, it contained the extraordinary suggestion that Einstein died of syphilis ('Why shouldn't a healthy and beautiful man have had bad luck in his youthful daredevil days and contracted a lues [syphilis]?'). Plesch insisted that Einstein's symptoms were entirely consistent with the disease, and boasted that in all his years of medical practice he had never once been wrong in tracing an abdominal aneurysm to this cause.

It appears that the same thoughts may have been occupying Seelig, for the cause of the aneurysm was a point on which he had been pressing Nathan. The latter replied that the doctors had 'not come to definite conclusions', but urged him not to bother them and suggested arteriosclerosis or 'an accident which Einstein suffered many years ago'. One is tempted to wonder whether the possibility of syphilis had occurred to Nathan too. Dr Harvey has stated that, medically speaking, Plesch 'had justification for thinking along those lines'. However, although he ran no blood tests for the disease, Dr Harvey saw no other anatomical evidence to indicate it. 'It is known that tertiary syphilis does cause aneurysms, but not in this location very often,' he said. 'Einstein's was not due to that.' The interest of Plesch's claim lies not so much in its accuracy, or lack of it, as in the fact that he made it at all. Plesch was a boaster and a spinner of yarns, of whom Dukas remarked 'everything is to be taken with a pound of salt,' but he had known Einstein well, and his writings showed a psychological insight that was often accurate even when his facts were awry. His remarks are further scurrilous but intriguing evidence of Einstein's reputation as a philanderer.

The provisions of Einstein's will had left Dukas and Nathan as the twin guardians of his name, by granting them control of his entire literary estate. All rights were eventually to pass to the Hebrew University of Jerusalem, but until then nothing from his personal papers could be made public without their approval. It would have been hard to find two individuals less prone to reveal Einstein's secrets. Both were devoted to preserving his public image, and had no wish to provide ammunition to the enemies he had made through his political campaigning. Dukas told Carl Seelig in 1953 that she always found intimate confessions disagreeable, and hardly talked about her own private life to her closest friends. 'It's a good job that I wasn't born Catholic – and it also looks like I'm no good for psychoanalysis,' she joked.

But there was a twist to their attitude that would shape the public perception of Einstein for years to come. Dukas and Nathan both came to know Einstein during his second marriage, and regarded Elsa and her daughters as his true family. Their sympathy for Mileva and her sons was limited, to say the very least. In the words of one Einstein scholar, 'Dukas and Nathan were not only interested in protecting the great god Einstein: they also hated anything that had to do with the first family. They considered themselves part of the second family.'

In the dark hours immediately after Einstein died, there was only unity. Hans Albert was with Dukas at Mercer Street when Dr Dean telephoned the news. Briefly she broke down, but then Hans Albert sat beside her and talked until morning came. She wrote that without his support she would not have known how to survive the night. It was as if his father were speaking to her, Dukas said. Over the following weeks, she distributed to the family some of the personal effects that Einstein had left her. Pipes, watches, a leather tobacco-pouch, a leather belt, a propelling pencil and a pen-holder – all were handed out with punctilious efficiency. Dukas even made arrangements for Eduard to be sent bundles of his dead father's clothing, from sweaters to underwear and the short-sleeved soft-collared sports tops that Einstein preferred to normal shirts. Although Eduard was 'rather fat', she hoped that he would fit some suits from the days when Einstein was 'handsomely broad'.

Dukas noted with approval that Hans Albert was 'very modest' in his selection from these spoils, asking only for a few of Einstein's scientific books. The demeaning position in which he had been placed seems not to have occurred to her: few sons would wish to apply to their father's secretary for the right to a posthumous memento of him – knowing as they did so that this secretary had been left the lion's share of the money, and enjoyed joint control over every word that their father had ever written, even to them. The humiliation for Hans Albert was not lessened by the fact that Nathan – the other literary trustee – was also sole executor of the will that so comprehensively froze him out.

Though Hans Albert hid his chagrin, his wife was openly outraged. After one tense encounter with Frieda, Dukas declared that 'it would be hard for more open greed and ill-will to be combined in one person. It would be funny if it was not so sad and so revolting.' There was nervousness besides indignation in Dukas's words, since she knew that Frieda was plotting to defy her in the most sensational manner. Frieda had found Mileva's cache of letters from Einstein when she cleared out the flat at Huttenstrasse in 1948. They had remained in her possession ever since, and had inspired her with an ambition to write the untold story of her father-in-law's private life, a venture that could help pay for Eduard's hospital bills. 'My mother decided that she would like to show the human side of Einstein,' Frieda's daughter Evelyn recalled.

Dukas and Nathan knew that the letters existed, but could not be sure of either their contents or how Frieda would use them. Their suspicions were enough to worry them deeply, and they also knew that Frieda was trying to track down the biographical sketch of Einstein by his sister. Nathan attempted to pump Hans Albert for information in the summer of 1955, after they happened to catch the same train on the way to Princeton. He failed. Friends and contacts such as Seelig were also pressed to pass on whatever they heard, but it was not until early 1957 that Nathan took direct action – asking Hans Albert to surrender copies of the letters for use in the embryonic Einstein archive. Dukas claimed that the request was framed 'very diplomatically', but it was turned down. Instead, Frieda submitted her now completed manuscript to the publisher Origo Verlag in Zurich. It consisted of extracts from Einstein's letters to Mileva, Hans Albert and Eduard, with an introduction by Frieda offering her own assessment of them. This made plain her opinion that Mileva was the one true love of Einstein's life.

Dukas and Nathan were appalled, convinced that the book was aimed simply to make money at the expense of Einstein's reputation. In 1958 they went to court in Switzerland to prevent its appearance, supported by Margot. The loyal Dukas wrote that Einstein would have been horrified had he known that private letters to his family – 'above all to Mileva' – would be made public. Her anger grew after Eduard's guardian, Dr Meili, became embroiled in the affair, claiming that his ward's interests were at stake and bombarding Nathan with aggressive letters. Dukas complained that Meili had been 'extraordinarily provocative, not to say low, towards poor Otto', whom she described as 'honour and unselfishness personified'. It genuinely dismayed Dukas that such an ugly dispute might be linked publicly with Einstein's name. 'The other side is not so sensitive – you would be amazed! – and uses it as a weapon!' she told Seelig.

Any affection that Dukas had felt for Hans Albert was now at an end, since he stood united with his wife and determined to see the book in print. Dukas told Seelig that she had been browsing through some of Hans Albert's old letters. 'He can be terribly rude, not to say brutal, and absolutely cold . . . Teddy was quite different – sensitive and genuine! It's too bad!' All Dukas's sympathy was now switched to the helpless and unthreatening Eduard. It was a shift that had been signalled three years earlier, quite soon after Einstein's death, when she remarked how strongly Eduard's face now reminded her of his father. In the past, she said, he had always seemed more like Mileva. The taint of this latter resemblance was now passed over to Hans Albert, as Dukas railed against him for previous evasiveness towards Nathan. 'What is almost worse than the greed and unprovoked hostility is the insincerity – exactly like Mileva,' she wrote to Seelig in June 1958. Then again, a few months later, 'He is the son of his mother – much more than Teddy – one can see it plainly.'

To the vast relief of Dukas and Nathan, the Swiss courts ruled in their favour. The legal team representing Frieda and Hans Albert argued that the manuscript contained family information, concerning their own lives, which they were entitled to make public if they wished; but these claims were set aside, on the basis that the letters were a literary work forming part of Albert Einstein's estate. Thus they came under the control not of his family but of the estate's two trustees. Without their permission, Hans Albert was forbidden from publishing letters written to him by his father.

Frieda Einstein-Knecht did not live to fight the ruling. She died in October 1958, after collapsing at a concert she attended in Berkeley with Hans Albert. The letters she had hoped to publish lay in Hans Albert's house in Berkeley until after his own death.

Hans Albert never overcame the pain of losing Frieda, but he could not face life alone. He married for the second time in June 1959, to Elizabeth Roboz, a Hungarian Jew who had emigrated to America in 1940. She was a neurochemist, and had met Hans Albert and Frieda through a mutual friend while working at Caltech in Pasadena. Elizabeth has provided her own account of the marriage, which stresses that – although very fond of each other – both continued to devote themselves to their separate academic disciplines. She writes that once, when Hans Albert was discussing hydraulics with colleagues, she told him that she could not understand their conversation. Hans Albert jokingly recalled his father's remark about being glad that Elsa did not understand physics. Elizabeth admits that she vowed to read up on basic hydraulics, to ensure she could defy the precedent, but never quite got round to it. 'We never did discuss those problems, and we continued to live in peace and harmony.'

The agony of Eduard continued. He reached his fiftieth birthday in the summer of 1960, and held a sad little celebration with Seelig, insisting that they send a greetings card to his brother in America. Seelig was shaken by Eduard's physical ill health:

> He didn't want to have anything sweet to eat, which has never happened with him before. Every few metres he has to stay standing, and during eating he came out in a cold sweat on his brow, so that he had to go out. Together with that, he smokes endlessly one cigarette after another. I think there are the signs of angina pectoris conditioned through the smoking, the corpulence, the indolence, the voices that he sometimes hears etc. He smiled at me often so sweetly and sadly that it cut my heart in two.

After their meal together, Seelig returned Eduard to the Burghölzli. He was now a resident there once more, and had increasingly limited contact with outside society. Hans Albert's daughter Evelyn had been sent to Switzerland to attend a boarding-school, and became one of her uncle's rare visitors. 'I felt rather abandoned, locked away in that Swiss school,' she said. 'I thought – he has been abandoned, I have been abandoned, maybe we should get together.' Evelyn found Eduard utterly institutionalized, with old clothes and his fingers yellowed by tobacco. He appeared helpless and docile, 'paunchy and ponderous in his movements'. In all their conversations, he never spoke of his parents. Instead, he beset his young visitor with bizarre questions that suggested a man cut off from reality – as if he had been closeted at the clinic all his life, and had known no other existence.

He asked me about automobiles and whether they had decided on using the internal combustion engine or whether they were going ahead with electric cars. His mind was darting all over . . . it was like this sponge that was being exposed to something from the outside world and he was trying to get as much information out of me as he could. I was allowed to take him to town. His eyes were as big as saucers and he was like a little kid. This all seemed new to him, and that again disturbed me.

Another visitor was the pastor, Hans Freimüller, who found Eduard in the clinic's nursery. He was standing in front of a pile of flowerpots, washing each one in turn under running water to clean them of clinging mud. 'That's now my work,' he said apologetically. They talked a little, but Eduard seemed distracted and painfully introverted. The pastor asked a member of staff whether Eduard still played the piano, remembering how music had been an invaluable therapy for Eduard when he had stayed with Freimüller's family in 1950. 'This is not possible with so many patients,' came the reply, 'otherwise all of them would want to play too.'

The same sad mood was captured later in a local newspaper article, entitled '*In Zürich vergessen*' – Forgotten in Zurich. The anonymous author described visiting Eduard in 1963 as he worked in the clinic's grounds, dressed in blue overalls and wooden shoes. A moustache helped to lend his pale face a startling resemblance to his father, intensified by his 'large, deep, luminous child's eyes'. He spoke of his frustration at not being allowed to play the piano (the staff had told him it disturbed other patients) and was unhappy that he no longer slept in a room of his own. But he seemed to have reconciled himself to his lot and, in the article's words, 'sought to defend those who had deserted him'. Throughout the conversation he stared at the ground, poking at it with his shoes. His sentences rambled, wandering off on complicated digressions, but his choice of words still revealed his education and intelligence. In the eyes of the article's author, Eduard was a man ruined by his own good nature, 'who had, alas, loved his fellows more than himself and been broken by it.'

Eduard suffered a stroke in 1964 and was visited by Hans Albert and his second wife. They talked to him as they pushed his wheelchair around the clinic's gardens. As he returned to the car, Hans Albert said with a mixture of sorrow and anger, 'What a miserable life Eduard has had.' Death came during the night of 25 October 1965. The announcement in the local press identified Eduard as 'son of the late Prof. Albert Einstein'. There was no mention of Mileva.

Hans Albert survived his brother by a little under eight years. He continued to give lectures around the world even after his retirement in 1971, and received several honours for his work in hydraulics and river management. His expertise had helped to shape development of the Mississippi, the Missouri, the Rio Grande and rivers in Thailand and India. Though he avoided writing books, claiming that his ideas were too ephemeral, his academic papers became some of the most widely cited in their field. His long years of work had brought him respect and prestige, even peace of a kind. And when all his work was done, on Sunday afternoons, Hans Albert would drive out to the Berkeley marina in his venerable Oldsmobile, with the radio permanently tuned to a classical-music station, to take his twenty-three-foot wooden sloop out to sea. The love of sailing that he had inherited from his father, and which began when they went boating together on Lake Zurich in his youth, stayed with him to the end. It was, he said, 'the best way of getting to nature'.

Hans Albert was looking forward to an afternoon sailing trip to the island of Martha's Vineyard when he suffered his fatal heart attack at Woods Hole, Massachusetts, in the summer of 1973. He was buried in a small cemetery overlooking the ocean at Vineyard Sound. Carved on his marble gravestone were the words 'A life devoted to his students, research, nature and music'. With a sentiment of which her father-in-law would have approved, his widow wrote, 'There was no escape from the sorrow of having lost my husband; no way to deal with my grief but to immerse myself in work.'

12

Keepers of the Flame

FOR well over a quarter of a century after Einstein died, his spirit lived on at his Mercer Street home. One of his last instructions on his deathbed had been 'Don't let the house become a museum.' Instead it survived as an entirely private memorial where Helen Dukas and Margot lived on into great old age, visited regularly by the equally long-lived Otto Nathan. Einstein's spartan rooms on the second floor were left much as they were when he was alive – with photographs of his mother and sister still on the walls, and his books and record collection still on the shelves – save for the addition of a few more plants and the replacement of a portrait of Newton by some abstract modern art. Would-be visitors to this sanctuary were discouraged. All the efforts of Dukas and Nathan were devoted to ensuring that Einstein retained his mystery, and that his reputation continued undimmed.

Biographers and researchers who attempted to investigate Einstein's life, or to make use of his writings, found their efforts constantly thwarted. Crucial sources of information were either suppressed or censored. Take, for example, the letters of Michele Besso, which were tracked down by Professor Pierre Speziali, a Swiss historian of science. He had got to know Besso while looking after the mathematics library at the University of Geneva following the Second World War. Every day, whatever the weather, a little white-haired man would potter in and sit absorbed among the books. They began to talk, and Speziali learned something of Besso's long relationship with Einstein. After Besso's death the professor approached his son, and in 1962 they discovered a hoard of letters that had been sitting in a cellar being nibbled by rats. These were augmented by further searches, and by 1968 well over two hundred letters between Besso and

Einstein had been located. Professor Speziali won permission from the Einstein estate to publish this revealing correspondence, but it did not appear until 1972. Nathan had required the excision of the most personal exchanges from the time of the divorce, to conceal the full extent of Einstein's hostility to Mileva. Nathan also ensured that the letters did not appear in English, by turning down proposed translations on the grounds that they were inadequate. The letters have been published only in German and French, ensuring that their contents failed to make much impact in the country where Einstein spent the last two decades of his life.

It was a source of regret to Nathan that he let Speziali publish as much as he did – particularly the most illuminating letter of all, in which Einstein admitted that he had 'failed rather disgracefully' in his marriages. Nathan claimed in 1982 that he gave permission for this letter's inclusion while still unaware of Einstein's aversion to the publication of personal material. He realized this aversion only later, he said, when he came across a letter in which Einstein refused to show his diaries to his early biographer Philipp Frank. For this to be true, Nathan would have needed to have ignored all the evidence of his eyes and ears during the entire time he spent at Einstein's elbow. One doubts, too, whether Hans Albert and Frieda would have credited Nathan with such naïvety in 1958. One can only conclude that he was horrified at his failure to realize the implications of the material, but could not bring himself to admit his mistake.

Nathan's sensitivity was clear in his reaction to the biography of Einstein by Ronald Clark, first published in America in 1971. Clark made only fleeting references to the Besso letters, but it was still clear to Nathan that he had seen them, including the censored passages. Nathan quickly deduced that the source was Dr Jagdish Mehra of the University of Texas at Austin, who had obtained photocopies of the entire collection. Mehra found himself pursued by a series of letters and angry telephone calls from Nathan, demanding that he surrender all the material to the Einstein estate. 'He was very angry with me for sharing it with Clark,' recalled Mehra. 'I told him to go to hell. It was simply that he wanted the whole story of Einstein's relationship with Mileva kept quiet. He did not want any attention drawn to the divorce or Einstein's unfortunate relationship with both of his wives.'

Even today, Mehra is bitter about the treatment that Nathan meted out to him and any others who dealt with the delicate matter of publishing Einstein correspondence, such as Max Born.

Clark had been warned by Hans Albert to expect trouble from Nathan and Dukas, and he got it. Besides warning Clark away from the best account of Hans Albert's side of the story – the Peter Michelmore biography to which we have often referred – Dukas made clear to him that she wanted no detailed discussion of Einstein's marital breakup. He was threatened with legal action against both himself and his sources, and was refused key copyright permissions for the UK edition of his book. Although Clark fiercely resisted, Nathan forced him partially to rewrite the work before its publication in London in 1973. Clark became convinced that Dukas and Nathan were trying to suppress his book because it hinted that Einstein possessed what he called 'an Achilles heel on both feet'. Privately he referred to the guardians of the estate as 'the St Einstein brigade'. It is instructive to compare Clark's acknowledgments in his American and British editions. The first begins by offering personal thanks to Nathan and Dukas (praising the latter for her 'generous and unstinting help') while observing that 'if two devoted colleagues and an impartial biographer were to take the same view all the time, there would be something wrong somewhere.' The later British edition says simply, 'I am grateful for permission to consult the Einstein Archive in Princeton.'

Despite their partial victory over Clark, the truth was that Dukas and Nathan were waging a war they could not win. The first steps towards uncovering Einstein's secrets had been made soon after his death – and with their own cooperation. They began when Philipp Frank set about arranging a memorial symposium for his old friend, and asked for help from one of his Harvard assistants, Gerald Holton. When Holton started to prepare his ground, he found that surprisingly little had been written by historians of science on the impact of Einstein's work. 'There was this vacuum of early-twentieth-century physics history,' he recalls, and it was one that he decided to fill.

Being fascinated by archives, Holton took up Frank's suggestion that he should visit Dukas. He knew she had some of Einstein's correspondence, but he was not prepared for what greeted him when he arrived at the Institute for Advanced Study. Holton entered the imposing red-brick main building – Fuld Hall – and made his way downstairs to the basement, where tiny windows let in a little light under a low ceiling covered with pipes and wiring. Walking through the deserted corridors to the west side, he found a huge walk-in safe. There, hard at work and flanked by twenty or so filing-cabinets, was Helen Dukas. Says Holton, 'I recall Miss Dukas sitting there by the light of the lamp – the only illumination in the room – very much like Juliet in the crypt, still answering letters that were coming in to Einstein – correspondence about his reprint rights, things like that.' As she opened the doors of the cabinets, she revealed a jumble of thousands of papers. There were letters and documents spanning the whole of Einstein's life – even a little geometry book that she thought (wrongly) was the 'holy' one that had fired his imagination as a boy. Many of the papers had only narrowly escaped seizure by the Nazis, and had been spirited to America from Berlin with the help of the French embassy. Holton felt as though he had fallen into a treasure house.

Soon Holton and some graduate students set about the task of creating an ordered archive from the chaos of paper. Even then, it was clear to him that Dukas had been selective about what had been placed in the files. Many letters – those she considered too private to mix with his scientific correspondence – remained in Einstein's house at Mercer Street. 'My function was to get Miss Dukas educated on what a historian of science needs,' says Holton. 'And so she ended up, bit by bit, bringing files from the house.' He believes that she was reverential towards every scrap of memorabilia, but other scholars suspect that vital material was kept hidden or destroyed. Mark Darby, librarian and archivist at the Institute, says, 'The rumour is, and I don't know if it's true, that they threw stuff out. Part of the problem, I guess, was with Helen Dukas and Otto Nathan, who did not – absolutely distinct, clear, did not – want anything to be made public that made Albert Einstein look anything less than perfect.' Among the items believed to have been disposed of are half a dozen missing originals of Einstein's early letters to Elsa.

In 1971 a contract was signed between Princeton University Press and the estate of Albert Einstein to publish his collected papers, volume by volume. Dukas and Nathan gave their permission in the apparent belief that they could prevent the inclusion of all the most personal data, while still producing a lasting monument to Einstein's achievement. All that was required was a historian of science to edit and oversee the massive project, which was originally expected to run to forty volumes. The length of time it took to fill the post reflects the extreme sensitivity of Dukas and Nathan. Various people were considered for the job, and one of them, Martin Klein, actually started work before withdrawing, initially retaining an advisory role and then becoming a senior editor. There were personal reasons for his decision, but he admits that he had a 'feeling in the pit of my stomach' that he would clash with Nathan and Dukas. 'I didn't want someone looking over my shoulder.'

The effort to fill the post continued through the persistence of the then director of Princeton University Press, Herb Bailey. It was fully five years before he approached John Stachel, an expert on the theory of relativity who had given an undergraduate course at Boston University on Einstein's life and times. Stachel was enthusiastic. To him, Einstein was more than just a scientific hero: he was a standard-bearer for political freedom. 'In the 1950s in this country, during the McCarthy period, Einstein was a beacon standing up for the right of the individual to resist the inquisition,' he says. Stachel also admired Nathan on similar grounds.

Stachel moved to Princeton to start work in January 1977. He found that dealing with Nathan and Dukas required all his diplomacy. 'Dukas herself was a repository of so much information about the archive that it was necessary to work with her,' he recalls. 'She could be very charming. I got along fine with her, but she certainly had a line about Einstein – he was represented as a heroic figure.' Stachel remembers that Dukas used to talk about her 'enemies list', and remarks, 'Access to the archives was very much on a personal basis, depending on how your relationship with her worked.' He could sympathize with her concern to see fair play, but it was an uneasy situation: 'Obviously, from a scholarly point of view, I had to have full independence as editor, and ultimately that led to friction.'

Six months after Stachel's arrival in Princeton, Nathan decided he wanted three editors instead of one. Though Herb Bailey and Stachel thought the plan unworkable, Nathan was keen to regain his grip on the project and was alarmed at the thought that funding from the US National Science Foundation would be conditional on maintaining editorial freedom. 'At this point,' says Stachel, 'Nathan decided that he did not want me to continue as editor under the terms that had been agreed. We signed a contract, the Press and I, but Nathan refused to sign.' The dispute went to arbitration, where Nathan lost, but he took it on to appeal through the legal system of New Jersey. 'The case dragged through the courts for a couple of years or so,' Stachel says. 'I was in limbo and could not proceed with the work on this project . . . it was a very unpleasant period.' The appeals were not exhausted until 1980, leaving the way open for publication. But by then Stachel's working relationship with Dukas and Nathan was in tatters.

With canny anticipation, Stachel had already laboriously made an exact duplicate copy of the Institute for Advanced Study's Einstein archive. Editorial work now proceeded on this backup copy at the nearby Princeton University Press. The project was later transferred to Boston, where Stachel still held a tenured professorship of physics.

Stachel and his colleagues did not confine their interest to the documents that Holton had found in the Princeton filing-cabinets. Instead, Hans Albert's daughter Evelyn remembers, they 'were poking their noses here and there and everywhere'. Stachel had picked up rumours of the letters left behind by Hans Albert, which were then in the hands of his widow, Elizabeth. He also knew that a book based on them had been blocked by the estate, and of the strained relations with Hans Albert's family that had resulted. The year he chose to contact Elizabeth was an auspicious one: it was 1979, the centenary of Einstein's birth. Biographies and memorial volumes were flooding on to the market, and various celebrations were planned, including one at the Institute for Advanced Study. The organizer of the guest list asked Stachel if Elizabeth should be invited. He replied, 'By all means: it would make a good occasion to try to smooth things over.' He then happened to mention the matter to Dukas. 'It was the only time in my life that I saw her lose her cool,' he says. 'She was a very charming person, and even if she were annoyed or angry she knew how to carry things off politely. But she really became almost hysterical. In retrospect I think I understand why: she knew what was in those letters, and she feared scandal.'

Elizabeth attended the centenary celebrations. She tried to talk to Dukas but was snubbed – not for the first time. Stachel, who was already at odds with Dukas, went to work on Elizabeth independently, both there and at a subsequent centenary meeting in Jerusalem. As a Jew, she sympathized with his suggestion that the letters be given to the Hebrew University in Jerusalem, which was subsequently to become the ultimate repository of the archive. But she may have felt under pressure closer to home to keep the letters in family hands, and eventually she placed them under a trust with Hans Albert's grandson, Thomas Einstein. Stachel did not know what the letters contained, and was desperate to find out how far they dated back. Elizabeth assured him there was nothing before 1914.

Helen Dukas finally expired on 10 February 1982, at the age of eighty-five. 'Einstein died a second death when she died,' Nathan told the press. 'She completely identified with Einstein.' Just before her death, Dukas and Nathan had handed control over Einstein's estate to the Hebrew University, in accordance with his will. The original documents of the archive were transferred to the Jewish National and University Library in Jerusalem. However, Nathan continued to harry the Einstein scholars in America until his own death on 27 January 1987, aged ninety-three. The biographer of Einstein's American years, Jamie Sayen, was close to both Dukas and Nathan. He remarked, 'Without passing judgement on the publication of Einstein's letters to Mileva, I can assure you that Helen and Otto would have been deeply grieved. I'm glad they died before publication.' Their passing was not mourned by many Einstein scholars: Jagdish Mehra remarked that 'everybody rejoiced' when Nathan died.

Hints of the Mileva letters were picked up by Robert Schulmann, a historian who had taught German history at the University of Pennsylvania and had started working on the Einstein papers project in the autumn of 1981, three years before it moved from Princeton to Boston. In November 1985 he attended a dinner party at the home of the Swiss physicist Professor Res Jost in a suburb of Zurich. Frau Jost said she had been told of the love-letters by Einstein's granddaughter-in-law, Aude Einstein, who had thought them 'most beautiful'. At the same dinner, Gina Zangger, daughter of Einstein's friend Heinrich Zangger, suggested that Schulmann visit Evelyn Einstein. This was a breakthrough in itself, for Evelyn had been deserted by her family after Hans Albert died. We have only her explanation of this: her stepmother, Elizabeth, has not answered our requests for information. But it seems significant to us that Elizabeth had never mentioned Evelyn to Stachel in all their discussions.

Robert Schulmann arranged to meet Evelyn in Berkeley, California, in 1986. She retained her mother's handwritten introduction to the banned book, and this contained snippets from some of the letters. As Schulmann looked through it, he saw that it drew on an extensive correspondence between Einstein and Hans Albert from 1914 to 1955. But, most exciting of all, he saw that Frieda had paraphrased what could only be the contents of the love-letters between Einstein and Mileva. For Schulmann, this was a glimpse of the promised land. As Frieda herself had written of her material, 'The reader is immediately drawn by its enchantment. Even a person familiar with Albert Einstein's personality looks at a world which has been closed to him.'

A still greater shock was in store for him. Evelyn offered to make a photocopy of Frieda's introduction after Schulmann left. As she took the manuscript out of its plastic cover, something caught her eye. 'I saw some sheets poking out underneath,' she says. 'I pulled them out and those were all Mileva's letters – not the originals, but copies quoting what obviously were the love-letters.' She rang Schulmann, who had not yet returned to Boston, to tell him, 'Hey, I have got some love-letters!' Armed with this material, the scholars knew what was at stake and could 'play a little hard ball', in Evelyn's phrase.

The Hebrew University and the Einstein papers project negotiated an agreement with the family trust under which Hans Albert's family was at last given permission to publish the suppressed manuscript in return for copies of all the letters. The project's editors also offered to pay a large sum of money, but Thomas Einstein saw the issue as one of principle alone. 'He never asked for one cent,' Stachel says. The deal was done, and the scholars at last put their hands on copies of the letters on the evening of 18 April 1986, in the office of the lawyer Michael Ferguson on Shattuck Avenue, Berkeley. Some time earlier, Mr Ferguson had prevailed on Hans Albert's widow to transfer the letters to a safe deposit at the Bank of America. A document setting out the agreement was signed by Stachel, Ferguson, Reuven Yaron of the Hebrew University and Thomas Einstein. Then the box fetched from the bank vaults was opened and two photocopies were made of every scrap of paper within it: one for Stachel and one for the Hebrew University. The copies were made on the spot, letter by letter, by Michael Ferguson. He remembers the atmosphere: 'It was one of enormous relief and, to some extent, exhaustion after a long day's negotiation.' Stachel says, 'There was nothing in that box that was not copied. Everyone was pleased we had reached agreement so amicably after those many years of bitterness on the side of the Einstein family and of the estate.'

In the event, Frieda's manuscript remains unpublished. She had chosen not to reveal all that was in the letters, and her attempts to put them in chronological order could not match the painstaking efforts that were now made by the Boston scholars. Schulmann was ready to check library opening-hours at the turn of the century to fix the date of a particular event. 'If there was a reference to a concert that Einstein attended,' recalls Stachel, 'Robert went to Switzerland and looked through the newspapers to find out when the candidates for that concert were.' A fellow member of the Einstein papers project team at the time, Jürgen Renn, remembers the mounting excitement as the letters began to reveal their secrets with the gradual transcription of the difficult Gothic German script and the subsequent translation. The wrangles with Dukas and Nathan had delayed the first volume of the Collected Papers by many years; work on these letters delayed it even more, says Renn, 'but on the other hand they added juice to the whole thing.'

When publication did eventually take place, in 1987, a few months after Nathan's death, it revolutionized our understanding of Einstein's early years. Most immediate attention focused on Lieserl and the possible contribution of Mileva to relativity, but this reflected only part of the collection's riches. One of the most surprising finds for Renn and Stachel was the wide range of scientific themes with which the young Einstein dealt, other than those for which he was known. 'Only some turned out to be successful,' says Renn. 'That makes him more human as well.'

Now this breakthrough has been followed by the release of Einstein's early letters to Elsa. They had formed part of around five hundred letters which Margot Einstein insisted be locked up until twenty years after her death in 1986. The originals first caught the eye of John Stachel while he was making the duplicate archive to forestall difficulties with Nathan. He noticed that they were not among the ordinary files of correspondence, having been put to one side by Dukas. After scanning their contents, he quickly realized their significance and made copies of all of them. Since then, at least six originals have disappeared – they did not make it with the other originals to the Einstein archives in the Hebrew University, Jerusalem. The first three letters, written in 1912, and another batch of three, written in December of the following year, now survive only as photocopies.

The most plausible explanation is that the originals were deliberately destroyed. In 1992, however, the Hebrew University gave permission for their contents to be published by Princeton University Press. It was a decision that marks a clean break with the censorship established by Dukas and Nathan, and the promise of a new era that will allow the systematic publication of all the papers. This, in turn, will allow an objective assessment of both Einstein the scientist and Einstein the man. All those interested in his life will be in the Hebrew University's debt.

Already, Einstein's private face can be seen more clearly than ever before. Perhaps it should be seen as a marvellous joke on humanity that such strength and such weakness, such wisdom and such obtuseness, could be combined in one man. For Einstein and those around him, however, the joke was very bitter. One of the most poignant reminders of this was included in a book co-edited by Helen Dukas and dedicated to Otto Nathan, which announced its intention to reveal Einstein's 'human side' with the aid of extracts from his archives. Unsurprisingly, the selection emphasized his compassion, wisdom and good humour. But it is almost impossible to dip into Einstein's non-scientific writings without producing hints of his personal troubles.

Dukas and her co-editor, Banesh Hoffmann, included one letter from Einstein's last years – a letter that may never have been sent, and that was discovered only in draft. Einstein was replying to a graduate student in psychology, who wrote for his advice in October 1951. The student was Jewish, but was considering marriage to a Christian girl. His parents had expressed their opposition, and, in the words of Dukas and Hoffmann, 'The young man was torn between his love for the girl and his desire not to alienate his parents and cause them lasting pain.' This was the reply that Einstein drafted:

> I have to tell you frankly that I do not approve of parents exerting influence on decisions of their children that will determine the shapes of the children's lives. Such problems one must solve for one's self.
>
> However, if you want to make a decision with which your parents are not in accord, you must ask yourself this question: Am I, deep down, independent enough to be able to act against the wishes of my parents without losing my inner equilibrium? If you do not feel certain about this, the step you plan is also not to be recommended in the interests of the girl. On this alone should your decision depend.

No suggestion appeared in Dukas's book of the relevance this exchange had to Einstein's own life, yet the echoes of his experiences with Mileva, his parents and his sons are clear. Deep down, had Einstein ever achieved full independence? Had he ever achieved 'inner equilibrium'? The answer appears to be no. That was one problem he had been unable to solve.

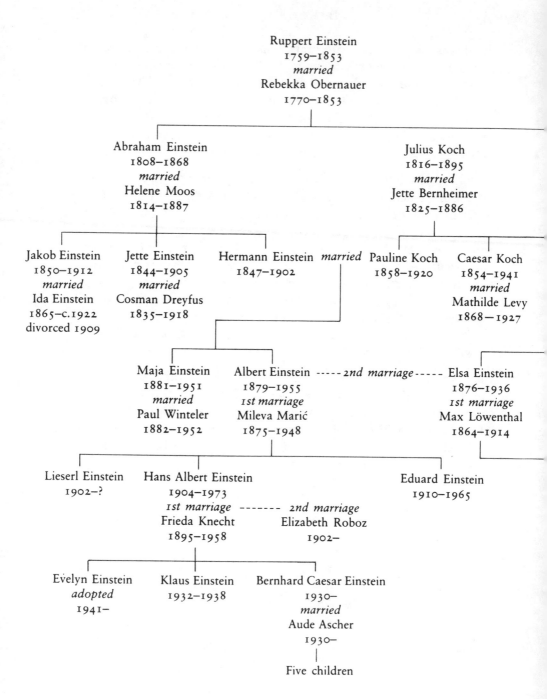

Ruppert Einstein
1759–1853
married
Rebekka Obernauer
1770–1853

Abraham Einstein
1808–1868
married
Helene Moos
1814–1887

Julius Koch
1816–1895
married
Jette Bernheimer
1825–1886

Jakob Einstein
1850–1912
married
Ida Einstein
1865–c.1922
divorced 1909

Jette Einstein
1844–1905
married
Cosman Dreyfus
1835–1918

Hermann Einstein   *married*   Pauline Koch
1847–1902   1858–1920

Caesar Koch
1854–1941
married
Mathilde Levy
1868–1927

Maja Einstein
1881–1951
married
Paul Winteler
1882–1952

Albert Einstein ----- *2nd marriage* ----- Elsa Einstein
1879–1955   1876–1936
1st marriage   *1st marriage*
Mileva Marić   Max Löwenthal
1875–1948   1864–1914

Lieserl Einstein
1902–?

Hans Albert Einstein
1904–1973
1st marriage ------- *2nd marriage*
Frieda Knecht   Elizabeth Roboz
1895–1958   1902–

Eduard Einstein
1910–1965

Evelyn Einstein
adopted
1941–

Klaus Einstein
1932–1938

Bernhard Caesar Einstein
1930–
married
Aude Ascher
1930–

Five children

284

Family Tree

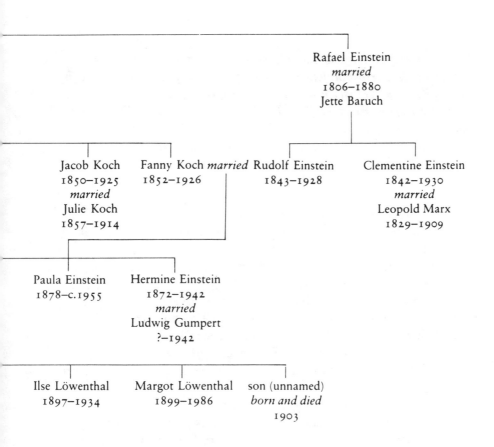

Rafael Einstein
married
1806–1880
Jette Baruch

Jacob Koch
1850–1925
married
Julie Koch
1857–1914

Fanny Koch *married* Rudolf Einstein
1852–1926   1843–1928

Clementine Einstein
1842–1930
married
Leopold Marx
1829–1909

Paula Einstein
1878–c.1955

Hermine Einstein
1872–1942
married
Ludwig Gumpert
?–1942

Ilse Löwenthal
1897–1934

Margot Löwenthal
1899–1986

son (unnamed)
born and died
1903

Notes and References

Where correspondence is quoted, the date of the letter is provided.
*/† Denotes correspondence provided with a provisional date by Frieda Knecht. Translations until 15 August 1922 were kindly provided by Evelyn Einstein (*); other translations are by Doris Highfield(†).

1 THE INHERITANCE

1 'summer of 1973' E. Einstein 1991: 77, 78
1 'warned by doctors' Evelyn Einstein, interview, 15 March 1992
1 'his greatest fear' Evelyn Einstein, interview, 15 March 1992
1 'beyond its natural term' Pais 1983: 477
1 'in a canteen queue' Evelyn Einstein, interview, 15 March 1992
1 'beyond professional matters' E. Einstein 1991: 103
2 'Chinese water torture' E. Einstein 1991: 44
2 'a permanent slight smile' E. Einstein 1991: 2
2 'a suppressed resentment' Evelyn Einstein, interview, 15 April 1992
2 'saintly golliwog' Goldsmith et al. 1980: 4
2 'a Jewish saint' Dukas & Hoffmann 1979: 63 (Letter to Paul Ehrenfest, 12 April 1926) and Albert Einstein to Betty Neumann, 21 September 1923
3 'such shifting foundations' Einstein 1991: 2–3, also quoted in Nathan 1961: v. Translation according to Frank 1948: 66
3 'odd nooks and crannies' Clark 1979: 55
3 'a pretty hefty ego' Goldsmith et al. 1980: 8
4 'merely personal' Schilpp 1959: 5
4 'our work' Renn & Schulmann 1992: 39 (27 March 1901)
4 'right hand' Beck & Havas 1987: 145 (August 1900)

4 'as strong and as independent' Renn & Schulmann 1992: 36 (3 October 1900)

5 'Newly released documents' Klein et al. 1993

5 'unvisited by his father' Evelyn Einstein, interview, 22 April 1993

6 'preceded me briefly' Speziali 1972: 537 (Albert Einstein to Vero Besso and Frau Bice Besso, 21 March 1955)

6 'home in Berkeley' Michael Ferguson, letter to Roger Highfield, 6 July 1992

6 'Einstein priests' Karlheinz Steinmüller, interview, 8 October 1992

2 FIRST LOVE

8 'It is discipline' Ernesta Marangoni, '*Momenti pavesi nella vita di Alberto Einstein*', *La Provincia Pavese*, 14 May 1955: 1

8 'unpleasantly critical edge' Frank 1948: 97

8 'mentally retarded' Beck & Havas 1987: xviii

9 'Cannot be answered' 20 Questions from Bela Kornitzer, 1948, Clark archive, Edinburgh

9 'question did not arise' Albert Einstein to Carl Seelig, 11 March 1952, ETH

9 'Janos Plesch wrote' Janos Plesch to Peter Plesch, 18 April 1955

9 'sought his bearings from his father' Reiser 1931: 27

11 'the soul of that odd household' Beck & Havas 1987: xv

11 'lonely and dreamy' 20 Questions from Bela Kornitzer, 20 September 1948, Clark Archive, Edinburgh

12 'but where are its wheels?' Beck & Havas 1987: xviii

12 '*Pater Langweil*' Reiser 1931: 29

12 'Music meant little' Reiser 1931: 28

13 'his progress was only workmanlike' Hoffmann & Dukas 1986: 20

13 'inner necessity' 20 Questions from Bela Kornitzer, 20 September 1948, Clark archive, Edinburgh

13 'through whom I say and I sing to myself' Beck & Havas 1987: 128 (28 July 1899)

13 'he would take refuge in music' Whitrow 1967: 21
13 'superlative ability' Dukas & Hoffmann 1979: 76
13 'and keep your mouth shut' Dukas & Hoffmann 1979: 63, 75
13 'about two per cent' Pyenson 1985: 3, 29
13 'far from devout' Schilpp 1959: 3
13 'not too malicious' Stachel et al. 1987: lx (3 April 1920)
14 'the anti-Semitism he felt' Beck & Havas 1987: 160 (27 March 1901)
14 'he refused to eat pork' Beck & Havas 1987: xx
14 'deep religiosity' Schilpp 1959: 3
14 'merely personal' Schilpp 1959: 5
15 'he wasn't even good at arithmetic' Beck & Havas 1987: xix
15 'top of the class' Beck & Havas 1987: 3 (1 August 1886)
15 'a great professor' Reiser 1931: 29
15 'learn gabble by rote' Hoffmann & Dukas 1986: 25
15 'a deceptive point of view' Schilpp 1959: 3
15 'a professorship of Greek grammar' Beck & Havas 1987: xx
16 'had real scientific knowledge' 20 Questions from Bela Kornitzer, 20 September 1948, Clark archive, Edinburgh
16 'a jolly game' Reiser 1931: 37
16 'with breathless attention' Schilpp 1959: 15
16 'these books were veritable revelations' Reiser 1931: 38
16 'key proofs of the general theory' Renn & Schulmann 1992: xxiii. These parallels have also been suggested by Frederick Gregory of the University of Florida.
17 'Out yonder there was this huge world' Schilpp 1959: 5
17 'God does not play dice with the world' Albert Einstein to Max Born, 12 December 1926. See also Pais 1983: 440
17 'how God created the world' Esther Salaman, *Listener*, 8 September 1968, Clark archive, Edinburgh
17 'cosmic religious experience' *New York Times*, November 1930
17 'the mind of God' Stephen Hawking, *A Brief History of Time*, Bantam, London, 1988, p. 175
18 'Lewis Carroll's Red Queen' Clark 1979: 33
18 'entirely man-made affair' Dukas & Hoffmann 1979: 63, 66

18 'sorry for the dear Lord' Albert Einstein to Ilse Rosenthal-Schneider in 1919

18 'deep and abiding impression' Schilpp 1959: 9 and Hoffmann & Dukas 1986: 9

18 'holy geometry book' Schilpp 1959: 11

19 'necessary lie' Reiser 1931: 41, 42

19 'well-to-do philistine atmosphere' Reiser 1931: 29

19 'only one friend' Reiser 1931: 34. However, later correspondence suggests he did have several friends.

20 'most cherished memories were destroyed' Beck & Havas 1987: xvii

20 'sweaty feet' Stachel et al. 1987: 277 (Military Service Book, 13 March 1901)

20 'engineer or technician' Reiser 1931: 43

21 'use his influence in Zurich' Plesch 1947: 219

21 'so-called child prodigy' Beck & Havas 1987: 7 (25 November 1895)

21 'little to prepare himself' Plesch 1947: 219

21 'an unforgettable oasis' Seelig 1956a: 21

22 'Albert's boarding costs' Beck & Havas 1987: 10 (29 October 1895)

22 'history, German and philology' Stachel et al. 1987: 388

22 'Esteemed Herr Professor' Beck & Havas 1987: 11 (30 December 1895)

22 'an old village schoolmaster' Beck & Havas 1987: 164 (10 April 1901)

22 'self-willed and complacent' Reiser 1931: 48

22 'Mamerl' Beck & Havas 1987: 33 (7 June 1897)

22 'A thousand greetings and kisses' Beck & Havas 1987: 34 (7 June 1897)

23 'somewhat late in the morning' Beck & Havas 1987: 34 (7 June 1897)

23 'as he did at home' Beck & Havas 1987: 10 (29 October 1895)

23 'a loner' A. Frish to Carl Seelig, 28 February 1952, Clark archive, Edinburgh, 0.219

23 'display of sentimentality' Seelig 1956a: 14

23 'conversations with birds' Robert Schulmann, interview, 20

February 1992; H. Kalshin to Carl Seelig, Aarau, February 1952, Clark archive, Edinburgh; and Klein et al. 1993: 46

24 'blind fate' Klein et al. 1993: 46 (3 November 1906)

24 'Marie was the prettiest' Robert Schulmann, interview, 20 February 1992; Marie Winteler was born on 24 April 1877.

24 'such exquisite care' Beck & Havas 1987: 11 (30 December 1895)

24 'more to my soul than the whole world' Beck & Havas 1987: 13 (21 April 1896)

25 'agreeable house-guest' Stachel et al. 1987: 18

25 'deep understanding' Beck & Havas 1987: 12 (31 March 1896)

25 'decked-up Pavia ladies' Beck & Havas 1987: 12, 13 (21 April 1896)

25 'teased her son' Beck & Havas 1987: 12 (21 April 1896)

25 'completely ideal love' Marie Müller-Winteler letter, Einstein archive, Boston, 71–183–5

26 'pretty as a picture' Marie Müller-Winteler letter, loc. cit.

26 'my beloved child' Beck & Havas 1987: 13 (21 April 1896)

26 'chase a light ray' Schilpp 1959: 53. Frederick Gregory of the University of Florida has also pointed out the link with the work of Aaron Bernstein.

27 'theoretical part of these sciences' Beck & Havas 1987: 15–16 (18 September 1896)

27 'would conjure up his image' Beck & Havas 1987: 31 (30 November 1896)

27 'why not sweetheart?' Beck & Havas 1987: 29 (November 1896)

27 'his dirty laundry' Renn & Schulmann 1992: xviii

28 'terribly long' Beck & Havas 1987: 30 (30 November 1896)

28 'has become frightfully lazy' Beck & Havas 1987: 31 (13 December 1896)

29 'bliss at the cost of new pain' Beck & Havas 1987: 32 (May 1897)

30 'I take him at his word' Robert Schulmann, interview, 19 October 1992

30 'in a delightfully mad way' Beck & Havas 1987: 33 (7 June 1897)

31 'the critical daughter' Renn & Schulmann 1992: 16 (September 1899)

31 'apologizing to Pauline Winteler' Beck & Havas 1987: 134 (11 September 1899)

31 'life of debauchery' Beck & Havas 1987: 174, 175 (28 May 1901)

32 'nervous illnesses' Robert Schulmann, interview, 20 February 1992

32 ' "confused" her' Aude Einstein, interview, 20 March 1993

32 'passing resemblance' Aude Einstein, interview, 20 March 1993

32 'affair with an older man' Stachel et al. 1987: 222 However, Seelig (1956a: 20) claims the older man wanted her hand. See also Stachel et al. 1987: 219 (August 1899).

32 'What a strange thing must be a girl's soul!' Beck & Havas 1987: 129 (August 1899)

3 JOHNNIE AND DOLLIE

33 'a large part of the population' Plesch 1947: 34

34 'little land of outlaws' Renn & Schulmann 1992: 3 (20 October 1897)

35 'Miloš would enter military school' E. Einstein 1991: 86

35 'quiet, kind, and always busy' E. Einstein 1991: 86

35 'patriarchal self-assurance' Trbuhović-Gjurić 1983: 153

36 'Watch out for this child' Trbuhović-Gjurić 1983: 21

36 'the woman saint' Trbuhović-Gjurić 1983: 22

36 'for boys only' Trbuhović-Gjurić 1983: 23

37 'sought special permission' Stachel et al. 1987: 380 and E. Einstein 1991: 88

37 'one of the first young women' E. Einstein 1991: 88

37 'I studied at a gymnasium' Gerald Holton, interview, 19 February 1992

37 'the highest awarded' E. Einstein 1991: 88 and Trbuhović-Gjurić 1983: 26

37 'inflammation of the lungs' Trbuhović-Gjurić 1983: 28 and E. Einstein 1991: 88

37 'a certain physical disability' Albert Einstein to Carl Seelig, 5 May 1952

38 'among the first in Europe' Anderson & Zinsser 1990: 188

38 'a pioneering Norwegian' Trbuhović-Gjurić 1983: 35

39 'a dear, sympathetic, shy girl' Stachel et al. 1987: 59, 212, 213 (20 October 1897, 16 February 1898, April–November 1898)

39 'a modest, unassuming creature' Seelig 1956a: 38, 35

39 'too serious and quiet' E. Einstein 1991: 89 and Trbuhović-Gjurić 1983: 53

39 'laughed a lot about it' Trbuhović-Gjurić 1983: 54

39 'a superannuated sheepdog' Nigel Calder, *Einstein's Universe: a Guide to the Theory of Relativity*, Penguin, London, 1982, p. 12

39 'muscular and quite powerful' Plesch 1947: 215

39 'an unusually strong man' In Goldman et al. 1980

40 'extraordinarily large shining eyes' *'Erinnerungen von Margarete von Uexküll, Frankfurt Allgemeiner Zeitung*, 10 March 1956

40 'at the house of Johanna Bächtold' Renn & Schulmann 1992: 79

40 'Mileva was the first person' *'Erinnerungen von Margarete von Uexküll'*, *Frankfurt Allgemeiner Zeitung*, 10 March 1956

41 'waited for boredom' Renn & Schulmann 1992: 4 (20 October 1897)

41 'Papa gave me' Renn & Schulmann 1992: 3 (20 October 1897)

41 'estranged from nature' Sayen 1985: 11

42 '1/100 of a hair's breadth' Renn & Schulmann 1992: 3 (20 October 1897)

42 'a high degree of self-consciousness' Renn & Schulmann 1992: xv

43 'notably those on physics' Beck & Havas 1987: 36 (December 1897 to June 1898; notes on H. F. Weber's lectures)

43 'little runaway' Renn & Schulmann 1992: 5 (16 February 1898)

43   'stimulating and informative' Renn & Schulmann 1992: 6 (16 April 1898)

44   'originality and independence' Renn & Schulmann 1992: 9 (August 1899)

44   'Dear Dollie' Renn & Schulmann 1992: 9, 17 (August 1899, 10 October 1899)

45   'My dear Johnnie' Stachel et al. 1987: 242 (1900)

45   'never have the courage' Seelig 1956a: 38

45   'She limped, she was moody' Gerald Holton, interview, 19 February 1992

46   'Best wishes *etc.*' Renn & Schulmann 1992: 8 (March 1899)

46   'plump as a dumpling' Renn & Schulmann 1992: 21 (1 August 1900)

46   'biggest kisses' Renn & Schulmann 1992: 20 (July 1900)

46   'fellow coffee-guzzler' Renn & Schulmann 1992: 17 (10 October 1899)

46   'each other's dark souls' Renn & Schulmann 1992: 11 (10 August 1899)

46   'a magnificent effect' Beck & Havas 1987: 138

46   'described as repulsive' Michelmore 1962: 52

46   'did not drink alcohol' Beck & Havas 1987: 155

46   'famous ailment' Beck & Havas 1987: 173 (May 1901)

46   'how closely knit' Renn & Schulmann 1992: 7 (March 1899)

47   'unpardonable Slav tendency' Clark 1979: 68

47   'Swiss-German house sprite' Seelig: 1956a: 59

47   'skilled hands' Renn & Schulmann 1992: 21 (1 August 1900)

47   'hen-like enthusiasm' Renn & Schulmann 1992: 25 (9 August 1990)

47   'such a great imagination' Renn & Schulmann 1992: 32 (13 September 1900)

47   'She judged people more quickly' Michelmore 1962: 36

48   'critical eye' Renn & Schulmann 1992: 4 (16 February 1898)

48   'don't be angry' Renn & Schulmann 1992: 6 (April 1898)

48   'Please don't be angry' Renn & Schulmann 1992: 6 (April 1898)

48   'bitter resentment' Renn & Schulmann 1992: 10 (August 1899)

48   'Don't pout about it' Renn & Schulmann 1992: 14 (10 September 1899)

48   'angry faces' Renn & Schulmann 1992: 31 (September 1900)

48   'You came vividly to my mind' Renn & Schulmann 1992: 7 (March 1899)

48   'your beneficent thumb' Renn & Schulmann 1992: 16 (September 1899)

48   'the mistress of our house' Renn & Schulmann 1992: 9 (August 1899)

48   'our household' Renn & Schulmann 1992: 10 (August 1899)

48   'a Zurich philistine' Renn & Schulmann 1992: 5 (16 February 1898)

48   'in May 1898' Stachel 1987: 245 and Trbuhović-Gjurić 1983: 54

48   'but not into your house' Renn & Schulmann 1992: 15 (September 1899)

49   'the nicest and cosiest place' Renn & Schulmann 1992: 15 (September 1899)

49   'memories of home' Renn & Schulmann 1992: 12 (August–September 1899)

49   'something for the household' Renn & Schulmann 1992: 17 (10 October 1899)

49   '5.7 out of 6' Stachel et al. 1987: 214

49   'fiddling' Renn & Schulmann 1992: 15 (September 1899)

49   'Don't you feel sorry for me?' Renn & Schulmann 1992: 13 (August–September 1899)

49   'knows what she wants' Renn & Schulmann 1992: 17 (10 October 1899)

50   'laughing on the outside' Renn & Schulmann 1992: 16 (September 1899)

50   'divine composure' Renn & Schulmann 1992: 9, 10, 15 (August 1899, August 1899, September 1899)

50   'straight 5s and a 4.75' records at ETH

50   'correspond to reality' Renn & Schulmann 1992: 10 (August 1899)

50   'fields and forces at work' The paper reads, 'Maxwell's electrodynamics . . . when applied to moving bodies . . . leads

to asymmetries . . . If the magnet is in motion and the conductor is at rest, there arises in the surroundings of the magnet an electric field . . . But if the magnet is at rest and the conductor in motion, no electric field arises.'

51 'The introduction of the term "ether" ' Beck & Havas 1987: 131 (August 1899)

51 'But enough of that!' Beck & Havas 1987: 133 and Renn & Schulmann 1992: 14 (10 September 1899)

51 'a veritable monster' Renn & Schulmann 1992: 11 (August 1899)

52 'somewhat petty and philistine' Renn & Schulmann 1992: 9 (August 1899)

52 'each and every day' Renn & Schulmann 1992: 11 (August 1899)

52 'so much like to be in Zurich' Renn & Schulmann 1992: 14 (10 September 1899)

52 'Little girl, small and fine' Beck & Havas 1987: 128 (August 1899)

53 'thousand warmest wishes' Renn & Schulmann 1992: 14 (10 September 1899)

53 'How could a young man' Stachel 1987: 219

53 'strict mother would never allow' Stachel 1987: 219

53 'in friendship and admiration' Seelig 1956a: 35

53 'sailed toy vessels' Albert Einstein to Hans Albert Einstein, 8 January 1917*

53 'travelling home by train together' Trbuhović-Gjurić 1983: 54

53 'plays beautiful violin' Trbuhović-Gjurić 1983: 54

54 'very amiable with me' Trbuhović-Gjurić 1983: 58

54 'the German, whom I hate' Stachel 1987: 245 (7 June 1900)

54 'very good but very wicked' Beck & Havas 1987: 139 (June–July 1900)

54 'My old lady sends her best' Renn & Schulmann 1992: 8 (March 1899)

54 'Best wishes to your family' Renn & Schulmann 1992: 11, 14 (August 1899, 10 September 1899)

54 'only imagined the story' Renn & Schulmann 1992: 11 (August 1899)

54 'I feel this is being disrespectful' Renn & Schulmann 1992: 13 (August–September 1899)

54 'parents teased him' Renn & Schulmann 1992: 18 (10 October 1899)

54 'common German prejudice' Gerald Holton, interview, 19 February 1992

54 'Pauline also distrusted Mileva' Beck & Havas 1987: 148 (August–September 1900)

55 'Do you think that she does not like me?' Beck & Havas 1987: 139 (June–July 1900)

55 'theses on the same subject' Stachel 1987: 244

56 'pass mark of around 5' Troemel-Ploetz 1990: 415–32

56 'Even the brightest female student' Troemel-Ploetz 1990

56 'terrible pedant' Renn & Schulmann 1992: 5 (16 February 1898)

56 'ease of understanding' Albert Einstein to Carl Seelig, 15 May 1952, ETH

56 'the same flaw as a student' Stachel 1987: 61. Einstein used the same German phrase: '*Leichtigkeit der Auffassung*'

57 'what will become of your Dollie now?' Beck & Havas 1987: 141 and Renn & Schulmann 1992: 19 (July 1900)

57 'Mama threw herself on the bed' Beck & Havas 1987: 141, 142 (July 1900)

4 THE DELICATE SUBJECT

59 'balm on her wounded mother-in-law's heart' Renn & Schulmann 1992: 22 (6 August 1900)

59 'a wife and a whore' Beck & Havas 1987: 144 (6 August 1900)

60 'I would have been smarter' Renn & Schulmann 1992: 26 (August 1900)

60 'and that means you' Beck & Havas 1987: 144 (6 August 1900)

60 'partaking of the holy sacraments' Renn & Schulmann 1992: 26 (August 1900)

60 'boasted that his parents' Renn & Schulmann 1992: 28 (20 August 1900)

60   'My parents are very worried' Renn & Schulmann 1992: 29 (30 August or 6 September 1900)

60   'I understand my parents quite well' Renn & Schulmann 1992: 23 (6 August 1900)

61   'quite frightened' Renn & Schulmann 1992: 29 (30 August or 6 September 1900)

61   'only now' Beck & Havas 1987: 143 (1 August 1900)

61   'he pitied the chaste Catholic nuns' Stachel et al. 1987: 253 (August 1900)

61   'When I'm not with you' Beck & Havas 1987: 144 (6 August 1900)

61   'but I belong nowhere' Renn & Schulmann 1992: 24 (August 1900)

61   'I lack self-confidence' Renn & Schulmann 1992: 26 (August 1900)

62   'people gone soft' Beck & Havas 1987: 143, 146 (1 August 1900, August 1900)

62   'hopelessly dull' Beck & Havas 1987: 143 (July 1900)

62   'a lower form of social evolution' Beck & Havas 1987: 144 (6 August 1900)

62   'found in Einstein' Einstein would read Schopenhauer and Nietzche for 'edification' according to Frank 1948: 67.

62   'If your abilities' Arthur Schopenhauer, *Essays and Aphorisms*, tr. R. J. Hollingdale, Penguin, 1970, p. 176

62   'thorough and incurable philistines' Schopenhauer, op. cit. p. 86

63   'talented and industrious' Beck & Havas 1987: 143 (1 August 1900)

63   'fattening her up' Beck & Havas 1987: 142 (1 August 1900); also 146 (14 August 1900)

63   'I can hardly wait' Renn & Schulmann 1992: 25 (August 1900)

63   'What a nice illusion!' Beck & Havas 1987: 149 (September 1900)

63   'O my! That Johnnie boy!' Renn & Schulmann 1992: 27 (20 August 1900)

64   'this sorry herd of humans' Renn & Schulmann 1992: 29 (30 August or 6 September 1900)

64 'You'll see, Dollie!' Renn & Schulmann 1992: 32 (September 1900)

65 'hardly any doubts' Beck & Havas 1987: 152 (3 October 1900)

65 'You'll never let yourself be told anything' Seelig 1956a: 29

65 'You, Herr Schmied' Beck & Havas 1987: xix

65 'There's nothing like a female' Renn & Schulmann 1992: 35 (3 October 1900)

66 'gypsy's life' Beck & Havas 1987: 153 (11 October 1900)

66 'focused on capillarity' Stachel 1987: 264

66 'You can imagine how proud' Beck & Havas 1987: 156 (20 December 1900)

66 'her praise was excessive' John Stachel, American Association for the Advancement of Science, February 1991

66 'worthless beginner papers' Renn & Schulmann 1992: xxi

66 'justly forgotten' Pais 1983: 68, 57

66 'If a law of nature emerges from this' Beck & Havas 1987: 152 (3 October 1900)

66 'our paper' Stachel 1987: 292, 294, 300 (15 April 1901, 30 April 1901, May 1901)

66 'that "we" had sent a copy' Beck & Havas 1987: 156 (20 December 1900)

67 'my theory' Beck & Havas 1987: 165 (14 April 1901)

67 'Any direct contribution' Beck & Havas 1987: 152 (3 October 1900)

67 'my work seems pointless' Renn & Schulmann 1992: 31 (September 1900)

68 'It is better so for his career' Beck & Havas 1987: 154 (11 December 1900)

68 'suffocate in his fat' Renn & Schulmann 1992: 34 (19 September 1900)

68 'slanders and intrigues' Beck & Havas 1987: 156 (20 December 1900)

68 'The lass cried' Beck & Havas 1987: 156 (20 December 1900)

69 'Soon I will have honoured' Beck & Havas 1987: 163 (4 April 1901)

69 'had it not been for Weber's underhandedness' Beck & Havas 1987: 165 (14 April 1901)

69 'he is oppressed by the thought' Beck & Havas 1987: 165 (13 April 1901)

69 'the poor souls' Beck & Havas 1987: 160 (23 March 1901)

69 'what a little sweetheart's love is' Beck & Havas 1987: 163 (4 April 1901)

69 'no longer sharing his feelings' Renn & Schulmann 1992: 42 (10 April 1901)

70 'not discouraged in the least' Renn & Schulmann 1992: 43 (10 April 1901)

70 'certainly poured out my heart' Beck & Havas 1987: 164 (10 April 1901)

70 'wonderful idea' Renn & Schulmann 1992: 45 (15 April 1901)

70 'I'll be so happy and proud' Beck & Havas 1987: 161 (27 March 1901)

71 'Michele is an awful schlemiel' Renn & Schulmann 1992: 39 (27 March 1901)

71 'almost unbalanced' Renn & Schulmann 1992: 39 (27 March 1901)

71 'our research' Renn & Schulmann 1992: 41 (4 April 1901)

73 'a young man, deeply in love' John Stachel, American Association for the Advancement of Science comments, 5 March 1990

73 'a wonderful job' Renn & Schulmann 1992: 45 (15 April 1901)

73 'did not let you forget' Beck & Havas 1987: 165 (14 April 1901)

74 'Mileva's pet hate' Stachel 1987: 229 (August–September 1899)

74 'The valiant Swabian is not afraid' Beck & Havas 1987: 166 (15 April 1901)

74 'how bright and cheerful' Renn & Schulmann 1992: 46 (30 April 1901)

74 'a thousand times more important' Renn & Schulmann 1992: 46 (30 April 1901)

74 'not only for having a good time' Beck & Havas 1987: 168 (2 May 1901)

75 'I became a little more cheerful' Renn & Schulmann 1992: 49 (3 May 1901)

75 'so much love for your Dollie' Renn & Schulmann 1992: 49 (3 May 1901)

75 'no words to describe the splendour' Beck & Havas 1987: 172 (May 1901)

76 'By submitting a dissertation' Stachel 1987: 300 (May 1901); see also Stachel 1987: 61, 260

76 'How beautiful it was the last time' Renn & Schulmann 1992: 51 (May 1901)

76 'I'll work very hard' Renn & Schulmann 1992: 52 (May 1901)

77 'a wonderful paper by Lenard' Renn & Schulmann 1992: 54 (May 1901)

78 'point out his mistakes' Renn & Schulmann 1992: 53 (May 1901)

78 'Do you still remember' Renn & Schulmann 1992: 55 (June 1901)

78 'a brilliant man' Renn & Schulmann 1992: 41 (4 April 1901)

78 'sad specimen' Beck & Havas 1987: 177 (8 July 1901)

78 'It is no wonder' Renn & Schulmann 1992: 57 (July 1901)

79 'irrevocable decision' Renn & Schulmann 1992: 57 (July 1901)

79 'sense of duty' Albert Einstein to Carl Seelig, 5 May 1952, ETH

79 'a really bad position' Renn & Schulmann 1992: 57 (8 July 1901)

80 'every moment' Renn & Schulmann 1992: 58 (July 1901)

80 'soured by her resentment' Senta Troemel Ploetz, *Index on Censorship*, 9/1990, p. 3

80 'vowed never again' John Stachel. In press.

80 'would have to be motivated by ambition' Beck & Havas 1987: 180 (July 1901)

81 'left the plane of pure human feelings' Renn & Schulmann 1992: 60 (July 1901)

81 'the thrashing that Marija Marić had promised to bestow' Renn & Schulmann 1992: 70 (17 December 1901)

81 'the charming behaviour' Beck & Havas 1987: 183 (23 November to mid-December 1901)

82 'No more fights' Beck & Havas 1987: 181 (November 1901)

82 'same feeling of disgust' Renn & Schulmann 1992: 64 (13 November 1901)

82 'a very wicked tongue' Beck & Havas 1987: 183 (23 November to mid-December 1901)

83 'great joy and admiration' Beck & Havas 1987: 183 (23 November to mid-December 1901)

83 'I'm sure he won't dare' Renn & Schulmann 1992: 66 (28 November 1901)

83 'It's really terrible' Renn & Schulmann 1992: 69 (17 December 1901)

83 'The thesis' Stachel et al. 1989: 170

83 'gifted young men' Renn & Schulmann 1992: 68 (12 December 1901)

83 'the only human pleasures' Renn & Schulmann 1992: 66 (28 November 1901)

84 'except when I'm with you' Renn & Schulmann 1992: 69 (17 December 1901)

84 'Long live impudence!' Renn & Schulmann 1992: 67 (12 December 1901)

85 'dizzy with joy' Renn & Schulmann 1992: 68 (12 December 1901)

85 'as if it were a bitter medicine' Beck & Havas 1987: 190 (28 December 1901)

85 'He is not quite as stupid' Renn & Schulmann 1992: 71 (19 December 1901)

85 'Only now that this terrible weight' Renn & Schulmann 1992: 70 (19 December 1901)

85 'students . . . as long as we live' Renn & Schulmann 1992: 68 (12 December 1901)

86 'Soon you'll be my "student" again' Renn & Schulmann 1992: 71 (19 December 1901)

87 'When you're my dear little wife' Renn & Schulmann 1992: 72 (28 December 1901)

5 MY ONLY COMPANION

88 'frightened out of my wits' Renn & Schulmann 1992: 73 (4 February 1902)

89 'impractical to continue' Robert Schulmann, interview, 20 February 1992

89 'I'm very sorry' Renn & Schulmann 1992: 78 (September 1903)

90 'belonging to foreigners like Mileva' Lewis Pyenson, *History of Science*, vol. 28, pt 4, no. 82 (December 1990), p. 368

90 'Illegitimacy was acceptable' Robert Schulmann, interview, 20 February 1992

90 'we strongly oppose the liaison' Beck & Havas 1987: 193 (Pauline Einstein to Pauline Winteler, 20 February 1902)

91 'with something important' Renn & Schulmann 1992: 64 (13 November 1901)

91 'a strange thing to write' John Stachel, interview, 21 February 1992

91 'letters from Mileva were destroyed' Robert Schulmann, interview, 20 February 1992

91 'compliments to your lady wife' Klein et al. 1993: 164, 173 (2 May 1909)

91 'Some day she might walk in' Gerald Holton, interview, 19 February 1992

92 'she approached contacts of Einstein' Don Howard, interview, 10 October 1992

92 'send a warning telegram' Frederick Lindemann, telegram to Hermann Weyl, 23 November 1935, Einstein archive, Boston

92 'I even began to see family resemblances' Plesch 1947: 221

92 'extraordinarily comic' Don Howard, interview, 10 October 1992

93 'Einstein disavowed all knowledge' Clark archive, Edinburgh, 0174; letter to Lindemann from Bertha Bracey. It appears that this has now been lost or removed from Nuffield archives.

93 'identified as Grete Markstein' F. Bial, report of 12 August 1936

93 'this is the right person' F. Bial, report of 12 August 1936

93 'All my friends are hoaxing me' From the German in Plesch 1947: 221

94 'Friends had noticed a change' Michelmore 1962: 42

94 'distrusting, taciturn' Albert Einstein to Carl Seelig, 5 May 1952, ETH

95 'dreamy, ponderous nature' Seelig 1960: 73

95 'blunt and stern' Frank 1948: 35

95 'knew that her love for the man was strong enough' Michelmore 1962: 42

96 'sailed away from N[üesch]' Beck & Havas 1987: 190 (4 February 1902)

96 'the mysteries of physics' French 1979: 9

96 'recalled the thunderous "Come in!" ' Pais 1983: 47

96 'I admired his extraordinarily penetrating mind' French 1979: 9

97 'expert in the noble arts' Klein et al. 1993: 8 ('AD 1903')

97 'President of the Academy' Seelig 1956a: 61

97 'far less childish than those respectable ones' Seelig 1956a: 57

97 'a general overview of physics' Gerald Holton in Woolf 1980: 49–50

97 'incorruptible scepticism and independence' Schilpp 1959: 21

97 'under a decorative arch of sausages' Klein et al. 1993: 8

97 'When Einstein ate something' French 1979: 10

98 'Einstein and Habicht took revenge' French 1979: 11

99 'I'd rather be going with you' Renn & Schulmann 1992: 77 (28 June 1902)

99 'the work was very dull' Renn & Schulmann 1992: 76 (17 February 1902)

99 'cobbler's job' Seelig 1956a: 56

99 'uncommonly varied' Klein et al. 1993: 6 (August–October 1902)

99 'more severe than my father' Clark 1979: 63

99 'haunted Einstein with guilt' Pais 1983: 47

100 'shattering sense of loss' Hoffmann & Dukas 1986: 39

100 'The banns' Klein et al. 1993: 10 and E. Einstein 1991: 91

100 'locked himself out' Seelig 1956a: 38, 61

101 'Now I'm an honourably married man' Klein et al. 1993: 10 (January 1903)

101 'even more attached to my dear treasure' Mileva Marić to Helene Savić, c. 20 March 1903; John Stachel, American Association for the Advancement of Science, February 1991

101 'to raise the child themselves' Renn & Schulmann 1992: 102

101   'morning sickness' Renn & Schulmann 1992: 78 (27 August
      1903)

101   'not the least bit angry' Renn & Schulmann 1992: 78 (Septem-
      ber 1903)

102   'her parents fully accepted the marriage' E. Einstein 1991: 92
      and Trbuhović-Gjurić 1983: 94

102   'who conquered Mileva's wayward heart' Seelig 1956a: 60

102   'the joke about the old whore' Michelmore 1962: 43

102   'laughed so much they thought they would die' Klein et al.
      1993: 227 (Maurice Solovine to Carl Seelig, 31 July 1955)

102   'Totally drunk' Postcard 12–429, Einstein archive, Boston

103   'Einstein found work in the Patent Office dull' Klein et al. 1993:
      7 (Mileva Marić to Helene Savić 20 March 1902)

103   'The Besso and Einstein families became almost inseparable'
      Jeremy Bernstein, 'A critic at large: Besso', New Yorker, 17
      February 1989, p. 89

103   'several scholars' Arthur Miller and Gerald Holton among
      others

103   'based on a "particulate" view' Jürgen Renn, interview, 27
      March 1992. For detailed discussion of the papers, see Stachel
      et al. 1989.

103   'of a predominantly aesthetic nature' In Woolf 1980: 55

104   'very revolutionary' Klein et al. 1993: 32 (Albert Einstein to
      Conrad Habicht, May 1905)

104   'sent to Annalen der Physik on 17 March' Beck & Havas 1989:
      103

105   'every Tom, Dick and Harry' Coveney and Highfield 1991: 114

105   'This was like a conjuring trick' French 1979: 3

105   'I discovered that, according to atomistic theory,' Woolf 1980:
      53 and Schilpp 1959: 47

105   'It was his friend Besso who pointed out' Renn & Schulmann
      1992: xxvi. See also Stachel et al. 1989: 206ff.

106   'existing ideas upside down.' Jürgen Renn, interview, 28 Febru-
      ary 1993

106   'absolute rest or absolute motion' This idea troubled Newton,
      who lamely suggested that 'in the remote regions of the fixed

stars or perhaps far beyond them, there may be some body absolutely at rest.'

107 'The Minute in Danger' Frank 1949: 79

107 'another short article' Albert Einstein, *Annalen der Physik*, vol. 18 (1905), p. 639: 'The mass of a body is a measure of its energy content.'

107 'the reverse is also true' Albert Einstein, *Jahrbuch der Radioactivität und Elektronik* vol. 4 (1907), pp. 411, 462

108 'Her intellect lives in those lines' Trbuhović-Gjurić 1983: 95

108 'Her part was not small' E. Einstein 1991: 98

108 'may have been the primary contribution' Evan Harris Walker, *Ms Einstein*, p. 15

108 'a fantasist' Boston University statement, February 1990

108 'I had no interest or motive of that sort' Evan Harris Walker, interview, 22 January 1993

109 'Mrs Einstein's claim to fame, relatively speaking' *The Times*, 20 February 1990

109 'jointly awarded the Nobel prize for physics' Abir-Am & Outram 1989: 66–7

109 'in recognition of his wife's contribution' Abir-Am & Outram 1989: 114

109 'passing references to Einstein's own early work' Pais 1983: 55

110 'Everything that I have created' Trbuhović-Gjurić 1983: 94

110 'interview with a Belgrade journalist' Attempts to find this interview have been unsuccessful – John Stachel, interview, 26 March 1993

110 'our great Serbian woman' Trbuhović-Gjurić 1983: 95

111 'unaccountable result' Pais 1983: 118–9, 172

111 'as capable of discovering the principles of relativity' Evan Harris Walker, *Physics Today*, February 1991, p. 123

111 'Einstein wrote to *Mileva* in 1899' John Stachel, p. 5 of draft reply to Walker for *Physics Today*, 1992

111 'very interesting' Renn & Schulmann 1992: 15 (September 1899)

111 'saw the originals while working as an assistant' Trbuhović-Gjurić 1983: 97

111 'in a 1955 Soviet physics journal' *Uspekhi Fizicheskikh Nauk*, vol. 57, no. 2 (1955), p. 187

111 'Einstein-Marity' John Stachel, p. 6 of draft reply to Walker for *Physics Today*, 1992

112 'Only if Joffe had actually seen the manuscript' Evan Harris Walker, *Baltimore Sun*, 30 March 1990

112 'one well-known Einstein biography' i.e. Seelig 1954 – John Stachel, p. 6 of draft reply to Walker for *Physics Today*, 1992

112 'If Röntgen read the paper' John Stachel, American Association for the Advancement of Science, 5 March 1990

112 'used the manuscript as scrap paper' Hoffmann & Dukas 1986: 69

113 'list of his close collaborators' Pais 1983: 483–97

113 'thrusting the papers into his desk' Reiser 1931: 67

113 'from Albert and his student' Klein et al. 1993: 26 (Albert Einstein to Marcel Grossman, April 1904)

113 'From the beginning' Gerald Holton, interview, 19 February 1992

113 'When people collaborate' Peter Bergmann, interview, 16 March 1993

114 'quietly, modestly' E. Einstein 1991: 98

114 'Mileva's great-grandson' Paul Einstein, interview, November 1992

114 'Mileva helped him [Einstein]' Michelmore 1962: 45, 46

114 'neglecting the subject' Schilpp 1959: 15

114 'against her mere 5' Stachel et al. 1987: 247. In computing averages, some grades were doubled and the *Diplomarbeit* grade was quadrupled.

115 'If he had needed help' Jürgen Renn, interview, May 1992. His dissertation did require a great deal of number-crunching.

115 'Mermaids?' Abraham Pais, letter to Roger Highfield, 3 November 1992

115 'speech he delivered in Japan in 1922' Pais 1983: 139. The figure of five or six weeks appears elsewhere: for instance, see Albert Einstein to Carl Seelig, 11 March 1952

115 'sounding-board' Arthur Miller, lecture at University College, London, 11 February 1992

115 'Besso also drew on his own studies' Renn & Schulmann 1992: xxvi
116 'Everyone at the Patent Office' Bernstein, Jeremy, 'A critic at large: Besso', *New Yorker*, 17 February 1989, p. 91
116 'so Mileva's defenders have rejected it' See Senta Troemel Ploetz, *Index on Censorship*, 9/1990, p. 36
116 'commented on almost everything' John Stachel, interview, 21 February 1992

6 STARVED FOR LOVE

118 'the response of the highly influential Max Planck' We do not know when this correspondence started, though Einstein does refer to it in a letter to Solovine on 3 May 1906
118 'I could not believe' Pais 1983: 151 and Seelig 1956a: 78; also Clark archive, Edinburgh, letter from Max von Laue to Carl Seelig 13 March 1952: 'I looked him up in the Patent Office. In the general waiting-room an official said to me: "Follow the corridor and Einstein will come out and meet you." I followed his instructions but the young man who met me made such an unexpected impression on me that I could not believe he could be the father of the relativity theory. So I let him pass and only when he returned from the waiting-room did we finally become acquainted.'
118 'confessing as an old man' Max von Laue to Margot Einstein, 23 October 1959, quoted in Holton 1988: 212
118 'A new Copernicus is born' Clark 1979: 116
118 'lazy dog' Hoffmann & Dukas 1986: 85
118 'a modest-sized crowd' Pais 1983: 151
119 'federal ink-shitter' Klein et al. 1993: 47 (5 January to 11 May 1907)
119 'our poor purse will stand the strain' 1906 letter to Helene Savić
119 'unbelievable questions' Trbuhović-Gjurić 1983: 100–1
119 'the happiest thought of my life' Pais 1983: 178
119 'I was sitting in a chair in the Patent Office' Pais 1983: 179 (November 1907)

120 'little machine' For a full discussion, see Klein et al. 1993: 52

120 'written by the Habicht brothers' Conrad Habicht and Paul Habicht, Elektrostatischer Potentialmultiplikator nach A. Einstein, *Physikalische Zeitschrift*, vol. 11 (1910), p. 532

120 'We are both only One Stone' Trbuhović-Gjurić 1983: 83

120 'A fleeting hint' Seelig 1956a: 60 – 'Their attempts to perfect it with occasional help from Mileva lasted several years.'

121 'his latest scientific enthusiasms' Klein et al. 1993: 116 (17 April 1908)

122 'the first person to publish work with him as a co-author' See, for instance, Pais 1983: 483 and Klein et al. 1993: 668.

122 'he disliked mountains' Helen Dukas to Carl Seelig, 9 September 1952, ETH

122 'even the sight of a mountain' Hans Albert Einstein, interviewed by Bela Kornitzer, *American Fathers and Sons*, Hermitage House, 1952; also in *Gazette & Daily*, York, Pa., 20 September 1948

123 'even the slightest comparison to Einstein's' Clark 1979: 134

123 'The story of Adler's self-sacrifice' Frank 1947: 95–6

123 'discussing a petition they planned' Speziali 1972: 105 (Albert Einstein to Michele Besso 29 April 1917)

123 'Adler knew he was really second choice' Robert Schulmann, interview, 20 February 1992

124 'among the most important theoretical physicists' Pais 1983: 185

124 'disagreeable qualities' Pais 1983: 185

124 'impersonal and of little interest' Seelig 1956a: 92

125 'heaven full of bass violins' Klein et al. 1993: 184 (12 May 1909)

125 ' "inappropriate" correspondence' Klein et al. 1993: 203 (23 May 1909)

125 'his intentions had been innocent' Klein et al. 1993: 202 (7 June 1909)

125 'spiritual equilibrium, lost on account of M[ileva].' Klein et al. 1993: 223 (17 November 1909)

125 'force it down one's gullet alone' Klein et al. 1993: 242 (28 April 1910)

125 'uncommon ugliness' Klein et al. 1993: 203 (27 July 1951)
125 'the first to shock him' John Stachel, interview, 21 February 1992
126 'hard and settled' Marianoff & Wayne 1944: 40
126 'harsh, almost coarse' Konrad Wachsmann, interviewed in Grüning 1990: 157
126 'She was a typical Slav' E. Einstein 1991: 20
126 'several weeks before it began' Arthur Miller, lecture at University College, London, 11 February 1992
127 'so many beautiful' John Stachel, interview, 21 February 1992
127 'among the leading German-speaking physicists' Mileva Marić to Helene Savić, 1909, in John Stachel. In press.
127 'The pressure that had often burdened his youth' Frank 1948: 97
127 'Messiah-feeling' Reichinstein 1934: 27–8
128 'he begged Habicht' Klein et al. 1993: 228 (17 December 1909)
128 'with such fame, not much time remains' John Stachel. In press.
128 'Stern? Severe?' Jerry Tallmer, 'Sons of the famous', New York Post Daily Magazine, 23 May 1963, p. 27
129 'the stork has brought us a healthy little boy' Klein et al. 1993: 254 (before 1 August 1910)
129 'In my relativity theory' Frank 1948: 96
129 'I don't believe he showed any particular' Bela Kornitzer, American Fathers and Sons, Hermitage House, 1952; also in Gazette & Daily, York, Pa., 20 September 1948
129 'one of the nicest toys' Whitrow 1967: 19
130 'He was sitting in his study' Seelig 1956a: 104
130 'I entered Einstein's room' Reichinstein 1934: 26
131 'expect to find her waiting' Reichinstein 1934: 26
131 'there are rather many musical occasions in our house' E. Einstein 1991: 95
131 'the beautiful time of our youth' Albert Einstein to Anna Meyer-Schmid, 17 December 1926
133 'because of material advantages' Mileva Marić to Helene Savić, January 1911
133 'a student petition was raised' Klein et al. 1993: 247 (23 June 1910)

133 'Would I too become so lazy' Beck & Havas 1987: 174 (May 1901)

134 'would ignore each other' Clark 1979: 143 and Trbuhović-Gjurić 1983: 111

134 'much joy' Pais 1983: 193

134 'neighbours complained' Levinger 1962: 53. They initially stayed in the Hotel Viktoria (Klein et al. 1993: 653).

134 'in the Smichov quarter' Illy 1979: 79

135 'a second-hand mattress' Levinger 1962: 53

135 'covered in bugs' Michelmore 1962: 54

135 'sinister brown liquid' E. Einstein 1991: 7

135 'fears about bubonic plague' Michelmore 1962: 54. Vivian Nutton of the Wellcome Institute for the History of Medicine confirms that bubonic plague was a threat at this time, though there was no outbreak in Prague.

135 'The filthier a nation is' Seelig 1956a: 129

135 'seriously ill' Klein et al. 1993: 320

135 'It doesn't matter much' Frank 1948: 102

135 'he sent a maid over' Albert Einstein to Heinrich Zangger, 7 April 1911, Einstein archive, Boston, 39–623. See also Illy 1979: 79

136 'without any goodwill towards their fellow men' Speziali 1972: 19 (Albert Einstein to Michele Besso, 13 May 1911)

136 'How one could use a man of your intelligence' Speziali 1972: 19 (Albert Einstein to Michele Besso, 13 May 1911)

136 'experimental adventures' (Albert Einstein to Heinrich Zangger, 1911)

136 'my beautiful subject' Speziali 1972: 45 (Albert Einstein to Michele Besso, 4 November 1912)

136 'an echo from this forest' (Albert Einstein to Heinrich Zangger, 1911)

136 'half-usable' Speziali 1972: 45 (Albert Einstein to Michele Besso, 4 November 1912)

136 'to the exalted Viceroy' Klein et al. 1993: 295 (7 April 1911)

136 'pen and ink shitting' Pais 1983: 193

137 'the man sent to repair the lights' Seelig 1956a: 120

137 'bowed and scraped in obsequious greeting' Klein et al. 1993: 440 (17 March 1912)

137 'an odd mixture of pomposity and servility' Speziali 1972: 19 (Albert Einstein to Michele Besso, 13 May 1911)

137 'He loved sitting under the trees' Marianoff & Wayne 1944: 50, 52

137 'at the home of Berta Fanta' Illy 1979: 82

137 'after drinking too much' Dreyer 1890: 309

137 'was helped in his observations' Abir-Am & Outram 1989: 46

138 'depressive and ill-tempered wife' Caspar 1959: 71, 175, 206

138 'something incomprehensible in its absence of emotion' Clark 1979: 145 and Frank 1948: 108

138 'only the same intolerance of received opinion' Max Brod to Albert Einstein, 22 February 1949, ETH, and to Carl Seelig, 1952

138 'quoted Brod at length' Frank 1948: 107

138 'jokingly compared himself to the lunatics' Frank 1948: 123. Illy 1979: 78 talks of overlooking a street and a shady garden surrounded by walls and buildings of the asylum.

138 'Those are the madmen' Frank 1948: 123

139 'Do not bodies act upon light at a distance?' Gjertsen 1986: 411ff.

139 'almost exactly the same' Pais 1983: 200

139 'Philipp Lenard had von Soldner's paper reprinted' Pais 1983: 200 and Bernstein 1973: 193

140 'a correspondence with Lorentz' Albert Einstein to Hendrik Lorentz, 30 March 1909

140 'I admire this man' Klein et al. 1993: 192 (Albert Einstein to Jakob Laub, 19 May 1909)

140 'stayed with the Lorentz family' An incidental pleasure of the visit was the Einsteins' reunion with Margarete von Uexküll, the fellow student at Zurich whose results Einstein had once so expertly forged, and who was now living in Leiden with her husband Anton Willem Nieuwenhuis, a Dutch doctor and ethnologist. Von Uexküll had lost contact with Albert and Mileva, and was mystified when Lorentz sent word that her old friends the Einsteins were asking to see her. The name meant nothing,

but on arrival she recognized Mileva instantly, with 'delighted amazement'. The announcement that Mileva was now Mrs Einstein still left her friend bemused, however, and it was only when Albert's familiar features emerged from an adjoining room that Von Uexküll recognized him. 'It was one of the most embarrassing moments of my life,' she recalled. (*'Erinnerungen von Margarete von Uexküll'*, *Frankfurt Allgemeiner Zeitung*, 10 March 1956)

140 'exactly the way a father looks' Klein 1970: 304

140 'ordered like a work of art' Address at the grave of H. A. Lorentz, Einstein 1991: 11

141 'pilloried as a scarlet woman' Abir-Am & Outram 1989: 64

141 'The penny dreadful story' Seelig 1956b: 43

141 'a sparky intelligence' Seelig 1956b: 43

141 'Mileva went along to the Congress' Trbuhović-Gjurić 1983: 115. E. Einstein 1991: 18 also says she went. However, the Einstein papers project has found postcards Einstein sent to Mileva.

141 'It must have been very interesting in Karlsruhe' Klein et al. 1993: 337 (4 October 1911)

142 'an inner fit of tenderness' Klein et al. 1993: 350 (28 October 1911)

142 'With that a dark point in my life diminishes' Klein et al. 1993: 389 (26 December 1911). When Marie had a child the following August, Einstein said he felt a kind of uncle to it (Maja was married to Paul Winteler).

142 'gave birth to an illegitimate child' Illy 1979: 79

142 'best teacher' Sayen 1985: 17–18

142 'hit it off instantly' Klein 1970: 178

142 'a meticulous diary' Robert Schulmann, interview, 20 February 1992

143 'She was at her husband's side' Klein 1970: 176

143 'She was there again to say goodbye' Illy 1979: 81

143 'Only when she left to go home' Klein 1970: 176

143 'dear dear boy' Klein et al. 1993: 616 (24 February 1912)

143 'He loves going to school' Mileva Marić to Michele Besso,

Clark archive, Edinburgh, 0291 (Prague 26 March). Year given by comparison with Klein et al. 1993: 443

143 'This was the start of a fascination' E. Einstein 1991: 7

143 'the discord became obvious' E. Einstein 1991: 18

7 I MUST LOVE SOMEBODY

145 'Elsa was judged prettier than Mileva' Herta Waldow, interview, 15 September 1992

145 'The resemblance of Mrs Einstein' Rabbi Harry Cohen, *The Jewish Spectator*, January 1969

146 'the same Swabian dialect' Vallentin 1954: 45 and Reiser 1931: 124

146 'they often played together' Hoffmann & Dukas 1986: 134. See also Reiser 1931: 124. The family sold the family textile business in Hechingen in order to retire to Berlin – John Stachel, interview, 26 March 1993.

146 'Elsa claimed that she fell in love with her cousin' Pais 1983: 301

146 'Biographies of Einstein' For instance Hoffmann & Dukas 1986: 134

146 'that shyness pussy cats have' Marianoff & Wayne 1944: 6, 16

147 'Contact was resumed' Klein et al. 1993: 657 and Illy 1979: 82

148 'I grew very fond of you' Klein et al. 1993: 465 (30 April 1912)

148 'made him promise to destroy all her letters' Robert Schulmann, interview, 20 February 1992

148 'especially beautiful letters' Klein et al. 1993: 467. The early letters were copied by John Stachel

148 'known to Marianoff' Marianoff & Wayne 1944: 54

148 'a nervous declaration of love' Klein et al. 1993: 465 (30 April 1912)

149 'I cannot tell you how sorry I feel' Klein et al. 1993: 468 (7 May 1912)

150 'he was writing to Elsa for the last time' Klein et al. 1993: 479 (21 May 1912)

151 'Hallelujah!' Seelig 1956a: 130

151 'he allowed himself to be swayed' Frank 1948: 150

151 'she could hardly feel homesick' Mileva Marić to Michele Besso, Clark Archive, Edinburgh, 0291 (dated Prague 26 March and year deduced from Klein et al. 1993: 443)

151 'with a heavy heart' Klein et al. 1993: 365 (23 November 1911)

151 'people will think I'm a Brazilian admiral' Frank 1948: 125

152 'a riot' Michelmore 1962: 59

152 'As he wrote to his cousin' Klein et al. 1993: 528 (23 March 1913)

152 'Grossmann, you must help me' Pais 1983: 212

153 'Compared with this problem' Pais 1983: 216

153 'Mileva's favourite' Trbuhović-Gjurić 1983: 120. See also Klein et al. 1993: 313

153 'Here comes the whole Einstein hen house.' Trbuhović-Gjurić 1983: 121 and Seelig 1956a: 112

153 'silent and gloomy' Trbuhović-Gjurić 1983: 120. (Trbuhović-Gjurić's book makes use of Lisbeth Hurwitz's diary, now lost.)

153 'Albert has devoted himself completely to physics' E. Einstein 1991: 96

153 'family matters' Trbuhović-Gjurić 1983: 122

153 'beat me up' Whitrow 1967: 21

153 'somewhat ill' Trbuhović-Gjurić 1983: 120–2. See Klein et al. 1993: 526

154 'sending him birthday greetings' Klein et al. 1993: 527

154 'If your ways ever lead to Zurich' Klein et al. 1993: 526 (14 March 1913)

154 'pressed Elsa with renewed force' Klein et al. 1993: 528 (23 March 1913)

154 'literally superhuman efforts' Klein et al. 1993: 533 (28 May 1913)

155 'The little drama was acted out' Klein et al. 1993: 544. There are various accounts – for instance Clark 1979: 169.

155 'because it got on my nerves to give courses' Pais 1983: 240

155 'whether I shall ever really lay another egg' Seelig 1956a: 148

156 'had sufficient guile' Clark 1979: 173

156 'the loving care of a female cousin' Pais 1983: 241

156 'to see you often, to run around with you' Klein et al. 1993: 547 (July 1913)

156 'with very mixed feelings because she is afraid of the relatives' Klein et al. 1993: 554 (August 1913)

157 'reflect the social embarrassment' Clark archive, Edinburgh, 0285

157 'Our parting occurred so quickly' Clark archive, Edinburgh, A3, p. 4

157 'Eduard was ill' Trbuhović-Gjurić 1983: 123

158 'the clearness of his mind' Clark 1979: 153

158 'sublime and unclouded' Albert Einstein 1935: 77

158 'Madame Curie is very intelligent' Klein et al. 1993: 554 (August 1913)

158 'Very few women are creative' Listener, 8 September 1968

159 'aggravated an ear infection' E. Einstein 1991: 97

160 'Hans Albert and Eduard were baptized' Trbuhović-Gjurić 1983: 124

160 'Eduard did his best to disrupt proceedings' E. Einstein 1991: 97

160 'a matter of indifference' Trbuhović-Gjurić 1983: 125. See also Seelig 1956a: 113.

160 'I am back in Zurich now' Klein et al. 1993: 568 (10 October 1913)

161 'Hairbrush is used regularly' Klein et al. 1993: 581 (November 1913)

162 'How crude and rough they are' Klein et al. 1993: 584 (December 1913)

162 'If I appear to be so unappetizing' Klein et al. 1993: 584 (December 1913)

162 'disinfecting and sterilizing distance' Klein et al. 1993: 596 (December 1913)

162 'the incorrigible dung finch' Klein et al. 1993: 596 (21 December 1913)

162 'travelling folk' Klein et al. 1993: 581 (November 1913)

162 'insatiable and painful ambition' Klein et al. 1993: 584 (December 1913)

162 'a more worthwhile occupation' Klein et al. 1993: 571 (16 October 1913)

163 'My mother consoled me' Klein et al. 1993: 568 (10 October 1913)

163 'icy silence' Klein et al. 1993: 583 (December 1913)

164 'Do you believe it is easy to get divorced' Klein et al. 1993: 583 (December 1913)

164 'why you are so terribly offended' Klein et al. 1993: 583 (December 1913)

164 'an unfriendly, humourless creature' Klein et al. 1993: 584 (December 1913)

164 'the sourest sourpot' Klein et al. 1993: 596 (December 1913)

164 'the atmosphere of a cemetery' Klein et al. 1993: 598 (December 1913)

164 'unpleasant and mistrustful' Klein et al. 1993: 596 (December 1913)

165 'if only he could be bothered' Klein et al. 1993: 596 (December 1913)

165 'love flourishes towards science' Klein et al. 1993: 596 (December 1913)

165 'really big things' Klein et al. 1993: 608 (February 1914)

166 'The less personal friction the better' Klein et al. 1993: 584 (December 1913)

166 'a certain danger' Klein et al. 1993: 604 (January 1914)

166 'refused to discuss his relatives' Klein et al. 1993: 598 (December 1913)

166 'This had its good side' Klein et al. 1993: 610 (February 1914)

166 'It is pleasant here in Berlin' Klein et al. 1993: 611 (5 March 1914)

167 'Life here is better than I anticipated' Seelig 1960: 247

167 'quite human' Seelig 1956a: 150

167 'She did not have any friends in Berlin' Michelmore 1962: 62

167 'believed they were going for a holiday' Michelmore 1962: 63 and E. Einstein 1991: 20

167 'Why the separation came' Whitrow 1967: 20

168 'Einstein wept' Pais 1983: 240

168 'born close to the water' Janos Plesch to Peter Plesch, 18 April 1955

168 'crying solely for the loss of his children' Vallentin 1954: 37 and Robert Schulmann, interview, 20 February 1992

168 'Without you, my life is no life' Beck & Havas 1987: 145 (August 1900)

8 AN AMPUTATED LIMB

169 'this sabre-rattling' Albert Einstein to Helene Savić (after 17 December 1912)

169 'Europe, in her madness' Klein 1970: 300 (Albert Einstein to Paul Ehrenfest, 19 August 1914)

170 'Apart from the general misery' (Albert Einstein to Heinrich Zangger, 17 May 1915)

170 'conscious disengagement' Albert Einstein to Heinrich Zangger, probably spring 1915; quoted in part by Pais 1983: 243

170 'That was probably the worst time' Whitrow 1967: 20

170 'the thought of a friendly relationship' Albert Einstein to Mileva Marić, 1914*

170 'without any ands, ifs or buts' Albert Einstein to Mileva Marić, 1914*

170 'send me news of my beloved boys' Albert Einstein to Mileva Marić, 18 July 1914*

171 'Einstein would sever all contact' Albert Einstein to Mileva Marić, 12 January 1915*

171 'He saw no reason why' Albert Einstein to Mileva Marić, 1 April 1916*

171 'my greatest passion' Albert Einstein to Hans Albert Einstein, 26 November 1916*

171 'practise the art of thinking' Albert Einstein to Hans Albert Einstein, 25 January 1915*

171 'too proud to ask her father' Trbuhović-Gjurić 1983: 132

171 'lent her music scores' Trbuhović-Gjurić 1983: 132, 134

171 'I would have sent you more money' Albert Einstein to Mileva Marić, 15 September 1914*

172 'yearly maintenance' Albert Einstein to Mileva Marić, 12 December 1914*

172 'nothing except the bare essentials' Albert Einstein to Mileva Marić, 12 December 1914*

172 'If I had known you' Albert Einstein to Mileva Marić, 12 January 1915*

172 'Einstein would continue to care for her' Trbuhović-Gjurić 1983: 134

172 'I have never been so serene and happy' Albert Einstein to Heinrich Zangger, 7 July 1915

172 'he and Elsa holidayed together' Albert Einstein to Heinrich Zangger, 7 July 1915

172 'the most restful time of his entire adult life' Albert Einstein to Heinrich Zangger, summer 1915

172 'people were like the ocean' Albert Einstein to Hans Albert Einstein, from Princeton, undated*

173 'Einstein had won her permission' Albert Einstein to Heinrich Zangger, 7 July 1915 and 28 May 1915

173 'a last-minute note' Albert Einstein to Heinrich Zangger, 7 July 1915

173 'So long as one is young' Albert Einstein to Heinrich Zangger, 7 July 1915

173 'travelled as far as southern Germany' Michelmore 1962: 67

173 'I will not visit you again' Albert Einstein to Hans Albert Einstein, 30 October 1915*

174 'Your letter sincerely pleased me' Albert Einstein to Mileva Marić, 15 November 1915*

174 'aware of since 1907' John Stachel, interview, 26 March 1993

174 'Einstein reported having had heart palpitations' Pais 1983: 253

175 'Every fibre of my body itches' Klein 1970: 302 (Albert Einstein to Paul Ehrenfest, 26 December 1915)

175 'even if I have to camp out at the border' Albert Einstein to Hans Albert Einstein, end of 1915*

175 'forcing him to beg' Albert Einstein to Mileva Marić, 1 April 1916*

175 'doing a lot of interesting things lately' Albert Einstein to Hans Albert Einstein, 1916*

176 'pick up vibrations' Frieda Bucky, Clark archive, Edinburgh, 0382a

176 'change our well-tested separation to a divorce' Albert Einstein to Mileva Marić, 6 February 1916*

176 'put herself in his shoes' Albert Einstein to Mileva Marić, dated as 'probably 1918',* but from a reference to Elsa's elder daughter it is probably 1915–16.

176 'I could not wish for anything better' Albert Einstein, to Mileva Marić, 8 April 1916*

176 'I would have been broken physically and mentally' Speziali 1972: 74 (Albert Einstein to Michele Besso, 14 July 1916)

177 'raise fears for her life' Trbuhović-Gjurić 1983: 138, but not sourced. Also Albert Einstein's reference to brain tuberculosis in Speziali 1972: 80 (Albert Einstein to Michele Besso, 24 August 1916)

177 'a series of heart attacks' Trbuhović-Gjurić 1983: 138

177 'lie motionless and avoid excitement' Speziali 1972: 90 (Michele Besso to Albert Einstein, 5 December 1916)

177 'taken in temporarily by Helen Savić' Trbuhović-Gjurić 1983: 138 and Milan Popović, interview, 16 March 1993

177 'You have no idea of the natural cunning' Albert Einstein to Michele Besso, 14 July 1916, ETH

177 'by far the largest part was simulated' Pauline Einstein to Elsa Löwenthal, 6 August 1916

178 'We men are lamentable, dependent creatures' Albert Einstein to Michele Besso, 21 July 1916, ETH

179 'That this should happen to a scientist!' Speziali 1972: 76 (Albert Einstein to Michele Besso, 21 July 1916)

179 'Einstein was grateful for the news' Speziali 1972: 124 (Albert Einstein to Michele Besso, 5 January 1918)

179 'my foster mother' Speziali 1972: 119 (Albert Einstein to Michele Besso, 3 September 1917)

179 'never before has anyone been so impudent to me' Speziali 1972: 126 (Albert Einstein to Michele Besso, 23 June 1918)

179 'Your silence reassures me' Speziali 1972: 78 (Albert Einstein to Michele Besso, 11 August 1916)

179 'my wife is slowly getting better' Speziali 1972: 80 (Albert Einstein to Michele Besso, 24 August 1916)

179 'with frequent spells in hospital' Trbuhović-Gjurić 1983: 139

180 'The boy had refused to show the contents to Mileva' Speziali 1972: 90 (Michele Besso to Albert Einstein, 5 December 1916)

180 'I will not bother her with the divorce' Speziali 1972: 81 (Albert Einstein to Michele Besso, 6 September 1916)

180 'I will see to it that she suffers no more' Speziali 1972: 84 (Albert Einstein to Michele Besso, 31 October 1916)

180 'so that you are not tricked by appearances' Albert Einstein to Heinrich Zangger, 17 May 1915

180 'thanked Savić for not condemning him' Trbuhović-Gjurić 1983: 139

180 'has stepped below freezing point' Speziali 1972: 80 (Albert Einstein to Michele Besso, 24 August 1916)

181 'Don't be frightened' Albert Einstein to Hans Albert Einstein, 13 October 1916*

181 'There can be absolutely no question that I will take Albert away' Speziali 1972: 96 (Albert Einstein to Michele Besso, December 1916)

181 'the idea of removing Albert from school' Speziali 1972: 101 (Albert Einstein to Michele Besso, 9 March 1917)

181 'nothing will occur *unless necessary*' Albert Einstein to Heinrich Zangger, late April 1917

181 'no consideration should be taken for my wife' Speziali 1972: 112 (Albert Einstein to Michele Besso, 8 May 1917)

181 'recite long passages from memory' E. Einstein 1991: 23

181 'enjoying newspapers by the time he entered primary school' Maria Grendelmeier, interview, July 1992

181 'delights of Goethe and Schiller' Rübel 1986: 11

181 'not to become a bookworm' Albert Einstein to Eduard Einstein, 1917*

182 'a delicate little chap' Heinrich Zangger to Albert Einstein, spring 1918

182 'persistent headaches and pains in his ears' Trbuhović-Gjurić
     1983: 151

182 'I'm pleased that everything goes well' Speziali 1972: 96
     (Albert Einstein to Michele Besso, December 1916)

182 'Who knows if it would not have been better if he had left the
     world' Speziali 1972: 101 (Albert Einstein to Michele Besso, 9
     March 1917)

183 'he preferred the child-rearing style of the ancient Spartans'
     Albert Einstein to Heinrich Zangger, 10 March 1917

183 'With thinly veiled sarcasm' Albert Einstein to Mileva Marić,
     31 January 1918*

183 'Tete must come back' Speziali 1972: 121 (Albert Einstein to
     Michele Besso, 22 September 1917)

183 'in a kind of disinfection machine' Albert Einstein to Heinrich
     Zangger, 6 December 1917

183 'his doctor diagnosed gall stones' Speziali 1972: 101 (Albert
     Einstein to Michele Besso, 9 March 1917)

183 'Zangger helped to procure the necessary foods' Speziali 1972:
     101 (Albert Einstein to Michele Besso, 9 March 1917)

184 'Berlin relatives supplemented his supplies' Pais 1983:
     299–301

184 'I find it hard to summon the necessary superstition' Speziali
     1972: 112 (Albert Einstein to Michele Besso, 8 May 1917)

184 'diagnosis shifted to a stomach ulcer' Speziali 1972: 124
     (Albert Einstein to Michele Besso, 5 January 1918)

184 'Why should I?' Seelig 1956a: 151 (Hedwig Born to Albert
     Einstein, 11 April 1938)

184 'to give Besso the impression that it was all her idea' Clark
     1979: 194

184 'He praised Elsa's home cooking' Pais 1983: 300, citing a
     letter to Heinrich Zangger

184 'You need have no scruples' Frank 1948: 154

184 'a unique occurrence in these times' Elsa Löwenthal to Pauline
     Einstein, September 1918

184 'a blob of oil' Albert Einstein to Heinrich Zangger, undated
     but probably late April 1917

185 'and learned to isolate myself' Albert Einstein to Heinrich Zangger, 10 March 1917

185 'which has revealed itself as an indescribable blessing' Michelmore 1962: 73

185 'always remain true to you' Michelmore 1962: 73

185 'Zorka herself swiftly showed signs of depressive mental illness' Trbuhović-Gjurić 1983: 140–1 and Heinrich Zangger to Albert Einstein, 21 February 1918

185 'Zorka was lodged at the Burghölzli' Heinrich Zangger to Albert Einstein, 22 October 1919

185 'Haber had every reason to feel especially moved' Goran 1967

186 'the best deal possible' Clark archive, Edinburgh, 0331

186 'very nicely' Albert Einstein to Heinrich Zangger, 22 April 1918

186 'his savings were in danger of being exhausted' Speziali 1972: 116 (Albert Einstein to Michele Besso, 15 May 1917)

186 'I will give Zangger what he laid out for me' Speziali 1972: 124 (Albert Einstein to Michele Besso, 5 January 1918)

187 'she would not see a penny more' Albert Einstein to Mileva Marić, 31 January 1918*. The sum matches that mentioned in his letters to Besso.

187 '32,000 dollars or 180,000 Swiss francs' Pais 1983: 503

187 'nominated for the prize of 1910' Pais 1983: 505

187 'comparing himself to Till Eulenspiegel' Speziali 1972: 128 (Albert Einstein to Michele Besso, 9 July 1918)

188 'he dreamt he had cut his throat with a shaving-knife' Speziali 1972: 132 (Albert Einstein to Michele Besso, 20 August 1918)

188 'The initiative had come from Zangger' Speziali 1972: 139 (Albert Einstein to Michele Besso, 8 September 1918)

188 'he was bound to his colleagues in Berlin' Speziali 1972: 139 (Albert Einstein to Michele Besso, 8 September 1918)

188 'a portfolio of shares' 7 December 1918, Einstein archive, Boston

188 'a Berlin register office' Clark 1979: 218

9 THE HOLY ONE

189 'the birth of the Einstein legend' Pais 1983: 309

190 'the emperor's new clothes' Albert Einstein to Heinrich Zangger, Christmas 1919

190 'he was like Midas' Clark archive, Edinburgh, 0314, and Albert Einstein to Max Born, 9 September 1920

190 'snip off a lock of his hair' *Daily Telegraph*, report on the meeting of the Committee of Intellectual Co-operation, 1922

190 'Do you exist?' Sayen 1985: 78

190 'compared her to Cerberus' Plesch 1947: 220

190 'She's there to protect me' Whitrow 1967: 54

191 'uniformly ugly' Vallentin 1954: 98

191 'the Biedermeier room' Herneck 1978: 14

191 'Pictures adorned the walls' Frank 1948: 154, and see Pais 1983: 301

191 'goldfish swam in a bowl' Herneck 1978: 84

191 'solid bourgeois comfort' Clark archive, Edinburgh, letter from Max Herzberger, 22 January 1970, who had visited Einstein in Berlin

191 'a bohemian guest in a middle-class home' Frank, 1948: 154

191 'abdominal cancer' Albert Einstein to Carl Seelig, 20 April 1952, Clark archive, Edinburgh, 304.15

191 'she was terminally ill' Speziali 1972: 147 (Albert Einstein to Michele Besso, 12 December 1919). He thought she would only live six months.

191 'She asked to be with her son' Pais 1983: 302

191 'too agitated to attend to his work' Speziali 1972: 147 (Albert Einstein to Michele Besso, 12 December 1919)

192 'her last illness sapped his energies' Born 1971: 21 (Albert Einstein to Max Born, 24 January 1920)

192 'terrible torments' Albert Einstein, to Heinrich Zangger, March 1920

192 'For Einstein wept, like other men' Clark 1979: 191

192 'to see one's mother suffer' Born 1971: 29 (Albert Einstein to Max Born, 18 April 1920)

192 'he was saddened but not heart-broken' Michelmore 1962: 89

193 'I don't really feel any pain' Klein et al. 1993: 610 (Albert Einstein to Elsa Löwenthal, February 1914)

193 'it did not strike observers as the love of a father' Grüning 1990: 160

194 'Misfortune suits humanity' Albert Einstein to Heinrich Zangger, end 1919

194 'Anti-Relativity Company' Sayen 1985: 54

194 'typical bloody-mindedness' Infeld 1950: 119–121. 'I remember too, that during the interval between two consecutive lectures, everyone was looking at the box in which Einstein sat. I don't know why he came but he seemed to have a wonderful time, greeting people and smiling broadly with a loud giggle and stealing the show just by his presence.'

194 'a German national, with or without swastika' Pais 1983: 316

194 'these damned pigs' Klein 1970: 321 (Paul Ehrenfest to Albert Einstein, 2 September 1920)

194 'That people can still disappoint and irritate you' Born 1971: 34 (Hedwig Born to Albert Einstein, 8 September 1920)

195 'Everyone has to sacrifice at the altar of stupidity' Born 1971: 35 (Albert Einstein to Max and Hedwig Born, 9 September 1920)

195 'separate bedrooms at opposite corners' Herneck 1978: 29

195 'day-time refuge' Herneck 1978: 16

195 'puritanical simplicity' Reiser 1931: 189

195 'but Einstein was adamant' Plesch 1947: 201

195 'Speak of you or me' Janos Plesch to Peter Plesch, 18 April 1955

195 'a lurking abyss' Dukas & Hoffmann 1979: 100

196 'as good as might be expected' Reiser 1931: preface

196 'Einstein wants this' Grüning 1990: 40

196 'As his mind knows no limits' Plesch 1947: 206. See also *Jewish Sentinel*, 1 September 1944, p. 50: Elsa 'watched over him as one might over a child.'

196 'a typical meal would begin' Marianoff & Wayne 1944: 15

197 'like a boy lost in a dreamworld' Pais 1983: 301

197 'were always inclined to look very critically' Frank 1948: 155

197 'Elsa's quick intelligence' Vallentin 1954: 45

198 'no compensatory feeling' Vallentin 1954: 59

198 'She kept herself in the background' Plesch 1947: 220

198 'He enjoyed having an audience' Clark archive, Edinburgh, 0331

199 'If I did not know you well' Born 1971: 38 (Hedwig Born to Albert Einstein, 7 October 1920)

199 'You do not understand this' Born 1971: 40 (Max Born to Albert Einstein, 13 October 1920)

199 'The whole affair is a matter of indifference to me' Born 1971: 41 (Albert Einstein to Max Born, undated)

199 'Einstein urged him to swap it' Albert Einstein to Hans Albert Einstein, 18 June 1919*. This date is believed to be incorrect because the book was published by Fontane, Berlin, in 1921.

199 'tolerant, and yet did not suggest' Moszkowski 1921b: 79ff.

200 'takes its revenge on women' Albert Einstein to Melania Serbu, 9 January 1929

200 'where you females are concerned' Born 1971: 153 (Hedwig Born to Albert Einstein, 11 April 1938)

200 'only women of a masculine disposition' Albert Einstein to Eduard Einstein, 27 March 1928*

201 'small minority' Peter Bergmann, interview, 16 March 1993

201 'It is psychologically interesting' Pais 1983: 347

202 'cat paradox' Imagine a cat placed in a box containing some radioactive matter and a flask of hydrogen cyanide. A mechanism is arranged so that, when an atom within the radioactive matter decays, a hammer will smash the flask and release toxic gas to kill the cat. Common sense says the cat is either alive or dead. However, radioactive decay is quantum mechanical and so can be predicted to occur only in a probabilistic sense. Using quantum mechanics, the box and its contents can thus be described by wave functions combining the two possible and mutually exclusive outcomes of the cat being alive or the cat being dead. Unless the box is opened to observe the cat – collapsing the wave function – it must be described mathematically by a combination of these two states.

202 'a sense of loss' Pais 1983: 443

203 'furnished with all the chicanery' Maja Einstein-Winteler to Theresia Mutzenbecher, 8 August 1930

203 'items of furniture from Haberlandstrasse' Erika Britzke, 19 October 1992

203 'indescribable joy' Albert Einstein to Mileva Marić, 4 July 1929,* and Michelmore 1962: 144, Plesch 1947: 224, and Peter Plesch, 'Einstein, Joffe and the Plesch family', lecture at the A. F. Joffe Physico-Technical Institute, Leningrad, 21 April 1989

204 'the most beautiful part of her visit' Maja Einstein-Winteler to Theresia Mutzenbecher, 30 September 1930

204 'majestic without compare' Albert Einstein to Eduard Einstein, undated*

204 'Every time his son' Chaim Tschernowitz, 'A day with Albert Einstein', *Jewish Sentinel*, September 1931

204 'recently published in German' Grüning: 1990

204 'He was aroused' Marianoff & Wayne 1944: 129

205 'in the fourth dimension' Clark archive, Edinburgh, 0224, and Seelig 1954: 134

206 'for several years he had a strong attachment' Pais 1983: 320. He states that the relevant correspondence is not in the Einstein archive.

206 'more emotionally felt' Abraham Pais, letter to Roger Highfield, 3 November 1992

206 'fell out badly with his friend' Giuseppe Castagnetti, interview, 20 October 1992

206 'visited him almost daily' Pais 1983: 489

206 'out of pity' Vera Weizmann, *The Impossible Takes Longer*, London, 1967, pp. 102–3

206 'robust child of nature' Janos Plesch to Peter Plesch, 18 April 1955

206 'Einstein loved women' Peter Plesch, interview, 13 August 1992

207 'sight of a pretty young woman' Konrad Kellen, Clark archive, Edinburgh, 0384

207 'He liked beautiful women' Herta Waldow, interview, 15 September 1992; also Herneck 1978: 48

207 'How long have you been married?' Herneck 1978: 133

207 'a wealthy and elegant Jewish widow' Herneck 1978: 146

207 'close friendship' Herneck 1978: 44

207 'Frau Mendel in Ontario' Clark archive, Edinburgh, 0346

207 'visits by Estella Katzenellenbogen' Herneck 1978: 71. Also referred to in Einstein's travel diaries in New York.

208 'a blonde Austrian, Margarete Lebach' Herneck 1978: 123 and Herta Waldow, interview, 15 September 1992

208 'the little angels sing' Albert Einstein, 'For Mrs Grete Lebach', Einstein archive, Boston, 31–064

208 'Frau Professor would always go into Berlin' Herneck 1978: 123

208 'a good acquaintance' Grüning 1990: 215

209 'silent vice to ostentatious virtue' Seelig 1956a: 114

209 'We do things' Marianoff & Wayne 1944: 186

210 'until her tongue lolled out' Plesch 1947: 207

210 'by an unimaginative pig' Janos Plesch to Peter Plesch, 18 April 1955

210 'slavery in a cultural garment' Grüning 1990: 159

210 'Marriage is the unsuccessful attempt' Sayen 1985: 80

210 'It's dangerous' Sayen 1985: 70

210 'My aim lies in smoking' Pais 1983: 302

210 'She probably suspected more' Grüning 1990: 159

210 'Where nature gave extravagantly' Clark Archive, Edinburgh, 0317, letter extract dated 1929, apparently to Hermann Struck, a writer and painter whom Einstein stayed with in Palestine

211 'bedridden for four months' Pais 1983: 317

211 'an hour sitting with a pretty girl' Sayen 1985: 130

211 'Without her nobody would know' Grüning 1990: 51

211 'to attack as "dung" ' Dukas told Ronald Clark on 30 November 1970 that Michelmore's book was 'dung'. See also Helen Dukas to Carl Seelig, 12 July 1952 and 30 July 1952: 'So much for Herr Reichinstein's love of truth. One experienced the same thing with the Marianoff book.' Commenting on Infeld's biography in a letter to Seelig on 27 August 1953, she said, 'Such very personal confessions are not agreeable.' On 27 September 1953 she dismissed Vallentin as a 'sob sister'.

212 'living on the empty stomach of Germany' the *Daily Telegraph*, 12 December 1930

213 'You will never see it again' Pais 1983: 318

213 'hoping to find arms' Frank 1948: 286

213 'make arrangements for emigration' Frank 1948: 324 and Pais
     1983: 450
213 'whip hand in Berlin' Cherwell papers, D51–69, Albert Einstein
     to Frederick Lindemann, 7 May 1933
214 'She was a very nice-looking lady' Micha Battsek, interview, 29
     October 1992
214 'dull and superficial' Speziali 1972: 204 (Albert Einstein to
     Michele Besso, 5 June 1925) 'where the professors thought they
     were clever' Albert Einstein to Eduard Einstein, from Princeton,
     undated*
214 'Never before have I experienced from the fair sex' Einstein
     1954: 7
215 'it had a sufficiently Einsteinian ring' Clark 1979: 274–5
215 'Professor Einstein returned again and again' Churchill Eisen-
     hart, 'Albert Einstein as I remember him', *Journal of the Wash-
     ington Academy of Sciences*, vol. 54 (1964) pp. 325–8
215 'I think that you are the most considerate, loving
     husband' Clark Archive, Edinburgh, 0222, Elsa Einstein to
     Leon Watters, 10 September 1936.
215 'Ilse was suffering from tuberculosis' Marianoff & Wayne
     1944: 176
215 'She had the courage to resume' Vallentin 1954: 172
216 'remained serene and worked constantly' Sayen 1985: 75 and
     Infeld 1941: 282
216 'anguished cries' Peter Bergmann, interview, 16 March 1993
216 'We discussed a serious difficulty' Infeld 1941: 257
216 'I have settled down splendidly' Born 1971: 128 (Albert Ein-
     stein to Max Born, undated)
217 'But as long as I am able to work' Albert Einstein to Hans
     Albert Einstein, 4 January 1937*

10 THE SEARCHER'S BURDEN

218 'to immerse himself' Albert Einstein to Carl Seelig, 5 May 1952
218 'mostly apart from his new wife' Trbuhović-Gjurić 1983: 142

218 'The schools there were excellent' Albert Einstein to Mileva Marić, 15 October 1919*

218 'an excellent man' Speziali 1972: 147 (12 December 1919)

218 'a fine technical college' Albert Einstein to Mileva Marić and family, 15 December 1920*

219 'an immense relief' Speziali 1972: 147 (12 December 1919)

219 'his sons would see more of him' Albert Einstein to Mileva Marić and family, 15 December 1920*

219 'she was in good health' Albert Einstein to Maurice Solovine, 24 April 1920, and Trbuhović-Gjurić 1983: 149

219 'frequent periods in hospital' Trbuhović-Gjurić 1983: 149

219 'a specialist hospital' Trbuhović-Gjurić 1983: 151

219 'It may be this trip' Trbuhović-Gjurić 1983: 155 (Mileva Marić to Milana Bota, 15 November 1916)

220 'simply ridiculous' Albert Einstein to Mileva Marić, 23 August 1920*

220 'plans for an autumn holiday' Speziali 1972: 151 (26 July 1920)

220 'he was especially grateful' Albert Einstein to Mileva Marić, 8 August 1921*

220 'They stayed in Florence' Speziali 1972: 170, 171 (20 October 1921, 26 October 1921)

220 'Eduard was deemed too young' Albert Einstein to Hans Albert and Eduard Einstein, 1921*

220 'The boy proudly showed off the gift' Trbuhović-Gjurić 1983: 151

220 'Besso was instructed to contact him' Speziali 1972: 171 (26 October 1921)

220 'an ebullient mood' Trbuhović-Gjurić 1983: 151

220 'He had assured his sons' Albert Einstein to Hans Albert and Eduard Einstein, 1921*

220 'I am staying with my first wife' Clark 1979: 380

221 'this objection left Einstein cold' Grüning 1990: 157

221 'almost no one knew that he had two sons' Grüning 1990: 39

221 'that he had influence on the newspapers' Albert Einstein to Mileva Marić, 15 August 1922

221 'The money was transferred to Mileva' Pais 1983: 503

221 'Lorentz, for example, wrote confidently to him' Clark 1979: 287

221 'it was used to buy three houses' Albert Einstein to Karl Zürcher, 8 January 1948

222 'I was doing some experiments in the bathroom' Georg Busch, interview, spring 1992

222 'special leave to call herself Mileva Einstein' Pais 1983: 301

223 'But that does not bear thinking about' Albert Einstein to Mileva Marić, 27 May 1925

223 'foreign type' Herneck 1978: 49

223 'But when Einstein came' Grüning 1990: 157

223 'once the clockwork of his body' Albert Einstein to Mileva Marić, 19 April 1924†

223 'Einstein told her' Albert Einstein to Mileva Marić, 13 June 1925†

223 'While it was there it was very strong' Michelmore 1962: 124

223 'a lifelong horror' Evelyn Einstein, interview, 15 April 1992

223 'was rather repressed' Evelyn Einstein, interview, 17 February 1992

223 'Once I remember a discussion' Evelyn Einstein, interview, 15 April 1992

224 'Have Mama tell you' Albert Einstein to Hans Albert Einstein, 1917*

224 'an unpleasant and touchy scene' Albert Einstein to Mileva Marić, 15 August 1922*

224 'Appealing for sympathy' Albert Einstein to Eduard Einstein, 15 July 1923†

225 'even if Elsa did get on one's nerves' Albert Einstein to Hans Albert Einstein, 5 February 1927†

225 'I am pleased that Albert has a strong interest' Albert Einstein to Mileva Marić, 1918*

225 'He declared that Albert has already begun' Albert Einstein to Heinrich Zangger, Early 1918

225 'Hans Albert was hostile to his father' Michelmore 1962: 79

226 'Rivers don't like to be changed' Jerry Tallmer, 'Sons of the famous', *New York Post Daily Magazine*, 23 May 1963

226 'My Albert has become a sound, strong chap' Speziali 1972: 197 (5 January 1924)

226 'Science is a difficult profession' Albert Einstein to Hans Albert Einstein, 7 March 1924†

227 'When someone else has picked up' E. Einstein 1991: 43

227 'never sought to impose his will' Bela Kornitzer, *American Fathers and Sons*, Hermitage House, 1952; also in *Gazette & Daily*, York, Pa., 20 September 1948

227 'Albert had such a hell of a time' Evelyn Einstein, interview, 17 February 1992

227 'overactive thyroid' Aude Einstein, interview, 20 March 1993

228 'alluded darkly to the Book of Exodus' Albert Einstein to Mileva Marić, 9 November 1925†

228 'It would be a crime' Albert Einstein to Mileva Marić, 23 December 1925†

228 'Hans Albert be sent to a pretty forty-year-old woman' Albert Einstein to Mileva Marić, 17 October 1925†

228 'he attempted to influence his son' Albert Einstein to Mileva Marić, 9 November 1925†. Anschütz-Kaempfe tried to convince Hans Albert not to marry Frieda. He also sent Einstein a memo giving an unflattering portrait of her. (Robert Schulmann, interview, 19 October 1992)

228 'to prevent a disaster' Albert Einstein to Mileva Marić, 28 January 1926†

228 'He implored his son' Albert Einstein to Hans Albert Einstein, 5 February 1927†

228 'they would make the inevitable divorce more complicated' Michelmore 1962: 131

228 'I don't understand it' Michelmore 1962: 130

228 'Fate will now take its course' Albert Einstein to Mileva Marić, undated, but refers to expecting a baby†

229 'Hans Albert's marriage was very happy' Albert Einstein to Eduard Einstein, 5 June 1929,† and an undated letter to Mileva Marić

229 'much better than her reputation' Maja Einstein-Winteler to Theresia Mutzenbecher, 13 August 1934

229 'He was definitely the genius' Evelyn Einstein, interview, 17 February 1992

229 'in a clear and intelligent manner' Rübel 1986: 21

230 'At the keyboard, Eduard seemed another person' Rübel 1986: 95

230 'I don't think it's right' Albert Einstein to Eduard Einstein, 28 January 1926†

230 'as happy as a baby with its bottle' Albert Einstein to Eduard Einstein, 17 December 1926†

230 'Drilling holes through thick pieces of wood' Albert Einstein to Hans Albert Einstein, 7 August 1927†

231 'I often sent my father rather rapturous letters' Eduard Einstein to Maja Schucan, undated

231 'could only parrot the ideas of others' E. Einstein 1991: 23; also in Trbuhović-Gjurić 1983: 146 and Michelmore 1962: 122, 131

231 'copied from another author' Albert Einstein to Eduard Einstein, summer 1929†

231 'a collection of Eduard's literary juvenilia' Rübel 1986: 81, 108, 109

231 'we are all two-legged animals' Albert Einstein to Eduard Einstein, 17 April 1926†

232 'memories of Maja Schucan and Waltrud Kappeler' The quotes that follow are based on interviews conducted at the end of August 1992 with Maja Schucan and Waltrud Kappeler.

233 'he described to me the nature of schizophrenia' Rübel 1986: 99

233 'believed his methods dubious – even fraudulent' Albert Einstein to Eduard Einstein, undated but believed to be late 1930 or early 1931†

233 'I always knew that you admired me' Sigmund Freud to Albert Einstein, 3 June 1936

233 'He had a picture of his hero' Eduard Einstein to Maja Schucan, undated

234 'a mature medical student' Eduard Rübel, letter to Roger Highfield, 5 April 1992

234 'she was too cunning for him' Albert Einstein to Eduard Einstein, undated†

234 'Being occupied with the opposite sex' Albert Einstein to Eduard Einstein, undated†. The 'unhappy love adventure' is also mentioned by Maja Einstein-Winteler in a letter to Theresia Mutzenbecher, 26 May 1932.

234 'Even a genius like Schopenhauer' Albert Einstein to Eduard Einstein, 30 July 1928†

234 'In one respect you should be pleased' Albert Einstein to Eduard Einstein, 5 February 1930†

234 'incoherent, pathetic and unhinged' Vallentin 1954: 141

235 'accused Einstein of abandoning him' Michelmore 1962: 146

235 'threatened to throw himself from the window' Trbuhović-Gjurić 1983: 169

235 'I would not have noticed her' Marianoff & Wayne 1944: 12

235 'He likened himself to a nomad' Albert Einstein to Hans Albert Einstein, 5 December 1930†

235 'He had an absorbed look' Vallentin 1954: 141

235 'intense and contradictory feelings' Michelmore 1962: 147

236 'with the greatest accuracy and soberness' Maja Einstein-Winteler to Theresia Mutzenbecher, 26 May 1932

236 'an institution with oppressively narrow horizons' Carl Jung, *Memories, Dreams, Reflections*, Fontana, London, 1993, p. 134.

236 'utterly failed in Eduard's case' Speziali 1972: 352 (11 November 1940)

237 'shock treatment had "ruined" his brother' E. Einstein 1991: 25

237 'thanking her for some poems' Eduard Einstein to Maja Schucan, 28 December 1932

237 'Sometimes my head aches for hours' Eduard Einstein to Maja Schucan, undated

238 'monastery-like treatment' Albert Einstein to Eduard Einstein, 8 October 1932†

238 'I have the feeling that nobody but I' Albert Einstein to Eduard Einstein, 27 July 1932†

238 'This sorrow is eating up Albert' Vallentin 1954: 141

238 'he could teach him psychoanalysis' Albert Einstein to Eduard Einstein, 8 October 1932†

238 'dear, good and old friend' Speziali 1972: 285 (18 September 1932)

239 'a "delightful" exchange of letters' Speziali 1972: 288 (17 October 1932)

239 'he had invited Eduard to visit him in Princeton' Speziali 1972: 290 (21 October 1932)

240 'a photograph' Sayen 1985: 133

240 'work of some kind would be the best cure' Albert Einstein to Mileva Marić, 25 June 1933†

240 'these included Freud himself' E. Einstein 1991: 24 and Michelmore 1962: 147

240 'gruesome swindle' Albert Einstein to Hans Albert Einstein, 11 January 1935†

240 'There also hangs over him a leaden melancholy' Maja Einstein-Winteler to Theresia Mutzenbecher, 20 April 1934

241 'but the words came slowly from his lips' Speziali 1972: 315 (19 June 1937)

241 'Besso's academic links with Zurich' Speziali 1972: 324 (5 September 1938)

241 'The deepest sorrow' E. Einstein 1991: 34

242 'Zorka promptly burnt the notes to ashes' Trbuhović-Gjurić 1983: 152

242 'Her body was found only several days after she died' Trbuhović-Gjurić 1983: 192

242 'Miloš carved out a successful career' Trbuhović-Gjurić 1983: 161

11 ALL AN ILLUSION

243 'the chaotic voices' Dukas & Hoffmann 1979: 52 (Albert Einstein to Elizabeth of Belgium, 20 March 1936)

244 'Have you read the Maxims' Dukas & Hoffmann 1979: 52 (Albert Einstein to Elizabeth of Belgium, 20 March 1936)

244 'the great stone face' Sayen 1985: 75

245 'I no longer care a straw' Speziali 1972: 330 (10 October 1938)

245 'Due to their wretched traditions' Sayen 1985: 146 (Albert Einstein to Otto Juliusburger)

245 'He encouraged Hans Albert' Albert Einstein to Hans Albert Einstein, 19 October 1942.† See also 10 July 1943, when he refers to being an 'advice centre' for the navy. Information on Hans Albert's work from Evelyn Einstein, interview, 22 April 1993.

245 'he was human enough' Clark 1979: 538

246 'Your father was responsible' E. Einstein 1991: 71

246 'rang day and night' Maja Einstein-Winteler to Theresia Mutzenbecher, undated

246 'Professor Einstein, they are newsmen' Sayen 1985: 286

246 'No statement' Helen Dukas to Carl Seelig, 2 March 1954, ETH

246 'Sometimes she would make the decision' Evelyn Einstein, interview, 17 February 1992

247 'I noticed she had a way' Mark Darby, interview, 30 April 1992

247 'at least one young visitor' Micha Battsek, interview, 29 October 1992

247 'privately alluded to it' Bucky 1991: 238

247 'In his will, Einstein left Miss Dukas' New York Times, Helen Dukas obituary, 14 February 1982

247 'so much like Einstein' Clark 1979: 577

248 'sailed like Odysseus' Sayen 1985: 132

248 'closer together than ever' Maja Einstein-Winteler to Theresia Mutzenbecher, 8 August 1940

248 'he has more right' Maja Einstein-Winteler to Theresia Mutzenbecher, July 1940

248 'only her husband was sure it was not of Einstein' Maja Einstein-Winteler to Theresia Mutzenbecher, 8 August 1947

248 'only because one strokes the dog' Maja Einstein-Winteler to Theresia Mutzenbecher, 15 December 1939

248 'the first person to whom Einstein would confide his thoughts' Maja Einstein-Winteler to Theresia Mutzenbecher, 15 July 1946 and 18 February 1948

249 'Since she was a very good listener' Whitrow 1967: 77

249 'Every day I look forward to this hour' Maja Einstein-Winteler to Theresia Mutzenbecher, 15 July 1946

250 'He politely declined' Sayen 1985: 78

250 'All of that is an illusion' Sayen 1985: 295

250 'an indefinable presence' Vladimir Prelog, letter to Roger Highfield, 7 July 1992

250 'bad-tempered and frightening' Evelyn Einstein, interview, 15 April 1992

250 'that alien child' Evelyn Einstein, interview, 17 February 1992

250 'Mileva's unfeigned joy' Maria Grendelmeier, interview, August 1992

251 'Similar reports of violence' Evelyn Einstein, interview, 15 March 1992

251 'It is a thousand pities for the boy' Speziali 1972: 352 (11 November 1940)

251 'nothing gives more joy and satisfaction' Albert Einstein to Eduard Einstein, date uncertain†

252 'One account of her last months' Trbuhović-Gjurić 1983: 196

252 'When the house has been sold' Albert Einstein to Karl Zürcher, 29 July 1947

253 'Frau Mileva has always made out that I neglected her' Albert Einstein to Karl Zürcher, 8 January 1948

253 'Perhaps she has hidden it' Albert Einstein to Hans Albert Einstein, 7 June 1948†

253 'she had suffered another stroke' Dord Krstić, letter to Roger Highfield, 11 April 1992, and Trbuhović-Gjurić 1983: 199

253 'She died alone' Maria Grendelmeier, interview, August 1992

253 'never to have spoken of his mother again' Trbuhović-Gjurić 1983: 203. This is borne out by all our interviews with those who knew Eduard in his later life.

254 'a hoard of 85,000 Swiss francs' Helen Dukas to Carl Seelig, 24 December 1956, ETH

254 'This is how legends arise' Helen Dukas to Carl Seelig, 24 December 1956, ETH

254 'dealing with a poor lunatic' Helen Dukas to Carl Seelig, 23 November 1957, ETH

254 'a growth in his abdomen' Pais 1983: 475

254 'the sword of Damocles' Helen Dukas to Carl Seelig, 8 May 1955, ETH

255 'her predicament in the last years' Albert Einstein to Hans Albert Einstein, 8 March 1946†

255 'recalled his first meeting' Hans Freimüller, letter to Paul Carter, 19 November 1992

255 'shock at seeing the sad figure' Nora Herzog, interview, July 1992

256 'furnishing me and my nose' Albert Einstein to Carl Seelig, 4 January 1954, ETH

256 'manna from heaven' Helen Dukas to Carl Seelig, 24 August 1954, ETH

256 'intense emotional inhibitions' Albert Einstein to Carl Seelig, 11 March 1952, ETH

256 'Seelig dined with Eduard' Carl Seelig to Albert Einstein, 22 March 1952, ETH

256 'no personal contacts of any sort' Albert Einstein to Carl Seelig, 26 March 1952, ETH

257 politely declined the offer' Albert Einstein to Carl Seelig, 12 May 1952, ETH

257 'whom he apparently found unsympathetic' Albert Einstein to Carl Seelig, 20 August 1952, ETH

257 'what Americans called "cushioning" ' Helen Dukas to Carl Seelig, 9 August 1952, ETH

257 'to hold back any bad news' Helen Dukas to Carl Seelig, 12 October 1954, ETH

257 'You have probably already wondered' Albert Einstein to Carl Seelig, 4 January 1954, ETH

257 'his famous name brought constant problems' Bela Kornitzer, *American Fathers and Sons*, Hermitage House, 1952; also in *Gazette & Daily*, York, Pa., 20 September 1948. At the time, Hans Albert was forty-seven.

258 'From school I went' Jerry Tallmer, 'Sons of the famous', *New York Post Daily Magazine*, 23 May 1963 .

258 'this stern dedication that Einstein praised' Albert Einstein to Hans Albert Einstein, 1 May 1954†

259 'but the very first sentence' Whitrow 1967: 21

259 'more of a historic relic' Leopold Infeld, 'As I see it', *Bulletin of the Atomic Scientists*, February 1965, p. 9

259 'It was distressing to see' Leopold Infeld, *Uspekhi Fizicheskikh*, vol. 59, no. 1 (1957), p. 174 Clark archive, Edinburgh, 291

259 'This is so simple' Hoffmann & Dukas 1986: 228

259 'Einstein was trying to solve the problems of his youth' Frank Wilczek, interview, 30 April 1992

259 'master key to the universe' Pais 1983: 350

260 'It is an imbecility' Albert Einstein to Hans Albert Einstein, 1 January 1950†

260 'to help protect him' H. Fleming, *Sunday Times Advertiser*, Trenton, NJ, 2 May 1955, Clark archive, Edinburgh

261 'leading a harmonious life' Speziali 1972: 537 (21 March 1955)

261 '*Aber* Frau Bice' Niccolo Tucci, 'The great foreigner', *New Yorker*, 22 November 1947

261 'A butterfly is not a mole' Speziali 1972: 390 (6 January 1948)

261 'an intense pain' Helen Dukas to Carl Seelig, 8 May 1955, ETH

262 'I want to go when I want' Helen Dukas to Carl Seelig, 8 May 1955, ETH

262 'I can die without the help' Sayen 1985: 299

262 'If I knew that I should have to die' Infeld 1941: 268

263 'An obituary cartoon' By Herbloc – see Hoffmann & Dukas 1986: 263

263 'a river not far away' Michelmore 1962: 262. However, Hans Albert Einstein told his daughter the ashes were scattered in the nearby ocean – Evelyn Einstein, interview, 22 April 1993.

263 'the idea of donating his body' Albert Einstein to Carl Seelig, 12 August 1954, ETH

263 'I just knew we had permission' Thomas Harvey, interview, 18 March 1993

264 'The family suffered' Charles Boyd, interview, 19 April 1993

264 'Einstein's brain differed' Marian Diamond, interview, 18 March 1993

265 'heritability of aneurysms' Charles Boyd, interview, 19 March 1993, and fax, 22 April 1993

265 'the less that is published' Otto Nathan to Carl Seelig, 26 May 1955, ETH

265 'one of the last to see him' Peter Plesch, interview, 13 August 1992

265 'a letter to his son' Janos Plesch to Peter Plesch, 18 April 1955

266 'not come to definite conclusions' Otto Nathan to Carl Seelig, 26 May 1955, ETH

266 'had justification' Thomas Harvey, interview, 18 March 1993

266 'with a pound of salt' Helen Dukas to Carl Seelig, 19 January 1956, ETH

266 'It's a good job' Helen Dukas to Carl Seelig, 27 August 1953, ETH

267 'part of the second family' Robert Schulmann, interview, 20 February 1992

267 'his father were speaking to her' Helen Dukas to Carl Seelig, 8 May 1955, ETH

267 'handsomely broad' Helen Dukas to Carl Seelig, 9 June 1955, ETH

267 'comprehensively froze him out' Albert Einstein to Karl Zürcher, 29 July 1947

267 'open greed and ill-will' Helen Dukas to Carl Seelig, 9 June 1955, ETH

268 'could help pay for Eduard's hospital bills' Aude Einstein, interview, 20 March 1993

268 'My mother decided' Evelyn Einstein, interview, 17 February 1992

268 'very diplomatically' Helen Dukas to Carl Seelig, 8 February 1957, ETH

268 'above all to Mileva' Helen Dukas to Carl Seelig, 11 February 1958, ETH

268 'extraordinarily provocative' Helen Dukas to Carl Seelig, 4 June 1958, ETH

269 'He can be terribly rude' Helen Dukas to Carl Seelig, 4 June 1958, ETH

269 'seemed more like Mileva' Carl Seelig to Helen Dukas, 29 September 1955, ETH

269 'What is almost worse' Helen Dukas to Carl Seelig, 29 June 1958, ETH

269 'He is the son of his mother' Helen Dukas to Carl Seelig, 3 December 1958, ETH

269 'ruled in their favour' E. Einstein 1991: 37

270 'her own account of the marriage' E. Einstein 1991: 59–78

270 'didn't want to have anything sweet' Carl Seelig to Otto Nathan, 3 August 1960, ETH

270 'I felt rather abandoned' Evelyn Einstein, interview, 15 April 1992

271 'That's now my work' Hans Freimüller, letter to Paul Carter, 19 November 1992, p. 3

271 'Forgotten in Zurich' 'M. W.', *Neuen Zürcher Zeitung*, 28 October 1965

272 'a stroke in 1964' E. Einstein 1991: 25

272 'the best way of getting to nature' Jerry Tallmer, 'Sons of the famous', *New York Post Daily Magazine*, 23 May 1963

272 'looking forward to an afternoon sailing trip' Evelyn Einstein, interview, 17 February 1992

272 'There was no escape' E. Einstein 1991: 79

12 KEEPERS OF THE FLAME

273 'Don't let the house' Clark 1979: 588

273 'left much as they were' Bernstein 1973: 11–12

274 'turning down proposed translations' Jeremy Bernstein, 'A critic at large: Besso', *New Yorker*, 17 February 1989, p. 92

274 'Nathan claimed in 1982' Sayen 1985: 312

274 'He was very angry' Jagdish Mehra, several telephone interviews during the summer of 1992

275 'Clark had been warned' Ronald Clark, 25 August 1971, Clark Archive, Edinburgh

276 'The rumour is' Mark Darby, interview, 30 April 1992

277 'pit of my stomach' Martin Klein, interview, 8 February 1993

277 'admired Nathan on similar grounds' *New York Times* obituary of Otto Nathan, 30 January 1987

277 'enemies list' John Stachel, interview, 29 February 1992

279 'Without passing judgement' James Sayen, letter to Roger Highfield, November 1992

279 'everybody rejoiced' Jagdish Mehra, telephone interview during the summer of 1992

279 'most beautiful' Hilde Jost, interview, 29 August 1992

280 'suggested that Schulmann' Robert Schulmann, letter to Roger Highfield, 12 June 1992

280 'drawn by its enchantment' Frieda Knecht, unpublished manuscript, p. 4

280 'I have got some love-letters!' Evelyn Einstein, interview, 17 February 1992

281 'Bank of America' Michael Ferguson, letter to Roger Highfield, 6 July 1992

281 'one of enormous relief' Michael Ferguson, letter to Roger Highfield, 6 August 1992

281 'candidates for that concert' John Stachel, interview, 21 February 1992

281 'they added juice' Jürgen Renn, interview, 4 May 1992

282 'locked up until twenty years after her death' Ze'ev Rosenkranz, letter to Roger Highfield, 30 March 1993

282 'not among the ordinary files' John Stachel, interview, 26 March 1993

282 'survive only as photocopies' Letters designated as ALSX (Autographed Letter Signed in Photocopy) by the Einstein papers project: 30 April 1912, 7 May 1913, 21 May 1912, before 2 December 1913, after 2 December 1913 and 21 December 1913.

282 'a book co-edited by Helen Dukas' Dukas & Hoffmann 1987

283 'The young man was torn' Dukas & Hoffmann 1987: 27, 28

Bibliography

ABIR-AM, PNINA, & OUTRAM, DORINDA, eds. 1989. *Uneasy Careers and Intimate Lives. Women in Science, 1798–1979*, Rutgers University Press, New Brunswick, NJ.

ANDERSON, BONNIE, & ZINSSER, JUDITH. 1990. *A History of Their Own, Volume 2*, Penguin, Harmondsworth.

BECK, ANNA, & HAVAS, PETER. 1987. *The Collected Papers of Albert Einstein, Volume 1*, English translation, Princeton University Press, Princeton.

BECK, ANNA, & HAVAS, PETER. 1989. *The Collected Papers of Albert Einstein, Volume 2*, English translation, Princeton University Press, Princeton.

BERNSTEIN, AARON. 1853–7. *Aus dem Reiche der Naturwissenschaft. Für Jedermann aus dem Volke*, 12 vols., Berlin, Besser.

BERNSTEIN, JEREMY. 1973. *Einstein*, Fontana, London.

BORN, MAX, ed. 1971. *Born–Einstein Letters*, Walker, New York.

BUCKY, PETER A. 1991. *Der private Albert Einstein*, ECON Verlag, Düsseldorf.

CASPAR, MAX. 1959. *Kepler*, Abelard-Schuman, London and New York.

CLARK, RONALD. 1971. *Einstein, the Life and Times*, World Publishing, New York.

CLARK, RONALD. 1979. *Einstein, the Life and Times*, Hodder & Stoughton, London.

COVENEY, PETER, & HIGHFIELD, ROGER. 1991. *The Arrow of Time*, Flamingo, London.

DREYER, J. 1890. *Tycho Brahe, a Picture of Scientific Life and Work in the Sixteenth Century*, Adam and Charles Black, Edinburgh.

DUKAS, HELEN, & HOFFMAN, BANESH. 1979. *Albert Einstein, the*

Human Side: New Glimpses from his Archives, Princeton University Press, Princeton.

EINSTEIN, ALBERT. 1935. *The World As I See It*, tr. Alan Harris, London.

EINSTEIN, ALBERT. 1954. *Ideas and Opinions*, Alvin Redman, London.

EINSTEIN, ALBERT. 1991. *The World As I See It*, Citadel Press, New York.

EINSTEIN, ELIZABETH. 1991. *Hans Albert Einstein: Reminiscences of his Life and our Life Together*, Iowa Institute of Hydraulic Research, Iowa City.

FRANK, PHILIPP. 1948. *Einstein: his Life and Times*, Jonathan Cape, London.

FRENCH, A. P. 1979. *Einstein: a Centenary Volume*, Heinemann, London.

FRIEDMAN, ALAN, & DONLEY, CAROL. 1990. *Einstein as Myth and Muse*, Cambridge University Press, Cambridge.

GJERTSEN, DEREK. 1986. *The Newton Handbook*, Routledge & Kegan Paul, London.

GOLDSMITH, MAURICE, MACKAY, ALAN, & WOUDHUYSEN, JAMES. 1980. *Einstein: the First Hundred Years*, Pergamon, Oxford.

GORAN, MORRIS. 1967. *The Story of Fritz Haber*, Norman, Oklahoma.

GRIBBIN, JOHN, & WHITE, MICHAEL. 1993. *Einstein: A Life in Science*, Simon & Schuster, London.

GRÜNING, MICHAEL. 1990. *Ein Haus für Albert Einstein*, Verlag der Nation, Berlin.

HERNECK, FRIEDRICH. 1978. *Einstein privat, Herta Waldow erinnert sich an die Jahre 1927 bis 1933*, Buchverlag Der Morgen Berlin.

HOFFMANN, BANESH, & DUKAS, HELEN. 1986. *Albert Einstein, Creator and Rebel*, Paladin, London.

HOLTON, GERALD. 1988. *Thematic Origins of Scientific Thought*, Harvard University Press, Cambridge, Mass.

ILLY, JOZSEF. 1979. Albert Einstein in Prague, *Isis*, vol. 70, no. 251, March.

INFELD, LEOPOLD. 1941. *Quest: the Evolution of a Scientist*, Gollancz, London.

INFELD, LEOPOLD. 1950. *Albert Einstein: his Work and its Influence on our World*, Scribners, New York.

KLEIN, MARTIN. 1970. *Paul Ehrenfest, Volume 1, The Making of a Theoretical Physicist*, North Holland, Amsterdam.

KLEIN, MARTIN, KOX, A. J., SCHULMANN, ROBERT, RENN, JÜRGEN, BRENNI, PAOLO, HENTSCHEL, KLAUS, RUETSCHE, LAURA, LEHAR, ANN, LÜBKE, RITA, PRINGLE, ANNETTE, & SMITH, SHAWN. 1993. *The Collected Papers of Albert Einstein, Volume 5*, Princeton University Press, Princeton.

LEVINGER, E. 1962. *Albert Einstein*, Dennis Dobson, London.

MARIANOFF, DIMITRI, & WAYNE, PALMA. 1944. *Einstein: an Intimate Study of a Great Man*, Doubleday Doran, New York.

MICHELMORE, PETER. 1962. *Einstein: Profile of the Man*, Dodd, Mead and Company, New York.

MOOK, DELO, & VARGISH, THOMAS. 1987. *Inside Relativity*, Princeton University Press, Princeton.

MOSZKOWSKI, ALEXANDER. 1921a. *Einstein: Einblicke in seine Gedankenwelt*, Hoffmann und Campe, Hamburg.

MOSZKOWSKI, ALEXANDER. 1921b. *Einstein the Searcher: his Work Explained from Dialogues with Einstein*, Fontane, Berlin.

NATHAN, OTTO, & NORDERN, HANS, eds. 1961. *Einstein on Peace*, Simon and Schuster, New York.

PAIS, ABRAHAM. 1983. *Subtle is the Lord . . . the Science and Life of Albert Einstein*, Oxford University Press, Oxford.

PLESCH, JOHN. 1947. *Janos: the Story of a Doctor*, Gollancz, London.

PYENSON, LEWIS. 1985. *The Young Einstein*, Adam Hilger, Bristol.

REICHINSTEIN, DAVID. 1934. *Albert Einstein, a Picture of his Life and his Conception of the World*, Prague.

REISER, ANTON (pseudonym of Rudolph Kayser). 1931. *Albert Einstein: a Biographical Portrait*, Thornton Butterworth, London.

RENN, JÜRGEN, & SCHULMANN, ROBERT, eds. 1992. *Albert Einstein/ Mileva Marić, the Love Letters*, Princeton University Press, Princeton.

RÜBEL, EDUARD. 1986. *Eduard Einstein*, Verlag Paul Haupt, Berne.

SAYEN, JAMIE. 1985. *Einstein in America*, Crown Publishers, New York.

SCHILPP, PAUL. 1959. *Albert Einstein, Philosopher-Scientist, Volume 1*, Harper Torchbooks, New York.

SEELIG, CARL. 1956a. *Albert Einstein: a Documentary Biography*, Staples Press, London.

SEELIG, CARL, ed. 1956b. *Helle Zeit Dunkle Zeit*, Europa Verlag, Zurich.

SEELIG, CARL. 1960. *Albert Einstein, eine Dokumentarische Biographie*, Europa Verlag, Zurich.

SOLOVINE, MAURICE, ed. 1956. *Albert Einstein, Lettres à Maurice Solovine*, Gauthier Villars, Paris.

SPEZIALI, PIERRE. 1972. *Albert Einstein–Michele Besso, Correspondance 1903–1955*, Hermann, Paris.

STACHEL, JOHN, CASSIDY, DAVID, SCHULMANN, ROBERT, RENN, JÜRGEN, GRIMINGER, OLGA, SMITH, GARY, & SUMMERFIELD, ROBERT. 1987. *The Collected Papers of Albert Einstein, Volume 1*, Princeton University Press, Princeton.

STACHEL, JOHN, CASSIDY, DAVID, RENN, JÜRGEN, SCHULMANN, ROBERT, HOWARD, DON, KOX, A. J., & LEHAR, ANN. 1989. *The Collected Papers of Albert Einstein, Volume 2*, Princeton University Press, Princeton.

STACHEL, JOHN. In press. 'Einstein and Marić: a failed collaboration', in Helene Pycior et al., eds, *Creative Couples in Science*, Rutgers University Press, New Brunswick, NJ.

TRBUHOVIĆ-GJURIĆ, DESANKA. 1983. *Im Schatten Albert Einsteins, das tragische Leben der Mileva Einstein-Marić*, Haupt, Berne.

TROEMEL-PLOETZ, SENTA. 1990. 'Mileva Einstein Marić, the woman who did Einstein's mathematics', *Women's Studies International Forum*, vol. 13, no. 5.

VALLENTIN, ANTONINA. 1954. *Einstein: a Biography*, London.

Index